The **Rough Guide** to

Yos

Natic

written and researched by

Paul Whitfield

NEW YORK • LONDON • DELHI

www.roughguides.com

Contents

◀◀ The Mist Trail and Vernal Falls ◀ Camping at Ottoway Lakes

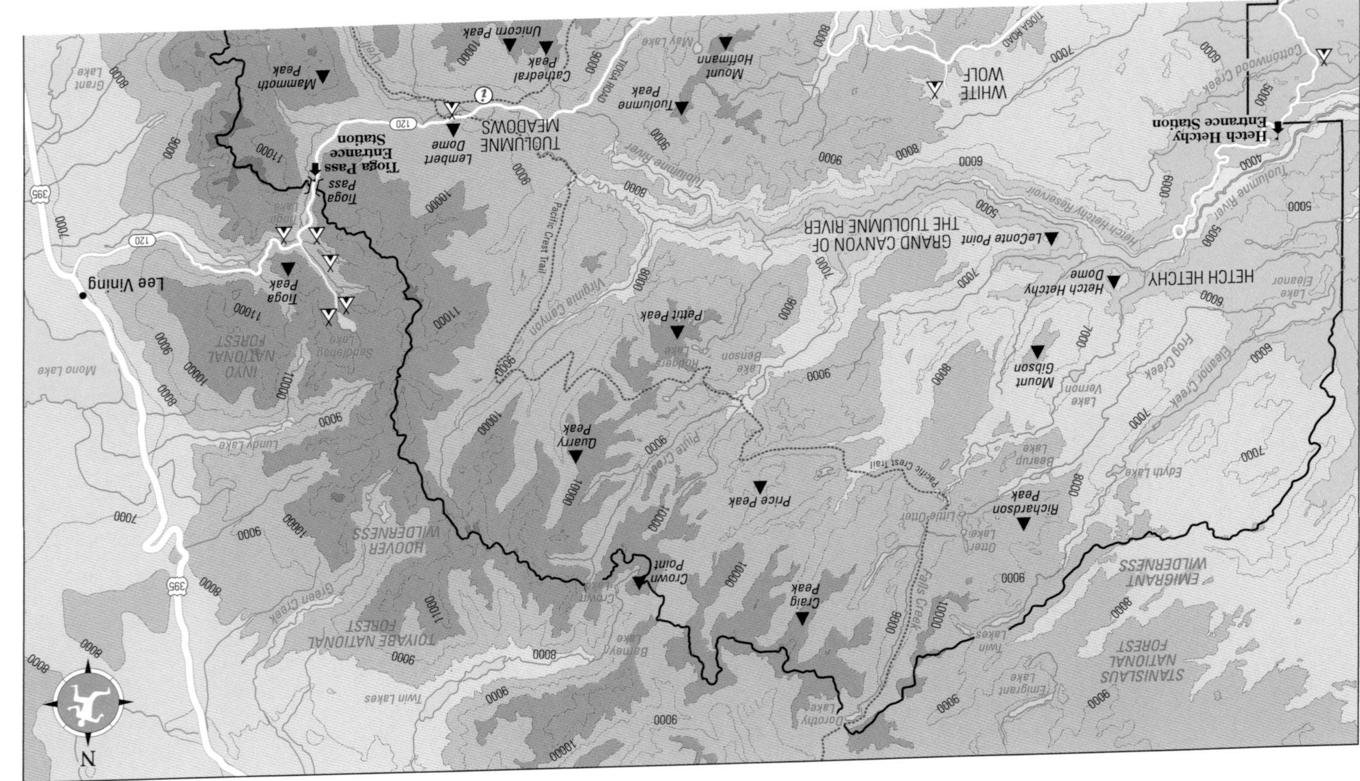

Lee Vining
Mono Lake
Tioga Peak
Tioga Pass
Tioga Pass Entrance Station
Mammoth Peak
Grant Lake
Lembert Dome
TUOLUMNE MEADOWS
Cathedral Peak
Unicorn Peak
Tuolumne Peak
Mount Hoffmann
May Lake
TIOGA ROAD
WHITE WOLF
Hetch Hetchy Entrance Station
Cottonwood Creek
Tuolumne River
Hetch Hetchy Reservoir
GRAND CANYON OF THE TUOLUMNE RIVER
LeConte Point
HETCH HETCHY
Hetch Hetchy Dome
Lake Eleanor
Eleanor Creek
Frog Creek
Mount Gibson
Lake Vernon
Edyth Lake
Bearup Lake
Richardson Peak
Otter Lake
Little Otter
Pacific Crest Trail
Price Peak
Pettit Peak
Lake Benson
Virginia Canyon
Quarry Peak
Piute Creek
Crown Point
Craig Peak
Falls Creek
Twin Lakes
Emigrant Lake
STANISLAUS NATIONAL FOREST
EMIGRANT WILDERNESS
Dorothy Lake
Barney Lake
TOIYABE NATIONAL FOREST
HOOVER WILDERNESS
Green Creek
Lundy Lake
INYO NATIONAL FOREST
Saddlebag Lake
Tuolumne River
N

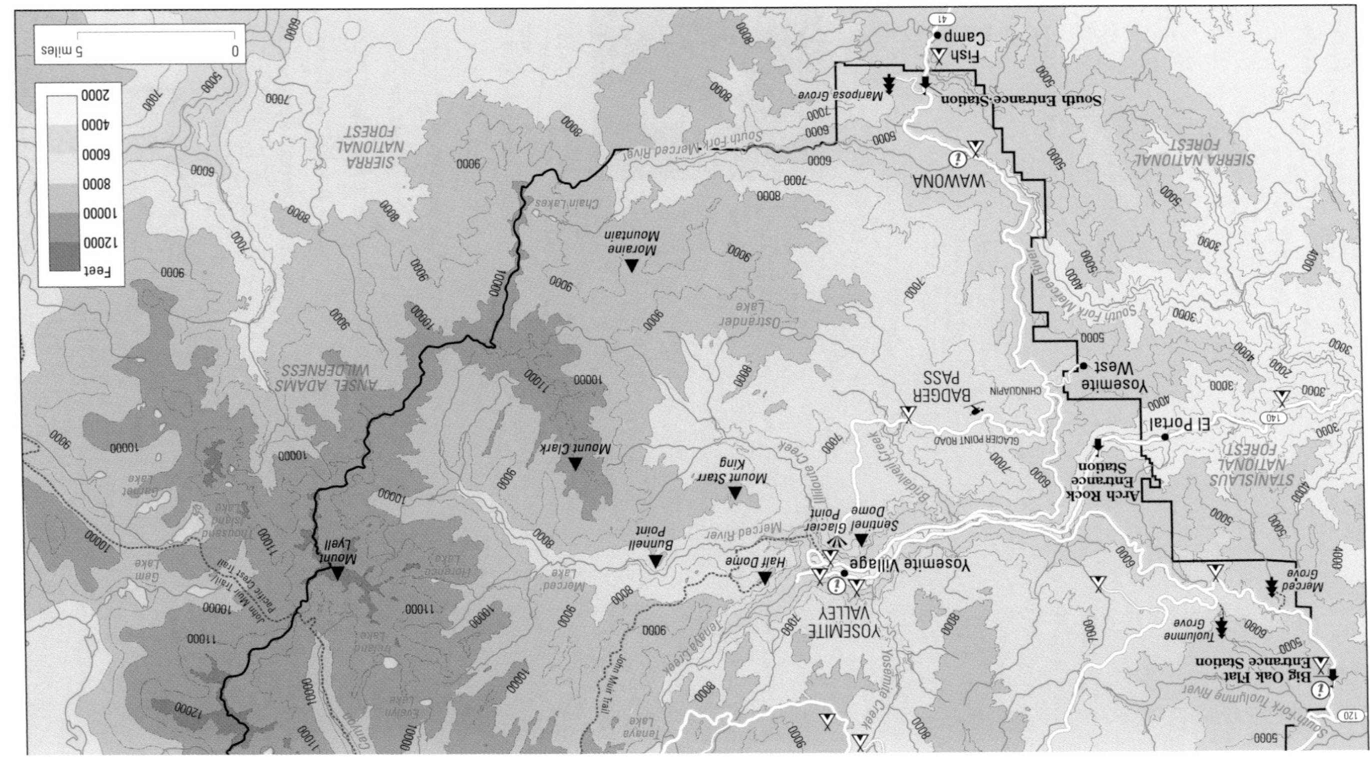
Feet
12000
10000
8000
6000
4000
2000
0
5 miles
YOSEMITE VALLEY
Yosemite Village
Half Dome
Sentinel Dome
Glacier Point
Bunnell Point
Mount Starr King
Mount Clark
Moraine Mountain
Mount Lyell
ANSEL ADAMS WILDERNESS
SIERRA NATIONAL FOREST
STANISLAUS NATIONAL FOREST
BADGER PASS
GLACIER POINT ROAD
CHINQUAPIN
WAWONA
Mariposa Grove
South Entrance Station
Fish Camp
Yosemite West
El Portal
Arch Rock Entrance Station
Big Oak Flat Entrance Station
Tuolumne Grove
Merced Grove
Merced River
South Fork Merced River
South Fork Tuolumne River
Tenaya Creek
Yosemite Creek
Bridalveil Creek
Illilouette Creek
Tenaya Lake
Merced Lake
Ostrander Lake
Chain Lakes
Florence Lake
Evelyn Lake
Ireland Lake
Thousand Island Lake
Garnet Lake
Gem Lake
Canyon
John Muir Trail
Pacific Crest Trail
41
120
140

Introduction to Yosemite

No temple made with hands can compare with the Yosemite. Every rock in its walls seems to glow with life. Some lean back in majestic repose; others, absolutely sheer or nearly so for thousands of feet, advance beyond their companions in thoughtful attitudes, giving welcome to storms and calms alike, seemingly aware, yet heedless, of everything going on about them.

John Muir, *The Yosemite*

More gushing adjectives have been thrown at Yosemite National Park than at any other part of California. But however excessive the hyperbole may seem, once you enter the Park and turn the corner that reveals Yosemite Valley you realize it's actually an understatement.

Simply put, **Yosemite Valley** – only a small part of the Park but the one at which most of the verbiage is aimed – is one of the most dramatic pieces of geology to be found anywhere in the world. From massive hunks of granite to the subtle colorings of wildflowers, the variations in the Valley can be both enormous and discreet. Just seven miles long and one mile across at its widest point, the Valley is walled by near-vertical, three-thousand-foot cliffs whose sides are streaked by cascading waterfalls and whose tops, a variety of domes and pinnacles, form a jagged silhouette against the sky. This is where you'll find some of the world's most famous rocks – **Half Dome** and rock climbing's holy grail of **El Capitan** – as well as many of America's tallest waterfalls, with **Yosemite Falls** topping the lot.

At ground level, too, the sights can be staggeringly impressive. The **Merced River** meanders among grassy wildflower meadows where mule deer graze, while black bears secretively forage the surrounding oak, cedar, and fir woods. The Valley's buildings blend into their surroundings with varying degrees of success, a few even contributing to the overall beauty of the place, not least **The Ahwahnee** hotel that adds grace to the landscape while providing opulent accommodation.

▲ El Capitan

All of this wondrous scenery is within half a day's drive of San Francisco, and not much further from Los Angeles, so it is understandable that the tourists are plentiful. Each year almost **three and a half million** people visit Yosemite Valley, which in July and August (and any summer weekend) is typically packed, though most of the crowds can be left behind by taking any path with much of a slope. Fortunately, the whole Park is diverse and massive enough to soak up the crowds.

Yosemite National Park can be experienced on a variety of levels: many people just spend a day here doing a quick whip around the top attractions. Others return frequently during their lifetime to photograph, explore, observe the wildlife, or just soak up the atmosphere. Whatever your interests, be sure to spend some time **hiking**, even if it is just around the Valley floor on one of the nearly-flat, paved trails. If you're willing to hike a few miles and perhaps camp out overnight you open up the 95 percent of Yosemite National Park that is designated **wilderness**, which essentially makes it off limits to everyone except hikers and those with pack animals.

▼ Hetch Hetchy

What to see

Located at 4000ft and with a relatively mild year-round climate, **Yosemite Valley** was an obvious place for the native Ahwahneechee people to make their home, and an equally comfortable spot for early pioneers, who established themselves here

Fact file

- Roughly fifty miles by forty miles, Yosemite National Park covers **747,956 acres** (1169 square miles) and is about the size of Rhode Island. 94.45 percent is designated **wilderness**.
- Sections of Yosemite came under federal protection as early as June 30, 1864, but Yosemite National Park itself was only created on October 1, 1890, making it the nation's **third national park** after Yellowstone and Sequoia.
- The Park was declared a United Nations **World Heritage Site** on October 31, 1984.
- Yosemite currently receives around 3.4 million visitors a year, down from a peak of almost 4.2 million in 1996.
- The Park varies in **altitude** from 2000ft in the west to the 13,114ft summit of Mount Lyell on the Park's eastern boundary.
- Some 85 species of **mammals**, 150 species of **birds**, 35 types of **tree**, and 1500 species of **flowering plants** can be seen from the 263 miles of roads and 800 miles of hiking trails.

from the late 1850s onwards. The pattern has continued, and Yosemite Valley remains at the geographic, spiritual and business heart of the Park. With over ninety percent of the Park's roofed accommodation, around sixty percent of the campsites, and almost all the restaurants, it is the hub for visitors who use the network of hikers and tour buses (or their own vehicles) to fan out into the rest of the Park.

In **northern Yosemite**, everyone flocks to the sub-alpine setting of **Tuolumne Meadows** (pronounced Too-ol-uh-me), perched at 8600ft and close to Yosemite's highest mountains on the Park's eastern border. The name is given to both a small collection of visitor facilities and the open high-alpine flatlands that surround them. Here there's a crisp, elemental atmosphere, great scenery and a good deal of peace and quiet. It is all best appreciated on some of the Park's finest hikes, which provide easy access to the wild backcountry beyond, especially into the ragged **Cathedral Range**, a place much loved by Yosemite's champion, **John Muir**, who was the first to scale the dramatically pointed **Cathedral Peak**. Trails quickly climb into the rarefied high country above 10,000ft, and by scrambling off-trail you can get among some of the Sierra's highest peaks, including Yosemite's highest point, the 13,114ft summit of **Mount Lyell**.

The Tuolumne River courses west through its own Grand Canyon down to **Hetch Hetchy**, once the scenic rival for Yosemite Valley but relatively little visited since its meadows were drowned under a controversial dam almost a century ago. Nonetheless, it remains a beautiful spot, best for a little tranquility among the wildflowers and spring waterfalls.

The spectacle continues into **southern Yosemite** around **Wawona**, little more than a lovely old wooden hotel and a campground set beside

Getting the most out of a short visit

With so much to see and do in the Park it is hard to pick favorites; what follows is a brief list of some of the most popular and worthwhile sights and activities.

Two hours If you're just driving through, be sure to loop around Yosemite Valley, take photos from Tunnel View then either take a quick look at the giant sequoias in Mariposa Grove or drive the Tioga Road east through Tuolumne Meadows.

Half a day Make straight for Yosemite Valley and stroll to the base of Lower Yosemite Falls, hike some or all of the Mist Trail to Vernal Falls and gaze up at El Capitan from El Cap Meadow.

Full day Do all the half-a-day activities, add in the walk to Mirror Lake, visit the museum and Indian Village and, if driving, admire the late afternoon views from Tunnel View on the Wawona Road then continue to Glacier Point for sunset and the stars after dark.

Two to three days Keen hikers shouldn't miss Half Dome, but they might also fancy the Four-Mile Trail or Upper Yosemite Falls Trail. Less ambitious visitors could float down the Merced River then repair to *The Ahwahnee* for a drink or a meal, and everyone should make side trips to Tuolumne Meadows and the Mariposa Grove at Wawona.

Over three days After three days in the Park, you'll begin to feel like a local; consider hiking out to one of the Park's less visited corners (perhaps Hikes 18, 34 or 42), taking a rock climbing course (see p.147 for details) or visiting an area outside the Park like Mono Lake, Bodie Ghost Town or Mammoth Lakes with its superb mountain biking.

a meadow that has partly been converted into a historic golf course. It is at the same altitude as Yosemite Valley but has a quite different feel, most of the low-key activity revolving around a diverting outdoor museum that brings together historic buildings from all over the Park. Nearby, the **Mariposa Grove** encompasses one of the most awe-inspiring forests of **giant sequoias** found anywhere. The immediate vicinity of Yosemite is equally rich. The former gold rush towns of **Groveland** and **Mariposa** make pleasant bases for visiting the Park, and **whitewater rafting** on the local rivers easily justifies lingering an extra day or so. To the east,

Yosemite is approached over the Sierra Nevada from the Owens Valley, a semi-desert punctuated by **Mono Lake**, with other-worldly tufa towers rising from its brackish waters. Immediately north of Mono Lake, the photogenic decaying structures of **Bodie**, make it the most appealing of all California's **ghost towns**, while to the south **Mammoth Lakes** makes a superb base for skiing and mountain biking.

▲ The John Muir Trail near Tuolumne Meadows

When to go

You can visit Yosemite at any time of year; choosing the best time to visit depends mostly on whether you've come for hiking, viewing waterfalls, or winter activities. Summer is generally dry with occasional thunderstorms; while spring and fall are more variable with highs in the Valley reaching the seventies. Winter means snowy trails and frozen waterfalls, though the frequent sunny days bring highs into the fifties and the low-angled sun casting the cliffs and domes in a flattering light.

May and June are fairly busy months, particularly in Yosemite Valley where the waterfalls are the big draw. Lowland snows should have melted, but throughout May and early June the high country is likely to be off limits with both Glacier Point Road and Tioga Road closed by snow. The Park is at its busiest in **July and August**, when daytime temperatures in Yosemite Valley and Wawona are regularly in the eighties and nineties, and the rivers and lakes are (just about) warm enough for swimming. This is a good time for hiking since almost all the high country snow has melted, though the more ephemeral waterfalls will have dried up. The limited summer rainfall tends to come in short thunderstorms, which dissipate in the evening to leave a clear, starry night.

If you don't mind missing most of the waterfalls, **September and October** are excellent months to visit, with smaller crowds but most activities still operating, and plenty of hiking that's both cooler and dry under foot. In October, the Valley and Wawona also put on a decent show of fall colors. **November** is getting marginal with snowstorms more likely and the

Smarter than the average bear

You may never see a **black bear** anywhere else in California, but spend a few days in Yosemite Valley and you've a fair chance of spotting one, probably at night, breaking into a car or roaming the campgrounds looking for a free meal. Banging pans and yelling – from a safe distance, of course – will probably drive them off, but their dependence on human food has led to several bears being shot each year. Yosemite bears are not deterred by tent walls or car doors, and safe **food storage** is now mandatory in the Park. As they say, "a fed bear is a dead bear," so do them and yourself a favor by keeping all food and smelly items – deodorant, sunscreen, toothpaste – either inside your room or in the metal lockers in campgrounds and parking lots, and at trailheads.

Out in the backcountry, campers must use portable plastic bear canisters to store food. Sows have taught their cubs to climb along slender branches to get at food, so the old method of hanging food seldom works. For more on bears and other local animals, see p.242.

Report all bear sightings on ☎209/372-0322.

high country roads likely to close early in the month. **December through March** are basically the winter months, with cross-country skiing and skating in full swing; tire chains are generally required. By **April**, Wawona and the Valley may well be free of snow, but late dumps are not uncommon. With a few lowland exceptions April is too early for much hiking.

Traveling **outside peak summer** season also offers rewards with rooms easier to come by and prices markedly lower.

Average temperatures and rainfall in Yosemite Valley

		Jan	Feb	Mar	Apr	May	Jun	Jul	Aug	Sep	Oct	Nov	Dec
Precipitation													
in		6.2	6.1	5.2	3.0	1.3	0.7	0.4	0.3	0.9	2.1	5.4	5.6
mm		157	155	132	76	33	18	10	8	23	53	137	142
Temperature													
Max	(°F)	49	55	59	65	73	82	90	90	87	74	58	48
	(°C)	9	13	15	18	23	28	32	32	31	23	14	9
Min	(°F)	26	28	31	35	42	48	54	53	47	39	31	26
	(°C)	-3	-2	-1	2	6	9	12	12	8	4	-1	-3

18 things not to miss

It's not possible to see everything Yosemite has to offer in one trip – and we don't suggest you try. What follows, in no particular order, is a selective look at highlights in and around the Park, including spectacular landscapes, thrilling activities, and the best places to relax and relive the day's excitement. The highlights are arranged in five color-coded categories, so you can browse through to find the very best things to see, do, and experience. All highlights have a page reference to take you straight into the guide, where you can find out more.

01 Sunset at Glacier Point Page **94** • The alpenglow on Half Dome and Clouds Rest assures stunning sunsets from Glacier Point.

02 Wildflowers Page **237** • California lupins are just some of the most visible of Yosemite's huge array of wildflowers, which stretch from the foothills to the subalpine meadows.

03 The Ahwahnee Page **61** • Luxurious rooms, classy dining, a cozy bar and sumptuous public spaces make *The Ahwahnee* an essential sight.

05 Hiking the Mist Trail Page **105** • Get drenched in spray following this fabulous hike to the top of Vernal Fall.

04 Rock climbing Page **147** • Climbers of all abilities will find boundless challenges both in Yosemite Valley and around the summertime crags of Tuolumne Meadows.

06 Winter in Yosemite Page **155** • Frozen waterfalls, pine boughs heavy with snow and a host of cold weather activities make Yosemite a great winter destination.

07 El Capitan Page **46** • Though stunning at first sight, El Cap's truly immense scale is only revealed when you spot the flea-like climbers on its face.

08 Yosemite Museum Page **58** • Superb basketware and a replica native village give the deepest insight into the lives of the Ahwahneechee.

09 Waterfalls Page **55** • Come in April, May or June to witness Yosemite's myriad waterfalls at their thundering best.

10 Horseback riding Page **150** • Gentle but unforgettably scenic rides head from stables in Yosemite Valley, Tuolumne Meadows and Wawona.

11 Mono Lake Page **214** • Outlandish tufa towers rise from the waters of Mono Lake creating a sci-fi world on the semi-desert of the Owens Valley.

12 Hiking Half Dome Page **111** • A steep cable "staircase" leads to the summit of Half Dome, an exhausting hike ending high above Yosemite Valley.

13 Mariposa Grove of Giant Sequoias Page **99** • It is always an honor to be among these forest giants, but better still at dawn or under a winter cloak of snow.

14 Watching wildlife Page 242 • Count yourself lucky if you see mountain lions, bighorn sheep and wolverines, but you've a good chance of spotting marmots and black bears, and mule deer are seemingly everywhere.

16 Pioneer Yosemite History Center Page 98 • Cabins and farm buildings from Yosemite's pioneering past are gathered here in Wawona beside a covered bridge.

15 Tuolumne Meadows Page 81 • The Sierra's most expansive meadows make a superb base for hiking in the surrounding mountains, but are also glorious for simply watching the day go by.

17 Iron Door Saloon Page 182 • One of California's oldest bars still serves up the good stuff in convivial surroundings, complete with swing doors straight out of the Wild West.

18 The High Sierra Camp Loop Page 146 • Yosemite's high-country highlights are linked by this hiking route, featuring much sought-after stays in catered tent cabins.

Basics

Basics

Getting there

With well-maintained access roads and over two hundred miles of highway within the Park, it is hardly surprising people opt to drive their own vehicles to Yosemite. While dropping visitor numbers has reduced summer traffic congestion, visitors are still being encouraged to park in nearby towns and enter Yosemite by bus, a more tempting option than it might sound. These buses mostly leave from the local transport nexus of Merced, eighty miles southwest of Yosemite Valley, where they link with Amtrak trains and Greyhound buses. Several companies also run tours either solely to Yosemite, or visiting Yosemite as part of a longer circuit.

International and out-of-state visitors will probably want to **fly** to California, more than likely using the international airports in Los Angeles and San Francisco, though Fresno is closer to Yosemite. Either rent a car at the airport or use public transportation to get to the Park.

By car

Contrary to popular belief, there is no restriction on driving your own vehicle into Yosemite, nor is there likely to be in the foreseeable future. Indeed, **driving to Yosemite** is straightforward. Of the Park's four road entrances, three are from the west and one traverses the Sierra Nevada from the Owens Valley in the east. The three western approaches are generally kept open all year (except immediately after snowfall), but the eastern approach (Hwy-120 East) over the 10,000-foot Tioga Pass is closed all winter (see box, p.20). The Park is around 200 miles from San Francisco (just under 4hr), 310 miles from Los Angeles (6hr) and 340 miles from Las Vegas (8hr).

Approaching Yosemite

Drivers have a choice of **four roads into Yosemite**. All have concentrations of lodging and eating establishments close to the Park boundary and your choice of route will most likely be determined by where you are starting. Towns along all four approach roads are covered in detail in Chapters 12–15.

From the west: Hwy-120 West

The most direct (though not necessarily the fastest) approach from the San Francisco Bay area to Yosemite is along **Hwy-120 West**, which can be picked up at Manteca, twelve miles south of Stockton, where the freeways I-5 and Hwy-99 meet. From there a fairly good road runs through **Oakdale** and **Chinese Camp** to the attractive former gold-town of **Groveland**. With its supply of appealing lodging and restaurants, Groveland makes a great base for western Yosemite, particularly Hetch Hetchy, though the Valley is still an hour's drive away.

For the next twenty-odd miles there's little in the way of services except for a good selection of accommodation, all heavily oriented to Yosemite visitors. The Park's entrance is at Big Oak Flat, where there's a small information station that's a good place to stop to check for both accommodation availability and wilderness permits.

From the southwest: Hwy-140

The fastest road into Yosemite from San Joaquin Valley in the west is **Hwy-140**, which cuts off Hwy-99 at **Merced**, an important transport interchange for Amtrak, Greyhound, and buses into the Park. Although Merced has good lodging, including a HI hostel, and some decent restaurants, it is really too distant from the Park to make it a good base. A better bet is **Mariposa**, about an hour's drive from the Valley, or even Midpines, where there's an excellent backpacker hostel and lodge.

A major **rockfall** in 2006 closed the highway around ten miles west of the Park entrance. A one-way traffic-light controlled detour now allows traffic to bypass the slip but can add 15 minutes to the journey and vehicle lengths are limited to 28 feet.

You'll enter the Park near **El Portal** at the Arch Rock entrance, from where it is a short drive directly into Yosemite Valley.

From the south: Hwy-41

Approaching from Los Angeles and the southern half of California, you'll most likely follow **Hwy-41**, which enters Yosemite through the South Entrance, near Wawona and the Mariposa Grove of Giant Sequoias. At Fresno, turn off Hwy-99 onto Hwy-41, which runs for forty miles through the Sierra foothills to the bustling but functional **Oakhurst**. There's accommodation here and on the road into Yosemite at **Fish Camp**. At the South Entrance you have a choice of roads: right for the Mariposa Grove of Giant Sequoias; left for Wawona and the rest of the Park.

From the east: Hwy-120 East

Visitors coming to Yosemite from Las Vegas or Death Valley during the summer and fall will approach along US-395, which runs through the dry sage-brush-covered hills of the Owens Valley past **Mammoth Lakes** to **Mono Lake** and **Lee Vining**. Here, you'll follow the only eastern approach to Yosemite, **Hwy-120 East** (generally open late May–early Nov) which cuts west up the Lee Vining grade past a number of good campgrounds to the Tioga Pass Park entrance at almost 10,000 feet. Tuolumne Meadows lies six miles ahead, but it's another hour and half in the car to Yosemite Valley.

Renting a car

If traveling from out of state or from overseas, chances are you'll want to **rent a car**. For short visits the convenience is a boon, and even for longer hiking or rock climbing holidays rental rates are low enough that when shared between two or more people the cost isn't prohibitive.

What **type of vehicle** you choose is pretty much a matter of taste and budget, though there are a couple of things to consider. That convertible you had your eye on

Tioga Road closures and winter driving conditions

For over half the year the only eastern entrance to Yosemite – the 10,000ft **Tioga Road** (Hwy-120 East) – is **closed by snow**. It usually shuts by mid-November (though late October is not unheard of), and typically reopens between mid-May and mid-June; for snow conditions and road closures call ⓣ209/372-0200. **Glacier Point Road** from the Badger Pass ski area to Glacier Point is also closed at about the same time.

All vehicles entering the Park (including four-wheel-drives) are required to carry **tire chains** whenever chain controls are in effect, most likely from November to April. Rangers probably won't stop you but the highway patrol occasionally checks compliance especially if a storm is expected. Rental cars are not usually equipped with chains, but they can be rented (around $20–30 for up to a week) from service stations and auto parts shops around the region; shop around as deals vary considerably. Since you have to return rented chains to their source, many people find it more convenient to buy: a basic set for a compact car should cost under $60 from the same outlets, though prices roughly double for SUVs and pickups. Within the park there are no chain rental facilities, but they are for sale at the Yosemite Valley garage (around $50 for cars, $120 for trucks).

In snowy conditions, signs along the highway indicate the **restriction levels** on open roads; R1: snow tires or chains; R2: 4WD or chains; R3: chains on all vehicles. Anyone not used to fitting chains should practice beforehand.

With no significant hills, Hwy-140 from Mariposa often stays open even if all other roads are snowed in, and it is usually the first to be plowed. Hwy-120 West from Groveland is the route most likely to have tire chain restrictions after snowfall.

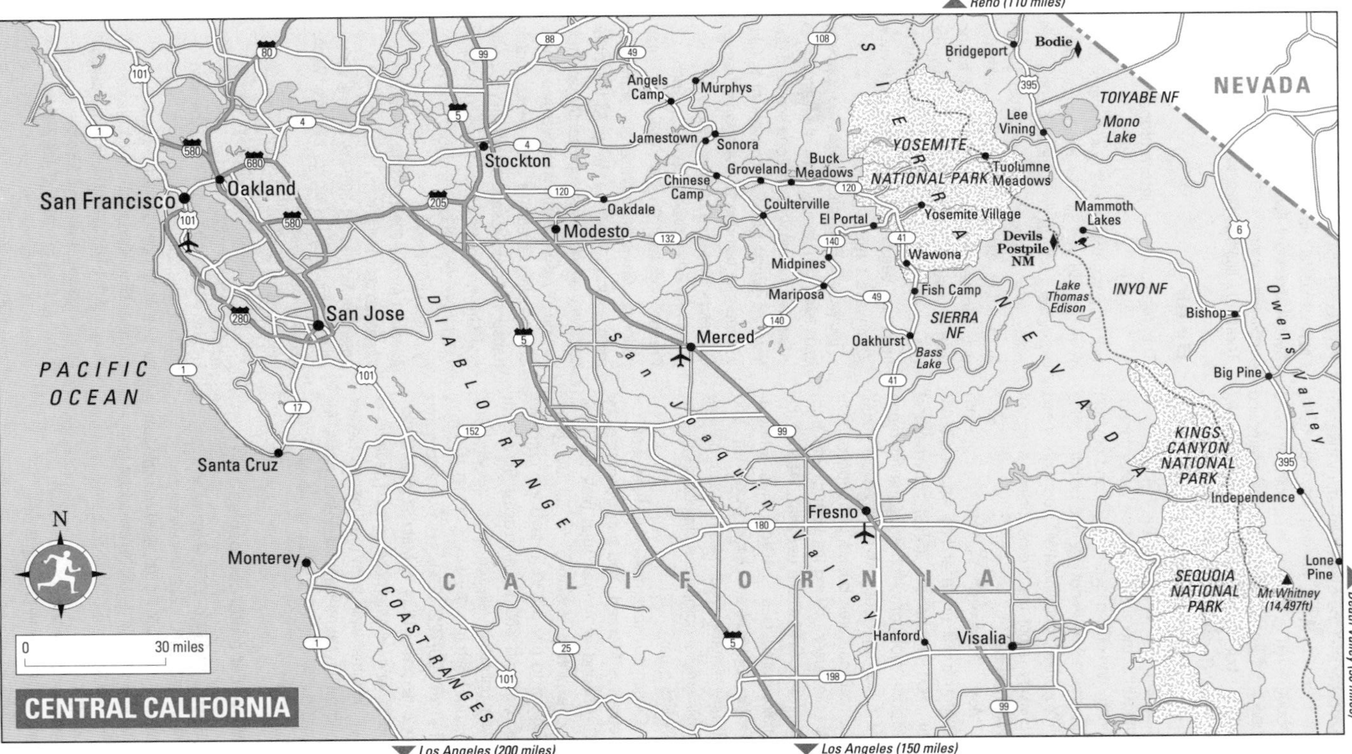
CENTRAL CALIFORNIA
Reno (110 miles)
Death Valley (50 miles)
Los Angeles (200 miles)
Los Angeles (150 miles)
NEVADA
TOIYABE NF
Mono Lake
Bodie
Bridgeport
Lee Vining
YOSEMITE NATIONAL PARK
Tuolumne Meadows
Yosemite Village
Mammoth Lakes
Devils Postpile NM
Wawona
Fish Camp
SIERRA NF
Bass Lake
Lake Thomas Edison
INYO NF
Bishop
Owens Valley
Big Pine
KINGS CANYON NATIONAL PARK
Independence
SEQUOIA NATIONAL PARK
Mt Whitney (14,497ft)
Lone Pine
S I E R R A N E V A D A
Angels Camp
Murphys
Jamestown
Sonora
Groveland
Buck Meadows
Chinese Camp
Coulterville
El Portal
Midpines
Mariposa
Oakhurst
Oakdale
Stockton
Modesto
Merced
San Joaquin Valley
Fresno
Hanford
Visalia
C A L I F O R N I A
San Francisco
Oakland
San Jose
DIABLO RANGE
PACIFIC OCEAN
Santa Cruz
Monterey
COAST RANGES
N
0
30 miles
1
4
5
6
17
25
41
49
80
88
99
101
108
120
132
140
152
180
198
205
280
395
580
680

probably isn't the best when left overnight in a Yosemite Valley parking lot with bears about. Even a hardtop isn't going to keep bears out if you've left something tempting inside, but a soft shell is inviting extra trouble. Generally an ordinary sedan works best, preferably something powerful enough to cope effortlessly with the hilly terrain. In the winter months it might be worth considering something with 4WD and/or high clearance. You're not going to be off-roading in Yosemite, but with 4WD you won't need to worry about tire chains (unless it snows very heavily).

Most Yosemite visitors flying into California will arrive at Los Angeles (LAX) or San Francisco (SFO) international airports, both of which have the full range of major agencies. At LAX, all car rental companies are based off-airport, with shuttle buses making frequent circuits from their depots to all the terminals. At SFO the major companies – Alamo, Avis, Budget, Dollar, Enterprise, Hertz, National, and Thrifty – have reservation desks on site while smaller companies provide shuttles to their depots.

Closer to Yosemite, the best bet for rentals is **Merced**. You can travel here by Greyhound or Amtrak then pick up a car for exploring Yosemite for a few days. Expect to pay a $30 a day for a compact and around $60 for a midsize SUV, both with unlimited mileage (plus tax and any insurance fees). Try Hertz, 1710 W Hwy-140 (ⓣ209/722-4200, ⓦwww.hertz.com), or Enterprise, 1334 W Main St (ⓣ209/722-1600, ⓦwww.enterprise.com). The latter is ten minutes' walk from the Transpo Center and offers three-day weekend deals for $20 a day providing you pick up on Friday or Saturday.

Major car rental companies

Alamo ⓣ1-800/462-5266, ⓦwww.alamo.com
Avis ⓣ1-800/331-1212, ⓦwww.avis.com
Budget ⓣ1-800/527-0700, ⓦwww.budget.com
Dollar ⓣ1-800/800-3665, ⓦwww.dollar.com
Enterprise ⓣ1-800/261-7331, ⓦwww.enterprise.com
Hertz ⓣ1-800/654-3131, ⓦwww.hertz.com
National ⓣ1-800/227-7368, ⓦwww.nationalcar.com
Payless ⓣ1-800/729-5377, ⓦwww.paylesscarrental.com
Rent-A-Wreck ⓣ1-800/944-7501, ⓦwww.rent-a-wreck.com
Thrifty ⓣ1-800/847-4389, ⓦwww.thrifty.com

By air

The nearest major **international airports** to Yosemite are San Francisco (4hr by car from the Valley) and Los Angeles (6hr), both served by all the major car rental agencies. Using a sequence of buses and trains (see opposite), it's possible to get from either airport to Yosemite within a day. **Merced Airport** is the closest airport with regional flights, though currently the only scheduled services are daily flights from Las Vegas with US Airways (ⓦwww.usairways.com).

The local YARTS bus service (see opposite) can take you direct from the airport to Yosemite, though with only one service a day from the airport it's more convenient to take a three-mile taxi ride to the town's Transpo Center, picking up a bus from there.

The only other airport worth considering is **Fresno** (officially Fresno Yosemite International; ⓦwww.flyfresno.org), some 95 miles south of Yosemite Valley. All the major car rental agencies are represented and you can be in Yosemite in a little over two hours. Unfortunately there is no direct public transportation to Yosemite, though you could ride Greyhound to Merced and pick up a YARTS bus from there. The following airlines fly direct into Fresno.

Allegiant Air ⓣ1-800/432-3810, ⓦwww.allegiantair.com. Flights from Las Vegas.
American Airlines ⓣ1-800/433-7300, ⓦwww.aa.com. Flights from Los Angeles, Dallas/Fort Worth, and Guadalajara, Mexico.
Delta Airlines ⓣ1-800/221-1212, ⓦwww.delta.com. Flights from Salt Lake City, Boise, Colorado Springs and Kansas City.
Frontier Airlines ⓣ1-800/432-1359, ⓦwww.frontierairlines.com. Flights from Denver.
Horizon Air ⓣ1-800/547-9308, ⓦwww.horizonair.com. Flights from Portland, Oregon.
Mexicana ⓣ1-800/531-7921, ⓦwww.mexicana.com. Flights from Guadalajara, Mexico.
United Airlines ⓣ1-800/241-6522, ⓦwww.united.com. Flights from Los Angeles, San Francisco, Denver and Las Vegas.

By train

There is **no direct train service** to Yosemite, though it is possible to get there by combining Amtrak (①1-800/872-7245, ⓦwww.amtrak.com) and bus services. The nearest train station is in Merced, where several services a day link with YARTS buses (see below) running straight to Yosemite Valley. You could conceivably visit Yosemite in one long day from San Francisco, but you'll only get around three hours in the Park.

The most convenient combination is from San Francisco, with five daily departures, though only a couple connect tolerably with bus services to Yosemite. The best is the early morning departure. Amtrak buses depart from the Ferry Building in San Francisco (7.05am), connect with trains across the Bay at Emeryville (7.40am), arrive at Merced in time to connect with YARTS buses (10.30am) and reach Yosemite Valley at 1.30pm.

On the return journey, the best bets are the YARTS departures at 10am and 4.15pm, that arrive at Merced Amtrak (12.27pm & 6.23pm) in time for the northbound train/bus combos (1.20pm & 6.49pm) which reach San Francisco at 5pm & 10.15pm.

From Southern California, Amtrak buses leaves Los Angeles' Union Station (4.10am & 10.45am) and connect with trains at Bakersfield (7.15am & 1.20pm), which reach Merced Amtrak (10.08am & 4.19pm) in time for YARTS departures (11am & 5.15pm) that arrive in Yosemite at 1.30pm and 8pm.

Leaving Yosemite heading south, departures at 10am & 4.15pm get you to Merced Amtrak (12.27pm & 6.23pm) in time for trains (12.59am & 6.31pm) which reach Los Angeles at 6.40pm & 12.30am the next morning.

Fares are lower if booked a few days in advance. Between San Francisco and Merced is costs roughly $34 each way, and from Los Angeles the fare is about $38 each way. Amtrak also sells tickets all the way to Yosemite ($48 from San Francisco; $45 from Los Angeles), which usually work out slightly cheaper than buying the two legs separately.

By bus

Buses are the only form of public transportation that will get you right into Yosemite National Park, with year-round scheduled Greyhound services to Merced where you can catch the local YARTS buses to Yosemite. In addition there is a summer-only YARTS service from Mammoth Lakes on the eastern side of the Sierra. Arriving by bus saves you having to pay the Park entrance fee.

Greyhound

Greyhound (①1-800/231-2222, ⓦwww.greyhound.com) runs buses from all over California to Merced (see p.19), the only viable jumping-off point for Yosemite. Greyhound is a little slower than the train and less convenient with few services that directly connect with YARTS buses. From San Francisco there are around four departures daily (4hr), with perhaps twice that number coming from Los Angeles (6–8hr), all calling at various towns along the way. **Fares** are lowest if booked a few days in advance. Generally you can get a round-trip ticket to Merced from either San Francisco or Los Angeles for about $66.

YARTS buses

The Park Service and local authorities have set up the Yosemite Area Regional Transportation System or **YARTS** (①1-877/989-2787 or 209/388-9589, ⓦwww.yarts.com) as a way of encouraging people to leave their vehicles outside the Park. While the service is excellent and quite cheap along the main Hwy-140 corridor from Merced into the Valley, it is less useful elsewhere with just a summer-only service from Mammoth Lakes over Tioga Pass and through Tuolumne Meadows to Yosemite Valley. No buses run along either Hwy-120 West from Groveland or along Hwy-41 from Oakhurst and Wawona.

Along the main route, Hwy-140 from Merced through Mariposa, Midpines and El Portal into the Valley, **fares** include the Park entry fee (potentially saving you $20) and each adult fare allows one child (12 and younger) to ride free: round trip from Merced is $25, from Mariposa and Midpines $12, and from El Portal just $7.

There are always connections to Amtrak trains at Merced, and some buses are

timed to coincide with the start of guided tours (see box, p.28) within the Park. **Timetables** are available on the YARTS website and from visitor centers in the area. There are four departures daily picking up at the Merced Transpo Center and the Amtrak station (around 7am, 8.45am, 10.30am & 5.15pm), then calling at Mariposa (after one hour) and Midpines (1hr 15min) before arriving in Yosemite Valley (after almost 3hr). A couple of convenient early-morning services start their run in Mariposa. All drop off at Yosemite Village, *The Ahwahnee*, and Curry Village before the final stop at *Yosemite Lodge*. **Tickets** can be bought on board. Return services leave the Valley at 10am, 4.30pm, 5.50pm and 8.20pm.

The summer-only YARTS service along Hwy-120 East from Mammoth Lakes through Tuolumne Meadows to Yosemite Valley is less useful for commuting into the Park. There's only one service a day (Yosemite bound in the morning, and Mammoth-bound in the afternoon) but it does mean you can stay in Mammoth and make day-trips to Tuolumne Meadows that still allow enough time for a hike or two.

Tours and guided trips to Yosemite

Generally speaking, anything called a **sightseeing tour** that begins outside the park will involve you in an unsatisfying race through the Valley. The following four organizations, however, buck this trend with backpacker-oriented niche packages that keep costs low.

California Dreamin' Tours Ⓣ1-866/440-4440 or 626/533-5529, Ⓦwww.caldreamin.com. These backpacker-oriented, minibus tours give excellent coverage of California, Las Vegas and the Grand Canyon but only spend a couple of days in Yosemite. Though generally LA-based, you can join the tour at other points by special arrangement. Several tours run through the summer months (late May to early Oct) and most meals are included. The eight-day trip which includes Yosemite costs $580.

Green Tortoise Ⓣ1-800/867-8647 or 415/956-7500, Ⓦwww.greentortoise.com. With their roots going back to hippy bus tours from the early 1970s, Green Tortoise offer a more alternative approach than most using converted buses which facilitate a more communal atmosphere, and allow you to sleep on the bus (lying down) as you travel. They're geared towards active, outdoorsy types who enjoy camping out with limited privacy and pitching-in. You'll need to be flexible, must help with food preparation and should bring a sleeping bag and general traveling gear (but not a tent or cooking gear). Their two-day weekend trips (mostly April–Sept; $129, plus $41 food fund) to the Valley and Mariposa Grove run roughly twice a month departing from San Francisco Friday evening at 9pm and returning around 7am Monday. The three-day trip (June to mid-Oct; $181, plus $49 food fund) departs at Monday and Friday evening around 9pm returning early Friday or Tuesday morning and additionally spends half a day in Tuolumne Meadows and time around Mono Lake and at some hot springs. Both trips involve camping just outside the Park boundary, free time for day hikes and a final fling at the *Iron Door Saloon* in Groveland (see p.182). The food fund covers almost all your meals and Park entry fees.

Incredible Adventures ⓣ1-800/777-8464 or 415/642-7378, ⓦwww.incadventures.com. Based in San Francisco, this group runs four tempting tours to Yosemite using biodiesel fifteen-seater minibuses. The rushed one-day trip ($129; all year 7am–9pm; departures Tues & Thurs–Sun) includes a quick whip around the main Yosemite Valley sights and gives you around three hours to explore and hike. The more satisfying three-day trip ($240; late-May to mid-Oct; departures Sun, Tues & Thurs) is a camping-based tour with everyone pitching in to prepare food. Trips spend three nights just outside the Park staying at the same campground each night and exploring by day, perhaps high-country hiking around Tuolumne or visiting the sequoias. Most meals are included in the trip price. You'll need your own sleeping bag or can rent one for $10. In spring they run six- and seven-day Backpack & Raft trips (from $759; June & July) and there's also a year-round two-day hotel-based trip ($269) staying at *Cedar Lodge* (see p.169), with varied departure times throughout the year.

Yosemite Bug Bus Tours ⓣ1-866/826-7108, ⓦwww.yosemitebugbus.com. The *Yosemite Bug Rustic Mountain Resort* (see p.169), located a few miles outside Yosemite National Park, run a number of excellent bus trips. The most frequent trip is the Two-Day-Two-Night Tour (all-year Mon, Wed & Fri; staying in a dorm $155, private room $175, en suite $195) starting in San Francisco and spending both nights at the *Bug*. Visits to Mariposa Grove, Sentinel Dome, Yosemite Valley and the Mist Trail are supplemented by swimming, biking or gold panning, meals (included for an extra $26) and campfires at the *Bug*. For something more adventurous, go for the five-day Yosemite Backcountry Backpacking trips (June–Sept; $320–400), which involve exploring the high country and camping out in spectacular locations: see the website for details.

Getting around

The abundance of public transportation available in Yosemite is unusual for a national park. Long-term plans call for even more, though if the current downward trend in visitor numbers continues, that vision will become increasingly blurred.

YARTS services from the eastern entrance on Hwy-120 East and the western entrance on Hwy-140 run through the Park to Yosemite Valley, where free **shuttle buses** ferry visitors around the main sights and accommodation areas at its eastern end. From here, **hikers buses** fan out to Glacier Point and also Tuolumne Meadows, where there's another free shuttle service along the most popular section of Tioga Road. **Guided tours** range even further with trips as far as Tuolumne Meadows, and the southern section of the Park, where a third free shuttle links Wawona to the Mariposa Grove of Giant Sequoias. Unfortunately, there is only limited public transportation from the Valley to Wawona.

Despite all this choice, for some of the farther-flung parts, having a **car** is ideal. **Cycling** is also a viable option, and even **hitching is permitted** (though not encouraged): some hikers choose to walk one way then hitch back to their car, hotel or campground.

Shuttles and hikers buses

At some point almost everyone visiting Yosemite uses one of the **free shuttle buses**. By far the most popular is the Yosemite Valley Shuttle Bus around the eastern end of Yosemite Valley, though other services around Tuolumne Meadows and Wawona are also very convenient. In winter, skiers and boarders can ride from the Valley to the skifield at no charge.

The Glacier Point and Tuolumne Meadows **hikers buses** are both fee-charged services running in conjunction with the Glacier Point and Tuolumne tours. Consequently you get a full commentary, either all the way to the destination, or as far as your chosen trailhead.

Yosemite Valley Shuttle Bus

In the Valley, drivers should park at Curry Village or in the day-use parking area at Yosemite Village (sometimes known as Camp 6), and get around on the frequent and **free shuttle buses**. Recently upgraded to quieter and less polluting diesel hybrids, they operate around the eastern end of the Valley floor – we've marked shuttle stops with stars on our Yosemite Valley map (see p.48). Services run counterclockwise on a loop that passes through, or close to, all the main points of interest, trailheads and accommodation areas. From May to September visitor shuttles run roughly every ten to twenty minutes between 7am–10pm to most sections of the Valley, with slightly reduced frequency and hours at other times: see *Yosemite Today* for the current details. Buses are designed with low floors for easy access.

El Capitan Shuttle Bus

To access the western end of Yosemite Valley use the **free El Capitan Shuttle** (June to early Sept daily every 30min 9am–6pm), which runs on a loop from the Valley Visitor Center (stop 5) along Northside Drive to El Capitan Picnic Area and El Capitan Meadow (for excellent views of the monolith), then back along Southside Drive past the Four-Mile Trailhead to stop 5.

Tuolumne Meadows Shuttle Bus

Getting around Tuolumne Meadows is best done on the handy and **free Olmsted Point/ Tuolumne Meadows/Tioga Pass Shuttle** (mid-June to mid-Sept daily 7am–7pm), which makes an eleven-mile run every half an hour from *Tuolumne Meadows Lodge* past the Tuolumne Visitor Center and several important trailheads to Tenaya Lake and the fabulous viewpoint at Olmsted Point. The last bus leaves Olmsted Point at 6pm.

Four times a day (9am, noon, 3pm and 5pm) the route is extended and the bus runs six miles eastbound from Tuolumne Meadows to the Park entrance at Tioga Pass opening up a handful of excellent hikes.

Mariposa Grove & Wawona Shuttle

Throughout the busy summer months, the Mariposa Grove parking lot is frequently full, so visitors are encouraged to make use of the **free Mariposa Grove & Wawona Shuttle Bus** (mid-April to early Oct daily 9am–6pm), which runs frequently from the Wawona Store to Mariposa Grove. There's an intermediate stop at the South Entrance, so drivers entering the Park from the south can park here and ride the shuttle to the Mariposa Grove, then pick up their vehicle on the way back. The last bus back leaves the grove at 6pm. The shuttle is also handy for hikers who want to ride one way then hike back to Wawona, downhill all the way (see box, p.101).

Wawona & Yosemite Valley Shuttle

With the arguable exception of the Grand Tour (see p.28), the only public transportation between Yosemite Valley and Wawona is this summer-only once-daily **free shuttle**. The bus leaves the *Wawona Hotel* at 8.30am and arrives at *Yosemite Lodge* a little over an hour later. The return journey leaves *Yosemite Lodge* at 3.30pm.

Tuolumne Meadows Hikers Bus

Getting between Yosemite Valley and Tuolumne Meadows is straightforward. You can drive it in about ninety minutes, hike the

John Muir Trail for a couple of days, ride the afternoon YARTS bus (see p.23), or catch the **Tuolumne Meadows Hikers Bus** (mid-June to early-Sept; $14.50 one way, $23 round trip, kids 5–12 half-price, section fares available). Run in conjunction with the Tuolumne Meadows Tour (see p.28) it opens up the trails that lead off Tioga Road (Hikes 14–22) and plenty more from Tuolumne Meadows. The bus makes a 2hr 10min run from the Valley (leaving Curry Village at 8am, then *Yosemite Lodge* at 8.20am) to Tuolumne Meadows with stops at Crane Flat, White Wolf, Tuolumne Meadows Lodge, and anywhere else you request. The return journey leaves at 2pm, giving around three and a half hours in Tuolumne if done as a day-trip. If you need to be picked up en route, call a day or two in advance (☎209/372-1240) to let them know to expect you, then pay the driver.

Glacier Point Hikers Bus

A combined tour bus and trail access service, the **Glacier Point Hikers Bus** (late May–Oct; $20 each way, seniors $18, kids $12, section fares available), runs from the Valley to Glacier Point and back (1hr 10min each way) and is particularly convenient for lazy hikers wanting to ride the bus up then hike down the Four-Mile Trail (Hike 9), or for masochists to hike up and bus back. The bus is also useful for reaching the trailheads for Inspiration Point (Hike 11), the Pohono–Panorama Trail Combo (Hike 44) and the hikes off Glacier Point Road (Hikes 35–40).

There are three round trips daily, leaving *Yosemite Lodge* at 8.30am, 10am (not Oct), and 1.30pm, and departing Glacier Point at 10.30am, noon (not Oct), and 3.30pm. Section fares mean that you won't necessarily be paying the full Glacier Point fare for shorter rides.

Badger Pass Bus

During the winter months when the Badger Pass ski area is open, visitors staying in the Valley can reach Badger Pass on the **Badger Pass Bus** (Dec to early April daily; free). It leaves the Valley each morning calling at Curry Village (8am & 10.30am), Yosemite Village (8.10am & 10.40am), *The Ahwahnee* (8.15am & 10.45pm), and *Yosemite Lodge* (8.30am & 11am), arriving at Badger Pass an hour later. The return services leave Badger Pass at 2 and 4pm, and there are extra services on busy days (particularly holiday weekends).

Driving

Traffic congestion spoils everyone's fun, particularly in July and August, and the Park Service is doing what it can to reduce snarl-ups without cramping people's style unnecessarily. You can drive into Yosemite Valley, but as part of the Yosemite Valley Plan (see p.245) there is a long-term strategy to reduce the number of parking spaces in the Valley and encourage people to use the improved public transportation. All sorts of legal challenges are holding the process up and little seems likely to change in the immediate future.

Visitors are encouraged to leave their vehicles in the surrounding towns, and ride buses (see p.25) into the Valley. These are more tempting than they may sound and for those staying outside the Park and popping into the Valley each day it definitely makes sense – there's more time for admiring the scenery, and you don't pay Park entrance fees. This only really makes sense along the Hwy-140 corridor with Mariposa, Midpines and El Portal being obvious bases. If you drive into the Valley, be sure to leave your rig in one of the parking lots and use the free Valley shuttle buses to get around.

For exploring areas outside the Valley – Tioga Road, Glacier Point Road and Wawona – a car is very handy, with parking easier to find. Roads within the Park are generally in good condition, but many are winding with unnervingly steep drops to the side. The **maximum speed limit is 45mph** (35mph in the Valley) though often you'll be traveling much slower, maybe trapped behind some lumbering RV with no passing lanes in sight. The 55-mile drive from the Valley to Tuolumne Meadows might easily take two hours, and it is best to **be patient** and make frequent short stops to admire the view. Wherever you drive, try to keep your eyes on the road, and remember that others will be rubbernecking the scenery and may stop or pull out unexpectedly. Stop only at designated turnouts and pull well off the road. In winter and spring watch out for icy patches where the road is shaded by rocks or trees. For winter driving conditions and information on snow chains, see the box on p.20.

Cycling

While roads are narrow and grades are steep in much of the Park, **cycling** remains one of the most enjoyable ways to get around Yosemite Valley, where wide, flat roads are augmented by twelve miles of traffic-free asphalt bike paths at its eastern end. Cycling through the Park can be pleasurable if you time your ride when there is minimal traffic – spring and fall are probably your best bets.

Most people just cycle gently between the main sights in the Valley on single-speed **rented cruisers** ($7.50 per hour; $24.50 per day), available from the *Yosemite Lodge* bike stand (summer daily 9am–6pm or 7pm; ⓣ209/372-1208) and the Curry Village bike stand (summer daily 9am–6pm or 7pm; ⓣ209/372-8319). Tandems are not available, but for those with kids there are six-speed bike and trailer combos ($13.50 per hour, $42 a day) and baby jogger **strollers** ($7.50 per hour, $11 a day). By law, anyone seventeen or younger must wear a helmet ($5 per day).

Park regulations prohibit cycling off-road or along hiking trails, so you can forget about serious **mountain biking** within Yosemite National Park. More rewarding options lie just outside the Park in the surrounding national forests. We've covered a couple of rides close to Hwy-140 near the Briceburg Visitor Center (see p.205) and the downhill biking mecca of Mammoth Mountain (see p.220), but there's more to be found in the Stanislaus National Forest to the northwest, and a wealth of rides near Oakhurst, where there's the added benefit of all-terrain bike rental (see p.210).

Guided tours from Yosemite Valley

If time is short and you don't mind being herded around, you could join one of the Valley-based **guided tours**, which let you see as many of the major sights as possible along with a breezy (and occasionally cheesy) commentary. All tours start from *Yosemite Lodge*, where you can buy tickets on the spot at the Tour Desk, though in July and August it pays to **buy a ticket** a couple of days in advance either through the tour desk at any of the Valley hotels or by calling ⓣ209/372-4386. Children four and under ride free; kids' rates are for ages 5–12 inclusive.

An additional tour – the **Big Trees Tour** around the Mariposa Grove in the southern section of the Park – is covered on p.101.

Glacier Point Tour (late May to Oct; 4hr; $32.50, seniors & kids $26) A round-trip bus tour from the Valley passing many of its most famous sights and spectacular vistas on the way to Glacier Point, climbing over three thousand feet along the way. Buses depart from *Yosemite Lodge* at 8.30am, 10am (not in Oct) and 1.30pm daily. You'll get just over an hour at Glacier Point, but for those who want to stay longer, it can also be ridden one way in its role as the Glacier Point Hikers' Bus (see p.27).

Grand Tour (late May to early Nov; 8hr; $62, seniors $55, kids, $33) An informative full-day bus tour visiting Glacier Point, Wawona and including the Big Trees Tour around the Mariposa Grove (see p.101). It departs from *Yosemite Lodge* at 8.45am and stops for lunch at Wawona where you can eat lunch at the *Wawona Hotel* (additional $8–10 if bought when you book the tour). Only worthwhile if you are desperate to see as much as possible in one day.

Moonlight Tour (May–Sept/Oct when full moon falls, 2hr; $22, seniors $18, kids $11.50) Essentially the Valley Floor Tour (see opposite) done in the evening on the three or four nights leading up to full moon, with departures from *Yosemite Lodge* at either 9.30 or 10pm, depending on how late the moon rises. The enchanting silvery views make it worth enduring the annoying megaphone commentary.

Tuolumne Meadows Tour (mid-June to early Sept; 8hr; $23, kids $11.50) A there-and-back bus tour with stacks of photo opportunities at all the main Tioga Road viewpoints and sites of interest. A break allows over three hours for gentle hiking in Tuolumne Meadows. The tour is also the

Tuolumne Meadows Hikers Bus (see p.26) and can be used for one-way rides or for accessing the high country. Departs Curry Village at 8am then *Yosemite Lodge* at 8.20am.

Valley Floor Tour (all year; 2hr; $22, seniors $18, kids $11.50, family rates available) A rather dull and predictable 26-mile tour along the Valley roads on a kind of open-air flat-deck tram car with seats (or a bus from late Oct to April), with a fairly informative commentary on the famous landmarks, history, geology, flora and fauna. You get to visit or gaze at Yosemite Falls, Half Dome, El Capitan, Bridalveil Fall and Tunnel View (see p.91), which is otherwise hard to get to without a car (or a long walk). Best exploited on extremely rushed visits, the tour leaves from *Yosemite Lodge* every hour or so in summer, and twice a day in winter.

Health and backcountry dangers

Most visitors leave Yosemite with little more discomfort than a sunburn or aching legs from hiking up Half Dome. Accidents, of course, do happen and it is sensible to take a few precautions. For starters, if injured or suffering any ill effects, get in touch with the **Yosemite Medical Clinic** in Yosemite Village (see p.57). Along with the safety advice given below, it's also worth being aware that **altitude sickness** (see box, p.87) can strike if you quickly travel from low to high altitudes and stay overnight.

Theft and threats to your **personal safety** are also rare, but as with anywhere that people congregate, there are risks: don't drop your guard just because you are on vacation.

Bears, rattlers and mountain lions

Visitors unfamiliar with bear territory often arrive in Yosemite with an irrationally heightened fear of the threat bears pose. Despite the presence of a grizzly bear on the California state flag, these majestic beasts have been extinct in California for over a century and all bears in Yosemite (no matter what shade their fur) are **black bears**. In recent years, the Park Service has gone to great lengths to reduce the bears' reliance on human food and minimize human–bear contact. Consequently the bad old days when dozens of cars were broken into each night in the Valley are a thing of the past, and bears wandering through campgrounds are increasingly rare. You are encouraged to **report bear-related problems** and sightings on ⓣ209/372-0322. For more details see our "Smarter than the average bear" box on p.11.

Most visitors are thrilled to see bears, though fewer are keen on an encounter with a **rattlesnake**. There's no need to be especially fearful, but it definitely pays to keep an eye out for the thick-bodied Western rattlesnake (the only poisonous snake you're likely to see). They are fairly common below 5000ft (and have been seen as high as 10,000ft), generally preferring moderate temperatures and even hunting at night in midsummer at lower elevations. You're most likely to encounter them in boulder-strewn areas where they warm themselves in the morning sun, or in the dappled shade of trees where their patchy markings camouflage them perfectly. Much of the hiking in Yosemite is above 5000ft where the risk is much reduced, but when hiking low down heavy footfalls generally ensure that snakes will keep out of your way. In particular, don't go turning over rotting logs and the like without checking for the presence of lounging snakes. If you get **bitten**, try to remain as calm as possible, stay put and send for help. The old advice to suck out the poison or tourniquet the limb is counterproductive and even gently binding the limb and using snakebite kits is no longer widely recommended. Get outside help as soon as possible.

Mountain lions live throughout the Park but are rarely seen. Count yourself lucky if you catch sight of one but minimize the chance of an attack by grouping together and trying to appear as large as possible. Don't advance or run away, but retreat slowly and if the lion attacks, fight back. Normal mountain lion prey doesn't do that, and the shock of being attacked themselves usually frightens them off.

Smaller critters and poisonous plants

Perhaps the most annoying of smaller critters is the **mosquito**. In summer they're around populated areas, particularly at dawn and dusk, but are particularly bad in the high country. If you are venturing backcountry, be sure to take long pants, a loose long-sleeved shirt and bug repellant. A number of "natural" non-DEET repellants are available in the Park and work quite well, but when the going really gets tough you'll be glad of something with around 30 percent DEET.

Anyone who sits down to snack on a sandwich will soon be pestered by small critters, especially ground **squirrels**, Douglas' squirrels and the bushy-tailed Western Gray squirrel. Mor e tiresome than dangerous, they do, however, carry rabies and other nasty diseases so don't encourage them.

In spring, hikers may be exposed to the western-blacklegged **tick**, which is known to transmit the bacteria causing **Lyme disease**. Ticks lurk in moist, cool environments and may latch onto you as you brush through shaded grasses and shrubs, especially under oak trees. If you're walking in such areas, wear light-colored clothing to show up any ticks, tuck long pants into your socks and apply tick repellant (available locally). More information is available from the Park on ⓣ209/379-1033.

In the Sierra foothills (up to 5000ft), watch out for **poison oak**, with its oak-like grouping of three dark-green-veined leaves that secrete an oily juice. It's highly allergenic, so avoid touching it. If you do, washing with strong soap usually helps, though you are better applying an oil removal product such as Tecnu as soon after contact as possible. In extreme cases, see a doctor.

Fire and ice

Fire is both a natural hazard and a forest management tool used by the Park Service to reduce the risk of catastrophic fires. Those caused by human error and any blazes that threaten to destroy property are extinguished as soon as possible, but other wildfires are frequently left to burn, often for weeks. During summer and fall days, it is not unusual to see columns of **smoke** out in the Yosemite backcountry. At night, the cooling air draws the smoke down into Yosemite Valley, meaning hotel guests and campers rise to an oddly beautiful hazy world with beams of light filtering through the oaks. The smoke, however, can be irritating, particularly for elderly people and those with respiratory problems, who should avoid strenuous activity at such times. Usually the smoke clears by midday. More information on fire and its management (including details of fires currently burning) can be found at ⓦwww.nps.gov/yose/fire.

One of the biggest health risks in Yosemite is **exposure** to the elements. With typically stable summer weather and mild nights it is tempting to head out hiking in just shorts and a T-shirt, but storms can arrive quickly and when they do temperatures drop rapidly, especially at altitude. Caught without shelter in wet, cotton clothes with the wind picking is no fun at all and can quickly lead to **hypothermia**. Be prepared, and follow our hiking checklist on p.140.

Safety around water

Every year people get into trouble trying to cross or swim in streams. It might sound obvious, but choose your swimming spots carefully. We've suggested a few good and relatively safe locales in Chapter 6, "Summer Activities" (see p.154), but there are numerous other tempting swimming holes beside trails. Never swim or wade above **waterfalls**, even if the water appears calm. People are swept over falls almost every year when caught by unexpected currents. In the spring, **snowmelt** turns Yosemite's rivers into raging torrents, often with underwater obstacles that can easily trap the unwary. At these times, stay away from riverbanks and avoid rock-hopping. Along the major trails, streams are all suitably bridged, but in places where there is no bridge look for a calm, safe spot to cross, and be prepared to turn back if you can't find anywhere suitable.

Swimming is best from July onwards: as the snowmelt abates the waters are safer, and by August the rivers are tolerably warm (at least on hot days). Most of all, **supervise children** closely when anywhere around water.

Water quality

Water from fountains and faucets throughout the Park is invariably drinkable, but water taken from streams and lakes may contain disease-bearing organisms that can spread **giardia**. The official line is that all such water should be treated, though giardia is relatively uncommon and you may wish to chance it. That said, the consequence of contracting the disease are not pleasant at all, so chose your source carefully: rushing side streams are a better bet than lakes or large rivers which have a wide catchment.

Hikers should carry all the water they need or be prepared to purify it in some way. Options for the latter include carrying a giardia-rated water filter, dosing the water with iodine-based tablets or solutions, boiling the water for three to five minutes, or using one of the new ultraviolet light irradiators.

To prevent the spread of disease, use toilets where provided. In other areas, **bury human waste** at least six inches deep at least 40 paces away from any lake or stream, and carry out your toilet paper – double plastic bags should do the trick. All washing should be done a similar distance away from water.

Travel essentials

Campfires

Summertime air-quality restrictions limit campfires in Yosemite Valley to 5pm to 10pm from May to mid-October. For ecological reasons, firewood must not be gathered in the valley or above 9600 feet, but is available for sale at stores throughout the park.

Costs

Visiting Yosemite can be expensive. Accommodation, restaurant and tour costs are fairly high, and those on a brief visit might balk at the $20 entrance fee. Outside the Park, prices are much the same as you might expect in rural California, though accommodation is still on the pricey side, especially in the peak summer months.

In contrast, much of what you'll be doing in Yosemite is free. The scenery costs nothing, and many of the landmark sights in the Valley are accessible by the free shuttle bus. Once you've obtained the appropriate gear, hiking isn't going to dent the pocketbook, and if you are tackling overnight hikes (for which permits are free) then you camp in the backcountry for no charge. In addition, the Park Service runs numerous free ranger programs and much of the evening entertainment cost little or nothing as well. In winter there's even a complimentary shuttle bus connecting the Valley with the Badger Pass ski area.

If you are camping, preparing the majority of your meals yourself, and avoiding most fee-charging activities you can scrape by on $20 a day per person. By staying in the cabins at Curry Village or *Housekeeping Camp*, or at the *Bug* hostel just outside the

Park, eating meals out at the cheaper places and perhaps going horse riding or taking a tour, you'll need to set aside $60–70 a day. If you're staying at *Yosemite Lodge* or the *Wawona Hotel*, you'll be paying $120–150 a day; and those sleeping in the luxury of *The Ahwahnee*, eating most meals there and not skimping on tours can easily rack up a tally amounting to $400 a day.

Crime and personal safety

With mass flooding in the Valley in 1997, a series of rockfalls and even murders taking place in recent years, Yosemite has received more than its fair share of bad press. For all that, the Park remains a very safe place to visit; *Outside* magazine once claimed that the chances of being killed in an American National Park are around two million to one, about the same as drowning in your own bath.

Of course you shouldn't let your guard down just because you're on holiday: keep hold of those valuables and temptingly shiny cameras.

Personal safety is under greater threat from the elements, flora and fauna, covered in detail under "Health and backcountry dangers" (see p.29).

Electricity

The US operates on 110V at 60Hz and uses two-pronged plugs with the flat prongs parallel. Foreign devices will need a plug adapter though laptops and phone chargers automatically detect and cope with the different voltage and frequency. Other appliances will also require a transformer.

Entry requirements and Park Passes

Yosemite is always open. All four roads entering the Park have entrance stations that are just a kiosk in the middle of the road staffed by rangers. In summer these are typically open daily from 8am to 8pm though only until 5pm at other times. When open you're required to stop and pay the Park entry fee of $20 per vehicle (including all passengers), and $10 for each cyclist or hiker. Passengers arriving by bus avoid any Park entry fee. One payment is good for seven days, and there are potential savings with a number of annual passes. In return for your fee you'll be given a handful of useful leaflets and one of the national park service's characteristically superb maps.

If the entrance station is closed, simply drive through and pay your fee at one of the visitor centers where you can also pick up the same leaflets. Rangers usually stop visitors leaving the Park to check they have paid their fee.

Park passes

As well as the standard Park entry tickets you can also buy a **Yosemite Pass** ($40) allowing unlimited Yosemite visits for a year. If your visit is part of wider travels it may be worth investing in the **America the Beautiful National Parks and Federal Recreational Lands Annual Pass** ($80), valid for entry to all US national parks, national forests, national historic areas, national seashores, etc for a year from the date of purchase. In addition, free lifetime access to all national parks is available to US citizens and residents 62 and over who buy the **Senior Pass** ($10), and US citizens and permanent residents with lifetime disabilities who obtain the **Access Pass** (free). The Senior and Access passes also give a fifty percent discount on camping fees in national parks: these are available at Yosemite entrance stations.

Gas

Gas is available for a good price in Oakhurst, and moderate prices in Mariposa and Groveland. Gas is fairly expensive in the Park, but is available year-round at Crane Flat (the nearest to Yosemite Valley, 16 miles distant) and Wawona, and also at Tuolumne Meadows whenever Tioga Pass is open. Hours are printed in *Yosemite Today* and all three have 24hr operation with credit and debit cards.

Internet

Yosemite isn't that great for Internet access but it is getting better. Still, it is a national park and many would argue that a few days out of touch isn't such a bad thing. There's **free** access at the Yosemite Village public library (Mon 8.30–11.30am, Tues 10am–2pm, Wed 8.30am–12.30pm, & Thurs 4–7pm; limited to one 30min session per week) located just west of the Yosemite Museum in a building signed "Girls Club." There are just three machines, and opening hours are inconvenient if you want to be out doing stuff during the day. Demand is high and it is first-come-first-served so turn up early.

The only other public-use computers are a handful of pay kiosks ($1 for 4min; bills and credit cards accepted) at the daytime-only *Degnan's Café* in Yosemite Village (see p.180) and a couple more in the lobby of *Yosemite Lodge*.

The lobby of *Yosemite Lodge* also has free **Wi-Fi** for guests and will let nonguests log on ($6 for 12hr, $10 for 24hr or $25 for 3 days). There are plans afoot to supply all rooms with Wi-Fi at which point the lobby connections may be cut off.

The Ahwahnee also has free Wi-Fi in the Great Lounge: this is intended for guests, but is currently unsecured, though that may change. Anyone seeking a **dataport** will need to stay at *The Ahwahnee* or *Yosemite Lodge*, the only hotels with phones in rooms.

The Park's only public Internet access outside the Valley is at the Bassett Memorial Library in Wawona (see p.99).

Kids

Yosemite is a great place for **kids**, but as elsewhere it needs a little thought to maximize their (and your) enjoyment. Younger members of the family probably aren't going to thank you for dragging them (possibly literally) on long hikes with only a bit of boring scenery to look at. On the other hand, if you break up the hike with lake swimming, time spent looking at plants and animal tracks and some good old-fashioned play, you can all have a great day.

One of the best ways to prepare for all this is to visit the **Nature Center at Happy Isles** (see p.66) which is specifically set up to introduce kids and their parents to what's out there alongside the trails. The staff here can introduce you to the **Junior Ranger** and **Little Cubs** programs (see p.185), aimed at focusing young minds.

Most of the standard **ranger programs** are suitable for kids – star gazing, learning about bears, etc – but there are also free **child-oriented ranger programs** and evening entertainment including campfire sing-songs and stories: see *Yosemite Today* for the latest schedule. There's more fun to be had at the **Yosemite Museum**, including learning how to play Miwok stick games, handling animal furs native to Yosemite, and watching a **basket-weaving** demonstration. And in winter the Badger Pass Ski Area has an extensive kids program.

Parents might also want to keep the kids entertained with **books** (all available from the Yosemite Association and most stores in Yosemite). Worthwhile examples include the native legends about the creation of El Capitan in *Two Bear Cubs*, the exploration of miniscule Yosemite in *The World of Small* (which comes with a magnifying glass), and *The Happy Camper Handbook*, an entertaining look at camping basics.

Traveling with kids can be expensive, but many of the events and activities you'll want to go on are free, and those that are fee-charging – tours, shows, rentals, etc – usually have **kids' prices**. Typically those four and under go free while kids five to twelve inclusive go for half-fare, and teenagers must pay adult rates. Sometimes there are **family fares** that offer savings for two adults and two or more kids.

There is no formal system for **babysitting** in the Park, but staff at *Yosemite Lodge* and *The Ahwahnee* can often arrange something for their guests. Infants have to be two or older and be out of diapers.

Laundry

See Showers and laundry on p.38.

Left luggage

Yosemite Lodge has a "bellman room" with limited space where nonguests can leave a backpack at no charge, but only during the day. For overnight storage, you'll find a few lockers (big enough for a medium-sized backpack) close to the tour desk and the shower block in Curry Village (75¢). The Wilderness Center, visitor centers, permit stations and ranger stations will not store food or equipment. For long-term storage, for example while away hiking, some people commandeer the bear-proof lockers at the Curry Village parking area or elsewhere: bring your own lock.

Library

A public research library (usually Tues–Fri 8am–noon & 1–5pm) is situated upstairs from the museum entrance in Yosemite Village and contains all manner of Yosemite, backcountry and climbing information including recent magazines and daily papers. There is also a public library that opens for a few hours a day (see "Internet," p.32). Outside the Valley you'll find a library at Wawona (see p.94), and more in the gateway towns.

Living and working in Yosemite

Opportunities for **seasonal work** in Yosemite are fairly limited. Almost everything is run either by the Park Service or by DNC, the Park concessionaire, both of which offer relatively low rates of pay in return for long hours that will probably include evenings, weekends and public holidays. In return you get a great location, time off to explore, and a pretty decent social scene. The **best starting point** for a job search is Ⓦwww.nps.gov/yose/jobs, which contains links to most employers offering work in the Park.

During the peak summer months (late-May to mid-Sept) **DNC** employs around 1800 people, mainly working in shops, restaurants and hotels. You might find yourself cleaning cabins and making beds, serving burgers or standing behind a cash register, most likely for minimum wage or not much better. With all the form filling, past employment verification, reference checks and pre-employment drug testing, it is a time-consuming process.

A list of **positions vacant** can be seen on their website (look for "Employment" under "About us" at Ⓦwww.YosemitePark.com) where you can also download an **application form**. These can also be obtained by writing/emailing DNC Parks & Resorts at Yosemite, Human Resources, PO Box 578, Yosemite, CA 95389 (Ⓣ209/372-1236, ⒺYosHR@dncinc.com). There are no online applications, so either way you have to mail it in. Applications are accepted year-round, but for the summer positions it is wise to apply in February or March as they try to get positions filled by Memorial Day weekend at the end of May. Positions do become available at short notice, so impulsive types can just show up in person at DNC's Human Resources Department in Yosemite Village (Mon–Fri 9am–5pm) in the hope of finding something.

All employees are required to show their Social Security Card, but **international applicants** may be able to find something by contacting Intrax International (Ⓦwww.intraxworktravel.com) to see if there is a partner organization near you.

For jobs with the **National Park Service**, check out the NPS seasonal employment program (Ⓣ1-877/554-4550, Ⓦwww.sep.nps.gov). There are usually more applicants than jobs available, especially at popular parks like Yosemite, and people with prior experience get priority making it hard for first-timers to break in. Jobs listed at Ⓦwww.usajobs.opm.gov are typically full-time permanent positions, and all Park Service jobs are only available to US citizens. For Yosemite-specific jobs try the NPS's Yosemite Human Resources Office on Ⓣ209/379-1805 as they sometimes have jobs that haven't been advertised on the nationwide sites.

Volunteering

With gradually declining visitation to Yosemite and the corresponding drop in revenue, **volunteering** is becoming an increasingly important way to get crucial projects done. Apart from feeling good about giving something back, you get to hang out in Yosemite in convivial company.

One of the best ways to contribute is to join the **Yosemite Association** (see p.40; annual membership $35) and sign up for one of their volunteer programs. **Work week volunteers** help the Park Service resource management division, typically working in groups of a dozen or so putting in four eight-hour days (with a day off midweek) on restoration and re-vegetation projects throughout the Park. It can be backbreaking work, but there are immediate rewards in seeing your handiwork repair a riverbank or rehabilitate a meadow. Five one-week sessions are planned each summer with volunteers sharing a camp and being fed three hearty meals a day: there's a $75 fee to cover costs. Schedules and application forms are available at ⓦwww.yosemite.org/helpus/volunteer.html.

With more time at your disposal, consider becoming a **long-term volunteer**. You'll get a $10 daily allowance, free camping in Yosemite Valley, Wawona, or Tuolumne Meadows, and will be offered a thirty percent discount on book purchases. Working four or five days a week through summer, volunteers are likely to be employed staffing information booths, assisting visitors at Happy Isles, as a docent at the Yosemite Museum, or helping at an outdoor adventure course in Tuolumne Meadows.

The Park Service also accept volunteers through their Volunteers in Parks program (VIP: ⓦwww.volunteer.gov/gov), perhaps working in the Valley but maybe providing summer staffing for a remote ranger station: apply early. For more information regarding Yosemite National Park volunteer program, contact the Park Volunteer Coordinator at ⓣ209/379-1850.

Mail

When it comes to sending those Ansel Adams posters home, you're well served at the **main post office** in Yosemite Village (Mon–Fri 8.30am–5pm, Sat 10am–noon), which also has general delivery (aka poste restante: Mon–Fri 8.30–9.30am & 11.30am–5pm). In addition, there's year-round service at *Yosemite Lodge* (Mon–Fri 11.30am–2.45pm) and Wawona (Mon–Fri 9am–5pm, Sat 9am–noon) and summer-only service at Curry Village (June to early Sept Mon–Fri 8–10am) and Tuolumne Meadows (mid-June to mid-Sept Mon–Fri 9am–5pm, Sat 9am–1pm). The latter has general delivery for hikers on the John Muir and Pacific Crest trails. The **zip code** for the whole of Yosemite National Park is 95389.

Maps

Armed with this Guide and the excellent **map** of the park that you are handed as you arrive, you'll have pretty much all the guidance you're likely to need, though hikers will want to get hold of more detailed maps (see below).

For detail of specific areas, consider buying one of the green and white concertina-folded maps published in cooperation with the Yosemite Association, which use an angled projection to clearly show the rock formations and key features. These cover the main areas – Yosemite Valley, Tuolumne Meadows, and Wawona & the Mariposa Grove ($2.95 each) – and are available in almost every shop and hotel in the Park.

Anyone headed into the backcountry should obtain a **topographic map**. The best general hiking map is the double-sided 1:100,000 scale National Geographic *Trails Illustrated Yosemite National Park* map (No. 206; $10), which marks trail distances, and shows which wilderness areas are barred to camping and open fires. Keen hikers, and especially those planning to hike off-trail, will want to use detailed USGS "quad" maps ($6 each) which each cover an area roughly eight miles by six at a scale of 1:24,000. You'd need 22 to cover the entire park, but two or three will cover most hiking requirements. Most are still available from stores, ranger stations and visitor centers around the park, but this series is being phased out and you are now encouraged to download maps tailored to your specific requirements directly from the USGS website ⓦwww.store.usgs.gov. This is wonderfully handy if you are prepared before you leave home, but little use once in Yosemite where you're unlikely to have a fast Internet connection or a printer.

Medical assistance

Yosemite Medical Clinic (ⓣ209/372-4637) has 24-hour emergency care and accepts appointments (Mon–Fri 8am–5pm). Consultations cost around $135, and medication is extra. Dental treatment (ⓣ209/372-4200 for hours) is also available. The nearest pharmacies to the Park are in Mariposa and Oakhurst. Serious emergencies are medivaced to Modesto.

Money

Of course you can pay by **credit card** almost everywhere in the Park, but for smaller expenses you'll want cash, accessible from

24hr **ATMs** (typically charging $3 on each transaction) located in most of the Park's stores and hotels; try Yosemite Village Store, outside the Yosemite Art & Education Center, in the lobby of *Yosemite Lodge*, inside the Curry Village Store, inside the Wawona Store and, just outside the park at the *Yosemite View Lodge* in El Portal. There are **no banks** in Yosemite but the Park concessionaire runs a **check cashing service** (Mon–Thurs 8am–2pm Fri 8am–4pm) in Yosemite Village in the lobby of the Yosemite Art & Education Center: they charge $5 for cashing each check.

The gateway towns all have full banking facilities, though nowhere nearby has provision for foreign currency exchange: those from outside the US should use US dollar **traveler's checks**, which can be used like cash in shops, restaurants and hotels.

Pets

The best advice is to leave your dog at home. The Park Service discourages pets by limiting where you can take them. All hiking trails and the backcountry are off-limits, dogs aren't allowed on shuttle buses or in any of the accommodation, restaurants or shops, and may not be left unattended in vehicles, tents or tied up anywhere. They can be taken (on a leash) anywhere on the Valley Floor, Happy Isles Nature Center, Mirror Lake Parking Lot, Pohono Bridge and on paved paths not designated as a foot or horse trail. Seeing-eye and "hearing" dogs are generally exempt from these rules. Dogs are, however, allowed in all campgrounds except *Camp 4*, *Tamarack Flat* and *Porcupine Flat*. Gentle, properly immunized dogs weighing more than ten pounds can be boarded at the kennels at the stables by North Pines (May–Sept; ⓣ209/372-8348).

Phones

The easiest way to boast to family and friends about your ascent of Half Dome is by phone. **Mobile coverage** is only provided by Verizon and AT&T/Cingular, and even then coverage is patchy. Yosemite Valley is tolerably well covered, and Tuolumne Meadows has reception, but Wawona has no signal. In the backcountry it is a lottery, though your chances are better at high points.

Public phones are abundant in places like the Valley, Wawona, Glacier Point and Tuolumne Meadows, as well as campgrounds and even popular trailheads. Keep a bunch of quarters handy for local calls but for long-distance and international calls you should either organize a calling card from you home phone service provider before setting out, or obtain one of the account-based **calling cards** from any of the Park stores. Typically available in denominations of $5, $10 and $20, these can usually be topped up with a credit card when they run low.

Photography

Yosemite is one of the most **photographed** places on earth. Ansel Adams (see box, p.64) spent more than half a century creating his splendid visual record of the Park, and his work continues to inspire professional photographers and casual amateurs alike.

We've given a few pointers to help improve your shots (see p.37), but for more guidance you should join one of the free **Photography Walks** (year-round 3–4 weekly; check *Yosemite Today* for details), run either by the Ansel Adams Gallery or by Canon. These take place in Yosemite Valley (and occasionally in Tuolumne), last around two hours, and look into exposure control and using different lenses. Sign up and meet at the Ansel Adams Gallery.

More committed photographers will learn a lot more on **photography courses** run by the Yosemite Association. Their website (ⓦwww.yosemite.org) lists each year's courses which range from a day honing skills in the Valley to three-day courses on, for example, autumn photography (all around $250). In addition, the Ansel Adams Gallery also runs a series of fairly specialist non-residential photography workshops (ⓣ1-800/568-7398, ⓦwww.anseladams.com). These range from four days in Yosemite Valley ($625–675) learning the skills of platinum printing or crafting fine B&W prints to a four days learning about digital printing and color management based at Mono Lake ($625–700).

Equipment

What **camera gear** you take to Yosemite will largely depend on what you have and are

Tips for taking quality photos

Yosemite's scenery is so striking that it almost seems you could press the shutter without looking and still produce something to be proud of, but by following a few **pointers** you can quickly improve your strike rate.

- Take photos in the early morning and late afternoon when light is softer and longer shadows give scenes a greater sense of depth and texture.
- Animals are often easier to see at dawn or dusk, but be sure to use fast speed settings (say 400 ISO) when shooting in low light conditions.
- On sunny days avoid deep shadows by getting people to face the sun and remove their hat.
- With such vast sheets of granite and towering spires, it is important to give a sense of scale by including people or a building in the foreground.
- Keep shooting when the weather turns nasty – some of the best photos of Yosemite are taken during (or just after) storms or with snow or mist all around.
- Avoid camera shake in low light levels by resting the camera against a railing or tree.
- Use a tripod whenever possible, even under good lighting conditions – if nothing else it help to concentrate on the perfect framing. Bring something lightweight but sturdy.
- Don't use a polarizing filter when shooting into the sun – streaks and flares can occur.
- On white-sky days, include less (or none) of the sky choosing to concentrate on subjects close at hand. The softer light of overcast days is excellent for photographing the subtle textures in close-up.

familiar with. An SLR camera (either film or digital) with suitable lenses will give the best results but the extra weight can be a deterrent and only the more committed photographers will want to be lugging a couple of bodies, several lenses and a tripod around the backcountry. Of course, Ansel Adams carried a massive plate camera around with a dozen glass slides, but then he often took a mule as well. Point and shoot film cameras and the ever more sophisticated digitals can return incredible images. As ever, it all depends on where you point the camera and when you push the shutter.

Common brands of print film at all the popular film speeds are available at virtually every store in the Park at moderate prices. For more specialized **photographic supplies**, visit the Ansel Adams Gallery (p.60) which stocks a range of professional quality color negative, black and white, and transparency film, along with tripods, flash cards and accessories. They will also **burn your digital images** onto CD charging $10 for the first disk and $5 for each subsequent disk.

Recycling

Just about everything imaginable – glass, plastic, cardboard, aluminum cans, newspapers, steel cans, automotive waste (batteries, oil, filters, anti-freeze, tires), propane canisters, etc – can be recycled at the Yosemite Village Store Recycling Center (summer daily 10am–5pm) and the Curry Village Recycling Center (summer daily 1–5pm), and locally bought beverage containers may be returned for a 5¢ deposit at all retail outlets. Green recycling receptacles are located by many campgrounds, picnic areas, and roadside pullouts as well.

Senior travelers

Yosemite is well suited to senior travelers, there are some impressive discounts available. Foremost is the Golden Age Passport ($10) giving unlimited free access to all US national parks, available to US citizens and residents aged 62 and over: obtain one as you enter the Park or at one of the visitor centers. Those in possession of the Golden Age Passport also get fifty percent break on all camping in national parks. Some tours within Yosemite also have a small (10–20 percent) discount for seniors, but for things like bike rental and horseback riding you'll be charged the full adult rate.

Getting around is fairly straightforward. You can drive close to most places you are likely to want to be, except in some places in Yosemite Valley where you need to park then either walk a few hundred yards or catch one of the free **shuttle buses** (see p.26). The current generation of buses have low floors to make access easier.

One of the main issues affecting seniors is **health**. Although there are medical facilities in Yosemite Village (see p.57) and some drugs are available over the counter in Park stores, it pays to bring any **medication** you might need with you, or buy in one of the gateway towns on your way into the Park. You'll also need to be aware of your own level of **fitness** and chose your activities accordingly. It might sound obvious, but if it is a while since you have done much hiking or biking be sure to build up slowly, perhaps trying one of the easy trails before stepping progressively up to the moderate and strenuous ones. **Altitude** can also be a issue, and while hikes around Yosemite Valley, Wawona and Hetch Hetchy aren't going to be a problem in this respect, those that head out of the Valley, and particularly those starting in Tuolumne Meadows and near Tioga Pass, all spend time above 8000ft and often top 10,000ft. At the very least you'll be out of breath and may suffer the effects of **altitude sickness** (see box, p.87). Lastly, those with breathing difficulties should avoid exertion at times when fires (see p.30) create a **smoke hazard**.

Showers and laundry

None of Yosemite's campgrounds have **showers**. To get clean in Yosemite Valley, visit the 24-hour facilities at Curry Village, which cost $3 and include the use of a towel (though outside peak times in summer there is often no one in attendance to provide a towel or take your money). *Housekeeping Camp* also has public showers (daily 7am–10pm; $5 including towel). Alternatively, pay to use the pools at *Yosemite Lodge* and Curry Village (both $5, kids under 12 $3.50) and clean up while you're there.

Outside the Valley campers can shower at *Tuolumne Meadows Lodge* (daily noon–3.30pm; $4). You'll find public coin-op **laundry** facilities at *Housekeeping Camp* (mid-April to mid-Oct daily 7am–10pm).

Taxes

Within Yosemite National Park, anything federally run is not subject to state tax, but you'll still have 7.75 percent tax added to meals, tours and most items bought in Park shops. We have excluded taxes from our accommodation price listings. Park campgrounds incur no taxes but you can expect to pay an additional 8–12 percent on all other accommodation.

Time

California runs on Pacific Standard Time (PST), which is eight hours behind GMT, and jumps forward an hour in summer (the second Sunday in March to the first Sunday in November). During most of this eight-month **daylight saving** period, when it is noon Monday in California it is 3pm in New York, 8pm in London, 5am Tuesday in Sydney, and 7am Tuesday in Auckland.

Tourist Information

Upon entering the Park you'll be provided with a free copy of a Yosemite National Park map, the *Yosemite: Your Complete Guide to the Park* booklet, and the current *Yosemite Today* listings newspaper which has stacks of useful information including current museum, shop and restaurant opening hours.

The three main sections of the Park – Yosemite Valley, Tuolumne Meadows, and Wawona – all have some form of **visitor center** along with somewhere for overnight hikers to obtain wilderness permits.

While visitor center staff field general questions about hiking in Yosemite, anyone planning serious treks and overnight camping trips should direct their enquiries to one of the **wilderness centers**, prime sources of backcountry information. In addition to issuing wilderness permits and providing advice on route planning and backcountry etiquette, they also sell maps and guidebooks, and rent bear-resistant food canisters.

Yosemite is entirely encircled by the Stanislaus, Toiyabe, Inyo and Sierra **national forests**, in parts as scenic as the national park but considerably less regulated and virtually empty of visitors. We've provided some information about the areas that immediately abut the Park in Chapters 12–15, but there's much more to uncover and the national forest ranger stations are the best place to start. Most of the **gateway towns** also have a visitor center of some description; see the relevant town accounts in Chapters 12–15 for details.

Virtually everything within the Park, from transportation to accommodation, is organized through the five groups listed under **Useful contacts**, though you'll also find heaps of activities and programs organized by the various **support groups** listed.

Visitor centers

Valley Visitor Center Yosemite Village (daily: June–Sept 9am–7pm, Oct–May 9am–5pm or 6pm; ⓣ209/372-0299; shuttle stops 5 & 9). The Park's main visitor center, where the staff are helpful but often at full stretch. Here you can pick up maps, study the latest weather forecast, learn about the ranger programs for that week, and see a number of displays and videos (for further coverage see p.57).

Big Oak Flat Information Station at the Park entrance on Hwy-120 West (Easter–Sept daily 8am–5pm, Oct–Easter sporadically open, mostly at weekends; ⓣ209/379-1899). Handy when arriving from the northwest, this small information station also has an accommodation-booking service and deals with wilderness permits.

Tuolumne Meadows Visitor Center Tuolumne Meadows (mid-June to Sept daily 9am–5pm or 6pm; ⓣ209/372-0263). Concentrates on information on the north of the Park, and sells books, maps and gifts.

Wawona Information Station inside Hill's Studio, Wawona (mid-May to mid-Sept daily 8.30am–5pm; ⓣ209/375-9531). Visitor information and wilderness permits for the southern part of the Park.

Wilderness centers

Valley Wilderness Center Yosemite Village (mid-May to June & early Sept to mid-Oct daily 8am–5pm, July–early-Sept daily 7.30am–5pm, closed in winter; ⓣ209/372-0745; shuttle stops 5 & 9). The foremost source of backcountry information, where a scale model of the Park facilitates route planning. They specialize in hikes from Valley trailheads, but the staff here has extensive knowledge of the entire Park. During the winter months when the Wilderness Center is closed, wilderness permits are issued at the Valley Visitor Center.

Big Oak Flat Information Station Hwy-120 West (April to mid-Oct daily 8am–5pm; ⓣ209/379-1967). Handy when entering the Park from the northwest.

Hetch Hetchy Entrance Station (mid-April to mid-Oct daily 9am–5pm or longer). On the road to Hetch Hetchy and specializing in that area.

Tuolumne Meadows Wilderness Center (mid-June to Sept daily 8am–5pm and later in mid-season). High country wilderness permits from an office near *Tuolumne Lodge*.

Wawona Information Station (mid-May to mid-Sept daily 8.30am–5pm; ⓣ209/375-9531). Wilderness permits in the southern reaches of the Park. Self-register when closed.

Ranger stations in the surrounding national forests

Groveland Ranger Station 24545 Hwy-120 West, eight miles east of Groveland (Mon–Fri 8am–4.30pm Sat & Sun 8am–3.30pm, winter closed Sat; ⓣ209/962-7825, ⓦwww.fs.fed.us/r5/stanislaus). Covers the Stanislaus National Forest.

Yosemite Sierra Visitors Bureau in Oakhurst (see p.210) and the **Mariposa County Visitor Centre** in Mariposa (see p.207). Both good for information on the **Sierra National Forest** (ⓦwww.fs.fed.us/r5/sierra) which occupies Yosemite's southwestern flank.

Mono Basin Scenic Area Visitor Center (see p.215) just north of Lee Vining. Covers the Owens Valley on the eastern side of the Sierra the **Inyo National Forest** (ⓦwww.fs.fed.us/r5/inyo).

Useful contacts

Delaware North Companies Parks & Resorts at Yosemite (DNC) lodging reservations ⓣ559/253-5635, tour reservations ⓣ209/372-1240, ⓦwww.yosemitepark.com. Resource for everything run by the Park concessionaire – hotels, restaurants, tours, shuttle buses, etc.

Recreation.gov ⓣ1-877/444-6777 or 518/885-3639, ⓦwww.recreation.gov. Advance Yosemite campground reservations.

Wilderness Permits ⓣ209/372-0740, ⓦwww.nps.gov/yose/wilderness. For obtaining permits for overnight stays in the backcountry.
YARTS ⓣ1-877/989-2787, ⓦwww.yarts.com. Handles bus transport into Yosemite Valley from Merced, Mariposa and Mammoth Lakes.
Yosemite National Park recorded info on ⓣ209/372-0200, ⓦwww.nps.gov/yose. Resource for everything managed by the Park Service.

Support groups and organizations

Sierra Club ⓣ415/977-5500, ⓦwww.sierraclub.org. America's most powerful outdoor recreation and conservation group, founded by John Muir in 1892 and still active in the Park with members serving as interpreters at the LeConte Memorial (see p.63).
Yosemite Association (YA) ⓣ209/379-2646, ⓦwww.yosemite.org. This educational, nonprofit, membership organization was started in 1923 and continues to be dedicated to supporting the national park. It offers field seminars, assists the Park Service in its interpretive programs, and sells Yosemite-related books and interpretive material (ⓦwww.yosemitestore.com). YA members (mostly volunteers) staff a number of places around the Park – the Nature Centre at Happy Isles and the Mariposa Grove Museum among them – and run book stores in Park Service visitor centers.
Yosemite Fund (YF) ⓣ1-800/469-7275, ⓦwww.yosemitefund.org. San Francisco-based nonprofit organization devoted to funding conservation and preservation projects in the Park – managing wildlife, restoring habitat, repairing trails, providing educational exhibits. When staying in Park lodging you have the option to donate to the Fund's "Dollar-per-night" program with a voluntary $1 a day added to your bill going straight to the Yosemite Fund.
Yosemite Institute (YI) ⓣ209/379-9511, ⓦwww.yni.org/yi. A private nonprofit organization fostering understanding of the natural and cultural heritage of Yosemite through environmental education programs for school groups and individuals. Operating since 1971, they offer residential field science programs for child and adult groups, often tailored to accommodate specific needs.

Travelers with disabilities

The National Park Service goes to great lengths to ensure that as much of the Park and its facilities are open and accessible to all: full **information** is available (along with a downloadable brochure) from ⓦwww.nps.gov/yose/pphtml/accessibility.html.

The Park waives the entrance fee: those eligible for the **Access Pass** (see p.32) get in free along with any passengers in the same vehicle. The Passport also gives a fifty percent discount on many fee-charging services, along with camping (provide your pass number when reserving).

There are disabled parking spaces close to most lodging and restaurants, and drivers can obtain a **Temporary Accessibility Placard** (from entrance stations and visitor centers) allowing the holder to drive on some roads normally only open to hikers and cyclists. This is particularly helpful for getting to Mirror Lake and along the Happy Isles Loop Road. Assistance is available at Park gas stations during business hours.

When you want to leave your car behind, use the Yosemite Valley **shuttle buses**, which are all equipped with wheelchair lifts and tie-downs. Should you need them, manual **wheelchair rental** ($7.50 an hour, $11 a day) is available from the *Yosemite Lodge* and Curry Village bicycle stands (see p.28), along with tandem bikes for the visually impaired ($7.50 an hour, $24.50 a day) and hand-cranked bikes ($7.50 an hour, $24.50 a day). *Yosemite Lodge* also has a few first-come-first-served chairs available free of charge to guests.

Outside the Valley, some of the buses used for the Tuolumne Meadows shuttle service have wheelchair lifts: ask the driver for details.

If you have the choice, plan your visit outside the peak season: if nothing else, you'll find rangers and Park staff have more time to assist you. Whenever you come, give the Park Service and your lodging as much notice as possible of your arrival. The Park Service may well be able to provide someone to help interpret ranger programs for the hard-of-hearing (ⓣ209/372-0298 or TDD ⓣ209/372-4726) and DNC will be able to ensure accessible **lodging** is available (TDD ⓣ559/255-4848). For TDD **camping** reservations call ⓣ1-888/530-9796.

Consult *Yosemite Today* when you arrive, as the paper indicates **ranger programs** accessible to those in wheelchairs with assistance, and also summer-only events with a sign language interpreter. The *Spirit of Yosemite* film (see p.57) has closed captioning and can be viewed with audio descriptions with a headset available from the visitor center nearby. While pets are discouraged in the Park, suitably leashed **guide dogs** can be taken into all Park buildings and on trails except for horse/mule trails.

For communications, the Valley Visitor Centre has a TDD phone for incoming **calls** (Ⓣ209/372-4726). For outgoing calls, TDD payphones can be found at the Curry Village registration area, inside the *Yosemite Lodge* lobby, at the Valley Visitor Center and at *The Ahwahnee*. The **ATM** at the Art & Education Center is set up for Braille use and has a socket for a headset.

None of the **hikes** we've listed in the guide are completely wheelchair accessible, though several (Hikes 1 and 43, for example) can be managed with assistance. Parts of other hikes are also accessible, including Hike 5 where smooth asphalt reaches as far as Mirror Lake.

Vehicle repairs

The Village Garage in Yosemite Village has a 24-hour towing service, sells propane until 4pm and is open for repairs (daily 8am–5pm; Ⓣ209/372-8320).

Weather

Current conditions and forecasts (including road conditions) are available on the Web at Ⓦwww.nps.gov/yose/planyourvisit/conditions.htm, or by calling Ⓣ209/372-0200.

Weddings and religious services

The park concessionaire DNC (Ⓣ559/253-5673) is well set up for helping you get hitched in Yosemite. Services can be held outside *The Ahwahnee*, on the lawns around the *Wawona Hotel* or in the historic chapel; then the hotels make excellent places for the reception, especially *The Ahwahnee*. **Religious services** are held for various faiths at locations around the Valley: consult *Yosemite Today* for service times, call Ⓣ209/372-4831, or visit Ⓦwww.yosemitevalleychapel.org.

The Park

The Park

1

Yosemite Valley

In the minds of many visitors Yosemite National Park is **Yosemite Valley**, a four-square-mile nugget of stupendous landscape that never fails to impress no matter how many times you've visited. Perhaps because the whole always seems greater than the sum of its parts, Ralph Waldo Emerson felt that it was "the only place that comes up to the brag about it, and exceeds it."

Along the Valley's narrow cleft you'll find the densest concentration of stupendous cliffs and waterfalls, with the face of **El Capitan** standing sentinel over the western entrance to the Valley, and **Half Dome** looking imperiously on a couple of miles to the east. In between, **Yosemite Falls** plummets over the lip of the Valley rim in a double cascade, which together make up the highest fall in the US. Opposite El Cap, delicate **Bridalveil Fall** wafts down to the glossy rocks below, and during the spring snowmelt just about every other cliff sprouts a waterfall for a few weeks.

Through it all runs the **Merced River**, which rises in the high country around Merced Lake to the east. The river expends much of its youthful vigor before entering Yosemite Valley, where it meanders among meadows – forcefully in spring; sluggishly in summer and fall. Placid lily-flanked pools offer picture-perfect reflections of the cliffs and waterfalls, while sharp curves harbor sandy beaches that shelve into the cool waters making perfect swimming spots or pull-out points for leisurely float trips. Along the banks, mule deer and black bears forage amid black oaks and incense cedars.

Millennia of rockfall from the surrounding cliffs have formed talus slopes, at the foot of which, over the last century and a half, people have built the infrastructure for year-round habitation. **Yosemite Village**, at the eastern end of the Valley, is effectively Yosemite's capital, home to the main visitor center, wilderness center, the **Yosemite Museum** and **Indian Village**, the **Yosemite**

Avoiding the summer crowds

Most of Yosemite is free of crowds year-round, but a few hotspots – Tuolumne Meadows, Wawona, and especially Yosemite Valley – get very congested in summer. Though the crowds may be less dense than some would have you believe, the scenic impact can be appreciably enhanced by following these few pointers:

Start early Aim to visit the most popular sights, particularly Lower Yosemite Fall and Bridalveil Fall before 9am when the low-angled light brings out the best in the scenery, and wildlife is most active.

Get off the beaten path The vast majority of visitors never stray more than twenty minutes' walk from their car and only visit the most popular sights.

Stay out late The hour or so before sunset is usually spectacular; the "golden hour" is no time to be in a restaurant or your hotel room.

Cemetery, and a slew of restaurants and shops. There's accommodation nearby at the ordinary **Yosemite Lodge**, and the extraordinary **Ahwahnee**. Much of the rest of the accommodation is across the river on the southern, shaded side of the Valley at **Curry Village**, with more places to eat and shop, and handy access to the family-friendly **Nature Center at Happy Isles**.

As it attracts the bulk of visitors, the Valley has the busiest **hiking** trails, some tracing the river gently along the Valley floor, but most climbing steeply up the walls to the rim of the Valley almost three thousand feet above. Between these two extremes the many hikes from the popular **Happy Isles trailhead** step up in difficulty from one offering a distant view of Vernal Fall to the full-day blow-out to the summit of Half Dome.

With all the lodging, restaurants and the bulk of the trailheads concentrated at the eastern end of the Valley, **getting around** is fairly easy. But with Northside Drive and Southside Drive (the main roads into and out of the Valley) meeting in a confusion of one-way roads, you're better served by parking your vehicle and making extensive use of the free shuttle buses (see p.26).

El Capitan, Half Dome and the big cliffs

Everyone is stunned by their first view of Yosemite Valley, with the vertical grey walls of **El Capitan** and **Half Dome** dominating a wealth of magnificent granite architecture. A permanent backdrop to your time here, their constant presence grabs you every time you step out of a shop or restaurant, and continues to hold your attention with the shifting angles of sun and moon, ever-changing cloudscapes and, in winter, a heavy blanket of snow.

El Capitan

Whichever way you approach the Valley, your view will be blocked by **El Capitan** (*Tu-tok-a-nu-la*), a vast monolith jutting forward from the adjacent cliffs and looming 3593ft above the Valley floor. Though there are cliffs in Alaska, Canada's Baffin Island and Pakistan that are bigger, "The Captain" remains one of the largest pieces of exposed granite in the world, a full 320 acres of gray-tan rock. It is seemingly devoid of vegetation and is so sheer it is a wonder anyone ever considered climbing it let alone making it the holy grail of rock climbing worldwide. El Cap's enormous size isn't really apparent until you join the slack-jawed tourists craning their necks and training binoculars and cameras on the rock-climbers on the face. Eventually you'll pick out flea-sized specks inching up what appears to be a flawless wall, though closer inspection reveals a pattern of flakes, fissures and small ledges. The most accessible sequences are connected by what is probably the most famous rock-climbing route in the world, **The Nose**.

Straight on, El Cap looks almost flat, but it really has two principal faces that meet at The Nose to form a kind of prow. To the left is the **Salathé Wall**, distinguished by a massive heart-shaped indentation a third of the way up. To the right is the **North American Wall** with its thousand-foot-high patch of dark rock that looks remarkably like a map of North America. Follow it down to the bottom of the dark stain and you'll find El Cap's only significant vegetation, a hundred-foot **ponderosa pine** rooted in the cracks and hunkered under an overhang.

Ahwahneechee legends of Tu-tok-a-nu-la and Tis-sa-yak

It is hardly surprising that El Capitan and Half Dome are as important in Ahwahneechee legend as they were to Ansel Adams or just about any visitor to Yosemite.

To the local people El Capitan is known as **Tu-tok-a-nu-la**, after the chant of the inchworm which rescued two bear cubs. The story goes that, in the time of the animal people, the two bear cubs slipped away from their mother and went for a swim in the river. Afterwards they dozed off on a flat rock nearby, and while sleeping the rock grew higher and higher up until the bear cubs scratched their faces on the moon. Their mother was distraught and asked her animal friends, but none had seen the cubs. Eventually the crane spotted them and all the animals rallied around to try and help. The field mouse, rat, fox, raccoon, mountain lion and all the other animals tried so hard to scale the slippery surface that their feet left dark scratches on the rock near its base. Still, none could make any progress until the inchworm fronted up. The other animals all laughed at his bravado, but off the little worm went, painstakingly making his way up the rock all the while chanting "Tu-tok, tu-tok, tu-tok-a-nu-la." The inchworm finally reached the summit, awoke the still-sleeping cubs and guided them back to the ground and safety. All were overjoyed, and to honor the inchworm they named the rock after his song.

At the other end of the Valley, equally dramatic mountain forming was going on. A woman named **Tis-sa-yak** and her husband Nangas lived on the arid plains to the east but had heard tell of the wonders of the valley of Ahwahnee. As they journeyed west, Tis-sa-yak carried a heavy basket of acorns and a baby carrier. Nangas followed with his bow and arrows. Tired, hungry and thirsty after the long journey Nangas lost his temper and struck Tis-sa-yak who fled up the Valley spilling acorns, which eventually grew into the oaks we see today. Reaching Mirror Lake she drank it dry, which further enraged the thirsty Nangas who hit her again. The gods seeing this breach of custom were greatly displeased and vowed to permanently separate them. When Tis-sa-yak was cornered by Nangas, she turned and flung the basket at him, at which moment they were turned to stone, she as Half Dome with the tears of remorse streaking her face, and he on the opposite side of the Valley as Washington Column with Basket Dome above.

A long thin pullout at the base of El Cap allows drivers to stop and gawp, while the adjacent **El Cap Meadows** are quite delicate and you are discouraged from walking out onto them (though few seem to take much heed). Geologists will tell you that El Cap formed in the same way as most of the granite around here, cooling slowly underground to leave a solid lump of hard rock, smoother and more uniform than rock found almost anywhere else. The Ahwahneechee offer a less prosaic explanation (see box above).

Half Dome

Impressive though El Capitan is, for most people it is **Half Dome** (*Tis-sa-yak*) that instantly grabs their attention. A stunning sight topping out at 8842ft, it rises almost 5000ft above the Valley floor, smoothly arching from northeast to southwest but cut off on each side. Its two thousand-foot northwest face is only seven degrees off vertical making it the **sheerest cliff in North America**. According to a member of the 1849 Walker Party it "looked as though it had been sliced with a knife as one would slice a loaf of bread" and to English naturalist and adventurer, Joseph Smeaton Chase it was a "frightful amputation."

It is easy to imagine that the "other half" of the dome was hewn away by a massive glacier, but actually it is faulting in the rock that is primarily responsible for its shape. The relatively young plutonic rock from which Half Dome is

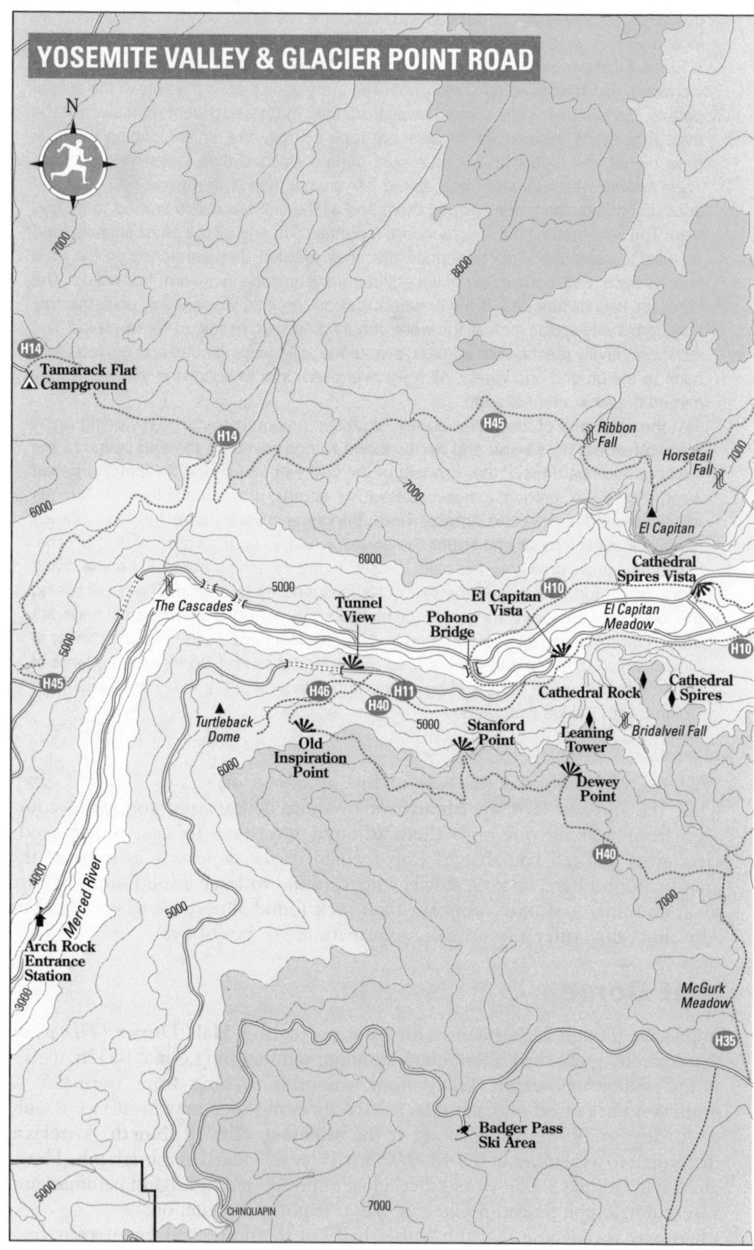
YOSEMITE VALLEY & GLACIER POINT ROAD
N
Tamarack Flat Campground
H14
H45
Ribbon Fall
Horsetail Fall
El Capitan
Cathedral Spires Vista
The Cascades
Tunnel View
El Capitan Vista
H10
El Capitan Meadow
Pohono Bridge
H46
H11
H40
Turtleback Dome
Old Inspiration Point
Stanford Point
Cathedral Rock
Cathedral Spires
Leaning Tower
Bridalveil Fall
Dewey Point
Merced River
Arch Rock Entrance Station
McGurk Meadow
H35
Badger Pass Ski Area
CHINQUAPIN
7000
8000
6000
5000
4000
3000

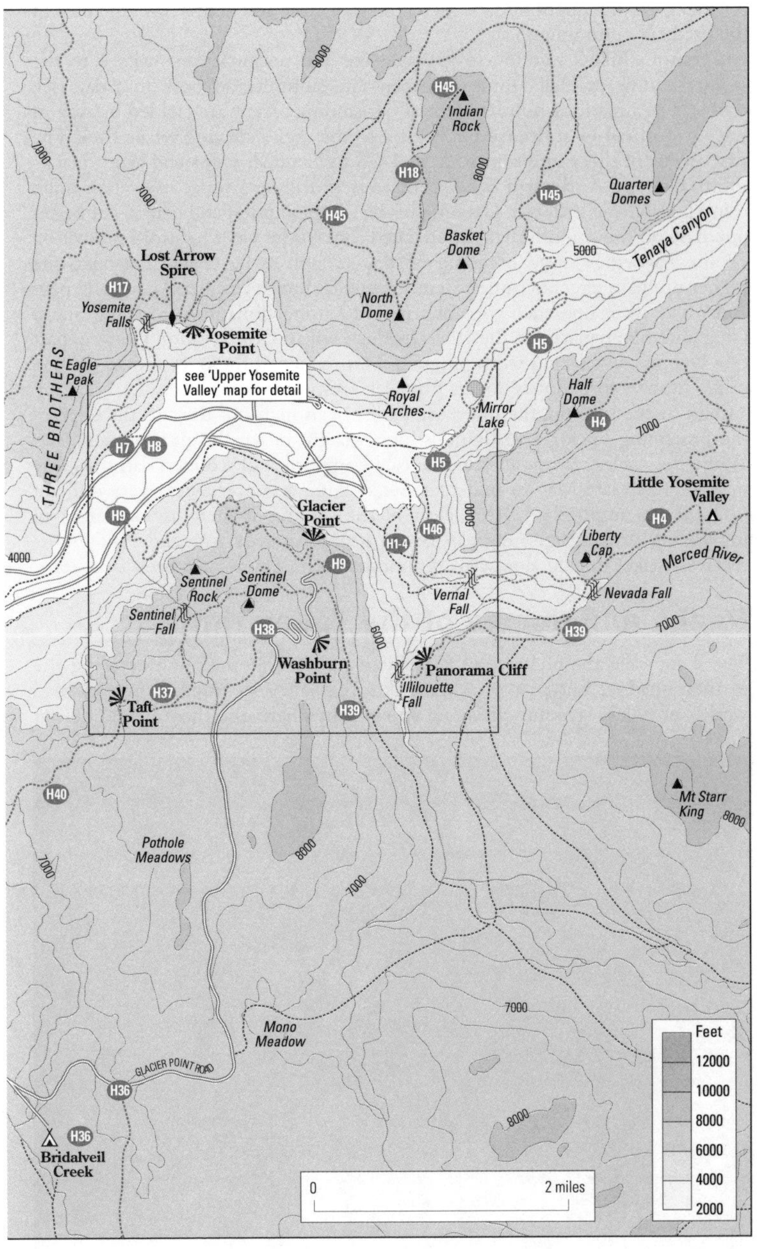
Lost Arrow Spire
Yosemite Falls
Yosemite Point
Eagle Peak
THREE BROTHERS
see 'Upper Yosemite Valley' map for detail
Indian Rock
Quarter Domes
Basket Dome
North Dome
Tenaya Canyon
Royal Arches
Mirror Lake
Half Dome
Little Yosemite Valley
Glacier Point
Liberty Cap
Merced River
Sentinel Rock
Sentinel Dome
Sentinel Fall
Vernal Fall
Nevada Fall
Washburn Point
Panorama Cliff
Illilouette Fall
Taft Point
Mt Starr King
Pothole Meadows
Mono Meadow
GLACIER POINT ROAD
Bridalveil Creek
H45
H18
H17
H7
H8
H9
H5
H4
H46
H1-4
H38
H37
H39
H40
H36
4000
5000
6000
7000
8000
Feet
12000
10000
8000
6000
4000
2000
0
2 miles

formed cooled slowly below ground under intense heat and pressure around 100 million years ago, and in the latter phase of this process the basic half-dome took shape. Subsequent glaciers merely shifted away any debris from the base of the gradually crumbling face.

Ambitious hikers wanting to get up close and personal can make it to the shallow saddle of Half Dome's thirteen-acre summit and back in a day (see p.111). The final four hundred feet of demanding ascent are tackled by way of a steep steel **cable staircase** hooked on to the rock's curving whale back. The first ascent of this route was made in 1875 by Scottish sailor and Valley blacksmith, **George Anderson**, who spent a week drilling a series of eyebolt holes using homemade drill bits. Daubing his feet in pine pitch and grit to get better purchase on the smooth rock, he attached ropes as he went to afford protection on the 45-degree slope. Standing on one eyebolt as he drilled the next one higher up he in effect became Yosemite's first technical climber. Andersons' pegs and ropes were upgraded to cables in 1919 using donations from the Sierra Club and then replaced in the 1930s by the Civilian Conservation Corps as part of a Depression-busting work program. This remained the only way to the top until climbers forged new routes from 1931 onwards.

Once at the summit, the brave (or foolish) can inch out towards the edge of the projecting lip for a vertiginous look straight down the near-vertical face. While the cables remain all year, the cable supports and wooden slats only stay in place from late May to mid-October, making a winter ascent very difficult (though not impossible). Keep clear of the summit if there are any signs of impending storms; lightning can occur at any time of year and Half Dome receives strikes during almost every thunderstorm. There have been fatalities.

Peaks and domes of the Valley rim

The sheer scale and presence of El Capitan and Half Dome put everything else in their shadow, but part of what makes the Valley so stunning is the sheer wealth of wildly striking **cliffs** and **spires**. Anywhere else these would be star

▲ The Three Brothers

The legend of Lost Arrow

Lost Arrow Spire is known to the Ahwahneechee as Hummo, and recalls the ancient tale of Tee-hee-neh and her fiancé, Kos-soo-kah. The day before their wedding Tee-hee-neh set about preparing acorn bread while Kos-soo-kah went hunting game for the wedding feast. At an appointed time he promised to fire an arrow to the bottom of Cholok (Yosemite Falls), the number of feathers indicating the success of the hunt.

Tee-hee-neh waited several hours then, concerned for her lover's safety, set off up the rough path to the top of the falls. She eventually saw him lifeless on a ledge with his empty bow beside him. It seemed he had been hit by rockfall in the very act of firing his arrow. By building a fire Tee-hee-neh summoned men from the village who managed to retrieve Kos-soo-kah's body. Any faint hopes for his survival were dashed and Tee-hee-neh, tears streaming down her face, fell forward onto Kos-soo-kah and died.

The two lovers were cremated on the spot along with the empty bow, but the arrow was lost forever and the spirits decided to acknowledge Kos-soo-kah's loyalty by placing a pointed column of rock beside the cliff where Kos-soo-kah fell.

attractions but here they're often relegated to a supporting role. As Muir put it, "every attempt to appreciate any one feature is beaten down by the overwhelming influence of all the others."

The north side

Entering the Valley along Southside Drive your best views are of the rock formations on the north side of the Valley, dominated by El Capitan. To the right (east) the **Three Brothers** step in symmetry up the Valley wall, triple gables which were given their name by John Boling who led the second expedition of the Mariposa Battalion in 1851. The story goes that Boling had a brief to chase out the Ahwahneechee, but the tribe had got wind of his imminent arrival and made themselves scarce. They left behind five scouts who were subsequently captured just east of El Capitan. Three turned out to be sons of Ahwahneechee chief Tenaya, and Boling couldn't help but name the rocks the Three Brothers. Their individual names haven't stuck and we now simply have **Lower Brother**, **Middle Brother**, and **Eagle Peak**, which at 7779ft tops the peaks along the north side.

After some more broken, lower-angled terrain you reach the sheer face bisected by Upper Yosemite Falls (see p.55), and to its right the **Lost Arrow Spire**. This thousand-foot-high column is completely detached from the rock wall for its uppermost two hundred feet, forming a slender pinnacle, its summit almost level with the top of the cliff. Barely visible throughout the middle of the day, the pinnacle is only clearly revealed in the low-angled morning and afternoon sunlight when it casts a shadow against the cliff behind. Occasionally you'll see climbers making a spectacular Tyrolean traverse using ropes strung out in space to regain the cliff from the top of the spire.

Yet further east, behind *The Ahwahnee*, lie the **Royal Arches**, a series of rock bands against the cliff face that overhang in places like giant raised eyebrows. In spring **Royal Arch Cascade** streaks down the cliff to the left: for the rest of the year it is just a black smudge.

Above the Royal Arches swells the smooth hemisphere of the **North Dome** (7525ft), which seems to be kept from sliding off the Valley rim by the rocky shoulder of **Washington Column**. Viewed from the south rim of the Valley

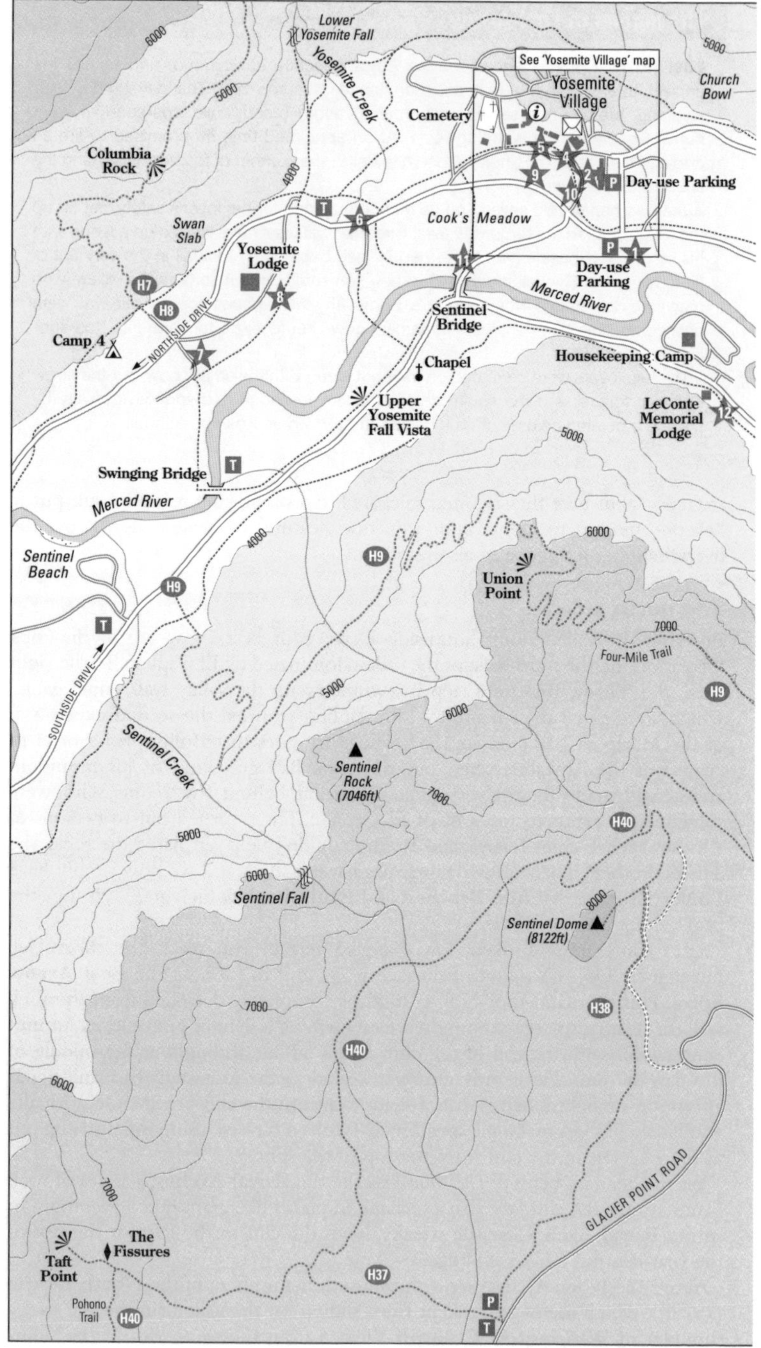
Lower Yosemite Fall
Yosemite Creek
See 'Yosemite Village' map
Yosemite Village
Church Bowl
Cemetery
Columbia Rock
Day-use Parking
Swan Slab
Cook's Meadow
Yosemite Lodge
Day-use Parking
Merced River
Camp 4
Northside Drive
Sentinel Bridge
Chapel
Housekeeping Camp
Upper Yosemite Fall Vista
LeConte Memorial Lodge
Swinging Bridge
Merced River
Sentinel Beach
Union Point
Four-Mile Trail
Southside Drive
Sentinel Creek
Sentinel Rock (7046ft)
Sentinel Fall
Sentinel Dome (8122ft)
Glacier Point Road
The Fissures
Taft Point
Pohono Trail

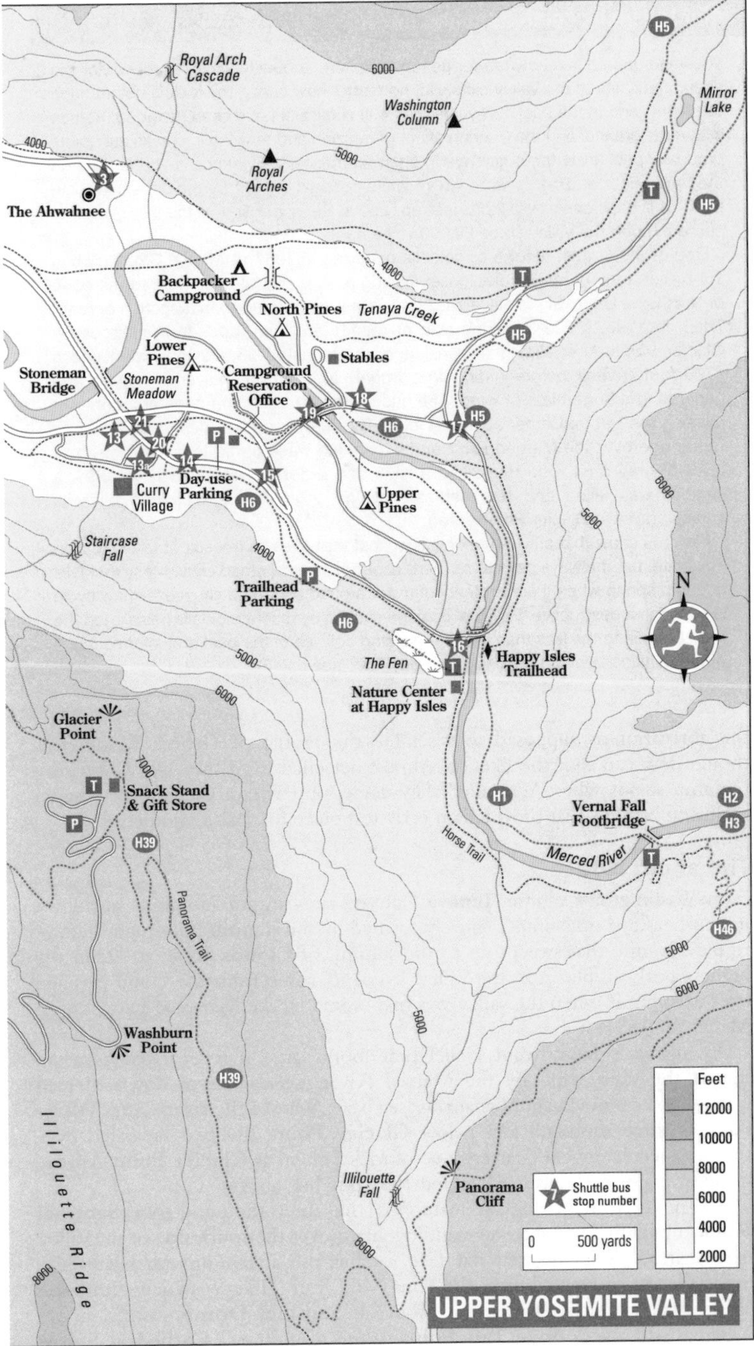
Royal Arch Cascade
Washington Column
Mirror Lake
Royal Arches
The Ahwahnee
Backpacker Campground
North Pines
Tenaya Creek
Lower Pines
Stables
Stoneman Bridge
Stoneman Meadow
Campground Reservation Office
Curry Village
Day-use Parking
Upper Pines
Staircase Fall
Trailhead Parking
The Fen
Happy Isles Trailhead
Nature Center at Happy Isles
Glacier Point
Snack Stand & Gift Store
Vernal Fall Footbridge
Horse Trail
Merced River
Panorama Trail
Washburn Point
Illilouette Ridge
Illilouette Fall
Panorama Cliff
Shuttle bus stop number
0 500 yards
Feet
12000
10000
8000
6000
4000
2000
UPPER YOSEMITE VALLEY

And the walls came tumbling down

Yosemite granite is renowned for its robust nature, a quality which accounts for the sheer verticality of the Valley cliffs. But no matter how hardy, the rock is not immune to gravity, and in the past 150 years over 400 **rockfalls** have been recorded. Forces within the granite, and the levering effect of freezing and thawing in cracks and joints gradually peel away the outer layers, often dramatically. Evidence is visible both on the Valley floor and on its walls where white patches are left by the detached rock, most of it originating over 2200 feet up, above the scour line of the last glacier to come through the Valley some 20,000 years ago.

One of the largest recorded rockfalls occurred in 1987 at Middle Brother when 1.4 million tons of rock broke loose, leaving a huge pile of talus right to the edge of Northside Drive. Signs still advise drivers not to stop along that section of road. Then, in 1996, a 500-foot-long slab of granite arch cut loose from cliffs below Glacier Point. After sliding over a ledge an estimated 68,000 tons went into a 1700-foot freefall before hitting the ground at 270mph, pulverizing itself and generating a huge blast of wind. The gust uprooted trees in a huge arc, only just missing the Nature Center at Happy Isles. The scattered trees destroyed a nearby footbridge over the Merced River and everything was coated in a two-inch-thick layer of gray dust. One tree killed a hiker and a dozen were injured. In 1999, a climber was killed and tent cabins in Curry Village were damaged by rock sweeping down Glacier Point Apron.

Records show that only ten people have lost their lives as a result of falling rock in Yosemite, but it always pays to be alert, especially below steep cliffs. Many rockfalls occur in spring when there is plenty of water around and the daily freeze–thaw cycle is at its most destructive. Physical damage caused by recent rockfalls has alerted the Park Service to the less than prudent building policies of the past and informs much of the thinking behind the Yosemite Valley Plan (see p.245).

this formation is supposed to resemble the profile of George Washington, though few can spot the likeness. Almost detached from the cliff, Washington Column stands where Yosemite Valley doglegs up Tenaya Canyon forming an enduring buttress that provided an early test piece for 1930s climbers.

The south side

From Washington Column, **Tenaya Canyon** runs toward Tuolumne Meadows, its southeastern side almost entirely formed by the smooth mile-high sheet of rippled granite that sweeps up to the summit of **Clouds Rest**, at 9926ft the highest peak visible from the Valley. It got its name from the cloud perched over its summit when the Valley was first visited by the Mariposa Battalion on March 28, 1851.

Moving back downstream, Half Dome looms large. It is separated from the rest of the Valley cliffs by the Merced River, which sweeps down Merced Canyon over Nevada and Vernal falls (see p.57). West of the river, Curry Village hunkers three thousand feet below **Glacier Point**, the two separated by a smooth, steeply angled quarter-cone of rock known as **Glacier Point Apron**, scene of major rockfalls in 1996 and 1999 (see box above).

The next large geological feature is the three-thousand-foot **Sentinel Rock**, a petrified watchtower standing guard over the south side of the Valley. The texture of its fissured flat face catches the afternoon sun beautifully, especially when viewed from the Four-Mile Trail (Hike 9) which climbs the Valley wall to the west. Looming above is **Sentinel Dome**, casting its eye west past the overlook of **Taft Point** to the magnificent **Cathedral Spires** and **Cathedral Rocks**, directly opposite El Cap. Just around the corner is Bridalveil Fall, and above it, the **Leaning Tower**, a vast slab of rock overhanging by twenty degrees.

The waterfalls

If there is one star in the Yosemite firmament that shines brighter than the rock architecture it is the stupendous **waterfalls** that stream down the canyon walls. Several are among the highest in the country, and nowhere else in the world is there such a spectacular array of cascades concentrated in such a small area. Come **in spring** or early summer and the cascades will be at their snowmelt best, though many dry up by August or September, and after a mild winter some might not make it beyond July.

The highest is the ever-popular **Yosemite Falls**, but **Bridalveil Fall**, **Ribbon Fall**, **Horsetail Fall** and **Sentinel Fall** all have their charm, and the combination of them all streaming into Yosemite Valley beats any individual cascade. Tucked away up the Merced River canyon, **Vernal Fall** and **Nevada Fall** make up for in power what they lack in height.

Yosemite Falls

At 2425ft, **Yosemite Falls** (or *Cholok*, "the fall"; shuttle stop 6) is widely claimed as the fifth highest in the world, and the highest in North America. It is a somewhat spurious assertion since it is actually two falls, separated by a couple of thousand feet of churning rapids and chutes known as **Middle Cascade** that drops a total of 675ft. Nonetheless, the 1430-foot **Upper Yosemite Fall** and the 320-foot **Lower Yosemite Fall** are magnificent, especially in May and early June when runoff from melting snow turns them into a foaming torrent. Cast your eyes up to the top where the water drops a short way (actually almost 100ft) then part of the flow hits a lip forcing plumes of water out into space and breaking up the flow so even a gentle breeze fans it out over a broad expanse of the cliff. When the falls are at their most powerful, a steady breeze blows from the base of the lower fall, pushed along by the force of the air drawn down with the water. If you are in Yosemite at full moon in spring and early summer, be sure to head for the base of Lower Yosemite Fall where the spray creates shimmering **moonbows**.

The flow typically dries up entirely by mid-August, but leaves a dark stain of algae and lichen to mark the spot. In winter the falls begin to flow again, but just enough to build up a 200- to 300-foot **ice cone** of frozen spray and fallen blocks of ice at the base of the upper fall.

Of course, John Muir couldn't resist an ascent and reported it in *The Yosemite*:

> Thus I made my way nearly to the summit, halting at times to peer up through the wild whirls of spray at the veiled grandeur of the fall, or to listen to the thunder beneath me; the whole hill was sounding as if it were a huge, bellowing drum. I hoped that by waiting until the fall was blown aslant I should be able to climb to the lip of the crater and get a view of the interior; but a suffocating blast, half air, half water, followed by the fall of an enormous mass of frozen spray from a spot high up on the wall, quickly discouraged me. The whole cone was jarred by the blow and some fragments of the mass sped past me dangerously near; so I beat a hasty retreat, chilled and drenched, and lay down on a sunny rock to dry.

The shuttle bus stops along Northside Drive at the start of a flat, quarter-mile, wheelchair-accessible asphalt trail which winds through the incense cedars and ponderosa pines to the base of the lower fall where a bridge crosses Yosemite Creek – an area always crowded with video camera-wielding tourists and kids playing among the rocks.

In the middle of the forest, a side trail leads to a viewpoint of Lower Yosemite Fall created a century back by early hoteliers who hacked down a passage through the trees so that their guests could see the falls from the hotel.

Bridalveil Fall

Perhaps the most sensual waterfall in the Park is the 620-foot **Bridalveil Fall**, a slender ribbon at the Valley's western end, which in Ahwahneechee goes by the name of *Pohono* or "spirit of the puffing wind." While Bridalveil seldom completely dries up, it is best seen from April to June when winds blow the cascade outwards up to twenty feet away from its base and draw the spray out into a delicate lacy veil. The spray-shrouded viewing platform near the base of the fall is at the end of an easy quarter-mile path from a parking lot four miles west of Yosemite Village. The shuttle bus doesn't go this far west, so unless you visit on the Valley Floor Tour (see p.29) you'll have to drive, cycle or come on foot.

Other falls

Come to the Valley in April or early May and you'll see numerous other falls, including the slender 1612-foot **Ribbon Fall**, the highest single-drop waterfall in Yosemite (and indeed in North America). It tumbles down the cliffs to the west of El Capitan and with its small, low-lying catchment is always the first waterfall to dry up each spring.

Moving round to the eastern side of El Cap you'll have to be here in winter or early spring to catch the 1000-foot **Horsetail Fall**, famous for its glowing display during any clear sunset for a few weeks in mid-February. As the last rays of the setting sun catch the cascade they create an ephemeral orange backlight

Area hikes

Yosemite's fifty best hikes are found in Chapters 4 and 5. The following hikes begin in and around Yosemite Village and Curry Village, and are consequently some of the Park's busiest. Hike early, late or out of season if you want to avoid too much company.

Day hikes

- Hike 1 Vernal Fall footbridge: see p.105
- Hike 2 Mist Trail to the top of Vernal Fall: see p.109
- Hike 3 Mist Trail to the top of Nevada Fall: see p.110
- Hike 4 Half Dome: see p.111
- Hike 5 Mirror Lake and Tenaya Canyon Loop: see p.112
- Hike 6 Eastern Valley Loop: see p.113
- Hike 7 Columbia Rock: see p.114
- Hike 8 Upper Yosemite Fall: see p.114
- Hike 9 Four-Mile Trail to Glacier Point: see p.115

Overnight hikes

- Hike 46 John Muir Trail: see p.142
- Hike 47 Merced Lake HSC: see p.144

that makes it looks like it is on fire. On the south side of the Valley, **Sentinel Fall** cascades off the rim of the Valley beside Sentinel Rock falling a total of two thousand feet in a series of stairstep drops.

Two of the Park's most striking falls are actually much shorter than these giants, and are guaranteed to be still active (though past their best) in September and October. Sequestered away from the road up the Merced River canyon, they can only be seen on foot from Happy Isles (see Hikes 1–4). It is a relatively easy walk to get a distant glimpse of the 317-foot **Vernal Fall**, a vertical curtain of water perhaps eighty feet wide that casts bright rainbows as you walk along the wonderful Mist Trail. It requires much more commitment to hike steeply upstream as far as the 594-foot **Nevada Fall**, but it is worth the effort for a close look at this sweeping cascade that drops vertically for half its height then fans out on the apron below.

Yosemite Village and around

Very much the heart of activity in the Valley, **Yosemite Village** is not really a cohesive "village" at all, but a scattered settlement of low shingle-roofed buildings tucked away among the pines and black oaks where mule deer wander freely.

There wasn't much here at all until the 1930s when tastes changed and people decided they preferred the warm side of the Valley to the cool. Most hotels and shops were formerly on the shady south side of the Valley close to the chapel, but virtually everything has now moved here.

Basically a service center for visitors as well as a home for Park employees, you'll find yourself returning time and again during your visit. The Park's **main visitor center** is here along with shops, restaurants and cafés, banking facilities, Internet access, and a post office. Close to the visitor center you'll also find the **Ansel Adams Gallery**, and beyond it the **Wilderness Center** (see p.39), essentially the visitor center for backcountry hikers.

The other main centers of activity on this side of the Valley are the restaurants and rooms at **The Ahwahnee**, half a mile to the east, and all manner of facilities at **Yosemite Lodge**, a similar distance west.

Yosemite Valley Visitor Center

The first stop for most people is the **visitor center** (daily: June–Sept 9am–7pm, Oct–May 9am–5pm or 6pm; ⓣ209/372-0299; shuttle stops 5 and 9), a single-story river-stone building that is essentially the hub of the Village. In addition to its visitor information (covered in detail on p.38), there's a good bookshop, boards with the latest weather forecast, and listings of ranger programs and activities. With a brief to help interpret Yosemite, the center gives a quick overview of the Park by means of an excellent relief map of the Valley, followed by displays on geology, flora, fauna and the people who have populated the place. Run your finger over examples of the different types of granite found throughout the Park, learn about the role of fire, and cast your eyes at photos of early inhabitants and the explorers and entrepreneurs who quickly replaced them. Hagiographic treatment is awarded to key players such as Galen Clark, Ansel Adams and David Brower.

Save time for the free 23-minute film *Spirit of Yosemite* (Mon–Sat 9.30am–4.30pm or later, Sun noon–4.30pm or later; free), which screens every half-hour in the West Auditorium, immediately behind the visitor center. Expensively made and with a somewhat overblown commentary, it is still well worth seeing for the great images of the Park through the seasons.

Yosemite Museum

Immediately west of the visitor center is the two-story **Yosemite Museum** (daily 10am–noon & 1–4pm with slightly longer hours in July and August; free; shuttle stops 5 and 9), its entrance flanked by a cedar-bark teepee and a hefty nine-foot **slice of a giant sequoia**, the rings suitably marked with significant dates going back to its sapling days in 923 AD. The museum's small but diverting exhibit of artifacts focuses on Native American heritage, specifically the local Ahwahneechee (see box, p.60) and their neighbors, the Mono Lake Paiute, with whom they traded and sometimes intermarried.

The objects on display illustrate the tribes' way of life and how it has changed since their first encounters with whites in the 1850s. There's little mention of the abominable way they were treated, with the exhibits instead concentrating on **basketwork**, one of the few crafts to flourish post-contact. Fine examples include a superbly detailed 1930s Mono Lake Paiute basket almost three feet in diameter which took close to three years to make, and its even larger Miwok/Paiute equivalent painstakingly created by the celebrated basket maker Lucy Telles. She appears with her basket in a photo next to a cabinet of more of her work. The intricate patterns of chevrons, red squares and black triangles were

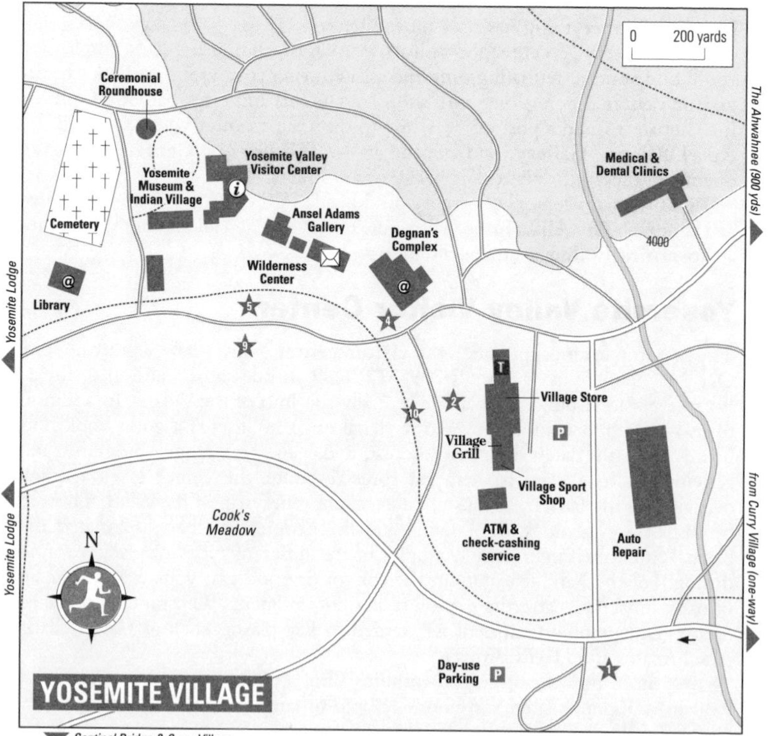

To focus your wanderings around the Yosemite Village area, pick up *A Changing Yosemite: A Self-Guiding Trail* (50¢) which follows a nature trail through the nearby meadows highlighting the evolution of the landscape. As you stroll, you'll often see **mule deer** nibbling shoots or searching for acorns. Though quite accustomed to people and willing to pose for photos, they are still wild animals and shouldn't be approached. For more on Yosemite's wildlife, see Contexts, p.236.

traditionally fashioned from sedge root and bracken fern root around a willow frame, and similar techniques are demonstrated by Ahwahneechee artisans throughout the day.

A couple of **feather-trimmed dance capes** warrant a look, as does the buckskin dress worn by natives in the 1920s and 1930s during demonstrations of basket weaving and dance. Though completely alien to the Miwok tradition, the Plains-style buckskin clothing and feather headdresses fulfilled the expectations of the whites who came to watch. Kids will enjoy being able to touch samples of animal fur native to the region, and can learn how to play Miwok stick and dice games.

The white man's history is remembered through an immensely detailed hotel **guest register** from the long-gone *La Casa Nevada* hotel which operated from 1870–91 near the base of Nevada Fall.

At the entrance to the museum there is a store (see p.193) selling finely wrought native crafts and jewelry, and upstairs hides a good research library (see p.34).

Indian Village of Ahwahnee

Wander through the Yosemite Museum (or, when closed, around its western side) to join a self-guided trail through the **Indian Village of Ahwahnee** (always open; free), a compact reconstruction of a Miwok village built in the 1920s as a venue for native dances on the former site of the largest native village in the Valley. A explanatory booklet available on site (*The Miwok in Yosemite*; $0.50) is rendered somewhat redundant by numerous signs describing the buildings and the uses of various plants such as black-oak acorns, which were ground into flour on a pounding rock and later made palatable by several washings to leach out the tannin. In the villages of all Sierra Indians the **acorn granary** was an essential repository of the principal source of carbohydrates. The granary here exhibits the usual features: high to keep it away from animals and bark-sheltered to keep the acorns dry.

The focal point of the Indian Village is its largest building, the semi-subterranean **ceremonial roundhouse** built in 1992 to replace a 1970s model. You can only peer into the gloomy interior, almost fifty feet across and crowned with a low-pitched cedar-bark roof that is of a design common in the post-contact period. The roundhouse is still used for ritual purposes by local Ahwahneechee throughout the year, as is the working **sweathouse** built in 1989 just behind the roundhouse. Traditionally used to rid hunters of human odors before a hunt, it is heated by an oak fire with each hunter spending a couple of hours inside before ritually bathing then rubbing down with scented bark and brush to disguise any remaining smells.

Along with a few traditional bark shelters, there's a Miwok cabin exhibiting strong Euro-American influence, which illustrates how native builders often had to make do with poorer or scavenged materials, building directly on the ground with a central fire pit and smoke hole in the roof. There are plans to improve the interpretation of the lives of Yosemite's native people but as yet it is undecided whether this will be on the existing "village" site or west of the *Camp 4* campground on the site of the last Ahwahneechee settlement in the Valley.

Yosemite Cemetery

Anyone familiar with Yosemite's history or simply drawn to graveyards should visit the **Yosemite Cemetery** (always open; free), fifty yards west of the museum. A peaceful spot in the shade of oaks and incense cedars, it holds some three dozen graves including a few poorly marked Ahwahneechee. The better-marked graves are all of early white settlers who attempted to farm the Valley, and often perished in its isolation. Most of the headstones, dating back to the mid-1800s, are identified by horizontal slabs of rock, some etched with crude or faded writing. Notables include **James Lamon**, who died in 1875 after establishing what is now known as Curry Orchard (an apple orchard which still bears fruit in the Curry Village), and Yosemite's first guardian, **Galen Clark** (1814–1910), whose grave is marked by an irregular hunk of granite with his name and dates inscribed on one smooth, weathered face. Clark honored Lamon by planting a sequoia beside his grave, then selected half a dozen sequoia saplings for his own resting place. Altogether five sequoias survive, though none are especially large. The visitor center stocks the detailed *A Guide to the Yosemite Cemetery* (see "Books," p.253).

Ansel Adams Gallery

Anyone with even the slightest interest in **photography** should devote some time to the **Ansel Adams Gallery** (daily: July & Aug 9am–6pm, Sept–June 9am–5pm; Ⓦwww.anseladams.com; shuttle stops 4, 5 & 9), which specializes in the work of the world-renowned photographer. Originally known as Best's

Edging out the Ahwahneechee

The **Ahwahneechee**, a subtribe of the Southern Miwok people, have to some degree occupied Yosemite Valley for three thousand years, gathering acorns and trading them for obsidian arrowheads. While three dozen inhabited sites have been identified, it is thought that there were seldom more Ahwahneechee here at any one time than the few hundred discovered by the Mariposa Battalion when they entered Yosemite Valley in 1851. Many members of the tribe were killed trying to escape capture, and the rest were temporarily bundled off to a reservation in California's Central Valley before being allowed to gradually filter back to Yosemite. Claims that the Ahwahneechee had signed away their land were never upheld, but the tribe became fragmented and marginalized in the increasingly white Valley. After the formation of the Park Service in 1916, the Indians became a sideshow, providing visitor entertainment disguised as cultural revival, and designer basket making flourished.

Behavior that the rangers deemed to be unacceptable was punished, and unsanitary living standards were used as an excuse to re-house natives away from their traditional villages. By the late 1920s the Ahwahneechee had been confined to one large village near the foot of Yosemite Falls; nevertheless a new Park superintendent sought their virtual eviction. Those whose claims to residency couldn't be denied eventually settled in cramped new cabins constructed west of *Camp 4* in the early 1930s. By the 1950s, only those with permanent jobs in the Park could stay, and in 1969 the last remaining residents were re-housed once again and the village razed. A few Ahwahneechee still live in government housing in the Park (some working as interpreters at the museum and Indian Village), but most live outside, returning primarily for ceremonial occasions.

Studio, this is the Park's oldest concession holder, owned by Harry Cassie Best who first set up shop as a landscape painter in the Old Village below Sentinel Rock in 1902. Ansel Adams used to drop by to practice the piano but eventually his interests shifted to Best's daughter, Virginia, whom he married in 1928. By the 1930s the business had relocated to it current site and as Adams became more famous the business eventually took his name. It is still in family hands, run by Ansel and Virginia's son, Michael.

Understandably, the gallery specializes in work by Adams, from postcards, calendars and photographic books to posters (from $30) and high-grade photographic prints (from $175 for a 10" by 8" unframed image), many produced by Alan Ross, a disciple of Adams who has been printing his work since the 1970s. Adams' successors are also represented, and there is usually a display of prints by some notable landscape photographer currently working in the field. The gallery also has a healthy selection of outdoors and ecology-based books on the Sierra and the greater American West, as well as a reasonable choice of novels. Photographers needs are also catered for (see p.36) with equipment and film sales plus free group photography lessons.

The Ahwahnee and around

Traveling east of Yosemite Village you soon leave the bustle behind, the pace calming appreciably as you approach the sedate confines of **The Ahwahnee**. A pleasant ten-minute walk or a short shuttle ride, it is a world apart, surrounded by meadows and with the Valley walls rearing up immediately behind. Aside from visiting *The Ahwahnee* there is little reason to come out this way, though some come to picnic at Church Bowl, the former site of a small chapel. Hymns have now been replaced by the chink of karabiners from the rock climbers on the cliffs that form the back of the "bowl." East of *The Ahwahnee*, walking trails continue to Mirror Lake (see p.67).

The Ahwahnee

Standing an imposing six stories above the meadows below the Royal Arches, *The Ahwahnee* (shuttle stop 3) warrants a stopover even if your budget doesn't stretch to staying in the plush rooms (see p.165). Drop in to eat in the restaurant, sip a cocktail in the bar (see p.179), or join one of the free hour-long **tours** which cover the hotel's history, architecture and its role in the national park: ask at the front desk for times.

A harmonious synthesis of a grand European hotel and a backwoods cabin and definitely the most architecturally successful buildings in the Valley, this National Historic Landmark was built in 1927 to attract wealthy tourists, something it still does fairly effortlessly. Over the years royalty, heads of state and movie stars have graced the hotel with their presence, including JFK, Greta Garbo and Queen Elizabeth II.

A young Los Angeles architect named **Gilbert Stanley Underwood** designed the hotel with instructions to make the building blend into the Valley – though that would seem barely possible when the original specification was for a hotel three times the size. The reduced article that was eventually built meets the original brief, the exterior structure appearing to be made of huge redwood beams, which were actually cast from concrete that has been skillfully wood-grained and stained.

While the hotel is officially for guests and restaurant patrons only, no one is likely to mind if you pop in for a few minutes to admire the wonderful baronial-style common areas on the ground floor. The finest room is the

Great Lounge, hung with grand chandeliers, and bookended by matching fireplaces large enough to live in (and blazing in winter). As with most of the hotel, the lounge is decorated with Native American motifs, Miwok basketware, and some wonderful rugs and oriental carpets. Along the walls old images of the Park blend with framed samples of old carpets and kilims that once graced the polished floors. French doors open both sides to the let in the summer breeze, and the sofas are a perfect place to relax, especially at 4pm when tea and cookies are served for guests to piano accompaniment. If you think the room looks familiar, it was used as the model (though not the actual location) for the interiors of the *Overlook Hotel* in Stanley Kubrick's *The Shining* – coincidentally, exterior shots of the film's haunted hotel are of Oregon's famed *Timberline Lodge*, another of Gilbert Stanley Underwood's designs.

At the southern end of the Great Lounge, the Solarium opens out to the grounds, and provides access to the **Mural Room** with its frieze of forest plants and animals, and the **Winter Club Room**, where old photos of skiing, ski-jumping and tobogganing line the walls. Back in the lobby, look out for the delicate Yosemite watercolors by Swede Gunnar Widforss.

Through the quieter seasons of the year *The Ahwahnee* continues to lure well-heeled guests for special events based on gourmandizing, imbibing and general revelry (see p.187). You don't have to stay at *The Ahwahnee* to attend most of the events, but to overnight elsewhere would undermine the spirit of the whole occasion: accommodation packages are generally available through DNC on ⓣ559/253-5635 or check ⓦwww.yosemitepark.com under "Special Events."

▲ Ansel Adams Gallery, Yosemite Village

Yosemite Lodge

A fair proportion of the Valley's visitors find themselves staying west of Yosemite Village at **Yosemite Lodge** (shuttle stop 8), built on the site of a US cavalry post which operated from 1906 to 1914. Some of the barracks were soon converted for use as a hotel (which opened in 1915) and several original buildings remained until the 1950s. All you see now is a fairly modern complex of low buildings open year-round with 245 rooms, a couple of restaurants, a bar, grocery and gift shops, tour desk, a public swimming pool, a post office, bike rental and an outdoor amphitheater used for slide shows and presentations (nightly in summer). All this is very convenient if you staying here, or across the road at the *Camp 4* campground, but otherwise you may only come here to visit the *Mountain Room Restaurant*, the bar or, perhaps, one of the ranger programs at the amphitheater.

Curry Village and the eastern Valley

At some point, everyone finds themselves at the eastern end of the Valley, either to hike the **Mist Trail**, explore the **Nature Center at Happy Isles**, stroll to **Mirror Lake** or visit the **stables** (see p.151). For many Yosemite visitors this is also "home" as the main campgrounds are here along with the permanent cabins of *Housekeeping Camp* and the tent cabin complex of **Curry Village**. The main **Southside Drive** runs through the area and is plied by frequent shuttle buses that always run to Curry Village and the campgrounds, and from early April to late October also make a loop past Happy Isles and the Mirror Lake trailhead.

LeConte Memorial Lodge

From the southern side of Sentinel Bridge, Southside Drive runs along a narrow strip between the foot of cliffs and the Merced River to *Housekeeping Camp* (see "Accommodation," p.166). Across the road is the **LeConte Memorial Lodge** (May–Sept Wed–Sun 10am–4pm; free; Ⓣ209/372-4542, Ⓦwww.sierraclub.org/leconte; shuttle stop 12), a small rough-hewn granite-block structure where the **Sierra Club** maintain displays on the Club's history, runs a conservation library and has a corner for kids with books and educational games. There's also a fascinating relief map of the Valley dating back to around 1885, and changing displays on topics relevant to the work of the Sierra Club. Their evening programs (usually Fri–Sun; free) are a little more highbrow than those elsewhere in the Park and might include a slide show or talk by some luminary: check *Yosemite Today* for details.

The Lodge itself was built by the Sierra Club in 1903 to commemorate one of its founding members, **Joseph LeConte** (1823–1901), who had died in Yosemite Valley and had expressed a wish to be buried there, but his relatives felt the family plot in Oakland was more appropriate. An eminent geologist, Le Conte was an early supporter of John Muir's glaciation theory on the creation of the Yosemite Valley.

Originally constructed in Camp Curry, where it served as the Valley's first visitor center and marked the northern terminus of the John Muir Trail, the Lodge was rebuilt to the original design (and fitted with the existing steep-pitched Tudor roof) in its current location in 1919. As the Sierra Club's Yosemite headquarters, it was managed for a couple of summers in the early

Ansel Adams

Few photographers have stamped their vision on a place as unforgettably as **Ansel Adams** has done with Yosemite Valley. He worked all over the American West, but it is here that he did much of his most celebrated work: icons of American landscape photography such as 1944's *Clearing Winter Storm*; *Jeffrey Pine, Sentinel Dome* from the following year; and *Moon and Half Dome* from 1960.

Adams once said "Sometimes I think I do get to places just when God's ready to have somebody click the shutter," but this ignores the years he spent toting his 10" x 8" view camera – and forty pounds of tripods, filters, lenses and glass plates – up Yosemite's steep gullies, and days spent waiting for that perfect moment. For some, Adams' images are dispassionate, perhaps too perfect and naïve for the modern world, and seemingly at odds with their creator, a man who one critic described as "as friendly, twinkle-eyed, excitable, and enthusiastic as a warm puppy."

Born in 1902 into a moderately wealthy San Francisco family, Adams was given his first camera – a Box Brownie – when he was fourteen, on his first trip to Yosemite. Though classically trained as a concert pianist, he claimed that he knew his "destiny" on that first visit to Yosemite. His mother pleaded "Do not give up the piano! The camera cannot express the human soul!" to which Adams replied "Perhaps the camera cannot, but the photographer can." Soon he turned his attentions to the mountains, returning every year and taking up a job as custodian of the Sierra Club headquarters.

He first made his mark in 1927 with *Monolith, The Face of Half Dome*, his first successful **visualization**. Adams believed that, before pressing the shutter, the photographer should have a clear idea of the final image and think through the entire photographic process, considering how lenses, filters, exposure, development and printing need to be used to achieve that visualization. This approach may seem obvious today, but compared to the hit-and-miss methods of the time, it was little short of revolutionary. Visualization was made easier by applying the **zone system** of exposure calculation which, though not new, was codified and promoted by Adams as the basis for his teaching. This blend of art and science divides the range of possible tones into ten zones from velvet black (I) through middle gray (V) to pure white (X), and allows precise tone control, something Adams felt was key to full expression through photography. This also marked Adams' transition from a nineteenth-century pictorial approach – soft focus and middle tones characterized by the desire to emulate painting – to a cleaner, more modernist "straight photography."

In 1932 Adams joined forces with like-minded photographers such as Edward Weston and Imogen Cunningham to form **Group f/64**, which was soon criticized for

1920s by **Ansel Adams**, who was happy to do anything if it meant he could spend more time in the Valley.

Curry Village

After Yosemite Village, the Park's largest concentration of visitor facilities is at **Curry Village** (shuttle stops 13, 13a, 13b, 14, 20 & 21), a rambling area of canvas tent cabins and wooden chalets centered on a small complex of restaurants, shops, pay showers, a post office and an outdoor amphitheater hosting ranger programs and evening shows. There's also a winter ice rink, a rock climbing school, bike rental and a kiosk renting rafts for use on the nearby Merced River.

The "village" is the direct descendent of **Camp Curry**, which was started in 1899 by David and Jeannie Curry, who were keen to share their adopted home in the Valley and charged just $12 a week for a "good bed, and a clean napkin being out of step with the social documentary photography fashionable in the class-conscious aftermath of the stock market crash. French photographer Henri Cartier-Bresson later declared "The world is going to pieces and people like Adams and Weston are photographing rocks." Adams held to his belief that the primal aspects of the earth had as much value as photographing breadlines, though that didn't stop him sensitively photographing Japanese Americans in internment camps during WWII.

As Adams fine-tuned his artistic theories through the 1930s, the idea of photography as fine art was still considered novel. Adams was therefore delighted when, in 1940, he was made vice chairman of the newly established **Department of Photography** at New York's Museum of Modern Art (MoMA). There was still very little money in photography and Adams continued to take commercial assignments, often producing promotional shots for the Yosemite Park and Curry Company and menu photos for *The Ahwahnee*. Commercial and personal work through the 1940s and 1950s earned Adams an ever wider audience. While still demanding the highest standard of reproduction, he had now tempered his perfectionism and allowed his work to appear on postcards, calendars and posters. By now, Adam was virtually a household name and for the first time in his life – in his early seventies – he began making money to match his status as the grand old man of Western photography.

His final triumph came in 1979, when MoMA put on the huge "Yosemite and the Range of Light" exhibition, which won him a *Time* magazine cover story. That same year, he was asked to make an official portrait of President Jimmy Carter – the first time a photographer had been assigned an official presidential portrait – and was subsequently awarded the nation's highest civilian honor, the Medal of Freedom.

Throughout his life, Adams had another great passion, one that he pursued with the same fervor as photography: **conservation**. Back in 1932, the artist had a direct hand in creating Kings Canyon National Park. Two years later, he became a director of the **Sierra Club**, a position he held until 1971, overseeing several successful environmental campaigns. He never quit campaigning for the cause of conservation, and, after an interview in which he suggested he'd like to drown Ronald Reagan in his own martini, agreed to meet the president to promote the environmental cause.

In his final years, Adams tired of printing the same old "greatest hits" and devoted his time to producing master sets of his best work for selected museums and galleries, and writing his autobiography. He died on April 22, 1984 aged 82, and has since become even more honored. The mountain which had been widely known as Mount Ansel Adams since 1933 now bears that name officially, and a huge chunk of the High Sierra south of Yosemite National Park is known as the Ansel Adams Wilderness.

every meal." Their first six guests stayed in tents below Glacier Point, but amenities soon improved with a dance hall, tennis courts, croquet lawns, and evening entertainment which culminated in the **Firefall** (see box, p.67). Through the Curry's daughter, Mary Curry Tressider, the business stayed in family hands until 1970 but is now run by the Park concessionaire.

The village isn't a place for sightseeing, but you can wander through the ageing apple trees of **Curry Orchard**, which was planted in the 1860s by the Valley's first year-round white resident, James Lamon. The trees are now past their best, but they still bear fruit, though it is mostly palatable only to the deer that come scavenging at night in late summer. Sadly the orchard now serves as a parking lot for Curry Village. Further sites of historic interest are visited on the Legacy of Curry Village trail, a half-hour stroll around Curry Village's precincts past signs explaining the likes of the Firefall and the old toboggan run.

▲ Oak Tree, Snowstorm, Ansel Adams

Nature Center at Happy Isles

Throughout the summer, shuttle buses continue from Curry Village along a car-free loop around the very eastern end of the Valley. First stop is the **Nature Center at Happy Isles** (early May to mid-Sept daily 10am–4pm; free; shuttle stop 16), a modern, river-stone and cedar-shingle building amid the pines on the site of a 1927 trout hatchery. It houses the most **family-friendly** set of displays in the Valley, and is the base for the Park's Junior Ranger Program, aimed at kids aged seven to ten (see p.185). Highlights include a mock-up section of forest that comes complete with stuffed examples of animals who make Yosemite their home – woodpeckers, owls, a coyote, a porcupine, pine martens, flying squirrels, a raccoon, even a mountain lion perched on a rock as though waiting to pounce. Hands-on exhibits allow you to touch the casts of animal footprints and feel how hunks of rough granite get weathered to river pebbles and eventually sand. There's also an "After Dark" section with a diorama featuring the animals which make up the Yosemite night shift, and an exhibit on a year in the life of a bear.

At the rear of the Nature Center, be sure to check out the **rockfall exhibit** (unrestricted entry) where a number of explanatory panels highlight the pulverized rock and flattened trees that resulted from the 1996 rockfall (see box, p.54). The air blast laid waste to everything up to the viewing spot, but already large bushes are beginning to recolonize the talus slope. Short trails nearby explore the various ecosystems around about – riparian, forest, talus, and fen.

Towards the Merced River, a couple of bridges lead out to the "**Happy Isles**" themselves, a string of three wooded islets first described in 1885 by Yosemite guardian W. E. Dennison: "No one can visit them without for the while forgetting the grinding strife of this world and being happy." A bit optimistic perhaps but hanging out at the swimming holes in summer is indeed quite relaxing.

Steps away on the eastern side of the Merced River lies the Valley's most important trailhead. From here the **Mist Trail** (see Hike 2) heads up to Vernal Fall, the **Half Dome Trail** (see Hike 4) continues to the summit of Half Dome, and the **John Muir Trail** (see Hike 46) spurs off to the Tuolumne high country.

Mirror Lake

The lure of Half Dome reflected in the glassy waters of Tenaya Creek makes the mile-long stroll to **Mirror Lake** (*Ahwiyah*, or "quiet water"; shuttle stop 17) one of Yosemite's most popular walks. We've included it as part of Hike 7 (see p.114), which continues a mile or so beyond the lake and returns along the south side of Tenaya Creek.

The Firefall

Hard to believe now, but for decades local hoteliers struggled to lure tourists to the Valley, even trying toboggan rides near Curry Village and organized bear feeding at the open dump in Church Bowl. From the beginning of the twentieth century to the late 1960s, the biggest draw was the spectacular **Firefall**, which took place every summer evening (and a couple of times a week in winter) at the end of Camp Curry's evening entertainment program.

As the music and vaudeville acts went through their routines, guests gazed up at Glacier Point, 3200 feet above, where a fire made from ten barrow-loads of red fir bark could be seen lighting the night sky. As the show drew to a close, the stentorian voice of camp owner David Curry would boom out "Hello Glacier! Is the fire ready?" The faint reply of "The fire is ready!" would waft back down, and at Curry's instruction "Let the Fire Fall!" the smoldering pile of embers would be raked over the cliff to create a thousand-foot fiery cascade that seemed to fall almost directly on the guests (but actually landed harmlessly on a ledge). The firefall, accompanied by solo rendition of "The Indian Love Call" or "America, the Beautiful", always took place at exactly 9pm, though one night in the early 1960s the proceedings were delayed for half an hour while President Kennedy finished his drink at *The Ahwahnee*.

The event was so popular that spectacle seekers crossed counties, clogged Valley roads, and trampled meadows to stake out the best vantage points. Though the cinders never caused a serious fire, the Firefall was eventually deemed inappropriate for a national park; the last one took place on Jan 25, 1968. Talk to older Park visitors who grew up with the Firefall and you'll uncover a deep fondness for the spectacle. A sense of what it was like can be gleaned from the periodic free slide shows on the topic (check *Yosemite Today* for times and venues) or seek out a copy of the 1954 Humphrey Bogart flick, *The Caine Mutiny*, which features a seven-second sequence.

Really just a wide spot in a stream, Mirror Lake is subject to seasonal variations and is best visited in spring and early summer when it is nearly bursting its banks. May is particularly spectacular with the dogwood blooms at their best. Long thought of as a lake in the process of turning into a meadow, ecologists now consider Mirror Lake a pool in a seasonal stream. Either way, there is little, if any, water left by August or September, but it is pleasant enough just wandering or biking along the broad asphalt path to admire the woods or gaze at the wondrous rock formations all around.

The lake's moneymaking potential was spotted early on and a toll road was installed here in the 1860s. A decade later there was a boathouse beside the lake, an inn and even a dance pavilion built out over the water. To raise the water level and improve the boating, the natural rock dam was built and the bottom dredged, a practice not halted until 1971. The area is now free from the trappings of early entrepreneurial ventures, but the self-guided **Mirror Lake Interpretive Trail** helps you identify the site of the dance pavilion and the location of an icehouse used to store winter-harvested ice for the summer demand. There's also extensive coverage of Native American use of the area, including the harvesting of bracken fern for the black elements in basketware.

Exploring the Valley loop road

The matchless beauty and variety of Yosemite Valley can't be fully appreciated from the developed areas around Yosemite Village and Curry Village, and you really need to explore further either on foot or along the road system. Two roads make up an eleven-mile one-way loop through the Valley with the westbound **Northside Drive** hugging the base of El Capitan and the Three Brothers, and the eastbound **Southside Drive** running parallel below Bridalveil Fall and Sentinel Rock. Set aside half a day, allowing time to take photos, have a picnic lunch in some sylvan spot beside the Merced River or hike the western end of the Valley by following Hike 10 (see p.116).

Northside Drive

Northside Drive heads west from Yosemite Village, initially along a two-way road with the open expanse of **Cook's Meadow** on the left and, on the right, regenerating **black oak woodland** blocking views towards **Lower Yosemite**

Area hikes

Yosemite's 50 best hikes are found in Chapters 4 and 5. The following hikes begin from the western end of Yosemite Valley and are considerably quieter than those at the eastern end.

Day hikes

- Hike 10 Western Valley Loop: see p.116
- Hike 11 Inspiration Point: see p.116

Overnight hikes

- Hike 44 Pohono–Panorama Combo: see p.141
- Hike 45 North rim of Yosemite Valley: see p.142

Wayside markers

Around Yosemite Valley and along roads throughout the Park, you'll see wayside markers with a letter and a number: V1–V27 in Yosemite Valley, G1–G11 along Glacier Point Road, T1–T39 along Tioga Road, and so on. These correspond to entries in the Park Service's *Yosemite Road Guide* (see "Books," p.253), which is useful for the completist, though you'll find that everything of importance is amply covered in the relevant section of our text. We've mentioned the nearest marker to points of interest where relevant.

Fall (V3; see p.55). Immediately beyond the Lower Yosemite Fall (shuttle stop 6) and *Yosemite Lodge* you pass the *Camp 4* walk-in campground and the Upper Yosemite Fall trailhead (V5), followed half a mile on by **Rocky Point** (V6) a mountain of boulders left by a major rockfall in 1987 (see box, p.54).

Drive on for a mile and a half to reach **Devil's Elbow**, a loop in the Merced River where the bank is being restored after the area was reclaimed from its earlier role as a parking lot. An unobtrusive cedar-rail fence keeps visitors back from the riverbank while regeneration of native willows and cottonwoods gets underway. At either end of the restoration area, there are sandy beaches good for swimming once the spring snowmelt abates. Opposite is the appropriately named **Cathedral Spires Vista** pullout, and a short trail leading to the base of El Capitan where climbers begin their multi-day ascents.

It is just a few hundred yards further to **El Capitan Bridge** (a possible return route over the Merced River to Yosemite Village) and **El Capitan Meadow** (V8), an open field with stupendous views of **El Capitan** (see p.46), which towers above, and Cathedral Spires across the Valley. Walking on the meadow is discouraged as it is becoming heavily impacted from thousands of people keen to spy on El Cap climbers. At the western end of the meadow, you can still pick out the abandoned route of **Old Big Oak Flat Road**, a very early toll road that climbs the Valley wall to the west.

Another quarter-mile on, the road suddenly dips (V9) as it descends a recessional moraine left by the last glacier to occupy the Valley. The Merced is swift here, as witnessed through a break in the trees revealing great views of Bridalveil Fall (V10). The river then slows again at **Valley View**, where you do indeed get a tremendous long view towards Half Dome.

Hwy-120 West and Hwy-140 now continue out of the Valley, or you can turn left and double back along Southside Drive towards Yosemite Village.

Southside Drive

Approaching the Valley along Hwy-120 or Hwy-140 you enter a one-way system at **Pohono Bridge**, which crosses the Merced and passes the small **Fern Spring** (V12) on the right. The road soon reaches the edge of **Bridalveil Meadow** where a marker (V13) records the spot where, on May 17, 1903, President Theodore Roosevelt and John Muir camped together and nutted out the conservation measures Muir felt were needed in the Park. Muir (and presumably the surroundings) obviously had some effect, because several of Muir's proposals were enacted over the subsequent years.

At the eastern end of the meadow, Hwy-41 comes in from Wawona. Turn right here for the parking lot for **Bridalveil Fall**, or left to continue the circuit. Next stop is **El Capitan Vista**, a broad section of road where RVs and buses regularly line the parking bays on both sides of the road for one of the most

From the western end of the Valley: Big Oak Flat Road heads northwest (see p.72) where you can pick up the Tioga Road (Hwy-120 West; see p.76); Hwy-140 heads west out of the Park towards Mariposa (covered on p.206); and Hwy-41 (see p.209) heads south past Tunnel View to Wawona with a spur to Glacier Point (see p.94).

celebrated views of the big stone. It looks its best early and late in the day when lower-angled light plays on the sheer granite walls, highlighting its features.

Cathedral Spires (V15) rise up on your right as you drive a mile or so on to a small side road to **Cathedral Beach picnic area** and **Three Brothers Vista** (V16). Another mile on, a side road leads to two more excellent waterside picnic areas, **Yellow Pine** and **Sentinel Beach**, the latter one of the nicest and most convenient picnic spots in the park.

Across the road a sign marks the **trailhead** for the Four-Mile Trail to Glacier Point (Hike 9). In the mid-nineteenth century this was the location of Lower Yosemite Village, home to Camp Ahwahnee and the Valley's original hotel, *Leidig's*, which saw its first tourists in 1856. The hotel was just a few muslin sheets stretched over a wood frame and is now long gone, but the name survives as Leidig's Meadow, reached across a very sturdy bridge from the **Swinging Bridge Picnic Area**.

Half a mile on, you get the first really startling view of Yosemite Falls from **Upper Yosemite Fall Vista** (V19), then reach the interdenominational **chapel**, (see p.70), a suitably alpine-looking structure with its vertical wooden battens, steep-pitched roof and short steeple. The oldest building in the Park still in use, the chapel was built in 1879 close to the base of the Four-Mile Trail, and later moved three-quarters of a mile to its current site. It is the last remaining building of the old Yosemite Village, once the main settlement in the Valley with a store, post office, park headquarters, hotel, saloons, and three photographers' studios. The site was chosen for its shade on hot summer days but tastes changed and during the 1930s most services were transferred to the sunnier and warmer northern side of the river. Several of the old buildings have ended up in the Pioneer Yosemite History Center in Wawona (see p.98).

A hundred yards further on, turn left over **Sentinel Bridge** to return to Yosemite Village, or continue straight ahead for Curry Village and the eastern Valley.

2

Northern Yosemite

Only ardent hikers prepared to spend several days in the backcountry get to see the true remoteness of **Northern Yosemite**, a vast expanse of angular peaks and glaciated valleys stretching beyond the northern Park boundary to the Hoover and Emigrant wildernesses. But between these wilds and the relative civilization of Yosemite Valley lies some of Yosemite's finest scenery, made accessible by **Tioga Road**, which virtually bisects the Park from east to west. Snowbound and impassable for all but the five warmest months, the road climbs up through densely forested high-country to the open grasslands of **Tuolumne Meadows**, surrounded by the polished granite domes and with a southern horizon delineated by the sawtooth crest of the **Cathedral Range**. It is a gorgeous and relaxing place simply to hang out, free from the bustle of Yosemite Valley but with access to the only significant cluster of visitor facilities in the Park's northern half. There are opportunities to go horseback riding, swimming in chilly but alluring alpine lakes, fishing in the Tuolumne River and simply picnicking among the meadow wildflowers, but the real draw is **hiking**. Nowhere else in the Park is such fabulous hiking country so close at hand or so easy to reach: starting at 8600 feet up, most of the hikes don't require a huge altitude-gaining slog at the start. We've outlined almost a dozen hikes in the area from a short stroll to the effervescent **Soda Springs**, to the two-day hike along a section of the **John Muir Trail** between here and Yosemite Valley.

East of Tuolumne Meadows, Tioga Road tops out at the 10,000-foot **Tioga Pass**, the Park's eastern boundary and the center of a historic mining area. To the west of Tuolumne, the best of the Tioga Road scenery is around **Olmsted Point**, where everyone stops to photograph the barren granite walls of Tenaya Canyon, and **Tenaya Lake**, surrounded by glacier-smoothed domes typically populated by rock climbers. Elsewhere, bumpy side roads spur off to wooded campgrounds and pass numerous trailheads, some feeding down to the northern rim of Yosemite Valley while others thread their way to alpine lakes and the sequoias at **Tuolumne Grove**.

The only other road-accessible section of Northern Yosemite is **Hetch Hetchy**, once a meadow-filled valley towards the Park's northwest border said to be the match of Yosemite Valley, but now controversially filled by the Hetch Hetchy Reservoir. It is an attractive area, nonetheless, particularly in spring when three lovely **waterfalls** spring to life among abundant wildflowers.

Big Oak Flat Road and northwestern Yosemite

Considering the quality of road access, the northwestern corner of Yosemite is surprisingly little visited. Plenty of people drive through the region along Hwy-120 West on the way from the Bay Area but few stop for long, except for a quick photo from one of the viewpoints or a leisurely stroll down to the **Merced Grove** of **giant sequoias**. The one major exception is **Hetch Hetchy**, notorious for being the only major dam in a national park, but still of interest as a springboard to hikes in the north of the park.

The Valley to Crane Flat

To get to the northern reaches of Yosemite from the Valley, drive northwest along **Big Oak Flat Road**, which starts climbing as soon as it spurs off Hwy-140 at the Valley's western end. There are great cliff views along the way as the Merced River rapidly drops away to your left; notice how the river leaves behind the U-shaped Yosemite Valley and takes on the classic V-shape of an unglaciated river canyon.

After two short tunnels lie two spectacular springtime waterfalls right beside the road. John Muir felt that the first, **Cascade Creek** (B2), was fittingly named, writing "as far as I have traced it above and below our camp it is one continuous bouncing, dancing, white bloom of cascades." The less dramatic **Tamarack Creek** takes its name from the lodgepole pines hereabouts, which early visitors thought looked like the eastern tamarack. The two creeks join forces just downstream and plummet five hundred feet into Merced River canyon as **The Cascades**. From here you can also look across the valley to **Elephant Rock** a granite lump vaguely resembling a great pachyderm.

Almost half a mile on, **Valley Portal** (B3) offers an excellent vista of the western half of Yosemite Valley. The longest of the three tunnels on this road runs almost a mile from here to a view of **Merced River canyon** (B4) and Half Dome. **Big Meadow Overlook** (B6), four miles on, affords views of the silted-up lake bed of Big Meadow, once used to grow hay to feed packhorses and now an important foraging area for the locally rare great gray owl. Four miles down a graded but unmade road on the edge of Big Meadow stands the private settlement of **Foresta**, around 150 homes on a plot of land that was grandfathered into the Park when it was created. It was a gorgeous spot until a 1990 wildfire swept through and burned virtually everything here along with 23,000 surrounding acres. The greenery is gradually returning and most of the houses have been rebuilt, usually to luxurious standards. The only reason to come here is if you are going to stay (see p.168). Big Oak Flat Road continues to climb over the next couple of miles, leveling off around 6200 feet at

Area hikes

Yosemite's fifty best hikes are found in chapters 4 and 5. The following hikes begin in northwestern Yosemite, where the relatively low altitude and light snow cover of Hetch Hetchy encourage early spring hiking when the waterfalls and wildflowers are at their best.

- Hike 12 Wapama Falls: see p.117
- Hike 13 Rancheria Falls: see p.117

Crane Flat, a small meadow where you'll find the Crane Flat Store and gas station and, across the road, Crane Flat campground. Here Tioga Road (Hwy-120 East) branches off of Big Oak Flat Road, heading east towards Tuolumne Meadows: our account of this route continues on p.118.

Merced Grove to Big Oak Flat Entrance

Just over three miles west of Crane Flat along Big Oak Flat Road a small pull-out provides parking for the **Merced Grove** of **giant sequoias**, which with only a couple of dozen trees is smaller and less spectacular than the Mariposa and Tuolumne groves. In compensation, it is the least visited of all the groves, and being satisfyingly free from barriers and signs is all the more appealing. A broad, sandy **trail** (1hr 30min–2hr round-trip; 3 miles; 600ft ascent on the way back) takes you to a dense cluster of five trees heralding the main section of the grove, clustered around the shuttered and gabled **Merced Grove Cabin** (closed to the public). Built in 1935 to exhibit the "highest evolution of log cabin construction," it has been restored and you can admire its bold exterior, featuring a hipped, shingled roof and log window boxes. It is managed by the Yosemite Institute (see p.40), and if a group is present you may get to peek inside. Beyond the cabin the grove thins out after one final fifteen-foot-diameter sequoia with a huge hemispherical burl across its entire width.

Continuing west on Big Oak Flat Road, **North Country View** (B11) gives a great view of Hetch Hetchy reservoir far below, filling the valley behind the dam. A couple of miles past the overlook stands the Park's **Big Oak Flat Entrance** (B12), where there is small **Information Station** (Easter–Sept daily 8am–5pm, Oct–Easter sporadically open, mostly at weekends; ⓣ209/379-1899) with a desk for obtaining wilderness permits, a free phone for reserving camp lodging, a campground reservations office (April to mid-Oct 8am–5pm), a few drink machines and toilets. Across the road, the *Hodgdon Meadow* campground (see p.175) sits on the site where Jeremiah Hodgdon and his family ran a horse and stage waystation until the 1890s, making the best of their location beside the original Big Oak Flat Road into Yosemite.

A mile west of the Big Oak Flat entrance, **Evergreen Road** heads north and re-enters the Park on the way to Hetch Hetchy. Our coverage of Hwy-120 West is covered on p.197.

Hetch Hetchy

John Muir's passion for Yosemite Valley was matched, if not exceeded, by his desire to preserve the beauty of **Hetch Hetchy** (open dawn–dusk only unless you have a wilderness permit), at one time a near replica of Yosemite Valley. At 3800ft it is around the same height as the Yosemite Valley floor and was considered by Muir to be "one of nature's rare and most precious mountain temples," with grassy, oak-filled meadows and soaring granite walls.

When Hetch Hetchy came under threat from power and water supply interests in San Francisco in 1901, Muir began a twelve-year losing battle for its preservation (see box, p.75). Eventually, in 1913, the cause was lost to a federal bill paving the way for the Tuolumne River to be blocked by the O'Shaughnessey Dam, creating the slender, eight-mile-long Hetch Hetchy reservoir. The dam, completed in 1923 and raised to its current height in 1938, drowned the meadows under a couple of hundred feet of water.

Despite Muir's rapture, it is hard to imagine that Hetch Hetchy was ever the equivalent of Yosemite Valley. The meadows may well have been very beautiful,

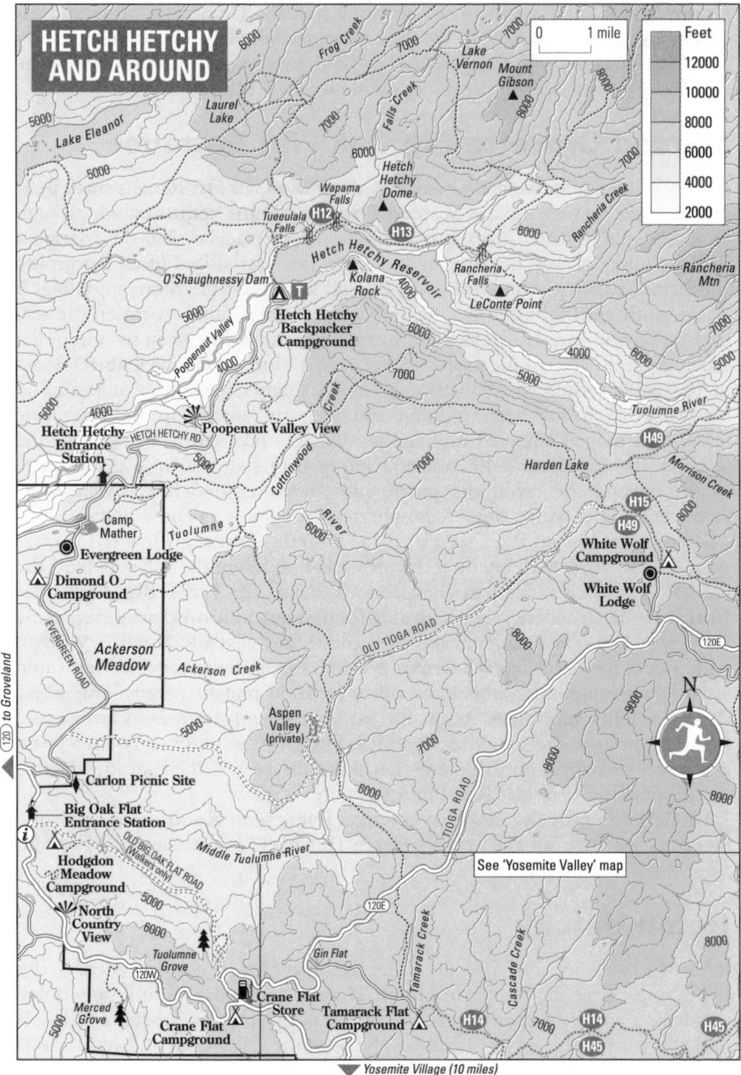

but the rocks all around could never quite equal Yosemite's majesty. It is certainly no match now, and with so much wonderful countryside competing for visitors' attention elsewhere in the Park, it isn't so surprising that Hetch Hetchy is little visited. That said, the view up the reservoir from the middle of the dam is stunning, with the bell-shaped dome of **Kolana Rock** dominating on the right and providing an active breeding ground for endangered **peregrine falcons**. Across the water, two beautiful falls drop over a thousand feet from the cliffs on the north side, both of them accessible on relatively easy hikes (see Hike 12 and Hike 13). The voluminous **Wapama Falls** roars away in its dark recess in dramatic contract to **Tueeulala Falls** (pronounced TWEE-lala), described by Muir as a "silvery scarf burning with irised sun-fire." Both are at their best from April to early June: Tueeulala Falls is usually dry by early June, with Wapama Falls hanging on for a couple more months.

Long before it was drowned by the reservoir, Hetch Hetchy valley was scoured out by glaciers, which ground down the valley between ten thousand and two million years ago. Their route was followed by the Tuolumne River, a passage used by Miwok peoples who named the area "Hatchatchie" after a type of grass with edible seeds once common hereabouts. **Wildflowers** are still abundant in the region in spring – look for bright California fuschia, waterfall buttercups in trickling cascades and shooting stars in damp meadows – along with California black oak, incense cedar, ponderosa pine and big leaf maple.

The only **facilities** at Hetch Hetchy are toilets, drinking water, phone and a backpacker campground (wilderness permit required), which makes a good starting point for treks into the near-deserted northern reaches of the Park. As the reservoir forms part of San Francisco's water supply, swimming and boating are not allowed, and **fishing** is only permitted from the shore if live bait isn't used.

The battle for Hetch Hetchy

"Dam Hetch Hetchy! As well dam for water-tanks the people's cathedrals and churches, for no holier temple has ever been consecrated by the heart of man."

John Muir, *The Yosemite*

As early as 1867 the burgeoning city of San Francisco, perched at the end of a dry peninsula, began searching for a dependable water supply. In 1900 the US Geological Survey recommended Hetch Hetchy valley as a potential source, where a relatively small dam would hold back a large body of water. San Francisco mayor James Phelan concurred, but Muir and his cohorts, instigating the first environmental letter-writing campaign to Congress and obtaining support from most of the country's influential newspapers, initially defeated the proposal.

At the time conservationists split into those favoring total preservation of "one of Nature's rarest and most precious mountain temples," and those advocating "wise use." Dam advocate William Kent described Muir as "a man entirely without social sense," while Muir retaliated by labeling his adversaries "mischief-makers and robbers" and "temple destroyers, devotees of ravaging commercialism."

The environmentalists eventually lost the battle in 1913 when commercial interests persuaded President Wilson to sign the Raker Act, allowing for the construction of the O'Shaughnessy Dam, which was built between 1914 and 1923. The *New York Times* reported "The American people have been whipped in the Hetch Hetchy fight," no one more so than Muir himself, who died dispirited in 1914.

Though Muir and company failed to stop the dam, their work led to the creation of both the National Park Service and the Sierra Club (see p.84), the latter a long-time advocate of **undamming Hetch Hetchy** and returning it to its original state. Since Muir's day, the construction of the huge Don Pedro reservoir (downstream from Hetch Hetchy) means that San Francisco's water supply would barely be affected; the bigger stumbling block would be the loss of power generation. With power shortages and rolling blackouts in recent years the proposal looks set to remain an environmentalists' pipe dream for the time being.

For more on the issues around Hetch Hetchy consult the appropriate section of the Sierra Club site (Ⓦwww.sierraclub.org/ca/hetchhetchy) or visit the site of the campaigning organization, Restore Hetch Hetchy (Ⓦwww.hetchhetchy.org).

If entering the Park from the east through Lee Vining, this section will work in reverse order: those driving from Yosemite Village should first follow our coverage of Northside Drive (see p.68), then our coverage of Big Oak Flat Road (see p.72).

Approaching Hetch Hetchy

The road into Hetch Hetchy (initially Evergreen Road, then Hetch Hetchy Road) cuts off Hwy-120 West a mile outside the Big Oak Flat Entrance, and twists north through the Stanislaus National Forest and then the Park for a total of sixteen miles to the O'Shaughnessy Dam. It is generally accessible without chains from mid-April to mid-October. A mile off Hwy-120 West, you pass the **Carlon Picnic Site** (hand-pumped water, fire rings and picnic tables) where you cross the South Fork of the Tuolumne River.

Another mile on, a rough road to the right follows a section of the **original Tioga Road** to Aspen Valley, a small area of private land that was homesteaded before the creation of the national park. A few people still have summer homes there, but it is off-limits to the general public. Round a few more bends, the forest opens out at **Ackerson Meadow**, once used by an early prospector for growing hay to sell to transport companies in Yosemite Valley. Six miles north off Hwy-120 West is the *Dimond O* campground (see p.176); continue a couple of miles to *Evergreen Lodge* (see p.168) and **Mather**, a former sheep ranch and later a stop on the railroad during the construction of the O'Shaughnessy Dam. It is now the San Francisco Recreation Camp, open to San Francisco residents by lottery. Turn right here to enter the Park at the **Hetch Hetchy Entrance** (closed dusk–dawn), with a kiosk acting as the **ranger station** where you can pick up wilderness permits.

The Hetch Hetchy Road climbs gently through **Poopenaut Pass** (H2) to reveal a view of the Grand Canyon of the Tuolumne River, the Hetch Hetchy reservoir and dam, and Wapama and Tueeulala falls. From **Poopenaut Valley View** (H3), a mile on, you can see Poopenaut Valley below the dam, where a few cabins remain from the small sheep and cattle herding settlement that once thrived there. It is a further three miles to Hetch Hetchy.

Tioga Road: Crane Flat to Tenaya Lake

Snow-covered and impassable for more than half the year, **Tioga Road** (Hwy-120 East: usually open late May–early Nov) runs 46 miles from Crane Flat through some of Yosemite's most breathtaking **high-country scenery** to the Park's sole eastern entrance at the 9945ft Tioga Pass, the highest road pass in California. Along the way it traverses alpine tundra and subalpine forests, cuts through glaciated valleys, and crosses the sublime Tuolumne Meadows. Throughout these varying zones are trailheads for numerous hikes and great places to stop, such as **Olmsted Point** with its tremendous views of Half Dome and Clouds Rest, and chilly **Tenaya Lake** where the brave can go for a swim from sandy beaches.

Tioga Road roughly follows a trading route used by the Mono Lake Paiute, which in 1883 was turned into the Great Sierra Wagon Road, opened by the Great Sierra Consolidated Silver Company who needed to transport machinery and supplies to their mines around Tioga Pass. Though realigned frequently over the years, parts of this road were still used until 1961. You can still get a sense of what travel was like in those times by exploring short sections of the old route which spur off to the May Lake trailhead and *Yosemite Creek* campground.

▲ Clouds Rest and Half Dome from Olmsted Point

Facilities along Tioga Road are limited to a handful of campgrounds, and the lodge, restaurant and store at White Wolf (both generally open mid-June–early Sept), before you get to Tuolumne Meadows. If you're planning to spend a few days exploring out this way, be sure to stock up with supplies in the Valley or at the Crane Flat store.

Tuolumne Grove

Just a half-mile north of the intersection of Big Oak Flat Road and Tioga Road at Crane Flat sits the first major sight in this direction, the trailhead for the **Tuolumne Grove** of **giant sequoias** (open all year, but usually snowbound from late November to April; free). With just a few dozen trees, it is far less impressive than the Mariposa Grove but is closer to the Valley and has the distinction of being the grove spotted by pioneer Joseph Walker and his party when they first entered Yosemite in 1833.

Access to the grove is on foot along a root-buckled asphalt road that once formed part of the **Old Big Oak Flat Road**, built in 1874 at a time when it took a day and a half of travel to get here from San Francisco. This stretch of the old road is inaccessible to vehicles (including bikes) but sees plenty of foot traffic on the way to the grove. The first sequoia is a mile down the road from the parking lot and marks the start of a mile-long loop trail that passes several more magnificent big trees. The huge **fallen giant** was known as the Leaning Tower Tree until, weakened by successive fire scars then laden with snow, it tumbled in 1983. Now hollow and fairly rapidly crumbling away, you can still crawl through. Nearby, the charred remains of a **tunnel tree** is distinguished by the car-sized hole that was bored through and undoubtedly contributed to its early demise. There were once several drive-through trees in California, though most have either toppled or access has been forbidden.

Beyond the sequoia grove, the long abandoned Old Big Oak Flat Road continues about four miles on to the *Hodgdon Meadow Campground*, opposite the

Area hikes

The following hikes are accessed off Tioga Road (in order heading east from Crane Flat) and most are usually under snow from November to early June.

Day hikes

- Hike 14 El Capitan from Tamarack Flat: see p.118
- Hike 15 Harden Lake: see p.118
- Hike 16 Lukens Lake: see p.119
- Hike 17 Yosemite Falls from Yosemite Creek: see p.119
- Hike 18 North Dome from Porcupine Creek: see p.119
- Hike 19 May Lake: see p.120
- Hike 20 Clouds Rest from Tenaya Lake: see p.120
- Hike 21 Polly Dome Lakes: see p.121
- Hike 22 Tenaya Lake circuit: see p.121

Overnight hikes

- Hike 48 Ten Lakes: see p.144

Big Oak Flat Entrance; again, cars, bikes and other vehicles are prohibited. The road takes its name from the former gold-mining town just west of the Park border that once had a population of 3000.

Tamarack Flat to White Wolf

Three miles east of the Tuolumne Grove parking lot, a drivable but winding and potholed section of the Old Big Oak Flat Road leads three miles southeast to the primitive *Tamarack Flat* campground (see p.175). Immediately past the turn-off, **Gin Flat** (T3) marks the spot where a bunch of delighted cowboys happened upon a barrel of gin lost off a passing wagon.

The next five miles run through a fire-scorched patch of forest, then parallel to the south fork of the Tuolumne River to **Smoky Jack** (T6), the former site of a simple campground which got its name from John Connel, who originally employed John Muir to tend his flocks. Much of the next four miles passes through an almost pure stand of **red fir forest** to the delightful, grass-fringed **Siesta Lake** on the right. Beyond, a narrow side road leads a mile north of Tioga Road to **White Wolf**, a lodge, restaurant (see p.182), campground (see p.175) and very small store (mid-June to early Sept daily 8am–8pm), which gets its name either from a misidentified coyote that happened by in the old days or a local chief. Surrounded by lush meadow and forests it is a good base for easy hikes to Harden and Lukens lakes (see Hike 15 & Hike 16).

Back on Tioga Road, a third of a mile drive east, a rough section of the Great Sierra Wagon Road heads five miles southeast down to the **Yosemite Creek campground**. The road was built in 1883 for taking machinery up to mines around Tioga Pass, and is still passable in ordinary vehicles. Hike 17 to the top of Yosemite Falls starts at the campground.

Clark Range View to Clouds Rest View

Beyond the White Wolf and Yosemite Creek crossroads, the Tioga Road leads into the high-country proper; eight thousand feet up, with trails heading off from the road to alpine lakes and craggy peaks. These lofty destinations are visible a couple of miles on from the **Clark Range View** (T11), offering extensive views south to the 11,522ft **Mount Clark** with its sharp-ridged back resembling the pointy plates of a giant stegosaurus. The first guardian of the 1864 Yosemite Grant, Galen Clark, would undoubtedly be proud to be honored with such a fine specimen.

To the east of the viewpoint lies the broad-shouldered gray granite mass of **Mount Hoffmann** (10,850ft), the geographical center of the Park and one of John Muir's favorite summits. The peak was named for Charles F. Hoffmann, chief topographer of Whitney's California State Geological Survey who initially appraised the area's topography. Its angular peak was never subjected to the ravages of glacial action, and stands in contrast to the smooth slabs of its lower flanks. When Tuolumne Meadows was two thousand feet under an ice sheet, it was the surrounding Hoffmann Range that divided the flowing ice into two distinct glaciers, one carving out the Tuolumne Canyon and Hetch Hetchy, and the other grinding down the Tenaya Canyon to sculpt Yosemite Valley.

The **Western Juniper** interpretive sign (T12), another mile and a half along, celebrates this relatively common tree which grows on rocky ridges in the sub-alpine forest and can live up to a thousand years. A road cutting a third of a mile on (T14) reveals a particularly clear example of **exfoliating granite**, the onion-like layers peeling off over the millennia in the same process that has created all Yosemite's domes. It is a process that continues today, gradually reshaping the landscape.

Three miles on, Tioga Road crosses Yosemite Creek, which crashes over Yosemite Falls seven miles downstream.

Four miles from the crossing, *Porcupine Flat* campground immediately precedes the 100-yard **Sierra Trees Nature Trail** (T18), along which are marked the various trees whose habitats overlap at this intersection of several climatic zones: Jeffrey pine, western white pine, lodgepole pine, white fir and California red fir.

From here it is half a mile to the **North Dome Trailhead** (T19; Hike 18), then a further mile to where a gap in the trees reveals the magnificent **Half Dome View** (T20), with Mount Starr King lurking behind the great, gray monolith. It is a little over another mile to **May Lake Junction** (T21), where a bumpy two-mile side road leads to the road-end trailhead for **May Lake** (Hike 19), a popular, pleasant hour-plus stroll that can be extended to the top of Mount Hoffmann, one of the Park's great viewpoints.

Back on Tioga Road, it's a mile to **Clouds Rest View** (T23), where you can gaze in awe at the vast, smooth sheet of granite sweeping at 45 degrees from the base of Tenaya Canyon five thousand feet up to the 9926-foot summit ridge of Clouds Rest. In case you were wondering why no trails seem to follow **Tenaya Canyon**, it is deemed too dangerous, with some sections requiring ropes.

Olmsted Point to Tenaya Lake

Almost two miles east of Clouds Rest View an expansive vista opens out at **Olmsted Point**, named after Frederick Law Olmsted, first chairman of the Yosemite Park Commission and joint architect of New York City's Central Park. Undoubtedly the most outstanding viewpoint from Tioga Road, it offers long views down Tenaya Canyon towards Clouds Rest and Half Dome, and up the canyon to Tenaya Lake with the sculpted, smooth monoliths of Tuolumne beyond. A quarter-mile trail leads to the top of a nearby dome where even more stupendous views await.

In the early 1960s when the Tioga Road was being re-aligned, Ansel Adams fought against routing the next section of highway past the cold, clear waters of

▲ Tenaya Lake

the mile-long **Tenaya Lake**. He failed and the road now skirts the northern shore of this beautiful alpine tarn, which fills a hollow gouged out the Tenaya Branch of the ancient Tuolumne Glacier. The lake takes its name from the native chief captured here by the Mariposa Battalion in 1851. The Ahwahneechee knew the lake as Py-wi-ack, or "Lake of the Shining Rocks," an apt description as its entire basin exhibits abundant evidence of glacial polish. Arrive in the early morning or evening and it can be a wonderfully peaceful place to appreciate the granite scenery and perhaps dangle a fishing pole.

As it skirts the lake, the road passes **Sunrise Lakes Trailhead**, marking the start of Hikes 20 and 22, then runs beside the sandy **beach** at **Murphy Creek**, where there's a small parking area that's popular on hot days. The **swimming** is good here, but generally deemed better at the far end of Tenaya Lake where a long strand is excellent for those afraid to brave the chilly waters.

You're now deep into **granite dome** country, which continues for the remaining five miles to Tuolumne Meadows. Overlooking Tenaya Lake on the north side of Tioga Road, you may see climbers tackling the relatively gentle slopes of **Stately Pleasure Dome**, presumably named by some fan of Coleridge's "Kubla Khan." Further on, **Pywiack Dome** rises above the south side of the road with a large pine growing out of its steepest face. **Mendicott Dome** is behind that, and further still is the blunt visage of **Fairview Dome**, the largest of them all. Rounding a bend, the low **Pothole Dome**, to the north, heralds the open expanse of Tuolumne Meadows.

Tioga Road: Tuolumne Meadows

The alpine area around **Tuolumne Meadows** – the "meadow in the sky" in the local Miwok tongue – has a very different atmosphere than that of the Valley, 55 miles (about ninety minutes' drive) away. Here, at 8575ft, it is much more open; the light is more intense, and the air has a fresh, crisp bite courtesy of temperatures fifteen to twenty degrees lower. There can still be good-sized blasts of carbon monoxide at peak times however, as this is the main high-country congregation point for visitors, and the only accommodation base in the area within easy reach of the park's eastern entrance at Tioga Pass.

The meadows themselves are the largest in all of the Sierra; twelve miles long, between a quarter and half a mile wide, and threaded by the meandering Tuolumne River. Snow usually lingers here until the end of June, forcing the **wildflowers** to contend with a short growing season. They respond with a glorious burst of color in July, a wonderful time for a wander. The distinctive glaciated granite form of **Lembert Dome** (Hike 29) squats at the eastern end of the meadows gazing across the grasslands towards its western twin, **Pothole Dome** (Hike 23), which makes for a great sunset destination.

It is abundantly clear why in 1869 John Muir asserted that "this is the most spacious and delightful high pleasure-ground I have seen...and though lying high in the sky, the surrounding mountains are so much higher, one feels protected as if in a grand hall." A little fanciful perhaps, but there's no denying that the mountain scenery is particularly striking to the south, where the **Cathedral Range** offers a horizon of slender spires and knife-blade ridges. This is best seen from **Soda Springs**, where the angled protuberant spire of **Unicorn Peak** is indeed most evocative of the mythical beast's horn. To its right is **Cathedral Peak**, a textbook example of a glaciated "Matterhorn," where glaciers have carved away the rock on all sides leaving a sharp pointed summit.

Tuolumne is a focal point for **hikers** who find the higher altitude makes this a better starting point than the Valley, and use it as a base from which to fan out into the surrounding High Sierra wilderness. The store here is the first provisioning point for southbound hikers on the **John Muir Trail** (see p.143), who typically take two days to get here from the Valley then start heading

Area hikes

The following hikes begin in and around Tuolumne Meadows (in order heading east to west) and are usually under snow from November to early June.

Day hikes

- Hike 23 Pothole Dome: see p.122
- Hike 24 Cathedral Lakes: see p.122
- Hike 25 Soda Springs and Parsons Memorial Lodge: see p.123
- Hike 26 Elizabeth Lake: see p.123
- Hike 27 Lyell Canyon: see p.124
- Hike 28 Dog Lake: see p.124
- Hike 29 Lembert Dome: see p.125
- Hike 30 Young Lakes: see p.125
- Hike 31 Glen Aulin: see p.126
- Hike 32 Waterwheel Falls: see p.126

Overnight hikes

- Hike 49 Grand Canyon of the Tuolumne: see p.145
- Hike 50 The High Sierra Camp Loop: see p.146

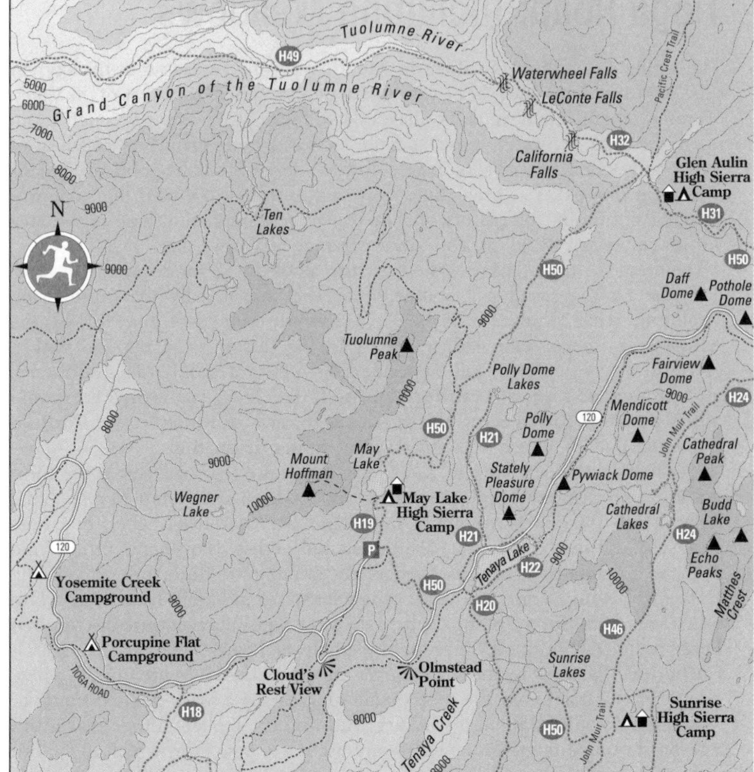

southeast towards Mount Whitney. Come in July and you may meet through-hikers on the 2650-mile **Pacific Crest Trail** from Mexico to Canada who'll be restocking for the next leg of their five-month journey.

Soda Springs and Parsons Memorial Lodge

If you've only got a short time in Tuolumne, take a stroll across the meadows to **Soda Springs**, one of the area's most popular and rewarding short **hikes**. It is included as part of Hike 25, but can also easily be visited by following a section of the old carriage road that spurs across the meadow three hundred yards east of the visitor center (see p.84). This takes you straight to the naturally carbonated springs, described in 1863 as "pungent and delightful to the taste." And so it is, though the Park Service discourages drinking warning of potential surface contamination. By 1885 the area was being homesteaded by the insect collector and so-called "hermit of the Sierra," **Jean Baptiste Lembert**, who raised goats on 160 acres and erected a small enclosure surrounding the springs, of which only the low walls now survive.

The area around the springs became one of the favorite camping spots of John Muir, who appreciated its location on a slight rise with a great view of the meadows and the jagged Cathedral Range to the south. Noting the

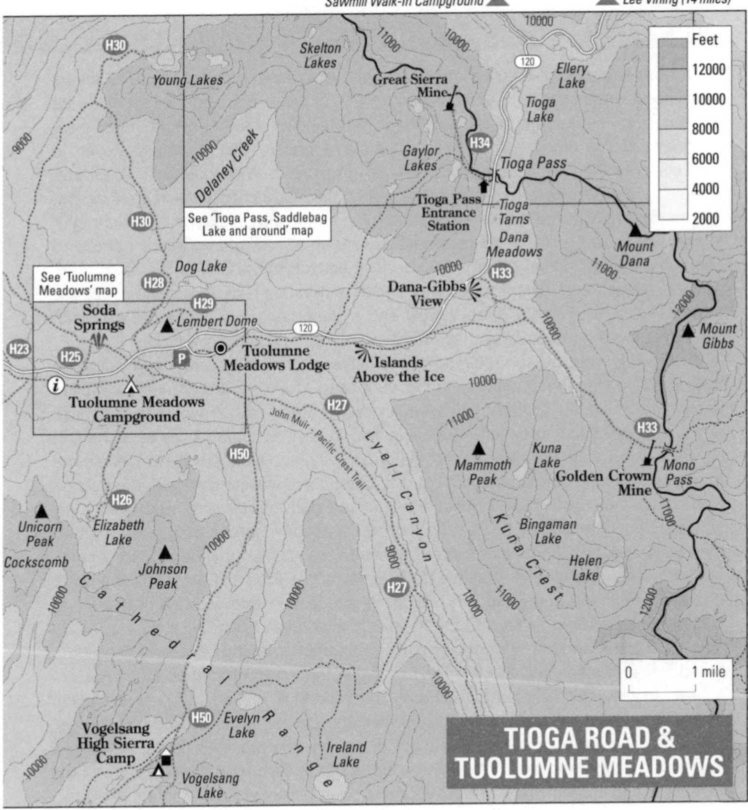

devastating effect sheep were having each summer when these "hoofed locusts" were herded up to the meadows from the lowlands for pasture, the avid conservationist, urged on by magazine editor **Robert Underwood Johnson**, campaigned for Tuolumne's protection as part of a newly created Yosemite National Park. Muir wrote two articles for *Century Magazine* outlining his proposal, and in the fall of 1890 Congress passed a bill along the lines that Muir advocated.

Muir's subsequent fight to save Hetch Hetchy (see box, p.75) was supported by high-country guide, Edward Taylor Parsons, who the fledgling Sierra Club honored posthumously by building the rugged but elegantly proportioned **Parsons Memorial Lodge** (mid-July to early Sept daily 11am–3pm or longer; free) right by the springs. Managed by the Yosemite Association, its single room houses displays on local environmental and campaigning issues, and hosts frequent talks and demonstrations (see *Yosemite Today* for details). The adjacent **McCauley Cabin** was built by the McCauley brothers, who bought Lembert's homestead after his death in 1897. It was subsequently sold to the Sierra Club who used it as a summer camp from 1912 to 1973, after which the Park Service bought it; the cabin is now closed to the public.

John Muir

John Muir was one of nature's most eloquent advocates, a champion of all things wild who spent ten years living in Yosemite Valley in the 1870s, and the rest of his life campaigning for its preservation. Born in Scotland in 1838, he had an austere upbringing which prepared him well for the life he chose. After his family moved to the United States when he was eleven, he grew up in Wisconsin where he later worked as a mechanical inventor until, aged 27, he nearly lost an eye in an accident. The incident galvanized his desire to search for something outside the normal run of things. Noting in his diary, "All drawbacks overcome ... joyful and free... I chose to become a tramp," he set off on a **thousand-mile trek** to the Gulf of Mexico by "the wildest, leafiest, and least trodden way" laden only with a New Testament, a volume of Keats' poems, Milton's *Paradise Lost* and a plant press. Dry bread and a twist of tea leaves were his sustenance, so he often slept hungry under the stars.

Arriving in Florida, he contracted malaria then spent time recuperating in Cuba. He then continued via Panama to California, supposedly for a short stay before doubling back to his real goal, South America. On arrival, he asked for "anywhere that is wild," and was pointed towards the Sierra; he is said to have shouted for joy when he first saw **Yosemite Valley**. So began months of camping and exploration with little more than a ragged blue notebook and a blanket. Often there was no particular destination since every path both posed questions and provided the answers, and every step was as rich as the last. Each night he'd chop down a few spruce branches for a bed then build a roaring fire to keep himself warm. Even in winter he'd be out, sometimes waking up under a mantle of snow. He later wrote "As long as I live, I will ever after hear waterfalls and birds and winds sing. I'll acquaint myself with the glaciers and wild gardens, and get as near to the heart of the world as I can."

In 1869 he spent the summer helping a shepherd **grazing sheep** in Tuolumne Meadows, a practice he soon learned to hate for the trampling damage their hooves caused to the delicate meadows. Later that year Muir moved to Yosemite Valley where he worked as a **sawmiller**, carpenter and part-time guide, living in a sugar pine shack he built himself. Unlike most of the Valley's other residents, he stayed year-round eschewing the wintertime comforts of the Bay Area in favor of the place that made him content. This, and his desire to spend every waking moment exploring the mountains and waterfalls made him something of an eccentric and put him outside Yosemite's social circles. He was regarded as nothing more than a "mere sheepherder" by the literary and scientific cognoscenti who came in search of enlightenment. Only gradually did Muir's star rise, largely thanks to the unflagging promotion of his Oakland friend, Jeanne Carr. She dispatched Berkeley geologist **Joseph LeConte** to visit him, and word of Muir's intelligence and understanding of

Tuolumne practicalities

Tuolumne is the sort of place you might base yourself for several days (or even weeks), heading out on long hikes or strolling the meadows taking photos, botanizing, or just lying in the sun by the river. You'll certainly not be pampered while staying here, but you can sleep and eat fairly well. Facilities are inconveniently scattered along a two-mile stretch of road, so visitors without their own vehicles will need to avail themselves of the **free Tuolumne Meadows Shuttle** (see p.26), which runs every half-hour west from *Tuolumne Meadows Lodge* past Tenaya Lake to Olmsted Point. There are also four daily runs eastbound from *Tuolumne Meadows Lodge* to the Park entrance at Tioga Pass.

The westernmost building of interest is the **Tuolumne Meadows Visitor Center** (mid-June to Sept daily 9am–5pm and later in mid-season; ⓣ209/372-0263), which has moderately interesting displays on alpine wildflowers (divided the Valley gradually got out. Even his hero, Emerson, visited him and began to spread the word.

Muir dubbed the Sierra Nevada the "**Range of Light**," and spent years developing his theory of how glaciers shaped the range. After Carr's constant imprecations, Muir quit his sawmill job in 1871 and began to write up some of his copious notes ensconced in *Black's Hotel* in the Valley. His first article, *Yosemite Glaciers*, was printed in the New York Tribune later that year and subsequent pieces gradually won him academic acceptance. The classic journal-based books for which he is known today – especially *My First Summer in the Sierra* and *The Yosemite* – were written much later, but mostly tell of his exploits at this time.

It was November 1872 before Muir returned to the city for the first time, signaling a gradual weaning off Yosemite, though the Sierra never left his heart. He **married** Louie Wanda Strentzel, nine years his junior, in 1880 when he was almost 42. They lived in Martinez, northeast of Oakland, and had two children, Wanda and Helen. Though Muir was a loving father, it seems he wasn't there all that much, often disappearing for weeks into the Sierra, taking off to Alaska, visiting Europe or making trips to Asia.

Muir was desperate to protect his beloved landscape from the depredations of sheep grazing, timber cutting and homesteading, and through magazine articles and influential contacts goaded Congress into **creating Yosemite National Park** in 1890. To act as a kind of watchdog for the new national park, two years later he set up the **Sierra Club**, an organization whose motto "take only photographs; leave only footprints" has become a model for like-minded groups around the world.

From the mid-1890s Muir was increasingly spending his time writing his books, but in November 1903, President **Theodore Roosevelt** asked to meet Muir. The pair managed to slip Teddy's minders and spent four happy days camping rough in the high country. Suddenly Muir had a very powerful ally, one who set aside five more national parks during his term, though this wasn't enough to save Hetch Hetchy from being drowned (see box, p.75). Still, the publicity actually aided the formation of the present National Park Service in 1916, which promised – and has since provided – greater protection.

Muir finally visited South America at the age of 74, almost fifty years after California had waylaid him. He died in 1914, aged 76, an event some claim was hastened by his failure to save his beloved Hetch Hetchy.

Muir's name crops up throughout California as a memorial to this inspirational figure, not least in the 211-mile **John Muir Trail** which twists through his favorite scenery from Yosemite Valley south to Mount Whitney, and the **John Muir Wilderness**, California's largest, located southeast of Yosemite.

into four characteristic zones of the region: forest, meadow, riparian and rocky), local geology and the area's human history. Kids get to touch bear fur, feel rams' horns and pick up a large but featherweight lump of Mono lake pumice. The wood and granite building was constructed by the Civilian Conservation Corps in 1934 in a style recalling Yosemite pioneer buildings, and was later used as a work crew mess hall.

It is over half a mile east to the **gas station** (mid-June to early Oct daily 9am–5pm or 6pm & 24hr with credit card) and Tuolumne Mountain Shop, which sells outdoor gear and **climbing** paraphernalia, and doubles as the summer home of the Yosemite Mountaineering School (see p.148). Next door a large, white plastic shed houses the fast-food style *Tuolumne Meadows Grill* (see p.181) and the Tuolumne Meadows Store (June to early Nov daily 8am–8pm), which stocks a reasonable selection of hiking and camping supplies, Coleman fuel, camping gas canisters, basic groceries, ice, booze, and firewood, and has a

▲ John Muir

small **post office** (mid-June to early Oct Mon–Fri 9am–5pm, Sat 9am–1pm). The huge *Tuolumne Meadows* campground (see p.175) is tucked behind, with the reservation office a hundred yards or so east of the store. Across the Tuolumne River it's another half mile past the Lembert Dome parking area to the **wilderness center** (see p.39) and another few hundred yards down a side road to the tent-cabins and hearty meals of *Tuolumne Meadows Lodge* (see p.166 & p.174), where nonguests can also take **showers** (mid-June to Sept daily noon–3.30pm; $4, towel supplied).

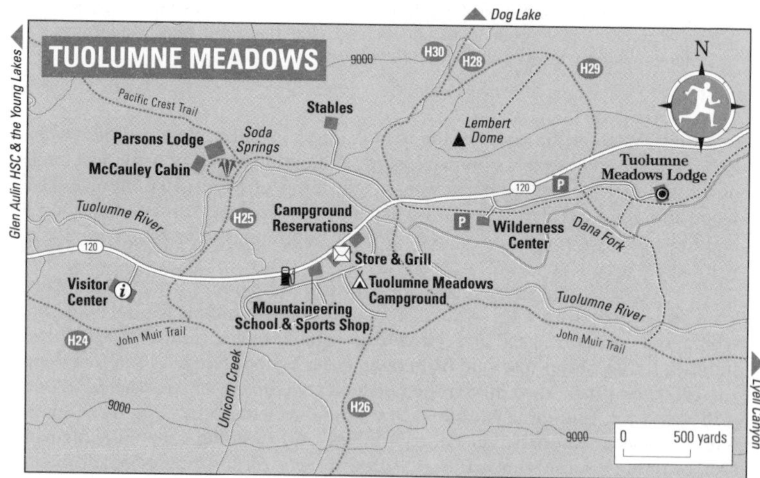

Altitude sickness

Though unlikely, it is possible to suffer **altitude sickness** in Tuolumne Meadows, especially if you spend the night here after coming up in one day from much lower elevations. You'll certainly feel short of breath, but older people and those with heart and lung diseases should consider spending at least one night in the Valley (4000ft) to acclimatize, and avoid high-fat foods and alcohol. If you find yourself suffering from headaches, nausea, shortness of breath, irritability and general fatigue, the only solution is to descend.

Hike, or drive, a mile down the road beside Lembert Dome to reach the Tuolumne Meadows Stables (see p.151), which offers **horseback rides** from a couple of hours to several days.

Tioga Road: Tioga Pass and the road to Lee Vining

At Tuolumne Meadows the Tuolumne River splits into two forks, the southerly Lyell Fork tracing the floor of Lyell Canyon towards Mount Lyell, while the Dana Fork runs six miles east to Dana Meadows and the Park entrance at Tioga Pass. Tioga Road follows the Dana Fork past the **Islands above the Ice** pullout where there's a distant view of Cockscomb, Unicorn and Echo peaks silhouetted against the horizon. Mount Gibbs (12,764ft) and the Park's second highest peak, Mount Dana (13,053ft), are both visible a mile further at **Dana-Gibbs View** (T36), from where you can admire their reddish ferriferous tinge, a striking contrast to the ubiquitous gray Yosemite granite.

Just past a stand of lodgepole pines, these mountains appear again as a backdrop to **Dana Meadows**, a quarter-mile wide and studded with erratics deposited by the ancient Tuolumne Glacier, the largest glacier in the Sierra Nevada, which receded twenty thousand years ago. Huge lumps of ice left behind as it receded formed a series of kettle lakes known as **Tioga Tarns**, now an extremely attractive collection of pools in boggy land beside the fledgling Dana Fork. At the eastern end of Dana Meadows, the road climbs the last few feet to **Tioga Pass** (T39), immediately preceded by the trailhead for the hike to Gaylor Lakes (see Hike 34).

For in-depth details of Tioga Road **closures** at the pass, see the box on p.20.

Lee Vining Grade

You might imagine that Tioga is a Miwok or Paiute word, but it actually means "where it forks" in Iroquois, a name appended by a native of Tioga County in New York State, who was then living in the area.

Leaving the Park you cross into the **Inyo National Forest** and quickly begin the rapid descent down what is known as the **Lee Vining Grade**, a steep and fast road that descends the heavily glaciated Lee Vining Canyon, dropping over

The following hikes start near Tioga Pass, both featuring history ruins and both reaching altitudes of over 10,000ft with relatively little effort.

- Hike 33 Mono Pass: see p.127
- Hike 34 Gaylor Lakes and the Great Sierra Mine: see p.127

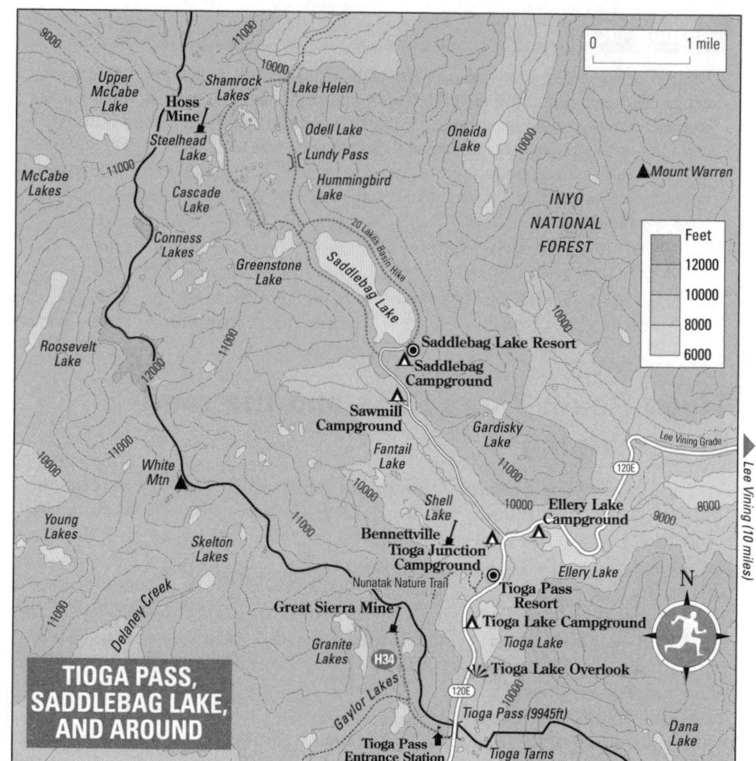

three thousand feet in six miles from lodgepole-pine studded meadows to low sage-covered hills. Beyond lies the small town of **Lee Vining** (see p.214) on the shores of **Mono Lake**.

Interpretive panels at **Tioga Lake Overlook**, less than a mile along, discuss the one-time town of Bennettville and introduce the work of early twentieth-century conservationist **Aldo Leopold**, whose thoughts on natural history and his "land ethic" are continued on more signs down the valley. A mile on, just past the *Tioga Lake* campground, the partly paved, quarter-mile **Nunatak Nature Trail** makes a pleasant place for a break among lodgepole and whitebark pines. Signs use the views of Mount Dana and the Dana Plateau – both untouched by the Lee Vining Glacier 20,000 years ago – to illustrate the creation of nunataks, angular pinnacles free of glacial erosion.

Half a mile further on, the *Tioga Pass Resort* offers rooms (see p.172) and has a good diner (see p.184). It sits right by the *Junction* campground (see p.177), from where a mile-long trail (350ft ascent; starting just by the pay station) runs to the former silver-mining town of **Bennettville**. The town flourished for two years from 1882 and was then abandoned, though it saw brief flurries of activity in 1888 and 1933. A couple of wooden shacks – the former assay office and a livestock wintering barn – can still be seen. Through the trees to the west you can glimpse the tailings and mine entrance: follow the obvious short trail to reach them.

Saddlebag Lake and 20 Lakes Basin

One of the best (and most popular) hikes on the eastern fringes of Yosemite heads around **Saddlebag Lake and 20 Lakes Basin** (8-mile loop; 3–5hr; 600ft ascent), a moderate trail with some gorgeous views of alpine lakes. Lingering snow in shaded areas means it is probably best ignored before July. You're already above 10,000ft when you start so you may want to take it easy, though the several short ascents do add up to 600ft. The less ambitious can just make a circuit around Saddlebag Lake (4 miles; best done counterclockwise) but it is well worth continuing north past little Hummingbird Lake (where there are a few campsites) and over the easy Lundy Pass. Past Odell Lake you reach Helen Lake where the trail continues around to the left. Rocky shorelines, wildflowers and whitebark pines characterize the area around Shamrock Lake and one to Steelhead Lake where a short side trip visits the abandoned Hess Mine. Complete the circuit past Waso and Greenstone lakes then along the western shore of Saddlebag Lake.

The *Junction* campground also marks the start of a three-mile gravel road past the *Sawmill* campground (see p.177) to **Saddlebag Lake**, a gorgeous area which is popular with **trout** fishers and opens up access to hiking in the 20 Lakes Basin (see box above). At the road end there's the first-come-first–served *Saddlebag Lake* campground (see p.177) and the Saddlebag Lake Resort (roughly mid-July to Sept daily 7am–7pm; Ⓦwww.saddlebaglakeresort.com), a 1930s former hunting lodge which is now an all-in-one store, café and boat rental place.

Back on Tioga Road, you continue down the Lee Vining Grade gradually gaining views of Mono Lake, and in the last few miles before Lee Vining pass side roads leading to a handful of Forest Service campgrounds collectively known as the *Lee Vining Creek* **campgrounds**.

3

Southern Yosemite

Roughly a quarter of the Park's total area, **southern Yosemite**'s broad swathe of sharply peaked mountains extends from the foothills in the west twenty miles to the Sierra crest in the east. This section of the Park is predominantly rugged country, though most visitors only see the thickly forested and more forgiving landscape of its very eastern fringes, accessed along **Wawona Road**.

In the 1860s and early 1870s Wawona Road was the stagecoach route from the San Joaquin Valley into Yosemite Valley, a harrowing journey typically broken up at the meadow-side homestead of Wawona. This is still where visitors to the southern part of the Park stay, either at the campground or in the *Wawona Hotel*, with its sweeping lawns and broad verandahs littered with Adirondack chairs. In recognition of Wawona's historic importance, it was elected as the site for the **Pioneer Yosemite History Center**, a well-designed open-air museum with cabins and significant commercial buildings rescued from around the Park and amassed beside the South Fork of the Merced River. Interesting though it is, the museum plays second fiddle to visitors' prime target, the **Mariposa Grove** of **giant sequoias**, part of the original 1864 Yosemite Grant that also set aside Yosemite Valley for preservation. Around five hundred enormous trunks make this easily the largest of Yosemite's three sequoia groves, and the most varied, with trees that have been hollowed out by fire, grown together, fallen over and been bored through to create a car-sized passage. While the Mariposa Grove suffers slightly from its own popularity, it still outshines Wawona's nine-hole **golf course**, the horseback trips from the **stables** and general outdoor pursuits at hand in southern Yosemite.

Partway along Wawona Road, **Glacier Point Road** cuts east through forests past the winter sports nexus of **Badger Pass Ski Area**, to the Park's **viewpoint** *par excellence* at **Glacier Point**, right on the rim of Yosemite Valley and on level with the face of Half Dome. It is a justly popular spot, especially at sunset when it seems as if half of the Park's visitors are here hoping to catch the last rays glinting off the distant **Sierra crest**.

South from the Valley: Tunnel View and beyond

Wawona Road (Hwy-41) leaves the Valley loop road near Bridalveil Fall and immediately starts to climb past a number of breaks in the trees which occasionally open up to reveal stunning views of the Valley, the best being from **Tunnel View**, a mile and a half up the road. Here, the whole Valley unfolds before you with El Capitan and Sentinel Rock standing as guardians to what lies beyond, notably Half Dome. From here it is easy to imagine the Valley swamped by its primordial lake, which gradually filled in to leave the existing flat floor.

The view will be immediately recognizable to anyone familiar with Ansel Adams image *Clearing Winter Storm*, with El Capitan and Sentinel Rock struggling to free themselves of cloud as Bridalveil Fall shines clearly on the right. Adams actually took the shot one rainy December day from **Inspiration Point**, a few hundred feet up the hill above Tunnel View. To get there, he would have used the original stagecoach road between the Valley and Wawona that was the regular route until 1933. Parts of it remain and can be seen by hiking the fairly steep first mile or so of the trail to **Inspiration Point** (see Hike 11) starting just across the road from Tunnel View.

Yosemite Valley View and the road to Wawona

Tunnel View immediately precedes a 0.8-mile tunnel – the longest in the Park – ending at **Yosemite Valley View**, where Valley-bound visitors get their first glimpse of El Capitan and Half Dome. Above the road is the exfoliated granite form of **Turtleback Dome**, and across the valley are falls known simply as **The Cascades**. Although you're not actually much higher here than in the Valley, the vegetation has already changed. Black oaks have been left behind and the ponderosa pines are joined by cinnamon-barked incense cedar, tall, slender Douglas fir, low, scrubby manzanita and canyon oak.

The next six miles pass through scorched forest to a road junction known as **Chinquapin**, from where Glacier Point Road breaks off to the northeast. South from Chinquapin towards Wawona, a side road soon spurs a mile off to

▲ Yosemite Valley View

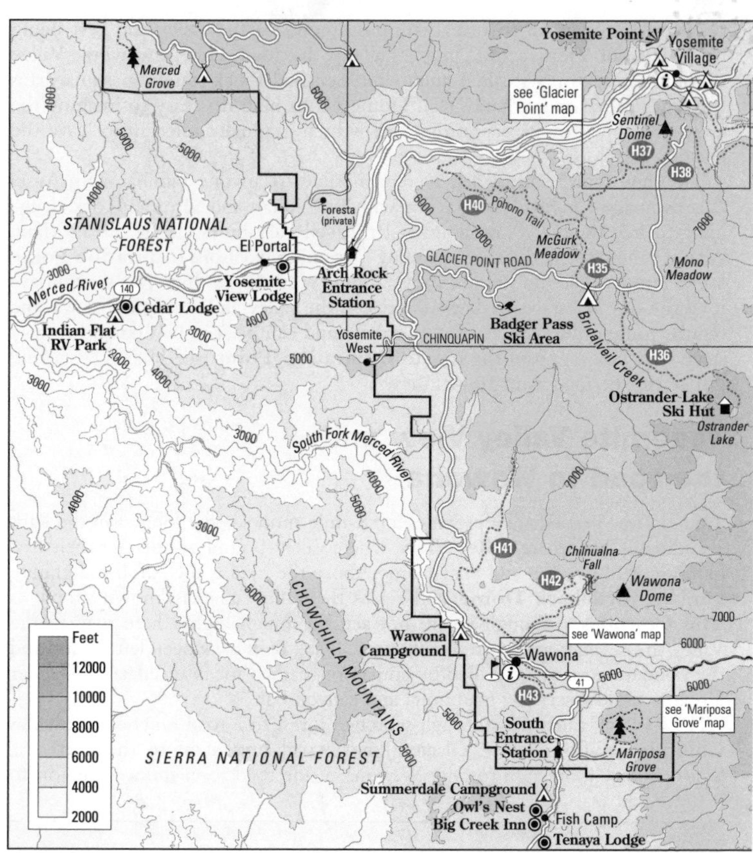

the right to **Yosemite West**, a private development just outside the Park's western boundary that's not worth visiting unless you plan to stay at one of the B&Bs (see p.167). About three-quarters of a mile down the access road there's a board showing the accommodation locations, though at last visit the pay phone to call them was out of action.

Back on Wawona Road it is an eleven-mile descent to Wawona, almost entirely through evergreens so thick they seldom reveal any views. Just before Wawona you pass the *Wawona* campground, site of the first Park headquarters from 1891 to 1906, and a small riverside picnic area.

Glacier Point Road

The sixteen-mile-long **Glacier Point Road** (usually open mid-May to late Oct) branches off northeast from Wawona Road and provides the principal access to **Glacier Point**, arguably the finest viewpoint in the whole Park.

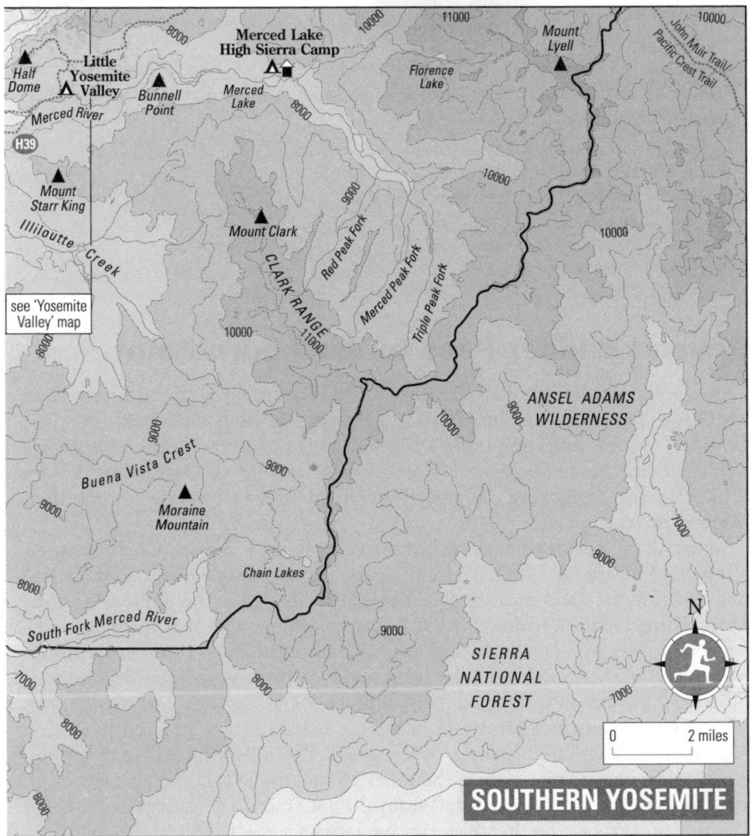

There's also some great hiking country hereabouts, with 7000ft trailheads saving hikers the grinding haul out of the Valley.

In winter the first five miles of the road is kept open to provide access to the **Badger Pass Ski Area** (chains are sometimes required); the only reason to stop before that is for the view down some 4500ft to Merced Canyon from a lookout (G1) a couple of miles along. Theoretically, you can see down to the San Joaquin Valley and the even to the Coast Mountains, but suitably clear days are rare.

Badger Pass Ski Area

Three miles past the viewpoint is the **Badger Pass Ski Area** (for full coverage see Chapter 7, "Winter Activities"), California's oldest skifield, established in 1935 at a time when the National Park Service was eager to attract as many visitors to Yosemite as possible. With a handful of short tows, a predominance of beginner and intermediate terrain, and superb cross-country skiing and snowshoe trails, it makes a great and unpretentious family destination. Once the tows stop and the snows melt, Badger Pass gets shut up until the next winter season.

Area hikes

Yosemite's fifty best hikes are found in chapters 4 and 5. The following hikes are accessed off Glacier Point Road and are listed in order from Chinquapin to Glacier Point.

- Hike 35 McGurk Meadow: see p.128
- Hike 36 Ostrander Lake: see p.128
- Hike 37 Taft Point and the Fissures: see p.129
- Hike 38 Sentinel Dome: see p.130
- Hike 39 Panorama Trail: see p.130
- Hike 40 Pohono Trail: see p.131

Beyond Badger Pass to Washburn Point

Three miles past Badger Pass, through forests brimming with red fir, sits the **McGurk Meadow** trailhead (Hike 35), immediately followed by the *Bridalveil Creek* campground (see p.176), located a quarter of a mile south off Glacier Point Road. Bridalveil Creek begins its life at **Ostrander Lake** (Hike 36) and eventually plummets over Bridalveil Fall before joining the Merced River.

Almost three miles further along Glacier Point Road you reach **Clark Range View** (G6) where the 11,522ft Mount Clark can be identified by the avalanche trail down its face and into the forest below. To the left is the domed **Mount Starr King** (9092ft), named for the Unitarian pastor who did much to alert America to the wonders of Yosemite through his writings in 1860. At **Pothole Meadows** (G7), a couple of miles later, five-foot-diameter natural depressions fill with snowmelt in spring and early summer.

The sight of **Sentinel Dome** from the G8 marker may tempt you to tackle Hike 38 from a trailhead parking lot just ahead. The mile-long trail leads to the 8122ft gleaming granite scalp of Sentinel Dome, topped by the remains of a gnarled Jeffrey pine. A second trail from the lot (Hike 37) leads west to **Taft Point**, a fine vantage on the Valley rim with views across to El Capitan. Nearby, the Valley rim's granite edges have been deeply incised to form the **Taft Point Fissures** and, with care, you can peer down hundreds of feet. Far fewer people follow this trail, perhaps because of the vertiginous drops all around, only protected by the flimsiest of barriers in one spot.

Glacier Point Road soon launches into a descending series of steep **switchbacks** marking the last two miles to Glacier Point. Stop halfway along at **Washburn Point** for a striking side view of Half Dome. From here you're looking at the vertical face side-on, helping make the granite monster look remarkably slim in profile. Below lies the Merced River canyon, where you can clearly see the so-called "Grand Staircase" of Nevada and Vernal falls with the smooth dome of Liberty Cap rising above. To the right Mount Clark and the rounded summit of Mount Starr King stand out.

Glacier Point

The most astonishing views of Yosemite Valley are from **Glacier Point**, the top of an almost sheer cliff 3214 precipitous feet above Curry Village, thirty slow and twisting miles away by road. From the lookout, the Valley floor appears in miniature far below and Half Dome fills the scene at eye level, backed by the distant snowcapped summits of the High Sierra. From here, Half Dome stands with its face angled slightly towards you, a stance that looks gorgeous when bathed in alpenglow just after sunset.

Right from the early days of tourism in Yosemite, Glacier Point's amalgam of boulders, pines and granite-formed viewpoints was an inescapable lure. The **Four-Mile Trail** (Hike 9) from the Valley was one of the earliest to be created, and even before the first road was constructed in 1883, visitors were coming up on mule-back to stay here (see box, p.96).

The hotels may be gone, but 150 years of tourism have left their mark with a network of viewpoints linked by smooth, asphalt pathways through the scattered pines. To learn something of the forces that created the wondrous landscape, drop in briefly at the open-sided **Geology Hut** on the eastern side of Glacier Point, then continue north to the Valley rim to inspect the **Overhanging Rock**, which reaches way out over the void. Postcards found in every Park store depict scenes of performers poised on the end of the rock doing handstands or precarious ballet steps. In one early promotional stunt, someone even drove a Dodge out onto the end. The rock is supposedly off-limits, though that doesn't seem to deter those with something to prove from wandering out there to be photographed with Half Dome in the background. Nearby, where the main approach path meets the Valley rim, the number 1982 on a metal railing marks the spot where the red fir bark fire was constructed then raked over the edge to create the **Firefall** (see box, p.67).

Practicalities

Though it is enjoyable to drive up here or ride the shuttle bus from the Valley, the moment of arrival at Glacier Point is much more rewarding if you hike to it on the very steep Four-Mile Trail (Hike 9). Most people take a couple of photos, raid the **gift store** (daily June–Oct 9am–6pm), grab something from the **snack stand** (daily June–Oct 11am–4pm), and then leave. But it is worth spending a couple of hours in the area, perhaps hiking to the summit of Sentinel Dome (there's a trail from here as well as that described in Hike 38) then returning to watch the lowering sun cast its golden hue over the mountain-scape. After dark the crowds will disappear and you'll have time for reflection as the moon casts its silvery glow on the surface of Half Dome. On most summer

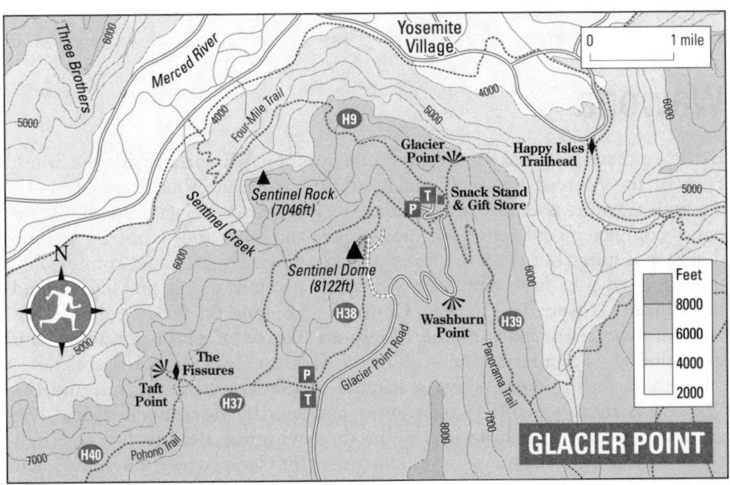

Life at Glacier Point

By the mid-1870s Yosemite Valley was seeing around a thousand visitors a year, a tiny number by today's standards, but enough to justify the creation of the Four-Mile Trail from the Valley to Glacier Point. Though built under the masterful eye of one John Conway, it was financed by James McCauley who then used the trail to transport materials for *The Mountain House*, a hotel built in 1876. Early guests would stand at the edge of the precipice impressed by the sheer scale of the drop to the Valley floor below. Some tossed things off, one visitor exclaiming "even an empty box, watched by a field-glass, could not be traced to its concussion with the Valley floor." McCauley would then front up with a hen under his arm and toss it off. As she fluttered to a speck, and then disappeared altogether, the visitors would turn aghast to McCauley who, with a wave of his hand, would dismiss their fear claiming the chicken was used to it and made the enforced journey every day during the summer season. Apparently it walked back up, visitors occasionally encountering the chicken on the trail.

By 1917, *The Mountain House* was joined by the *Glacier Point Hotel*, and visitors could stay in grand style, lounging on the verandah which looked east with the best views to Half Dome. Both stayed open over the summer months, and in winter caretakers would protect the properties, shoveling snow and feeding winter visitors who skied or snowshoed in from Badger Pass (much as they do today). Both hotels burned down in 1969, and revised Park authority policies didn't allow either to be rebuilt.

evenings, the remodeled 150-seat granite amphitheater overlooking Half Dome hosts free ranger-led talks. The half-hour **Sunset Talk** (usually on something topical) is frequently followed on Friday and Saturday evenings by the hour-long "Stars over Yosemite," explaining the mysteries of the night sky: see *Yosemite Today* for details.

Oddly, the Park concessionaire sees fit to close the gift store and snack stand well before a large number of people arrive for sunset, meaning there are no facilities for late arrivals. Pack accordingly especially if you're staying for an astronomy talk: you may find it hard to get served dinner if you get back to the Valley after 9pm.

Wawona

In the southern half of Yosemite, everyone heads for **Wawona**, beside the South Fork of the Merced River, 27 miles south of Yosemite Village on Hwy-41. Though Wawona is at the same altitude to Yosemite Valley (around 4000ft) it has a completely different feel, more open and surrounded not by granite domes and spires, but by dense forest and meadows. There's also a considerably more relaxed pace here with visitors playing a round of golf, ambling around the **Pioneer Yosemite History Center** or hopping on the free shuttle bus that runs the seven miles to the **Mariposa Grove** of **giant sequoias**, and guests lounging around the grounds of the *Wawona Hotel* (see p.167).

For those feeling more active, a handful of **hikes** start in the area and the Wawona Stables (see p.151) offer short and full-day **horseback rides**. The area's best **swimming hole** is close by the **Swinging Bridge**: follow Forest Drive for two miles to the Seventh Day Adventist Camp, where you branch left for a quarter of a mile along a dirt road then park and walk five minutes to a deep, crystal-clear pool with big white boulders.

Some history

The meadows of Wawona were originally known as *Pallachun*, or "good place to stop" to Native Americans making their way from the Sierra Nevada foothills to Yosemite Valley. Here they hunted game and gathered acorns and basket-making materials, until their lifestyle was destroyed by the 1851 arrival of gold miners and the Mariposa Battalion (see "History," p.230). In 1856, 160 acres of the area were homesteaded by 42-year-old **Galen Clark** who had suffered a severe lung hemorrhage and headed for the hills to live out his last days, but ended up surviving until he was 96. The area's giant sequoias had been "discovered" as early as 1851, but it wasn't until 1857 that Clark and trail-building entrepreneur Milton Mann thoroughly documented the big trees. Clark called the forest "Mariposa Grove" and renamed his homestead **Big Trees Station**.

Close to the current site of the *Wawona Hotel*, Clark ran a sawmill and blacksmith's shop, and provided for visitors traveling the original carriage road from Mariposa to Yosemite Valley. When Mariposa Grove became part of the Yosemite Grant in 1864, Clark was made guardian. He sold Big Trees Station in 1874 to the Washburn brothers who built the original *Wawona Hotel*, which burned down four years later. By 1879, the existing main building was built, the meadow was fenced for grazing animals, and produce was grown for hotel guests. Within three years, the area's name had changed again, this time to **Wa-wo-nah**, the local Indian name for the big trees, and the sound of the call of their guardian spirit, the owl.

In the early twentieth century the Washburns' son Clarence persuaded his parents to build a golf course to lure the newly car-mobile visitors. By 1925, planes were landing on the meadow, and there were daily mail and passenger flights until 1932 when the Wawona area was incorporated into Yosemite National Park. As with many national parks, areas that were previously occupied became "inholdings" where residents were entitled to keep living. One such homesteaded section lies along Chilnualna Falls Road about a mile from the *Wawona Hotel*. You'll see it if you head to the start of the Chilnualna Fall trail (Hike 42) and may even chose to stay there in the private homes of *The Redwoods in Yosemite* (see p.167).

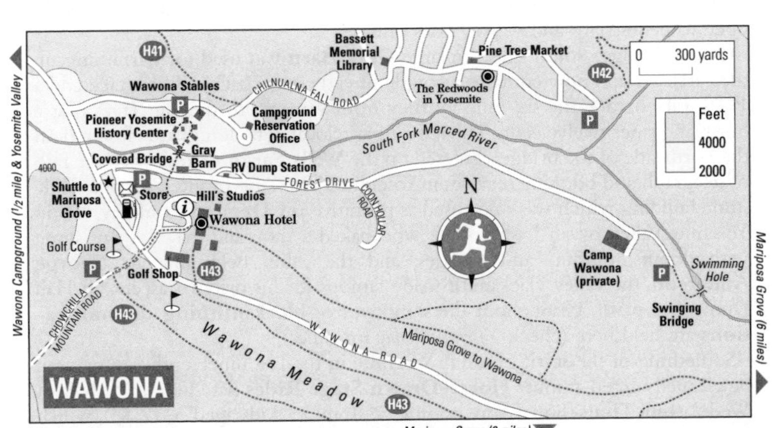

Area hikes

The following **hikes are accessed from in and around Wawona**, plus there's an additional hike from Mariposa Grove back to Wawona (see box, p.101).

- Hike 41 Alder Creek: see p.132
- Hike 42 Chilnualna Fall: see p.132
- Hike 43 Wawona Meadow Loop: see p.133

Wawona Hotel

Pretty much everything in Wawona revolves around the landmark *Wawona Hotel*, California's second oldest hotel (after the *Coronado* in San Diego). Started in 1876 as a small cluster of white-painted, wooden buildings, it was soon joined by the Washburn brothers' main two-story building with its encircling broad verandahs and Adirondack chairs. The entire complex is set in expansive grassy grounds with incense cedars and ponderosa pines all about.

The hotel (see "Accommodation," p.167) boasts a small **swimming pool** for guests only, a **tennis court** open to all ($2 racquet rentals from the golf shop), and a **nine-hole golf course** with fairways sprawled across the meadows, just over the road. The course is open to the public (mid-April to Oct; $30 for 18 holes, $19 for 9, plus optional cart rental $25 for 18 holes, $15 for 9, ⓣ209/375-6572 to a reserve tee time). Alternate tees turn this into a par seventy eighteen-hole course, with grazing mule deer as an added obstacle. The site of Galen Clark's first residence is marked behind the seventh green.

Pioneer Yosemite History Center

Though most of Yosemite's historic buildings have been lost to fire or simply knocked down, around a dozen have been gathered together at the **Pioneer Yosemite History Center** (self-guided walking tour all year; free), two minutes' walk north of the *Wawona Hotel*. Most were brought here in the early 1960s and arranged either side of the **covered bridge**, which spans the South Fork of the Merced River. The bridge was originally built by Galen Clark in 1868, but was covered in 1878 (to prevent snow build-up in winter). All Yosemite-bound traffic used to come this way, and though a modern bridge nearby now takes the strain, age has taken its toll. Now restored, the bridge is open to pedestrians and wagon rides only.

On the bridge's south side, the large **Gray Barn** was used for harnessing-up the carriages and now contains a couple of early stagecoaches, horse tack and a 1916 toll board – the six-mile journey from Wawona to the Big Trees cost a horse and rider twelve cents. The remaining relocated buildings are clustered on the north side of the bridge, centered on the **Wells Fargo office**, once the hub of telegraph and booking services in Yosemite Valley. Also of interest are: a dank, stone building which was once used as primitive jail; **Degnan's bakery**, run in Yosemite Valley by an Irish couple who baked a thousand loaves a day along with donuts, muffins and cookies; and the cabin belonging to **George Anderson**, the Valley blacksmith made famous for his original ascent up Half Dome (see p.50). Throughout the summer, free **blacksmithing demonstrations** are held here (check *Yosemite Today* for times).

Something of the spirit of life in Yosemite in the late nineteenth century can be gleaned on ten-minute **Horse-Drawn Stage Rides** (late June to early Sept Wed 2–4pm Thurs–Sun 10am–noon & 2–4pm; $3, kids aged 3–12 $2), which start outside the old Wells Fargo office. When funding permits, Park staff dress in period costume and open up some of the History Center's buildings.

Wawona practicalities

Wawona is just over an hour's drive south of Yosemite Valley and a shade under five miles north of the Park's South Entrance. There is no convenient public transportation to Wawona from Yosemite Valley or anywhere outside the Park, though you could visit Wawona and the Mariposa Grove on the guided Grand Tour from the Valley (see p.28). Once in Wawona, make use of the free **Mariposa Grove & Wawona Shuttle Bus** (see p.26), which runs frequently from the Wawona Store to the Mariposa Grove parking lot, with an intermediate stop at the South Entrance. It is particularly handy in midsummer when the Mariposa Grove lot is so full that the access road is closed to cars. The last bus back leaves the grove at 6pm.

Information and wilderness permits are available from the **Wawona Information Station** (mid-May to mid-Sept daily 8.30am–5pm; ⓣ209/375-9531), housed in Hill's Studio, once the workshop of landscape painter Thomas Hill. Snacks, camping supplies and a limited range of **groceries** are available from the Wawona Store (daily: June–Aug 8am–8pm, Sept–May 8am–7pm), and from the **Pine Tree Market** (similar hours), a mile along Chilnualna Falls Road. The Wawona Store also has a **post office** (Mon–Fri 9am–5pm, Sat 9am–noon), and the Bassett Memorial **Library**, 7971 Chilnualna Falls Rd (late May to early Sept Mon–Fri 1–5pm Sat 10am–2pm, early Sept to late May Wed–Fri noon–5pm Sat 10am–3pm), has free **Internet access**.

Evening **entertainment** hereabouts is limited. Several nights a week there's a **ranger campfire program** at the campground (open to all; free: check *Yosemite Today* for details), but if the opportunity arises don't miss the show put on by **Tom Bopp** (April–Oct Tues–Sat 5.30–9.30pm Nov–March some weekends; free) in the *Wawona Hotel* lounge. A fixture since 1983, Tom mostly just plays the piano as guests drink cocktails and wander in to dinner, but roughly twice a week (check with the hotel for details) he performs an hour-long interpretive session. While bashing out songs from Yosemite's past (mostly vaudeville, but anything goes) on a piano once used to accompany the Firefall at Curry Village (see box, p.67), he reels slides pertinent to the pieces being played. Pitched for all ages, some might find it all a bit cheesy, but Tom's obvious passion and enthusiasm always carry the evening.

Mariposa Grove

The biggest and most spectacular stand of **giant sequoias** in Yosemite is **Mariposa Grove** (snowbound in winter, but open at all times; free), at the end of Mariposa Grove Road, two miles east of the Park's South Entrance. Eight-foot diameter ponderosa pines and huge cedars are dwarfed by approximately five hundred mature sequoias, some up to three thousand years old, spread over an area roughly two miles by one mile. You can see sequoias all around the entrance area parking lot at an altitude of 5500ft, but to see the best, you really need to walk – not far, but all the trails lead gradually uphill. The sequoias straggle across a hillside gaining 1500ft from the **Lower Grove**, home to most of the biggest trees, to the **Upper Grove** where there is a greater concentration of sequoias but fewer really enormous specimens.

First explored by Galen Clark in 1857, the Mariposa Grove and Yosemite Valley were jointly set aside as the **Yosemite Grant**, the world's first public preserve in 1864. This afforded some protection at a time when sequoias were being cut for lumber and generally mistreated: one tree in the Calaveras Grove, north of Yosemite, died after its bark was stripped for display on the East Coast and in Britain. Clark was appointed as the first guardian, but wasn't able (or willing) to prevent tunnels being cut through two of the trees during his guardianship. Mariposa Grove was finally incorporated into Yosemite National Park in 1916.

Cars are now banned from the grove, but anyone with a modest level of fitness should have no trouble exploring some of the two and a half miles of well-maintained **trails** on foot: take your time heading uphill and enjoy the quick stroll back down at the end. If you can't cope with the terrain, join the hour-and-a-quarter-long **Big Trees Tram Tour** (June–Oct daily 10am–5pm, every 20min; $16, seniors $14, kids 5–12 $10; ⓣ209/372-4386) and get towed along a paved road on a flat-deck trailer with seats. Headphone narration comes in several languages. There are stops at the Fallen Monarch, Grizzly Giant and Clothespin Tree, and you are allowed to get off at the museum and board a later tour if you wish, though at busy times you may have to wait for a place. **Tickets** can be bought at the Mariposa Gift Shop, by the parking lot (April–Oct daily 9am–6pm), which also sells a limited range of **snacks**.

▲ Wawona Tunnel Tree, before it fell

Hiking the loop: Mariposa Grove to Wawona

Throughout much of the year, visitors traveling from Wawona to Mariposa Grove are encouraged to use the free Mariposa Grove & Wawona Shuttle Bus. Rather than take the bus in both directions, consider riding the shuttle to the grove, exploring at leisure, then hiking back to Wawona. It is not an especially spectacular hike by Yosemite standards, but it is downhill all the way and gives you the flexibility to stick around Mariposa Grove after the last shuttle bus has gone.

The hike from **Mariposa Grove to Wawona** (6.5 miles one way; 2–3hr; 2000ft descent) is a pleasant forest walk signposted off the grove's Outer Loop Trail. After 0.7 miles, a left fork is signed to Wawona. Continue steadily downhill through trees allowing sylvan views of Wawona Dome and the Wawona basin. After an hour or so you come to a small roadside parking bay and, at a trail junction 200 yards beyond, take the left fork and follow it along a broad undulating ridge used by horses. Keep going straight to reach the hotel for a well-earned cocktail on the verandah.

Mariposa Grove suffers slightly from its own popularity, so you should try to **arrive early or stay late** to avoid the crowds. A winter visit can be fantastic, though you'll need snowshoes or cross-country skiing equipment. You can even camp here in the snowy season (see p.176).

Grove highlights

After a century and a half of tourism, Mariposa Grove is presented as something of a sequoia freak show. While it is impressive enough just coming face-to-bark with these giants, throughout the grove unusual trees are singled out for attention: ones which have grown together, split apart, been struck by lightning, or are simply staggeringly large.

In the Lower Grove signs lead to the **Fallen Monarch**, made famous by the widely reproduced 1899 photo of cavalry officers and their horses standing atop

The life of the giant sequoia

The **giant sequoia** is the world's most massive tree, and yet it grows from a tiny seed, hundreds of which are packed into the hen-egg-sized cones which take a couple of years to mature. Cones may then stay on the tree for up to thirty years waiting for the right conditions. They don't fall of their own accord but require the aid of the chickaree (the Douglas squirrel) and the long-horned wood boring beetle to free them from their host. **Fire** too is a critical element in their propagation. The cones then need intense heat to open them, but even then, few of the tiny seeds (something like 90,000 to the pound) actually sprout. Perfect conditions are needed, usually where a fallen tree has left a hole in the canopy, allowing light to fall on rich mineral soil.

Young trees are conical, but as they mature the lower branches drop off to leave a top-heavy crown. There is no tap root so the trees rely on a shallow, wide root system to keep them upright. The cinnamon-colored bark of young sequoias is easily confused with that of the incense cedar, but as they age, there's no mistaking the thick spongy outer layer that protects the sapwood from the fires that periodically sweep through the forests.

Eventually heavy snowfall or high winds topple aging trees, but with its tannin-rich timber a giant sequoia may lie where it fell for hundreds of years. John Muir discovered one still largely intact with a 380-year-old silver fir growing out of the depression it had created. For more discussion of these magnificent trees, see our *Wild Yosemite* color section.

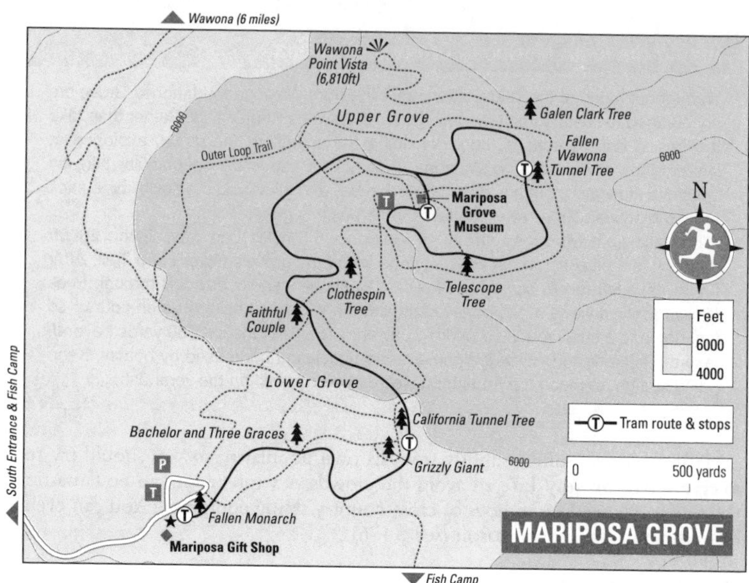

the prostrate tree. No one knows when it fell, but the tannin-rich heartwood doesn't seem to have deteriorated much in the hundred years since the photo was taken. Following the path beyond the elegant cluster four trees known as the **Bachelor and Three Graces**, you arrive at the largest tree in the grove (and the fifth largest in the world), the **Grizzly Giant**, thought to be somewhere between 2700 and 3500 years old. Its lowest branch is said to be thicker than the trunk of any non-sequoia in the grove, a claim that is easy to believe even when viewed from a hundred feet below. Adjacent is the **California Tunnel Tree**, bored out in 1859 for stagecoaches to pass through, but only accessible to pedestrians since the road was realigned in 1932.

It is a ten-minute walk to reach the **Faithful Couple**, two trees that seeded close to one another and appear to be united. Up the hill a bit further, the **Clothespin Tree** is indeed shaped like an old-fashioned clothespin with a 40-foot-high inverted V right through its base where it was hollowed out by fire. Continuing uphill you reach a fine stand of trees that marks the beginning of the slightly more open **Upper Grove**, where you'll also come upon the one-room **Mariposa Grove Museum** (June–Oct daily 9.30am–4.30pm; free), built in 1930 on the site of Galen Clark's original cabin. It contains modest displays and photos of the mighty sequoias, and sells Yosemite- and woodland-related books and educational materials.

Most visitors don't go much further so you'll have more peace and quiet as you stroll up to the **Telescope Tree,** where you can walk into the fire-hollowed base and peer up the length of the trunk to a tiny disc of sky. A little further on you'll see the **Wawona Tunnel Tree** lying beside the trail where it fell under a heavy load of snow in 1969. The tunnel dated from 1881 when the Yosemite Stage and Turnpike Company paid the Scribner brothers $75 to enlarge an old burn scar to a tunnel 26 feet long, 8 feet high and up to 8 feet wide.

If you've still got the energy, tackle the half-mile spur trail to **Wawona Point**, at 6810ft the highest point in the grove, for great panorama of High Sierra and along the South Fork of the Merced River.

4

Day hikes

However magnificent the roadside scenery, it is no substitute for striking out on foot along some of the eight hundred miles of **hiking trails** weaving through Yosemite National Park. The solitude and scenic grandeur quickly get their hooks into you, and many people are so captivated by the experience they end up doing far more hiking than they ever imagined.

Novice hikers may want to join one of the excellent guided day hikes, but it is really very easy to head out on your own along one of the less strenuous walks we've listed. More **experienced hikers** may feel restricted by our day-hiking recommendations and should flip straight to Chapter 5, "Backcountry hiking and camping."

Guided day hikes

If you are uncertain of your ability to navigate, fancy a little commentary about the journey, or are just looking for a little companionship, the answer might be to join a **guided hike**. As well as their rock climbing instruction (see p.148) and backcountry hikes (see p.135), the Yosemite Mountaineering School (Ⓣ209/372-8344, Ⓦwww.yosemitemountaineering.com) run a series of organized group hikes mostly from late May to early September. You'll be teamed up with other hikers and will be led by a knowledgeable guide. The school's guided day hikes include:

Cliffs and Climbers Hike A great taster spending a couple of hours or so ferreting around the base of cliffs where rock climbers ply their trade. Guides tell-tales of colorful characters and their exploits. $10 per person; kids under 10 free.

Discovery Hike Head out for 3–4 hours, perhaps following a gentle loop trail around the eastern end of Yosemite Valley (similar to Hike 6), or hiking from Tunnel View to Inspiration Point (Hike 11). The emphasis is on appreciating the scenery, flora, fauna and local history. $20 per person; kids under 10 free.

Adventure Hike Six hours of exploration giving the group time to explore wider. $40 per person; kids under 10 free.

Custom Hikes Hikes tailored to your needs and tastes. Rates are for half a day ($58 a head for 3–7 people, $160 total for 1–2); an eight-hour day ($75–86 a head for 3–7 people, $96 a head for two); or an extreme 10hr day ($125 a head for 3–7 people, $290 total for 1–2).

Companies based **outside the Park** also run guided hikes in the Park. One of the best is Yosemite Guides (Ⓣ1-866/922-9111, Ⓦwww.yosemiteguides.com), based at *Yosemite View Lodge* on Hwy-140 (see p.169), who offer five-hour naturalist-led walks. Try the High Country Trails ($65) or the Sunset Walk ($70), which explores the Valley rim around Sentinel Dome. Also worth checking out is the extensive program of specialist hikes run by the Yosemite Association (Ⓦwww.yosemite.org; see p.40).

Gentle hikes can be undertaken without leaving the Valley floor, but to get away from the crowds you only need to tackle any path with a bit of a slope. Some of the finest and most accessible trails, including the stunning **Mist Trail** and the demanding route up **Half Dome**, start from the **Happy Isles trailhead** at the eastern end of Yosemite Valley. In other areas of the Park, **Tuolumne Meadows** has the greatest concentration of high-country walks, though there are also plenty along **Tioga Road** and several more around **Wawona** and at **Hetch Hetchy**.

Hiking practicalities

Since wilderness permits are not required for day hikes, you need only get yourself to the trailhead and set off. In Yosemite Valley there is no trailhead parking so you must park in one of the day-use lots and ride the free Valley shuttle to the trailhead. Elsewhere in the Park, either ride the Glacier Point or Tuolumne Meadows hikers buses, or drive your own vehicle to the trailhead; you'll usually find enough parking, along with steel **bear-resistant lockers** in which you must stash any food and scented toiletries. Remember to pack out all **trash**, bury **bodily waste** at least six inches deep and a hundred feet from any water, and stand quietly aside for **horseback riders**.

Staying on track

Every major trailhead and trail junction in the Park sprouts a cluster of **stenciled metal signs**, many dating back to the 1950s. These state the distance to several prominent landmarks or destinations in each direction. Most trails are easy to follow, and sometimes have fallen tree trunks aligned with the path to guide you. Where the trails cross bare rock, look for **cairns** (small piles of rocks also known as "ducks") marking the way. In addition, you may also come across a rectangle or letter "T" cut from the bark of trailside trees, remnants of an outdated practice of trailblazing.

It is hard to get lost if you stick to the trail, but that shouldn't stop you from carrying a **compass** and a detailed **topographic map** of the Park. Hikers going **off-trail** should be equipped with the relevant topographic map (see p.35).

Safety

Safety on the trail is mostly common sense, but in an effort to reduce injuries the Park Service offers considerable precautionary information online (Ⓦ www.nps.gov/yose/wilderness/safety.htm). They make no attempt to keep track of hikers in the Park, so always let someone know where you are going (and tell them when you get back), especially when hiking alone.

Before setting off, check the **weather forecast** at visitor centers or by calling Ⓣ 209/372-0200. Yosemite's weather is generally stable, short sudden summer and fall thunderstorms are quite common, especially in the afternoons. Keep clear of exposed places, viewpoints and lone trees that are susceptible to **lightning strikes**, and always carry warm, waterproof clothing; **hypothermia** is a killer.

For all our hikes we've given an indication of the **normal hiking season**, when the trail is likely to be snow-free. It still pays, however, to check trail conditions through visitor centers or online (Ⓦ www.nps.gov/yose/wilderness/trailconditions.htm). In the high country it can still snow as late as June and as early as October. Beside inclement weather, other **potential backcountry hazards** include creatures big and small, from mountain lions to mosquitoes, along with the likes of poison oak; see Basics, pp.29–30 for details.

What to take

For full details on what to wear and what equipment to lug along with you, see pp.139–141 in Chapter 5, "Backcountry hiking and camping." In brief, your most important decision is what to **wear**. Several layers of light clothing work best so that you can bundle up or strip off as required. Cotton is a liability when wet, so bring at least one layer of either wool or one of the numerous "technical" synthetic materials available; always carry a light waterproof shell as well. Apart from the easiest excursions, the hikes listed below are mostly along rough paths. Day hikers carrying a light load may be happy with ordinary sneakers, but it's safer wearing **boots with ankle support**, preferably a relatively light and well-broken-in pair. For summer hiking heavy leather boots are overkill as you'll seldom come across wet or muddy terrain.

Always take more **food** than you think you are going to need, and on longer hikes, have some means of **water purification**. Also take a map, mosquito repellant, sunscreen, sunglasses and a wide-brimmed hat. Day-packs and other outdoor equipment can be rented from the Mountain Shop in Curry Village (see p.193).

Hikes from Yosemite Valley: Happy Isles trailhead

The hikes in this section all start from the **Happy Isles trailhead**, at the eastern end of Yosemite Valley (shuttle stop 16). They all initially follow the Merced River, and each hike builds on the previous one.

H1 Vernal Fall footbridge

Difficulty Strenuous
Distance 7 miles round trip
Estimated time 5–8hr
Elevation gain 1900ft ascent
Season May–Nov. Falls are best May–June; good fall colors Oct & Nov.
Trailhead location Map p.111, shuttle stop 16 near the Nature Center at Happy Isles.
Comments Crowds thin towards Nevada Fall where you get a high-country feel.

If you don't have time for the Mist Trail (see Hike 2), try this moderately steep path over broken asphalt to a perfect pine-framed view up the Merced River to Vernal Fall. It follows part of the John Muir Trail (JMT: see box, p.143), starting just east of the road bridge over the Merced River. The path leads upstream past a detailed trail distance sign and starts climbing. There are plenty of chances to catch your breath, as breaks in the pines and black oaks reveal the churning river below and views up to the 370ft **Illilouette Fall** lurking in the shadows of Illilouette Canyon. The fall is formed by Illilouette Creek, which drains the country west of Glacier Point Road then plunges over what is known as **Panorama Cliff** to join the Merced River below.

The trail continues to a footbridge over the Merced from where you'll get a great view of Vernal Fall. With the river crashing over huge boulders in the foreground it's a dramatic vantage point, usually crowded with people photographing their friends with the falls in the background. **Vernal Fall** gets its name from the Latin for spring, and the 317ft fall indeed looks its best during the spring snowmelt when the curtain of water is perhaps eighty or a hundred feet wide.

There are toilets and drinking water at the footbridge: return the way you came.

Yosemite's 50 best hikes

Hike	Name	Grade	Length (miles)	Time (hr)	Ascent (feet)	Season	Waterfalls	Best in Spring	Wildlife	Wildflowers	Kid-friendly	Swimming spots	Solitude	Panoramic views	Historic features
	HAPPY ISLES TRAILHEAD														
1	Vernal Fall footbridge	Easy	1.6	1	500	All year									
2	Mist Trail to the top of Vernal Fall	Moderate	3.0	2–3	1100	All year	✓				✓				
3	Mist Trail to the top of Nevada Fall	Strenuous	7.0	5–8	1900	May–Nov	✓								
4	Half Dome	Very strenuous	17.0	9–12	4800	Late May to mid-Oct	✓							✓	
	THE REST OF YOSEMITE VALLEY														
5	Mirror Lake and Tenaya Canyon	Easy	4.2	2	100	All year		✓			✓				✓
6	Eastern Valley Loop	Easy	2.6	1–2	50	All year		✓	✓		✓				✓
7	Columbia Rock	Moderate	2.0	1.5–3	1000	All year		✓				✓		✓	
8	Upper Yosemite Fall	Strenuous	7.0	4–7	2700	April–Dec	✓	✓						✓	
9	Four-Mile Trail to Glacier Point	Strenuous	4.8	2.5–4	3200	Mid-May to Oct								✓	
10	Western Valley Loop	Easy	6.5	2.5–3.5	350	All year		✓			✓				✓
11	Inspiration Point	Moderate	2.4	1.5–2.5	600	Mid-May to Oct						✓	✓	✓	
	HETCH HETCHY														
12	Wapama Falls	Easy	5.0	2–3	400	Mid-April to Nov	✓	✓		✓	✓				
13	Rancheria Falls	Moderate	14.5	5–8	800	Mid-April to Nov	✓	✓		✓			✓	✓	

Yosemite's 50 best hikes

	TIOGA ROAD														
14	El Capitan from Tamarack Flat	Strenuous	16.5	7–10	1240	June–Oct							✓	✓	
15	Harden Lake	Easy	6.0	2–3	270	June–Oct			✓	✓	✓				
16	Lukens Lake	Easy	1.6	1	200	June–Oct				✓	✓				
17	Yosemite Falls from Yosemite Creek	Strenuous	12.0	5–7	700	June–Oct	✓						✓	✓	
18	North Dome from Porcupine Creek	Moderate	9.0	4–6	650	June–Oct						✓	✓	✓	
19	May Lake	Easy	2.5	1	400	June–Oct				✓	✓				
20	Clouds Rest from Tenaya Lake	Strenuous	14.5	7–10	1800	June–Oct								✓	
21	Polly Dome Lakes	Easy	5.0	2–3	500	Late June–Oct				✓	✓		✓		
22	Tenaya Lake circuit	Easy	3.0	1–1.5	50	June–Oct					✓				
	TUOLUMNE MEADOWS														
23	Pothole Dome	Easy	0.5	1	200	June–Oct					✓			✓	
24	Cathedral Lakes	Moderate	8.0	4–6	1000	June–Oct								✓	
25	Soda Springs and Parsons Lodge	Easy	4.0	2	50	June–Oct				✓	✓	✓			✓
26	Elizabeth Lake	Moderate	4.8	3–5	900	June–Oct				✓		✓			
27	Lyell Canyon	Easy	11.0	4–5	100	June–Oct			✓	✓		✓	✓		
28	Dog Lake	Easy	3.2	1.5–2.5	600	June–Oct					✓	✓			
29	Lembert Dome	Moderate	3.7	2–3	850	June–Oct					✓	✓		✓	
30	Young Lakes	Strenuous	13.5	7–10	1500	June–Oct							✓	✓	
31	Glen Aulin	Moderate	11.0	6–8	600	June–Oct	✓					✓			
32	Waterwheel Falls	Very strenuous	17.5	8–12	2100	June–Oct	✓					✓	✓		
	TIOGA PASS														
33	Mono Pass	Moderate	8.0	4–6	1000	June–Oct			✓				✓	✓	✓
34	Gaylor Lakes and the Great Sierra Mine	Moderate	3.0	2–3	500	June–Oct			✓			✓	✓	✓	✓

Yosemite's 50 best hikes (*Contd.*)

Hike	Name	Grade	Length (miles)	Time (hr)	Ascent (feet)	Season	Waterfalls	Best in Spring	Wildlife	Wildflowers	Kid-friendly	Swimming spots	Solitude	Panoramic views	Historic features
	GLACIER POINT ROAD														
35	McGurk Meadow	Easy	1.6	1	150	Mid-May to Oct				✓	✓				✓
36	Ostrander Lake	Strenuous	12.6	5–7	1600	Mid-May to Oct			✓				✓	✓	✓
37	Taft Point and the Fissures	Easy	2.2	1	250	Mid-May to Oct						✓		✓	
38	Sentinel Dome	Easy	2.2	1	250	Mid-May to Oct					✓			✓	
39	Panorama Trail	Moderate	9.0	6–8	800	Mid-May to Oct	✓							✓	
40	Pohono Trail	Strenuous	13.8	5–8	2800	May–Oct			✓			✓	✓	✓	
	WAWONA AND MARIPOSA GROVE														
41	Alder Creek	Moderate	12.0	5–7	1700	April–Nov		✓	✓	✓			✓		
42	Chilnualna Fall	Moderate	8.2	4–6	2200	April–Nov		✓						✓	
43	Wawona Meadow Loop	Easy	3.5	1–2	200	March–Dec		✓	✓		✓	✓			✓
	OVERNIGHT HIKES														
44	Pohono–Panorama Combo	Very strenuous	23.0	2–3 days	3600	Mid-June to Oct	✓		✓				✓	✓	
45	North rim of Yosemite Valley	Very strenuous	30.0	2–3	5700	Late May–Oct	✓					✓	✓	✓	
46	John Muir Trail	Strenuous	20.0	2 days	6100	June–Oct	✓		✓			✓		✓	
47	Merced Lake HSC	Very strenuous	27.0	2–3 days	3300	June–Oct	✓		✓	✓		✓	✓	✓	
48	Ten Lakes	Strenuous	22.0	2 days	4500	June–Oct			✓			✓		✓	
49	Grand Canyon of the Tuolumne	Very strenuous	28.0	2–3 days	4000	June–Oct	✓					✓	✓		
50	The High Sierra Camp Loop	Moderate	47.0	6 days	8000	June–Sept	✓		✓	✓		✓		✓	✓

Hiking and backcountry camping guidelines

- **Stay on the trail** Walk single file, avoid cutting switchbacks, and limit track-broadening by walking through any wet areas.
- **Pack out all trash** If you pack it in, pack it out. Some hikers even carry a plastic bag and pick up stuff dropped by less considerate souls.
- **Bury bodily wastes** Use the vault toilets found at most trailheads, but if you get caught short, bury waste at least six inches deep and over forty paces away from any stream or river.
- **Pack out toilet paper** Attempts to burn it have caused wildfires in the past.
- **Stand aside for horses** On some trails horses and mules are common. Stop on the side of the trail to let them pass.
- **Purify drinking water** see p.31.
- **Use existing campsites** Use the campsites in Little Yosemite Valley, next to High Sierra Camps and other spots that are regularly used.
- **Camp away from water and trails** Wherever you camp, make sure you are over forty paces away from lakes and streams, and out of sight of nearby trails.
- **Camp on firm ground** Avoid setting tents on fragile, untouched vegetation.
- **No "improvements"** Don't build windbreaks or new fire rings, dig trenches or cut vegetation for bough beds.
- **Limit campfires** Fires are banned above 9600ft, and are discouraged elsewhere. Use stoves, and if you must have a fire, burn only dead and down wood.
- **Wash clean** Avoid putting anything in the water. Carry washing water away from lakes and streams. Even "biodegradable" soap pollutes.
- **Be bear safe** Always store food and any odorous items in bear canisters unless you are preparing a meal.

H2 Mist Trail to the top of Vernal Fall

Difficulty Moderate
Distance 3 miles round trip
Estimated time 2–3hr
Elevation gain 1100ft ascent
Season Accessible all year; the falls are best in May & June but run year round.
Trailhead location Map p.111, shuttle stop 16 near the Nature Center at Happy Isles.
Comments Fairly crowded and you can expect to get drenched in spring.

If you only do one hike in Yosemite, this should be it. During the spring snowmelt this short walk really packs a punch as it twists up a path so close to **Vernal Fall** that a rainbow often frames the cascading water, and hikers get drenched in spray; bring a raincoat or plan to get wet. Though hardly dangerous, the Mist Trail demands sure footing and a head for heights.

How tough is the hike?

All fifty hikes in this guide have been given a rating in one of four categories:

Easy Generally a walk of up to a couple of hours on relatively smooth surfaces across flat or gently sloping ground.

Moderate A hike with some gradient but on well-maintained trails, taking up to several hours.

Strenuous A tougher proposition on fairly steep and occasionally rough ground, usually consuming most of the day.

Very strenuous A trek of at least eight hours negotiating steep terrain on uneven ground.

Start by following Hike 1 to the Vernal Fall footbridge, after which the crowds thin appreciably. Continue 150 yards past the bridge to a junction where the John Muir Trail (and all the mule traffic) goes right. Take the pedestrian-only left-hand path marked **Mist Trail**, which starts climbing steadily along a fairly narrow path built over large wet boulders. If you're lucky, the sun will be playing on the spray thrown up by the roaring falls creating beautiful rainbows. Railings protect you from the edge and provide support for the final haul up slippery steps cut into the rock. At the top of the fall you can rest on the smooth slabs beside the deceptively placid **Emerald Pool**. Water flows into the pool over the **Silver Apron**, a thirty-yard-wide shelf of slick rock that looks very tempting as a slide. Rocks in the pool at the bottom have caused numerous injuries and signs ban both sliding and swimming, not that that seems to stop people. Once the spring snowmelt abates it certainly is a lovely place to swim, but take great care, and don't dive into the submerged rocks.

Either retrace your steps to the trailhead, or return via the JMT (slightly longer but easier), reached along the path leading uphill from near the footbridge just above the Silver Apron.

H3 Mist Trail to the top of Nevada Fall

Difficulty Strenuous
Distance 7 miles round trip
Estimated time 5–8hr
Elevation gain 1900ft ascent
Season May–Nov. Falls are best May & June, good fall colors Oct & Nov.
Trailhead location Map opposite, shuttle stop 16 near the Nature Center at Happy Isles.
Comments Crowds thin towards Nevada Fall where you get a high-country feel.

This hike expands on Hike 2, adding an extra 800ft of ascent and taking in more expansive views of the high country, including a **close-up view of the 594ft Nevada Fall**, higher and perhaps even more striking than Vernal Fall. It takes its name from the Spanish for snowy (as in Sierra Nevada, "snowy range") and forms a relatively narrow cascade falling vertically for half its height then fanning out on a steep, smooth granite apron for the remaining 300 feet.

Follow Hike 2 as far as the Silver Apron then cross the footbridge immediately above it. Except on the busiest summer weekends you'll have few fellow hikers as you wind through the forest passing a flat spot which, from 1870 until 1897, was the spray-drenched location of *La Casa Nevada*, also known as *Snow's Hotel*. Guides apparently used to boast of being able to show their clients eleven feet of snow, even in summer. They then introduced them to the six-foot tall Albert Snow and his five-foot wife, Emily.

The path then follows a series of switchbacks climbing up the side of Nevada Fall with the rounded peak of Liberty Cap rearing above. Roughly level with the top of Nevada Fall you meet the JMT (toilets). Half Dome hikers turn left here, but turn right and you'll soon reach the Merced River at the top of Nevada Fall. Peer over the lip at the cascade below from one of numerous excellent viewpoints, then relax on the smooth gray slabs of rock tucking into your lunch. Some vigilance is required to stop the squirrels spiriting away your sandwiches. This is another (technically illegal, potentially dangerous, but very popular) spot for swimming in late summer and fall.

For the return journey, rejoin the JMT and continue downhill passing an intersection with the Panorama Trail (Hike 39). The JMT now cuts across a cliff face, the path almost carved into the rock face with dripping overhangs above and a solid stone wall separating you from the vertiginous drop. This section can be icy in spring before the summer sun warms the shady corners. The trail then

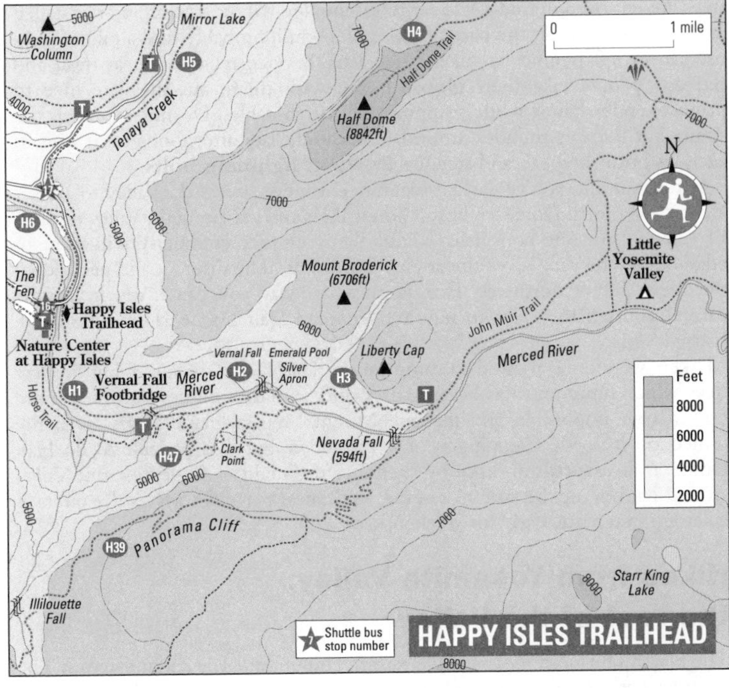

eases with some great views of Half Dome, and across the Valley to the Yosemite's northern reaches.

H4 Half Dome

Difficulty Very strenuous
Distance 17 miles round trip
Estimated time 9–12hr
Elevation gain 4800ft ascent
Season Late May to mid-Oct; cable stays are removed from Half Dome in winter.
Trailhead location Map above, shuttle stop 16 near the Nature Center at Happy Isles.
Comments Understandably the Park's most popular hard hike; well worth the effort.

The summit of **Half Dome** is the most alluring target of ambitious day hikers, who are rewarded with stupendous views from the broad flat top almost five thousand feet above the Valley floor. The route is a full day undertaking and hikers should start at the crack of **dawn**, initially following either Hike 3 to the top of Nevada Fall or following the JMT to the same point; for variety take the other route on the way down. From the junction of the two trails, follow the JMT as it skirts the backcountry campground in **Little Yosemite Valley** and follows Sunrise Creek steeply uphill. Split off the JMT along the **Half Dome Trail** passing the **last water** on the track (a small spring half a mile past the junction on the left), then reaching the base of Quarter Dome. Steep steps lead up across smooth slabs until you reach the base of **steel cables** and wooden slats lashed to Half Dome's extremely steep curved back. This is the only way to ascend the last 400 vertical feet to the summit, and short sections are at an intimidating angle of sixty degrees. The steps are removed in mid-October to discourage winter ascents and reinstalled at the end of May. At the base of the cables you'll probably find a pile of free-use gloves left behind by hikers. The Park Service regards this as trash and requests people take their **gloves** home with them, but they are nice to protect tender hands while gripping the rough cables. Do not approach the summit if there is thunder around (commonly late afternoons from Aug to Oct), as both the peak and steel cables attract **lightning bolts**.

At the summit, you've earned magnificent views across the Valley to Basket Dome and North Dome, right to Clouds Rest and left along the Valley towards El Capitan. Anyone concerned about their outdoor credibility will want to edge out to the very lip of the abyss – known as "The Visor" – and peer down the sheer 2000ft northwest face. Return the way you came. You have now earned yourself the right to buy a "I climbed Half Dome" T-shirt from the Village Store.

Hikers were once allowed to camp on the Half Dome's summit, but the few trees which hung on soon became firewood, sanitary facilities on bare granite proved near impossible, and the rare Mount Lyell salamander was given the protection it needs. Camping is now forbidden, but it is possible to do Half Dome as an **overnight hike** by spending the night at Little Yosemite Valley around halfway up: be sure to reserve wilderness permits early as the quota is taken up fast, particularly for weekends.

Hikes from Yosemite Valley: the rest of the Valley

The hikes in this section start at the eastern end of the Valley and move west. The main features on these walks are discussed in depth throughout Chapter 1.

H5 Mirror Lake and Tenaya Canyon Loop

Difficulty Easy
Distance 4.2 miles round trip
Estimated time 2hr
Elevation gain 100ft ascent
Season All year, but best in May & June. Mirror Lake is often dry by July.
Trailhead location Map p.111, shuttle stop 17, east of Curry Village.
Comments This very popular walk is pleasant but can be a little disappointing once Mirror Lake dries up.

This undemanding walk calls at **Mirror Lake**, one of the Valley's premier sights, then continues into the lower reaches of **Tenaya Canyon**; it is good all year but particularly gorgeous in May and June when the dogwoods are in bloom.

Starting at shuttle stop 17 (easily accessible on foot from Curry Village), follow the traffic-free road to Tenaya Creek Bridge, where you'll return at the end of the hike. The road continues all the way to Mirror Lake, but two hundred yards past the bridge a broad dirt path angles off to the left, offering a quieter, asphalt-free alternative route. The paths meet at the compellingly calm Mirror Lake where you can follow an interpretive trail and, early in the summer when the lake is full, photograph **Half Dome** reflected in its meditative stillness.

Beyond Mirror Lake you're in more peaceful territory, and soon cross an area where a rockfall came down in 1997. About a mile on, the Snow Creek Trail heads up out of Tenaya Canyon to the left; instead bear right and walk over Tenaya Creek on Snow Creek Bridge. Turn right and keep the river on your right as you follow the path downstream until you complete the loop

Active Yosemite

Visitors to Yosemite barely need to step out of their cars to revel in its scenic glory. Indeed, it is a sad fact that the majority of people never go more than half an hour's walk from the nearest road. Shame on them. They miss out on fabulous waterfalls tucked away up side canyons, magnificent Sierra vistas, refreshing swims in high-country lakes and the subtleties of the Park's meadows and wildflowers. All this is accessible along well-maintained hiking trails that thread the entire Park.

Hiking

The only way to really get to know Yosemite is to strike out on foot, and with 800 miles of trails the Park can occupy a lifetime of **trekking**. The majority of visitors only see a handful of the most popular trails, but they're fashionable for good reason. Bagging the five hikes we've listed below will quickly introduce you to a wonderful cross section of Yosemite's finest features.

The rest of the Park is left to hardy souls heading out into the backcountry. Despite Yosemite's three-million-plus annual visitors, only one in one hundred spends a night in the **backcountry**. You can walk for days only seeing a handful of people, and camp alone with just that big starry sky for company.

El Capitan ▲

Trail sign along the High Sierra Loop ▼

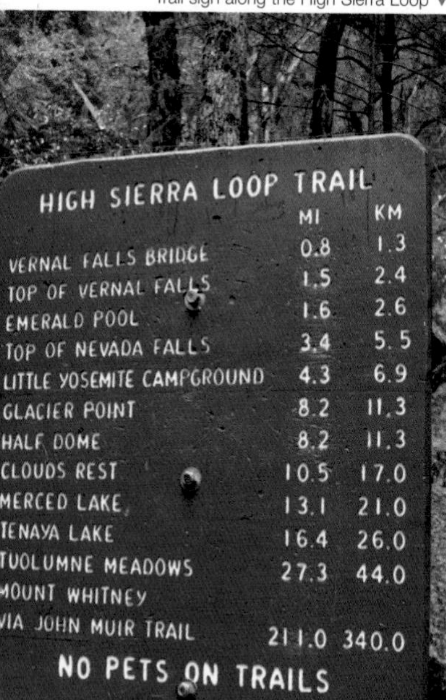

Five favorite hikes

▸▸ **The Mist Trail** (Hike 2): Precarious spray-drenched steps beside one of the Park's finest waterfalls make this the best short-ish hike in Yosemite.

▸▸ **Half Dome** (Hike 4): The summit in a day is a big effort, but well worth it for the haul up the steep cables and great views from the vertiginous summit.

▸▸ **Cathedral Lakes** (Hike 24): Relatively easy subalpine hiking to gorgeous lakes and sublime views of Cathedral Peak.

▸▸ **Waterwheel Falls** (Hike 32): Head into northern Yosemite past numerous wonderful cataracts and swimming holes. Best done overnight.

▸▸ **The High Sierra Camp Loop** (Hike 50): Superb multi-day hike through the Yosemite high country, with optional stays in seasonal tent cabins.

Horseback riding

It is hard to beat arriving at your mountain-girt campsite after a hot day on the trail, unhitching saddles and leading your pack animals down to the river to drink, then heading back to the tents for a meal that's far more luxurious than anything hikers would be prepared to carry.

Most of Yosemite's backcountry trails are open for **horseback riding**, so getting out into the wilderness doesn't have to involve backpacking-style hardship. It's an altogether more relaxing experience, evocative of early pioneering times when traveling with horses and mules was standard practice. Such trips can be organized through the stables in Yosemite and through pack outfitters based just outside the Park.

In practice, most people take a more spontaneous approach, just riding for a few hours for the sheer joy of being on horseback. Each of Yosemite's three **stables** – in Yosemite Valley, Tuolumne Meadows and Wawona – offer two-hour trips following river-banks or heading out across meadows in magnificent scenery. Half-day trips stray further afield and give you a chance to really get used to your steed. If you are saddle-hardened, go for a full-day trip, like the ride up to the base of **Half Dome** where you dismount for the final summit ascent.

▲ Enjoying the Park on horseback

▼ Badger Pass

Snowshoeing and skiing

With its silent blanket of pure white snow, and visitor numbers at a fraction of their summertime peak, winter is a fine time to be in Yosemite. Closed roads limit access to the high country, but that makes the destination all the more appealing

for those prepared to head out on **cross-country skis** or **snowshoes**.

Most people make straight for the modest downhill slopes of **Badger Pass** where you can rent gear and take lessons. The classic trip is then to journey along the snowbound Glacier Point Road to Glacier Point itself, where the winter-gripped Sierra stretches to the horizon in every direction, and you can look straight down on the skaters at the Curry Village ice rink in Yosemite Valley. There are even organized trips that stay overnight at Glacier Point for that moonlit vista of Half Dome.

Whole books have been written on cross-country skiing routes through the Yosemite backcountry, and with your own gear the options are limitless, especially if you are prepared to snow-camp. In fact, one of the winter highlights is a night spent in **Mariposa Grove** with massive sequoias all around, their gargantuan boughs weighed down by a fresh dump of powder.

Rafting

Enjoying the scenery **on the water** in Yosemite is a leisurely affair. Pick a sunny day, stock up with supplies for your journey, bring along your swimsuit and assorted aquatic toys and settle in for a stately drift past the towering cliffs and spires of the Valley walls. A few ripples provide a hint of adventure, but this is more about cruising downstream, occasionally dipping your paddle in the water, rolling over the stern for a refreshing dunking, then pulling up at a sandy beach for a picnic. Of course, if you've got friends in an adjacent raft, pirate-boarding antics are pretty much essential.

at Tenaya Creek Bridge. You're likely to encounter horse traffic along this final section.

H6 Eastern Valley Loop

Difficulty Easy
Distance 2.6 mile loop
Estimated time 1–2hr
Elevation gain 50ft ascent
Season All year
Trailhead location Map p.52, main parking lot at Curry Village.
Comments A gentle stroll around Curry Village and the Happy Isles area close to most of the campgrounds.

This gentle hike weaves through some of the most populated sections of Yosemite, but is surprisingly peaceful as it loops around the eastern end of the Valley past its main features and some attractive riverside scenery.

Starting from the main parking lot at Curry Village, head east along the broad path that runs between tent cabins until you reach the shuttle road. Turn right, and then almost immediately go right again into a parking lot used by overnight

▲ El Capitan, Half Dome and Bridalveil Fall

hikers. From the lot's eastern corner, a dirt track cuts half a mile through incense cedars and ponderosa pines to a swampy area known as **The Fen**, its soggy ecosystem explained by an interpretive panel. A trail from here leads you to the Nature Center at Happy Isles beside the Merced River where there is an impressive view of **North Dome** and Washington Column. Take a few minutes to visit the Nature Centre (see p.66) and don't miss the display on rockfall around the back.

Cross the Merced on the road bridge and turn left to follow the dogwood-shaded riverbank, gradually veering further left as you approach the Valley stables; there are especially good views of Upper Yosemite Fall along this stretch. At the stables, walk over Clark Bridge then immediately turn right into the **Lower Pines campground** and follow the campground roads to the far northwestern end. Here a narrow path cuts through trees to Stoneman Meadow. Cross over the long boardwalk and continue straight to return to Curry Village.

H7 Columbia Rock

Difficulty Moderate
Distance 2 miles round trip
Estimated time 1hr 30min–2hr 30min
Elevation gain 1000ft ascent
Season All year, but generally free of snow mid-May to October.
Trailhead location Map p.52, *Camp 4* parking lot accessed from shuttle stop 7.
Comments About the only winter and spring hike that climbs out of the Valley.

The most easily accessible views on the north side of the Valley are from **Columbia Rock**, a small promontory part way up the route to the top of Upper Yosemite Fall (see below). The south-facing slopes catch the sun for most of the year, quickly melting most snowfall and keeping this trail open when others are snowbound. The hike starts behind *Camp 4*, and quickly climbs through glades of canyon live oak. You'll probably want to catch your breath a couple of times in the first half-hour until the trail gradually bends to the right and eases. Breaks in the trees reveal the Valley far below, but the best vista is saved for Columbia Rock, from where Half Dome dominates to the east.

H8 Upper Yosemite Fall

Difficulty Strenuous
Distance 7 miles round trip
Estimated time 4–7hr
Elevation gain 2700ft ascent
Season April–Dec, but best in spring and fall when it isn't too hot.
Trailhead location Map p.52, *Camp 4* parking lot accessed from shuttle stop 7.
Comments Very popular trail but rewarding both physically and visually.

This perennially popular, energy-sapping hike climbs steeply to the north rim of the Valley with great views of Upper Yosemite Fall for much of the way, and the opportunity to sit virtually on the edge of the fall and gaze down at the Lilliputian activity below in Yosemite Village. As with the Columbia Rock hike (see above), the sun keeps the trail largely snow-free, but that also means you'll want to get an early start in summer when it's best to set off by 7am. If you've got lots of stamina, consider exploring **Yosemite Point**, a mostly level mile from the top of Upper Yosemite Fall, and perhaps **Eagle Peak**, a two-mile hike from the fall with an 1100ft ascent.

The Upper Yosemite Fall trail starts far to the west of the base of Yosemite Falls and follows Hike 7 to Columbia Rock. It then descends gradually until you round a corner revealing the full majesty of **Upper Yosemite Fall** – all

1430ft of it – straight ahead. During the meltwater period, the power and volume of the water become increasingly apparent as you draw nearer. In the morning light, the cascade casts ever-changing shadows against the rock wall, and you can also pick out **Lost Arrow Spire** standing apart from the cliff face to the right of the fall.

Climbing again, the track gradually pulls out of the trees into the full force of the sun just as the switchbacks get really steep. This is where you'll wish you'd gotten out of bed an hour earlier. When you get into some shady Jeffrey pines and red firs, a sign points to the top of the fall just a couple of hundred yards away.

There are numerous vantage points at the top, but the best is just to the right of the fall (facing downstream) where you can follow a narrow path to a rock shelf below, very close to the top of the fall. In July and August the low water flows combine with Valley winds to frequently blow the spray back over the shelf.

A popular alternative to a tiring day hike is to come up in the cool of the afternoon and **camp up here**, though regulations dictate you'll need to be back a quarter-mile from the Valley rim. Wilderness permits are required, and can be tricky to obtain for summer weekends.

H9 Four-Mile Trail to Glacier Point

Difficulty Strenuous
Distance 4.8 miles one way
Estimated time 2hr 30min–4hr one way; 5–8hr round trip
Elevation gain 3200ft ascent
Season Mid-May to Oct
Trailhead location Map p.52, on Southside Drive, two miles west of Curry Village.
Comments One of the more popular Valley rim hikes and steep enough to be best avoided in the summer heat. Ambitious hikers can combine the Four-Mile Trail with the Panorama Trail (see Hike 39) for a very strenuous full-day circuit.

Glacier Point can be reached by car and the hikers bus, but neither approach is as rewarding as hiking the very popular **Four-Mile Trail**, which climbs the southern wall of the Valley ascending switchbacks the whole way. Originally constructed in 1872, the track was financed by James McCauley, who intended it as a toll route to his hotel at Glacier Point. Remodeled and lengthened since, it now starts from a trailhead parking lot accessible by the El Capitan shuttle. Alternatively, get off the Valley shuttle at stop 7 and walk west along Northside Drive, then take the paved bike and footpath half a mile across the Valley to the trailhead.

The trail surface has been largely neglected, leaving a lot of broken asphalt underfoot. This is now covered in sand, making it fairly slippery; consequently it is safer to hike up than down. The trail starts steeply, but you're in shade for much of the way, and views become ever more expansive as you rapidly gain height. After about an hour, you'll reach the first really fantastic views of Half Dome, Cathedral Rocks, Tenaya Canyon and Washington Column. Further up, you're level with the near-sheer face of **Sentinel Rock**, its fissures cast in relief by the afternoon light. Soon you'll leave the last of the switchbacks behind and skirt some small cliffs with the Valley far below and Yosemite Falls on the far side. After a brief descent, the final forested climb brings you to Glacier Point, and a well-earned ice cream.

If you can organize friends to drive round and meet you for sunset at Glacier Point this also makes a wonderful hike to do in the late afternoon.

H10 Western Valley Loop: El Capitan and Bridalveil Fall

Difficulty Easy
Distance 6.5 mile loop
Estimated time 2hr 30min–3hr 30min
Elevation gain 350ft ascent
Season All year, but perhaps best for fall colors in Oct & Nov.
Trailhead location Map p.48, El Capitan Bridge, three miles west of Yosemite Village.
Comments Though never far from a road this is a serene way to tour the Valley's western end. Take a picnic.

This fairly long but easy and usually peaceful hike visits the meadows and viewpoints at the western end of Yosemite Valley, involving intimate encounters with **El Capitan**, **Cathedral Spires** and **Bridalveil Fall**. The trail largely follows the road but is a lot more pleasurable than the equivalent stop-start sightseeing drive, and being shaded makes it a good hike on a hot day.

Drive or take the El Capitan shuttle to El Capitan Bridge, then walk east for a couple of hundred yards along a path beside Northside Drive. When you cross over to the north side and into the forest on the trail marked "Bridalveil Fall 4.1," El Capitan's North American Wall will be straight ahead, and you'll soon cross climbers' paths leading to El Cap's base. Continuing west with the road about fifty yards off to the left, the trail bridges Ribbon Creek which is dry in late summer but violent in spring when Ribbon Fall (just upstream) is in full flow.

Just past a view of Bridalveil Fall, you'll cross **Pohono Bridge** to the southern side of the Valley following a track that sticks close to the Merced River. You are now headed upstream with the river on your left. Don't bother crossing the road to see Fern and Moss springs, and instead press on to Bridalveil Meadow, keeping close to the road until you meet Wawona Road coming in from the right. After visiting Bridalveil Fall, pick up the wide path that heads east, parallel to Southside Drive. A sign announcing 5.5 miles to Curry Village marks the start of the only significant climb on the walk, which gradually ascends a moraine to reveal great treetop views across to El Cap. It is pleasant undulating walking for the next half-hour or so until you reach the "El Capitan 1.4" sign, where you'll turn left and follow a footpath north across Southside Drive. After wandering through young ponderosa pines you'll be back at El Capitan Bridge.

Paths along both sides of the Valley link up with the loop described here making it possible to form an **extended loop** from *Yosemite Lodge* or Curry Village of 11–12 miles.

H11 Inspiration Point

Difficulty Moderate
Distance 2.4 miles round trip
Estimated time 1hr 30min–2hr 30min
Elevation gain 600ft ascent
Season Mid-May to Oct when it is generally free of snow.
Trailhead location Map p.48, Tunnel View a mile and a half west of Bridalveil Fall.
Comments Shun the roadside viewpoint crowds for the peace of one of Yosemite's great vistas.

This short but taxing hike leads you away from the crowded viewpoint at Tunnel View and takes you to **Inspiration Point**, an even more magnificent spot for viewing Yosemite Valley, not least because you'll most likely be alone. This is where Ansel Adams came to shoot his famous "Clearing Winter Storm."

Inspiration Point was once easily accessed from the main road from Wawona to the Valley and there's still a disused asphalt track visible, but few people come this way now. Head up in the late afternoon, switchbacking steeply through manzanita, oak and conifer woods with plenty of glorious wayside viewpoints, making use of good photo ops to catch your breath. Cross the asphalt road and continue uphill for another ten minutes or so. Inspiration Point isn't marked, but the magnificent view through a clearing in the trees announces your arrival.

Hikes from Hetch Hetchy

There's really not a great deal to do at **Hetch Hetchy** except go hiking. Fortunately a couple of excellent hikes cross the O'Shaughnessy Dam and head along its northern shore to some fine waterfalls. They're at their best in spring, which is also a good time visit as the higher reaches of the Park are still under a mantle of snow.

H12 Wapama Falls

Difficulty Easy
Distance 5 miles round trip
Estimated time 2–3hr
Elevation gain 400ft ascent
Season Mid-April to Nov, but best in spring when the falls are in spate.
Trailhead location Map p.74, where Hetch Hetchy Road meets the O'Shaughnessy Dam.
Comments Great waterfall views for very little effort.

This is a relaxing trail in a quiet corner of the Park, following the north shore of Hetch Hetchy reservoir and ideal for accessing the foaming **Wapama Falls**. Low altitude and a northerly aspect ensure that the path is clear of snow early in the season, which coincides with the falls' best display from late April to June; it generally dries up by August.

Park your vehicle beside O'Shaughnessy Dam and cross its concrete curve, gazing across the reservoir at the hefty bell-shape of **Kolana Rock**. At the far end of the dam a short tunnel brings you to the trail, which flows mostly on level terrain just above the water. The hike is especially nice in the spring, when wildflowers are abundant, and for a few weeks **Tueeulala Falls** plunges down the cliff to the left of the trail, its veils of spray wafting onto the path until it dries up in mid-June. At all times keep an eye out for **rattlesnakes** that might be camouflaged in fallen leaves dappled by the shade of live oaks. Further on, **Wapama Falls** drops 1400ft from the Valley rim in two steps before pouring over rocks as a braided stream, all best seen from a couple of footbridges on the route.

After you've had your fill of the falls, either head back the way you came, or continue a further five miles to Rancheria Falls (Hike 13).

H13 Rancheria Falls

Difficulty Moderate
Distance 14.5 miles round trip
Estimated time 5–8hr
Elevation gain 800ft ascent
Season Mid-April to Nov, but best early in the season.
Trailhead location Map p.74, where Hetch Hetchy Road meets the O'Shaughnessy Dam.
Comments More effort than Hike 12 but rewarded by great scenery.

As an extension of Hike 12, this hike is similar in character but more arduous, and with a gorgeous springtime reward in the form of **Rancheria Falls**. From Wapama Falls, the trail climbs towards the base of **Hetch Hetchy Dome**, eventually reaching a magnificent viewpoint high above the water and directly opposite Kolana Rock. Here you can look back to the dam, and up the lake towards your goal (still an hour and a half ahead) where Rancheria Falls courses down over smooth rock, the flow disturbed by shelves, ledges and scattered rocks that get in the way. **Overnighters** can camp at the backcountry site beside the falls.

Hikes from the Tioga Road

The hikes in this section are listed in trailhead order from Crane Flat east to Tuolumne Meadows.

H14 El Capitan from Tamarack Flat

Difficulty Strenuous
Distance 16.5 miles round trip
Estimated time 7–10hr
Elevation gain 1240ft ascent on the way back
Season June–Oct
Trailhead location Map p.82, at *Tamarack Flat* campground, four miles east of Crane Flat.
Comments Hike to this little-visited summit without climbing The Nose.

While the summit of **El Capitan** is the goal of some of Yosemite's most spectacular and intense rock climbs, it is also accessible by trail from Tamarack Flat, three miles off Tioga Road. Begin hiking along a disused section of the Old Big Oak Flat Road at the eastern end of *Tamarack Flat* campground, crossing Cascade Creek after a couple of miles. Continue downhill for another half mile or so to a point where a log jam forces you left onto a narrower path which climbs steadily for almost three miles, following a ridge to the diminutive Ribbon Meadow. There are potential **campsites** where you cross Ribbon Creek, just before the rim of El Capitan Gully gives you your first really good Valley views. El Cap dominates the scene ahead, its sheer face topping out not with a plateau but with a surprisingly steep slope rising back from the lip to a domed summit. The trail skirts the top and continues east along the Valley rim, with just a few cairns marking the way down to the lip. Watch your footing as you head to the edge for tremendous views up the Valley towards Tenaya Canyon and Half Dome, and across to the face of Sentinel Rock and the knife-blade ridge of Mount Clark. Return the way you came.

H15 Harden Lake

Difficulty Easy
Distance 6 miles round trip
Estimated time 2–3hr
Elevation gain 270ft ascent
Season June–Oct
Trailhead location Map p.82, at *White Wolf* campground, 15 miles east of Crane Flat and 25 miles west of Tuolumne Meadows.
Comments One of Yosemite's finest wildflower walks.

What this hike lacks in scenic splendor it easily makes up for in the glorious profusion of wildflowers, good from late June to August but especially vibrant in July. Heading north on the gravel service road from *White Wolf*, follow signs for **Harden Lake**, which bring you alongside a tributary of the middle fork of the Tuolumne River where the banks shimmer with the blue, pink, purple and white of lilies and lupines. Elsewhere in the area the red and yellow flowers of columbine mix with the delicate pink of Lewis' monkey flower. The lake itself fills a pleasant enough forest clearing, and you've got the walk back to look forward to.

H16 Lukens Lake

Difficulty Easy
Distance 1.6 miles round trip
Estimated time 1hr
Elevation gain 200ft ascent
Season June–Oct
Trailhead location Map p.82, 17 miles east of Crane Flat and 23 miles west of Tuolumne Meadows.
Comments Meadows and a beautiful lake are an easy hike from White Wolf.

This popular walk is notable for its colorful display of delicate flowers, and also has the added benefit of a beautiful destination in the form of the serene **Lukens Lake**. Partly filled with photogenic semi-submerged logs, Lukens Lake is bounded at one end by meadows where lush growth creates a waist-high grassland thick with wildflowers. The path winds through red fir and white pine forest from a trailhead on Tioga Road, but is also accessible directly from *White Wolf* campground (see p.175) along a well-signposted track. Both camping and fires are prohibited here and even picnicking isn't always pleasant with the summertime menace of mosquitoes: bring repellant.

H17 Yosemite Falls from Yosemite Creek campground

Difficulty Strenuous
Distance 12 miles round trip
Estimated time 5–7hr
Elevation gain 700ft ascent on the way back
Season June–Oct
Trailhead location Map p.82, at *Yosemite Creek* campground, 15 miles east of Crane Flat then five miles down a dirt road.
Comments An unusual (and gentler than normal) approach to a popular destination.

The top of **Yosemite Falls** is a justly popular hiking destination from Yosemite Valley, but you can cut out much of the ascent by using this alternate approach from *Yosemite Creek* campground, five miles off Tioga Road. A longer hike, but on primarily gentle terrain, it follows Yosemite Creek as it cuts its way first through forest, then down small granite canyons choked with rocks.

The path starts beside a trail-junction sign by the campground's entrance, and heads south, slowly descending through woods until reaching a section where Yosemite Creek is confined between high banks; take a few minutes to watch smooth sheets of water break up over cascades then calm themselves in deep blue pools. Broad sandy areas alternate with thicker forest and offer a few potential **campsites** along the way as you cross Blue Jay Creek and eventually pass a trail junction for Eagle Peak. Half a mile on you'll encounter exhausted hikers ascending the Upper Yosemite Fall trail. Join them for the final couple of hundred yards to the falls, best viewed from a wonderful viewpoint (see Hike 8). There are potential side trips to **Yosemite Point** and **Eagle Peak** before returning the way you came.

H18 North Dome from Porcupine Creek

Difficulty Moderate
Distance 9 miles round trip
Estimated time 4–6hr
Elevation gain 650ft ascent on the way back
Season June–Oct
Trailhead location Map p.82, 25 miles east of Crane Flat and 15 miles west of Tuolumne Meadows.
Comments Great Valley views from this little-visited dome.

It is almost all downhill from Tioga Road to the top of North Dome, giving this hike the unusual distinction of approaching a Valley viewpoint from above. From the Porcupine Creek trailhead, you'll plunge into pine and fir forest broken up by occasional meadows. Follow signs for North Dome and start climbing as the forest begins to open out to reveal expansive vistas. A little over an hour from the start a sign points along a 500-yard spur trail to **Indian Rock**, a slender rock arch perhaps thirty of forty feet across; not much by Utah standards, but an unusual feature in granite. Return to the track and drop steeply along Indian Ridge with Basket Dome off to the left, until you reach **North Dome**. Here, perched high above the Royal Arches and Washington Column, you find yourself face to face with the enormous bulk of Half Dome. Clouds Rest, too, is prominent, and the daily activity of Curry and Yosemite villages goes on below, with only the distant sounds of shuttle buses to disturb the tranquility.

This can be turned into an overnight hike by **camping** at the low saddle behind North Dome, though finding water can be a problem once the last of the snow has melted.

H19 May Lake

Difficulty Easy
Distance 2.5 miles round trip
Estimated time 1hr
Elevation gain 400ft ascent
Season June–Oct
Trailhead location Map p.82, 2 miles north of Tioga Road some 27 miles east of Crane Flat and 15 miles west of Tuolumne Meadows.
Comments The prettiness of May Lake is easily surpassed by the views from the summit of Mount Hoffmann.

This short hike is one of the most popular outside the Valley, chiefly for its destination, the gorgeous crystal-clear May Lake, huddled in the shadow of looming Mount Hoffmann, and home to the most accessible of the High Sierra Camps (HSC: see p.174).

From the trailhead, two miles north of Tioga Road, it is a short but fairly steep hike through woods and open granite-boulder fields with great views down Tenaya Canyon towards Clouds Rest and the back of Half Dome. As the trail levels out you'll see **May Lake**, reached through the scattered tents of a camping area. Nearby, prime lakeside positions are occupied by the white tent cabins of the HSC, which uses lake water for its supply; swimming is not allowed, but you're free to fish.

Anyone keen to see just why the summit of **Mount Hoffmann** was one of John Muir's favorite spots in the Park can continue along a three-mile track to the top.

H20 Clouds Rest from Tenaya Lake

Difficulty Strenuous
Distance 14.5 miles round trip
Estimated time 7–10hr
Elevation gain 1800ft ascent
Season June–Oct
Trailhead location Map p.82, 31 miles east of Crane Flat and 9 miles west of Tuolumne Meadows.
Comments Great views of Half Dome and the Cathedral Range.

The easiest and most popular approach to **Clouds Rest** is from Tenaya Lake; it is still a strenuous undertaking but involves only a third of the ascent you'd have to negotiate if starting in the Valley.

From the trailhead at the western end of Tenaya Lake you first cross a small creek and then turn south through meadows before beginning to climb to the rim of **Tenaya Canyon**. Follow Clouds Rest signs past a junction that leads to the Sunrise Lakes HSC, and drop down to a little meadow near the foot of Sunrise Peak. The small creek at the lowest point is your last chance for water. Ascend until you pass another trail junction, then continue through white pine as the knife-edge peak of Clouds Rest comes into view. At the base of the summit ridge a poorly signed path marked by cairns on bare rock rises to the top. Alternatively follow the horse trail that skirts the ridge on the southern side, then join a better-marked track from the western end of the ridge. Either way, be sure to watch your footing around the summit. The views from Clouds Rest, the highest peak visible from Yosemite Valley, are breathtaking; Half Dome dominates to the west, the Cathedral Range bristles to the east, and below you a wave of smooth granite sweeps down to the base of Tenaya Canyon.

H21 Polly Dome Lakes

Difficulty Easy
Distance 5 miles round trip
Estimated time 2–3hr
Elevation gain 500ft ascent
Season Late June–Oct
Trailhead location Map p.82, 32 miles east of Crane Flat and 8 miles west of Tuolumne Meadows.
Comments Pleasant hike with evidence of glacial action underfoot.

From a trailhead midway along the north side of Tenaya Lake, this gentle and little used track follows **Murphy Creek** through lodgepole pine forest to its source at **Polly Dome Lakes**. Polly Dome itself rises above, and there's good camping all about. Much of the second half of the hike is across rock slabs with abundant evidence of glacial action. The area is littered with erratics, and the polished surface is punctuated by "percussion marks" where boulders embedded in the base of the glacier have gouged their signature of multiple matching divots in the rock.

H22 Tenaya Lake circuit

Difficulty Easy
Distance 3 miles round trip
Estimated time 1hr–1hr 30min
Elevation gain 50ft ascent
Season June–Oct; Aug and early Sept are warmest for a dip.
Trailhead location Map p.82, 33 miles east of Crane Flat and 7 miles west of Tuolumne Meadows.
Comments Great views all round and even a beach.

One of the easiest hikes along Tioga Road is this circuit of **Tenaya Lake**, which mostly stays out of the trees and affords open vistas of granite domes the whole way. It starts at the picnic area at the eastern end of Tenaya Lake where there is access to a lovely beach that's popular for sunbathing in summer, though the water is too cold for most adults; kids, however, seem immune to the temperature.

The hike loops around the southern side of Tenaya Lake staying pretty close to the water's edge. In summer, you'll traverse fields of wildflowers, and the views across the water to the climbers' playground of Stately Pleasure Dome are an added highlight. The route rejoins Tioga Road at the major trailhead at Tenaya Lake's western end, from where you can either retrace your steps or complete the lake circuit by hiking along the road.

The hike can be accessed from Tuolumne Meadows by riding the free Tuolumne Meadows shuttle (see p.26), and if you time your walk right, riding the shuttle back from the far end thereby avoiding the road section.

Hikes from Tuolumne Meadows

The hikes in this section are listed in sequence moving west to east.

H23 Pothole Dome

Difficulty Easy
Distance 0.5 miles round trip
Estimated time 40min–1hr
Elevation gain 200ft ascent
Season June–Oct
Trailhead location Map p.26, 38 miles east of Crane Flat and 2 miles west of Tuolumne Meadows.
Comments A perfect, photogenic sunset hike.

This short but fairly steep walk ascends **Pothole Dome**, which marks the western limit of Tuolumne Meadows. The relatively small dome commands great views of the Meadows, Cathedral Range and virtually all of the High Sierra, seen to best effect in the hour before sunset. A ten-minute walk around the base of the dome is followed by a short, stiff scramble up bare granite: wear the stickiest shoes you have. The more-or-less level summit is a lesson in glaciation. The rock here is **porphyritic granite**, its fine granular structure embedded with feldspar crystals an inch or two long. As glaciers ground over the rock, it was planed smooth leaving a beautiful mosaic that shimmers in the low light. Notice, too, the glacial erratics deposited on the summit, now elegantly juxtaposed with stunted pines.

▲ Glacial erratics on Pothole Dome

H24 Cathedral Lakes

Difficulty Moderate
Distance 8 miles round trip
Estimated time 3–5hr
Elevation gain 1000ft ascent
Season June–Oct
Trailhead location Map p.82, 39 miles east of Crane Flat and 1 mile west of Tuolumne Meadows.
Comments A justly popular hike with views of Cathedral Peak from several angles.

A candidate for the best Tuolumne day hike, this route follows several miles of the JMT as far as **Cathedral Lakes**, a pair of gorgeous tarns in open alpine country with long views to a serrated skyline.

From the trailhead just west of the Tuolumne Meadows visitor center, the path climbs moderately steeply through lodgepole forest and small meadows. The blunt end of Cathedral Peak seen from this early section of the trail is barely recognizable as the same spiky two-pronged mountain you'll see further on. Its aspect changes as you continue through rolling woods to a junction at three miles. Here, a half-mile side trail leads to **Lower Cathedral Lake**, a divine spot lodged in a cirque now partly filled with lush meadows and split by a ridge of hard rock polished smooth by ancient glaciers. Looking back the way you came, the twin spires of **Cathedral Peak** catch the afternoon light beautifully and, on still days, may be reflected in the lake's waters.

Return to the JMT, turn right and continue for half a mile to reach **Upper Cathedral Lake** at 9585ft. Here, there's a more open feel though you are still ringed by mountains: the truncated ridge of Tressider Peak to the south, Echo Peaks rising up to the east, and Cathedral Peak always drawing your eye to the northeast.

There's great **camping** at both Lower and Upper Cathedral lakes. Return the way you came.

H25 Soda Springs and Parsons Lodge

Difficulty Easy
Distance 4 mile loop
Estimated time 2hr
Elevation gain 50ft ascent
Season June–Oct
Trailhead location Map p.86, Tuolumne Meadows visitor center.
Comments Visit the highlights of Tuolumne Meadows on this easy loop hike.

This is an easy meander around some of Tuolumne Meadows' best and most accessible features. Start from the visitor center and walk about 300 yards east along Tioga Road before turning left on a track across the meadow which was once part of the original Tioga Road. While it is a pleasant walk at any time, in June and July the wildflower display along here is superb – look out for penstemon, shooting stars, yellow goldenrod and white pussytoes. On the meadows' far side, you cross the Tuolumne River beside a small path leading up to **Soda Springs** and **Parsons Lodge** (see p.83). From here, take the wide path following signs for Tuolumne Meadows stables and the Lembert Dome parking lot; it is essentially a nature trail, lined with panels explaining flora, fauna, glaciation and a little history. An alternative route from Soda Springs picks up a narrow unmarked riverside trail winding upstream past beautiful small rapids and pools. The two routes meet close to the base of Lembert Dome from where you can walk to the visitor center along the road, or ride the shuttle bus, saving a two-mile walk.

H26 Elizabeth Lake

Difficulty Moderate
Distance 4.8 miles round trip
Estimated time 3–5hr
Elevation gain 900ft ascent
Season June–Oct
Trailhead location Map p.86, at the *Tuolumne Meadows* campground.
Comments Steep granite slopes hem in this pretty lake.

One of the more popular day hikes around Tuolumne Meadows, this trail culminates where the idyllic Elizabeth Lake nestles in a hollow scooped out by an ancient glacier, surrounded by pine trees.

The trailhead is at the back of the *Tuolumne Meadows* campground, most easily found using a free campground map from the kiosk near the entrance. The trail soon crosses the JMT and climbs steadily through forest, steeply at first and then more gradually alongside Unicorn Creek. Shortly after the track bridges Unicorn Creek you arrive at the glistening waters of **Elizabeth Lake**, perhaps not quite as exquisite as Cathedral Lakes (Hike 24), but still a gorgeous spot surrounded by steep craggy mountains and ringed by paths which provide access to spots ideal for fishing, a picnic, or, for the brave, a swim. There's no camping at the lake, and you'll have to return by the same route.

H27 Lyell Canyon

Difficulty Easy
Distance 11 miles round trip
Estimated time 4–5hr
Elevation gain 100ft ascent
Season June–Oct
Trailhead location Map p.86, *Tuolumne Meadows* campground.
Comments Follow the John Muir Trail as far as you can manage.

This long but gentle and virtually level walk follows the John Muir and Pacific Crest trails (see box, p.143) through the somewhat mis-titled **Lyell Canyon**, a quarter-mile-wide valley flanked by wooded slopes rising a couple of thousand feet on either side. There's no real destination, so if you don't fancy hiking the full eleven miles, just go as far as you please then retrace your steps.

Pick up the JMT at the eastern end of the *Tuolumne Meadows* campground where you immediately start following the **Lyell Fork** of the Tuolumne River, climbing very slightly as you pull out of the forest and into more open country. The river courses hurriedly amid fields thick with wildflowers in early summer but by September is reduced to a steady trickle through grasses burned golden by the high-country sun. Swimming in the river is particularly nice (if cold) in late summer, and anytime of year there is decent wildlife spotting for anyone with patience. The broad-shouldered Mammoth Peak is initially almost directly ahead, and as the trail swings to the south you get distant views to some of Yosemite's highest peaks; in fact, the further you go, the better the mountain scenery.

> Anyone with an interest in **scrambling** (see p.147) might fancy an assault on the needle summit of **Unicorn Peak**, a round trip of about three hours from Elizabeth Lake (Hike 26). Just use a little common sense and keep heading uphill until you can go no further. From the top there are great views of Cockscomb, Cathedral Peak, Echo Peak and the end of Matthes Crest.

H28 Dog Lake

Difficulty Easy
Distance 3.2 miles round trip
Estimated time 1hr 30min–2hr 30min
Elevation gain 600ft ascent
Season June–Oct
Trailhead location Map p.86, Lembert Dome parking area.
Comments Meadows, mountain views and a great destination for a picnic lunch. Can be easily combined with Hike 29 (4.5 miles total; 2hr 30min–4hr; 900ft ascent).

This relatively easy there-and-back hike ends at the small, attractive **Dog Lake**, where you might linger for a picnic lunch, an afternoon with a book, or maybe a bracing swim.

From the Lembert Dome parking area follow a trail through trees across a flat patch of polished granite and keep heading right at a series of trail junctions. The climb then turns steep, but only for a mile or so, until you fork left for an easy stroll to Dog Lake. The right fork goes to the summit of Lembert Dome (Hike 29). Find a spot to relax amid the lodgepole pines and small patches of meadow, or continue right around the lake for good views back to the Cathedral Range. The circumnavigation is most easily done in late summer when it is drier underfoot.

H29 Lembert Dome

Difficulty Moderate
Distance 3.7 miles round trip
Estimated time 2–3hr
Elevation gain 850ft ascent
Season June–Oct
Trailhead location Map p.86, Lembert Dome parking area.
Comments Hike up the back of Tuolumne's most prominent dome.

As the most prominent feature on the Meadows' perimeter, **Lembert Dome** has an immediate lure – the expansive views from the summit, with interesting glacial features found there adding to its attraction.

Follow Hike 28 as far as the trail junction where the Dog Lake path bears left. At this point head right, initially steeply but with the gradient easing until you reach the northeast corner of Lembert Dome. Here a series of cairns mark the fairly steep route across bare rock to the summit. After exploring the exposed stunted pines, glacial erratics and long views across Tuolumne Meadows and up Lyell Canyon, return to the trail and turn right for the descent to Tioga Road. Cross the road to the wilderness center where you can pick up a track running west and back to your starting point.

H30 Young Lakes

Difficulty Strenuous
Distance 13.5 miles round trip
Estimated time 7–10hr
Elevation gain 1500ft ascent
Season June–Oct
Trailhead location Map p.86, Lembert Dome parking area.
Comments An excellent overnight camping destination from Tuolumne.

At the end of this hike, the three beautiful **Young Lakes** make a suitable reward for your efforts, as do the spectacular vistas of the Cathedral Range en route. From the Lembert Dome parking area follow signs for Dog Lake (Hike 28) for the first mile and a half. At a trail junction, follow the Young

Lakes sign to some wide-open meadows bordered to the east by Mount Dana and Mount Gibbs. After a long and steady climb over a forest ridge and past a granite dome you emerge on a hillside studded with stunted trees and backed by the gap-toothed Ragged Ridge. Here you get a grandstand view back across Tuolumne Meadows to the whole of the **Cathedral Range**. Nowhere else do you get such an incredible panorama for relatively little effort. Mount Lyell and its acolytes stand above everything else at the left and scanning right you can pick out Unicorn Peak, Echo Peak, Cathedral Peak, Fairview Dome and the distant Mount Hoffmann.

After a short ascent the trail descends for a while and then climbs again up forested moraine to the first of the lakes, with barren rocky ridges all around. Take a break beside the water's edge before exploring higher up (using informal and unsigned trails) where two smaller lakes nestle in marshy meadows. Though an excellent day hike, Young Lakes also makes a great backpacking destination with ideal lakeside **camping**.

H31 Glen Aulin

Difficulty Moderate
Distance 11 miles round trip
Estimated time 6–8hr
Elevation gain 600ft ascent on the way back
Season June–Oct
Trailhead location Map p.86, Lembert Dome parking area.
Comments Hike alongside the tumbling Tuolumne River all the way.

This there-and-back hike to Glen Aulin is one of Tuolumne's finest, following the Tuolumne River all the way as it cascades its way to a beautifully situated High Sierra Camp and campground.

From the trailhead at Lembert Dome, hike along the broad, flat path to Soda Springs then follow signs for Glen Aulin along a good track that's made less pleasant by the evidence of all the mule traffic headed for the HSC. With lodgepole pines all about, the trail begins to dip slowly, the trees often pulling back to reveal fabulous views of the surrounding mountains. The river, too, is wonderfully picturesque all the way. Frenetic during the snowmelt in early summer, the water courses down the canyon over house-sized boulders, slithers over slickrock and eases into deep, bottle-green pools lined with polished river stones. By autumn the torrent subsides, making the pools between the cataracts calm enough for bathing. The classic photo stop is at **Tuolumne Falls**, the most vertical drop along this stretch, and there are more cascades as you continue further downstream with the descending trail switchbacking to **White Cascade** and the HSC. Press on a few hundred yards downstream to **Glen Aulin** itself where shallows provide access to a deep pool below a marvelously sculpted rock chute. Here you can rest a while before embarking on the long uphill hike back.

H32 Waterwheel Falls

Difficulty Very strenuous
Distance 17.5 miles round trip
Estimated time 8–12hr
Elevation gain 2100ft ascent
Season June–Oct, but best in June and early July.
Trailhead location Map p.86, Lembert Dome parking area.
Comments A big day out with waterfalls galore.

This hike is an extension of Hike 30, continuing past Glen Aulin, following the Tuolumne River as far as Waterwheel Falls. Beyond Glen Aulin the trail passes

Donohue Pass

The **John Muir Trail** runs for twelve miles through **Lyell Canyon** (Hike 27) to the 11,000ft **Donohue Pass**, where it leaves the Park. Robust hikers can make it from Tuolumne to Donohue Pass and back in a day climbing 2000ft in the last three miles through some stunning alpine scenery with views of the Park's highest mountain, Mount Lyell, and its attendant glacier. Around nine miles from Tuolumne Meadows you reach Lyell Base Camp (9040ft), a popular waystation for John Muir Trailers and a base for assaults on Mount Lyell and Mount McLure. Here the valley loses its bottom and the stream you've been following disappears into a rocky chasm heard but unseen from the trail which cuts away to the right. Climb through woods to about 10,000ft where Mount Lyell comes into view and continue across more alpine country to Donohue Pass.

a two-mile-long almost unbroken series of cascades officially called **California Fall**, **LeConte Fall** and Waterwheel Falls. In reality, each fall tumbles into another with little to distinguish where one ends and another begins. As the path winds down alongside, you get occasional views before **Waterwheel Falls** themselves, where a couple of midstream rocks on a smooth chute throw the snowmelt torrent up twenty feet into the air like a pair of paddle-wheels.

Hikes from Tioga Pass

The hikes in this section are listed in trailhead order from Tuolumne Meadows east towards Tioga Pass and Lee Vining. In addition to these hikes inside the Park we have covered the excellent "Saddlebag Lake and 20 Lakes Basin" hike which is just outside the Park, on p.89.

H33 Mono Pass

Difficulty Moderate
Distance 8 miles round trip
Estimated time 4–6hr
Elevation gain 1000ft ascent
Season June–Oct
Trailhead location Map p.82, 4.5 miles east of Tuolumne Meadows and 1.5 miles west of Tioga Pass.
Comments Trade in granite and waterfalls for old miners' shacks and red rocks.

Some old miners' cabins, delightful alpine tarns and mountain scenery geologically distinct from most of the Park make this an interesting day hike. There are opportunities for camping in Inyo National Forest just over **Mono Pass**, an area with a beautiful high-country meadow right on the Sierra crest, overlooked not by granite but by the iron-rich red rocks of Mount Gibbs and Mount Lewis which lured late nineteenth-century miners here.

The hike starts six miles east of the Tuolumne Meadows store, and climbs steadily pretty much all the way, alternately passing through meadows and lodgepole forest. After three miles you'll reach the treeline and then break out into open country before closing in on the 10,600ft Mono Pass. Several small lakes mark the pass and make a pleasant lunch spot. Mine hounds should retrace their steps for a couple of hundred yards and head south for ten minutes along an unmarked path. This drops briefly then climbs over a ridge to reach what remains of the **Golden Crown Mine**, just five primitive and strikingly weathered but well-preserved cabins.

H34 Gaylor Lakes and the Great Sierra Mine

Difficulty Moderate
Distance 3 miles round trip
Estimated time 2–3hr
Elevation gain 500ft ascent
Season June–Oct
Trailhead location Map p.88, right at Tioga Pass, 6 miles east of Tuolumne Meadows.
Comments The easiest hike that gets you above 10,000ft.

A couple of pretty alpine lakes in open country above the treeline and the opportunity to explore some meager silver-mine workings make this a particularly rewarding short walk. The lakes can be fished, but there is no camping in this area.

From the trailhead right beside the Tioga Pass entrance station, the track is initially quite steep, and unless you're accustomed to being at 10,000ft you'll quickly become breathless. At the crest of a blunt ridge there are views back to the scattered pools in Dana Meadows, and north beyond Granite Lake to the Sierra crest. The path then drops down into the shallow **Gaylor Lakes** basin, almost entirely filled by the lower Gaylor Lake. Bear right around the lake and start climbing gently towards the upper of Gaylor Lakes, with Gaylor Peak on your right. After skirting the left side of this lake, climb a ridge to reach the ruins of a stone cabin, virtually all that remains of the **Great Sierra Mine**. A hundred yards on, just on the Park boundary, you'll find a couple more dilapidated stone huts and the vertical shaft that briefly sustained the mine.

Hikes from Glacier Point Road

The hikes in this section are listed in trailhead order from Chinquapin east to Glacier Point.

H35 McGurk Meadow

Difficulty Easy
Distance 1.6 miles round trip
Estimated time 1hr
Elevation gain 150ft ascent on the way back
Season Mid-May to Oct
Trailhead location Map p.92, 9 miles east of Chinquapin and 7 miles southwest of Glacier Point.
Comments Visit a pretty meadow and a slice of old Yosemite.

McGurk Meadow makes a peaceful destination for this stroll through lodgepole pine forest. The trail starts almost opposite the entrance to *Bridalveil Creek* campground, and visitors staying there can walk straight from their site. Otherwise, park a couple of hundred yards east of the trailhead at a small turnout, then head into the forest. Descend gently until you notice a tumbledown summer sheepherders' cabin. Wildflower-filled McGurk Meadow is just beyond.

H36 Ostrander Lake

Difficulty Strenuous
Distance 12.6 miles round trip
Estimated time 5–7hr
Elevation gain 1600ft ascent
Season Mid-May to Oct
Trailhead location Map p.92, 9 miles east of Chinquapin and 7 miles southwest of Glacier Point.
Comments A rugged, stone, lakeside lodge makes a suitable destination.

Best known as a winter cross-country skiing destination, **Ostrander Lake** makes an equally good summer goal, either as a day hike or to **camp** near the waterside Ostrander Lake Ski Hut, which is managed by the Sierra Club. Originally known as Pohono Lake, Ostrander Lake feeds Bridalveil Creek, which enters the Valley as Bridalveil Fall (or Pohono). Whatever you call it, it is a fine spot nestled in a hollow with the rocky exfoliating scarp of Horse Ridge on the far side.

From the trailhead on Glacier Point Road, about a mile east of *Bridalveil Creek* campground, the path is initially flat as it winds through lodgepole forest burned in 1987 and where the saplings are already over six feet high. After three miles the trail begins a steady climb which continues until just before the lake. Occasionally you emerge from the forest onto the bare rock slopes that run down from Horizon Ridge, the route waymarked by small cairns. As you crest the ridge, breaks in the trees allow views of Half Dome, the Clark Range and Mount Starr King. A final descent brings you to the lake and **Ostrander Lake Ski Hut** (for winter bookings see p.158) built in rustic style with heavy beams and chunky rock, and named after Harvey Ostrander, a sheepman who had a cabin near Bridalveil Fall. The hut was constructed in 1940 by the Civilian Conservation Corps at a time when it was hoped to turn Yosemite into a premier ski resort.

The Ostrander Lake trail can also be accessed from the southern end of *Bridalveil Creek* campground: head towards the horse camp and just before you cross Bridalveil Creek turn right. After about a mile and a half a trail bears left to link up with the Ostrander Lake Trail.

H37 Taft Point and the Fissures

Difficulty Easy
Distance 2.2 miles round trip
Estimated time 1hr
Elevation gain 250ft ascent on the way back
Season Mid-May to Oct
Trailhead location Map p.95, 14 miles east of Chinquapin and 2 miles southwest of Glacier Point.
Comments Stand astride a fissure with hundreds of feet of air between your legs. This hike can be easily combined with Hike 38 (5 miles, 2–3hr; 600ft ascent) using a couple of miles of the Pohono Trail.

▲ Great Sierra Mine near Tioga Pass

For such an easily accessible and wonderfully scenic spot overlooking the Valley, Taft Point is surprisingly little visited; all the more reason to hike this trail.

From the Sentinel Dome parking area the dusty and undulating path heads west across a meadow, descending all the while. As you enter a patch of forest you cross a small creek where wildflowers flourish in the damp margins, then descend more steeply until you emerge from the trees just before Taft Point: the **fissures** are just to the right, the prow of **Taft Point** itself just beyond. Unlike crowded Glacier Point with its walkways and barriers, Taft Point has just a flimsy railing in one spot to protect you from the vertiginous drops all around. A hundred yards to the right, the granite edges have been deeply incised to form the **Taft Point Fissures**, narrow thirty-foot slices carved out of the Valley rim where you can stand astride a gap with hundreds of feet of air between your legs.

You can't see Half Dome from Taft Point, but that is more than compensated for by the view of the monstrous face of El Capitan, the staircase of the Three Brothers, and the slender white streak of Upper Yosemite Fall.

H38 Sentinel Dome

Difficulty Easy
Distance 2.2 miles round trip
Estimated time 1hr
Elevation gain 250ft ascent on the way back
Season Mid-May to Oct
Trailhead location Map p.95, 14 miles east of Chinquapin and 2 miles southwest of Glacier Point.
Comments It's a pity the famed tree has gone, but great Half Dome views anyway.

The most popular hike for Glacier Point visitors is to the gleaming granite scalp of **Sentinel Dome**; the Valley floor isn't visible from the summit, but just about everything else is. Sentinel Dome is directly accessible from the Glacier Point parking lot, but most people set off from a trailhead two miles back along Glacier Point Road. From here, the track crosses sandy ground with little shade; bring plenty of water as you won't find any at the trailhead. Sentinel Dome becomes visible on the left and the trail gradually curls around towards it, following waymarkers and getting progressively steeper. The final push to the summit takes you up the east side, the lowest angled (but still steep) approach.

Now you're a thousand feet higher than Glacier Point and views extend to the Park boundary in almost every direction, with Half Dome dominant to the east. The summit is crowned by what's left of a famous **Jeffrey pine**. Well known from Ansel Adams' atmospheric 1940 image prosaically titled "Jeffrey Pine – Sentinel Dome," the tree still bore cones until the mid-1970s when a drought and old age finally killed it off. Its skeletal form stood until its root system finally collapsed in 2003, leaving the fallen spindly trunk gradually succumbing to the elements.

H39 Panorama Trail

Difficulty Moderate
Distance 9 miles round trip
Estimated time 6–8hr
Elevation gain 800ft ascent, 4000ft descent
Season Mid-May to Oct
Trailhead location Map p.95, at Glacier Point.
Comments Catch the bus to Glacier Point then hike back along this trail.

One of Yosemite's oldest routes, the **Panorama Trail** passes the top of the otherwise inaccessible **Illilouette Fall**, skirting above the Panorama Cliff with its views down towards Glacier Point Apron and Happy Isles.

The Panorama Trail links Glacier Point with the top of Nevada Fall, and can either be tackled as a there-and-back trek from Glacier Point, or combined (as we've done here) with the John Muir Trail to make a one-way hike from Glacier Point to the Happy Isles trailhead in the Valley. Either ride the Glacier Point Hikers Bus to Glacier Point, or go for a very strenuous day hiking up the Four-Mile Trail (Hike 9) and down the Panorama Trail.

Just south of the gift and snack store at Glacier Point, a large sign announces the start of the several hiking routes. Follow directions for the Panorama Trail and start a two-mile-long descent to Illilouette Creek. Forest burned in 1987 provides little shade, but has regrown a hardy understory of chinquapin (with its distinctive chestnut-like fruit) that provides ideal cover for California blue grouse. Beyond the junction with the trail to Mono Meadow, switchback down into the forest, keeping an eye out for a short path on the left which leads to one of the only places with a good view of Illilouette Fall. The route soon crosses Illilouette Creek near some cascades and rock chutes just above the fall. It is a perfect spot for a break, but camping is not allowed.

Climbing steeply away from the fall, the track passes the unsigned but fairly obvious Panorama Point and continues up until **Nevada Fall** comes into view. After a trail junction you descend on switchbacks to meet the JMT. Before turning left to head down to the Valley, it's worth detouring right a quarter of a mile to the top of Nevada Fall.

H40 Pohono Trail

Difficulty Strenuous
Distance 13.8 miles round trip
Estimated time 5–8hr
Elevation gain 2800ft ascent
Season May–Oct
Trailhead location Map p.95, at Glacier Point.
Comments Infrequently hiked trail past several great Valley views.

The **Pohono Trail** ties together all the viewpoints along the south rim of the Valley, emerging from the forest periodically for magnificent vistas, each one significantly different from the last. Often tackled as part of a longer backpacking trip (see Hike 44), the Pohono Trail can be done in a day, either combining it with the Four-Mile Trail to form a very strenuous loop or using the Glacier Point hikers bus for one leg of the journey. Neither the starting nor finishing points are close to where you're likely to be staying, so transport considerations are paramount.

From Glacier Point, signs guide you onto the Pohono Trail, which initially ascends through forest then skirts the north side of Sentinel Dome, seen on the left. Occasionally views can be glimpsed through the trees, but none prepare you for **Taft Point** and its fissured fringes (see Hike 37). For the next couple of miles you drop down to **Bridalveil Creek**, a good spot to take a break, bathe and refill water bottles. Late in the season many creeks dry up, so this may be your last decent supply. Climbing out of the watershed, ignore the trail cutting south to *Bridalveil Creek* campground, and continue back to the Valley rim at **Dewey Point**, distinguished by several isolated rocky viewpoints accessible with a little easy scrambling. The end of the trail at Wawona Tunnel is visible below and to the left, still over four miles away. Press on to nearby **Crocker Point**, where you can look directly across to the top of El Cap, and down on

Bridalveil Fall. **Stanford Point**, another half-mile on, offers a slightly different perspective before you begin the final forested descent. The last viewpoint is **Inspiration Point** (see Hike 11) from where it is a mile down to the Tunnel View parking area.

Hikes from Wawona and Mariposa Grove

The hikes in this section are listed north to south following Wawona Road. (For details on the two- to three-hour hike from Mariposa Grove back to Wawona, see p.101).

H41 Alder Creek

Difficulty Moderate
Distance 12 miles round trip
Estimated time 5–7hr
Elevation gain 1700ft ascent
Season April–Nov
Trailhead location Map p.92, on Chilnualna Fall Road.
Comments Solitude and cascading water are your rewards here.

Alder Creek Trail faces south and is mostly at low elevation, so it sheds its layer of snow early in the season making it perfect for springtime hikers, especially those keen to catch the first of the wildflowers. At any time of year it is a lovely but little-used path gradually climbing a forested ridge to a **sixty-foot fall on Alder Creek**.

The route starts on Chilnualna Fall Road and follows a former railbed used for extracting timber from the area's enormous trees. This is initially fairly open country with long views to distant ridges, but as the trail ascends the forest gradually hems you in. After almost three miles the track meets a side path down to Wawona Road, but the Alder Creek Trail continues uphill, crosses into the Alder Creek watershed and finally reaches the falls themselves. This is a great place to relax, and makes a good **camping** spot if you're thinking of exploring the area further.

H42 Chilnualna Fall

Difficulty Moderate
Distance 8.2 miles round trip
Estimated time 4–6hr
Elevation gain 2200ft ascent
Season Mid-May to Oct
Trailhead location Map p.92, on Chilnualna Fall Road.
Comments Stiff but rewarding hike; avoid the midday sun.

South-facing and at low elevation, the Chilnualna Fall trail is perfect in early spring and fall. Though it gets quite hot on summer days, you can cool off in deep pools along Chilnualna Creek.

The route starts 1.8 miles along Chilnualna Fall Road: if you hit a gravel road you've gone too far. The first few hundred yards of ascent is among granite boulders alongside roaring cascades, where the water continues to carve out channels and hollows in the rock. Moving west away from the river you continue ascending through manzanita, deer brush and bear clover, and return briefly to the river before again looping west to a point with long views down to Wawona and across the valley to Mariposa Grove. All along the way, wildflowers bloom throughout spring and early summer. Finally the trail rejoins the creek at the top of **Chilnualna Fall**, an intimidating spot where snowmelt gathered in the high country thunders down into the narrow chasm below your feet. Catch it in early spring when the spray clings onto the walls in an organ pipe accumulation of icicles.

Take a break here, but don't turn back yet. Instead, continue upstream to yet more tumbling cataracts; use caution where the spray coats the slick riverside rock, making it very slippery. Return the way you came.

H43 Wawona Meadow Loop

Difficulty Easy
Distance 3.5 miles round trip
Estimated time 1–2hr
Elevation gain 200ft ascent
Season March–Dec, but best for wildflowers April–June.
Trailhead location Map p.97, at the *Wawona Hotel*.
Comments Best for wildlife and wildflowers around the fringes of Wawona's golf course.

This circuit of **Wawona Meadow** is the easiest of the walks around Wawona, and is consequently popular: you'll be sharing it with cyclists, horses and even Wawona dog walkers. It is mainly of interest for the plethora of wildflowers bursting forth in April, May and June.

From the *Wawona Hotel*, cross Wawona Road and follow the paved footpath through the golf course to a small parking area. The road straight ahead is the Chowchilla Mountain Road, first pushed through to Wawona in 1856 as a toll trail from Mariposa to Yosemite Valley. Four years later, Galen Clark developed it into a stage road to lure coaches to his hotel at Clark's Station (now Wawona). Don't follow Chowchilla Mountain Road, but instead turn left and follow the loop trail with the Wawona golf course on the left. This soon gives way to meadows as the route follows a fire road through ponderosa pine and incense cedar. Keep an eye out for wildlife, especially mule deer who favor the forest margin.

After almost circumnavigating the meadow, the trail meets Wawona Road, which you'll cross to return to the *Wawona Hotel*.

5

Backcountry hiking and camping

There's no denying the appeal of spending the night under the open skies with the last rays of sun glinting off the granite domes and a pearlescent alpenglow silhouetting the tall pines. Add in a hearty meal hard-earned after a day hiking up past thunderous waterfalls and you have a recipe for a magical experience. By camping out you'll also open up the majority of Yosemite's **backcountry**, essentially anywhere more than a mile from a road. The seven detailed backcountry itineraries that follow cover some of the most popular overnight trials and, with the accompanying advice, will give you all the grounding you need for a lifetime of exploring the rest ofYosemite's eight hundred miles of trail.

Much of the backcountry is pristine with very little evidence of human impact. The exceptions are **Little Yosemite Valley**, at the top of Merced Canyon, which sees almost a quarter of all wilderness travelers, and the five **High Sierra Camps** (HSCs: see p.174), semi-permanent clusters of frame tents designed to cater to those who don't relish lugging a tent and cooking gear. All six places have adjacent primitive campgrounds (free) with pit toilets, bear boxes and a water source.

Before heading out on your selected overnight hike, be sure to obtain a **wilderness permit** (see p.137). Hikers leaving from the Valley, or using one of the hikers buses to get to the start of the trail must park their vehicles in the **backpackers parking area** between Curry Village and Happy Isles: you receive a dashboard parking permit when you get your wilderness permit. In Tuolumne Meadows, backpackers need to park beside the wilderness center, and should note that vehicles are not allowed to remain overnight at Tioga Road trailheads (including Tuolumne Meadows) after mid-October, effectively ruling out overnight hikes starting here at that time. When hiking in other areas of the Park, you can often leave your **vehicle** right at the trailhead.

Backcountry hikers should also read our introduction to the **Day Hikes chapter**, beginning on p.103.

Backcountry information and practicalities

Backcountry information is best gleaned at one of the **wilderness centers** (see p.39), particularly those in Yosemite Valley and Tuolumne Meadow, which are both close to numerous trailheads. They'll help you sort out a wilderness permit and enlighten you on backcountry safety and etiquette. Wherever you go, be

Guided overnight hikes

Yosemite Valley-based **Yosemite Mountaineering School** (YMS; ⓣ209/372-8344, ⓦwww.yosemitemountaineering.com), not only runs guided day hikes and rock climbing courses, but also leads **guided backpacking trips** (late July to mid-Sept only). Trips start from the Mountain Shop in Curry Village and include transportation from Curry Village to the trailhead, all meals, tents, stoves, pans, water filters and wilderness permits; all you need is your personal gear plus a backpack and sleeping bag (both available for rent, see p.139). Along with the trips listed below, **custom trips** going wherever you want them to can be arranged; rates run $133 per day, per person for groups of 4–7; $138 each for three; $160 per day for two; and $256 per day if solo. All camping equipment and food is included.

Learn to Backpack Aimed at backpacking neophytes this is a two-day trip carrying tent, sleeping bag and all food, typically leaving the Valley and hiking for 3–4 miles. Prices start at $200 a head ($276 each for three; $320 for two; $512 for one).

Grand Canyon of the Tuolumne A four-day trip north of Tioga Road that's similar to our Hike 49, though done in the opposite direction from White Wolf to Tuolumne Meadows. Three departures in July and August. Rates ($400 a head with groups of four or more) include meals and use of tents and cooking gear.

Young Lakes to Mount Conness trip A three-day trip north of Tuolumne Meadows with a relatively easy first day to the campsite near Young Lakes (our Hike 31). The second day is spent hiking up the 12,590ft summit of Mount Conness (ropes are not needed). Around four trips are scheduled each summer, all leaving on Friday morning and returning on Sunday afternoon. Rates are $300 per person assuming a group of four or more.

Tuolumne Meadows to Yosemite Valley A four-day scheduled trip from Tuolumne Meadows to Yosemite Valley (more downhill than up) mostly avoiding the John Muir Trail and taking in Vogelsang Pass and Merced Lake. The trip includes a rest day with an optional hike up Half Dome. The four annual trips all start on Thursday morning and return on Sunday afternoon. Rates are $400 per person assuming a group of four or more.

sure to **leave an accurate itinerary** with family or friends, as it will be their responsibility to initiate a search if you do not return as scheduled. Several of the hikes we've listed start and/or finish away from the Park's main centers and you'll find it convenient to make use of Yosemite's **hikers buses** (see p.26), which run from the Valley to Glacier Point and Tuolumne Meadows.

Maps and selecting a backcountry campsite

With trails so well marked, you may find that the maps in this book along with the Yosemite map provided when you enter the Park are all the guidance you need, but most serious hikers will feel naked without a decent **topographic map**. For recommendations see "Travel essentials" on p.35.

Once out in Yosemite's backcountry, you are free to camp wherever you wish, subject to a few limitations. In the more popular sections of the Park though, you are encouraged to aim for and camp in existing **primitive campgrounds**, each with fire rings and some form of water source (though this may need to be treated). The most popular such areas are Little Yosemite Valley (on the John Muir Trial just south of Half Dome), and beside the five High Sierra Camps (see p.174).

Away from these areas, you are free to set up camp almost anywhere as long as the following **backcountry regulations** are met.

▲ Backcountry campers

Do not camp within four miles of any settlement (principally Yosemite Valley, Tuolumne Meadows, Hetch Hetchy, Glacier Point and Wawona), within one mile of any road, or less than a quarter of a mile from the Yosemite Valley rim. In addition, select a site at least a hundred feet from any watercourse, away from fragile and untrammeled vegetation, and out of sight of hikers on nearby trails. In practice, many commonly used sites don't meet all these criteria, but you should make sure yours does: the rules are designed to ensure everyone has a quality wilderness experience.

Hikers' passage into and out of the backcountry is eased by the existence of drive-in **backpacker campgrounds** (no reservations necessary; $5) in Yosemite Valley, Tuolumne Meadows and Hetch Hetchy. Here, hikers with valid wilderness permits have a place to camp for their last night before a trip and a place to stay when turning up late in the day after several days hiking.

Water and waste disposal

In the vast majority of the backcountry there is no guaranteed safe **drinking water**, so hikers must be prepared to treat their supply (see p.31).

Wilderness permits

Anyone planning to spend the night in the backcountry (including at High Sierra Camps) must obtain a **wilderness permit**. Each trailhead has a daily quota, with sixty percent of permits available in advance and the rest available on a first-come-first-served basis the day before your first planned hiking day. Remember that quotas are trailhead (rather than destination) based, and you may find that you can start from a slightly different spot and still do largely the hike you wanted to.

Outside busy times (or for less popular trailheads) it is usually easy enough to obtain an **on the spot permit** (free) in person early on the day before you want to start hiking. Line up outside any of the wilderness centers or information stations (see p.39), though preferably the one nearest to your trailhead. If you can't get a day-before permit for your desired trailhead, it is worth checking **after 10am on the day you plan to leave**. Any advance permits not picked up by this time then become available to all-comers.

During the busiest period from mid-July to the end of August you should **reserve in advance** for all trailheads. Most summer weekends are also busy enough to justify making reservations for those hikes beginning at popular trailheads such as Happy Isles and Upper Yosemite Falls in Yosemite Valley, May Lake along the Tioga Road, Sunrise Lakes at the western end of Tenaya Lake, and Cathedral Lakes and Lyell Fork from Tuolumne Meadows.

Advance wilderness permits ($5 per person) are available from 24 weeks to two days ahead of your trip online at Ⓦwww.nps.gov/archive/yose/wilderness/permits.htm, where you can also check availability. Alternatively, book either by phone (Ⓣ209/372-0740), or by writing to Yosemite Association, PO Box 545, Yosemite, CA 95389, stating your name, address, daytime phone, the number in your party, method of travel (foot, ski, snowshoe or horse), start and finish dates, entry and exit trailheads and main destination, along with possible alternate dates and trailheads. Checks should be made payable to the Yosemite Association, and credit card bookings must include the expiration date. Those mailing reservation requests will be notified of their success (or otherwise) by mail.

With the exception of the far north of the Park and a couple of areas in the far southeast, **bear canisters** are now required throughout the backcountry area of Yosemite. Almost everyone seeking a wilderness permit will need to rent a bear canister (see p.39) or show they already have one.

In winter (mid-Sept to mid-May), when demand is at its lowest, there is no need to reserve in advance and wilderness centers are closed. Free wilderness permits are available at several places: the visitor center in Yosemite Valley, the ski hut in Tuolumne Meadows, and the ranger station at the Badger Pass Ski Area. Winter hikers starting near Wawona and Big Oak Flat can self-register outside the nearest visitor center.

Climbers spending the night on a wall are not required to have a wilderness permit, but it is illegal to camp at the base of a wall, and when bivvying at the summit all Park regulations must be followed.

During the spring snowmelt there is no shortage of supply, but as the summer wears on creeks dry up and you should plan your hike with this in mind. That said, even creeks that aren't flowing often have stagnant pools which will satisfy your needs when necessary.

Except when using the vault **toilets** at Lower Yosemite Valley and the High Sierra Camps you're expected to bury human waste to protect water quality. It should be buried more than six inches deep in mineral soil at least a hundred feet (forty paces) from watercourses; portable plastic shovels are available from the wilderness centers for $3. When **washing**, be sure to carry water well away from the watercourse; even so-called "biodegradable" soaps

Camping stoves and fuel

Airlines are increasingly wary about letting passengers carry any form of **camping stove**: the faintest whiff of fuel and they'll confiscate your equipment. Consequently those flying to Yosemite should consider their stove systems in advance. Stoves requiring fuel carried in a special pressurized bottle are particularly tricky as it is virtually impossible to rid them of all odors, and both the bottle and any pump are likely to be seized. Some airlines allow such equipment to be professionally cleaned then carried, but it is hardly worth the effort. A better bet is to rely on butane and propane gas stoves. You can't carry the fuel canisters, but at least there is no problem with carrying the stove itself.

Butane/propane: Yosemite Valley's outdoor stores have a pretty good range of common brands – including Gaz, MSR, Kovea and Primus – but in more remote stores such as Tuolumne Meadows and Wawona the stock is limited. If buying a new stove, get one that accepts several types of canister.

Gasoline: Gasoline is available in Tuolumne, Wawona and at Crane Flat but is not available in the Valley. More expensive white gas (such as Coleman Fuel) is just a refined type of gasoline, works well and can be bought in stores all over the Park.

Methylated spirits: Trangia stoves burn meths, which is known in the US as denatured alcohol and can often be found in hardware stores. Supplies are not abundant in Yosemite.

pollute the water. All other waste – packaging materials, food scraps, etc – must be carried out. Do not burn or bury trash (including toilet paper): **pack out what you pack in**.

Campfires and cooking

No special permits are required to light **campfires** in the backcountry, but to preserve Yosemite's delicate ecology and limit pollution you should try to manage without a fire, or at least build a small warming one rather than a large bonfire. Where they exist, **fire rings** should be used, and be sure to only use dead and down wood. There are seldom all-out fire bans, but fires are not allowed above 9600ft where trees grow slowly and suitable wood is scarce. For cooking it makes sense to take a **portable stove**: fuel is available for most types of stove within the park (see box above).

Bear awareness

Yosemite Valley **bears** (see box, p.11) may be smart, but their backcountry cousins are no less adept at obtaining food from hikers. They're too timid to ambush humans, but unless you're happy to go hungry for the rest of your hike it is absolutely essential to correctly store your provisions overnight.

You may be familiar with the idea of **hanging food** in trees or the more advanced **counterbalance method** designed to prevent bears getting at your food. Neither are effective in Yosemite, and each year bears routinely obtain properly hung food. Sows even teach their cubs to go out along thin branches that wouldn't hold the weight of a full-grown bear. Consequently, the Park Service requires anyone overnighting in the backcountry to have a **bear-resistant food canister** (BRFC or just bear canister) – the only effective way for backpackers to store food in the wilderness. These three-pound plastic cylinders fit in your backpack and store enough food for 3–5 days for one person. You typically leave them outside your tent at night. When first introduced, bears were determined to get at the contents and hikers would frequently find their canister several hundred feet away. Having repeatedly failed, bears now walk past your tent in the night and ignore the canister.

Hikers headed for campsites at Little Yosemite Valley and beside the High Sierra Camps may be able to use the *in situ* bear boxes found there, but these may be moved out in future, and in any case you increase your campsite selection freedom by carrying a bear canister. **Rental** is $5 per trip (for up to two weeks; plus $75 deposit) and they can be rented from the Yosemite Valley Wilderness Center, the Crane Flat Store, the Wawona Store and the Hetch Hetchy Entrance Station. Reservations are neither available nor necessary, and canisters can be returned to any location after your trip. You can also **buy canisters** (around $75) from most wilderness centers and outdoor-oriented stores throughout the park. If you own your own bear canister, make sure it is approved for use in Yosemite. A list of currently **approved canisters** can be found at ⓦwww.nps.gov/yose/wilderness/bfoodstorage.htm.

Backcountry equipment and packing

Many a backpacking trip has been ruined by taking the wrong **equipment** – take too little and you're unprepared, but too much can make each day a painful march. Getting it right is an art learned over many trips: the following won't make you an expert overnight, but it will help in avoiding the biggest pitfalls.

What to wear

Wearing **layered clothing** within the Park is essential, as you must be able to adapt quickly to the varying conditions. In summer you'll be hiking in shorts and a T-shirt all day then as soon as the sun goes down you'll be quickly scrabbling for that warmer gear, particularly at high-country campsites where temperatures drop rapidly. At places like Vogelsang in September you'll be in your sleeping bag an hour after the sun goes down.

Cotton is great when the weather is hot and dry (as it will often be in Yosemite's main hiking season), but it is virtually useless when wet and actually makes you feel colder encouraging hypothermia. Always have a change of dry clothes handy. Try a light and comfortable base layer (next to the skin), preferably one of the modern fabrics that wicks away moisture and dries quickly when washed. If you carry two of these, rinsing one out each day, your hiking companions need never complain about your camping hygiene. In summer, you can probably do without a middle layer and just carry a warm, wind-breaking **outer layer** for when the sun goes down. This might be waterproof, or you may have an additional waterproof layer.

In summer and fall you're unlikely to come across bogs and very uneven ground, so relatively lightly constructed **hiking boots** will be fine, especially if you can keep your load down. Ankle support is always a good idea, but may not be essential – many hike for days with a relatively light pack in nothing more

Equipment rental

Although it pays to arrive in Yosemite fully prepared for your hike, a fairly extensive range of camping equipment and clothing is for sale in the Valley. You can also **rent** outdoor equipment from the Yosemite Mountaineering School (ⓣ209/372-8344) at the Mountain Shop in Curry Village, including two-person tents ($15.50 per day), overnight packs ($15.50), day-packs ($5.50), sleeping bags ($13), foam sleeping pads ($2.50), gaiters ($3), rock climbing shoes ($8.50), helmets ($7) and snowshoes ($19.50).

than strong sneakers. Whatever you wear, be sure they're broken in, and wear good **socks**.

What gear to take

Obviously you'll need a **tent**. John Muir may have been happy bedding down under the stars on newly hewn fir boughs with a raging fire nearby, but then he didn't mind waking up with a four-inch blanket of snow over him. Ideally you'll want a light, three-season tent that will stand up without having to be pegged out. Mosquito-proof mesh is good except when the temperature drops, so tents that allow you to zip over the mesh panels are good, though this adds to your load.

The cozy **sleeping bag** you use for car camping is likely to be too bulky for backpacking. Consider getting a lightweight, easily stored bag rated to 20°F, which should be fine for most uses. For a comfortable night's sleep, most people prefer to carry some form of **sleeping pad**. High-tech inflatable pads such as Thermorests are light and relatively luxurious, but it is worth considering a much cheaper closed-cell foam roll mat. They're almost as good at night, and much more useful for lunch breaks and lolling around the campsite.

A hiking gear guide

Weather conditions and personal preferences obviously dictate exactly what you'll need to take on a hiking trip, but the following checklist should point you in the right direction. Overnight hikers will need everything in the first two sections plus some of the additional overnight gear.

Day hiking

- Strong hiking shoes or light boots
- Good hiking socks
- Waterproof coat
- Water bottles
- Sunscreen
- Sunglasses
- Sun hat
- Water
- Snacks and emergency food
- Camera (optional)
- Binoculars (optional)

Essential overnight gear

- Wilderness Permit
- Map
- Waterproof tent
- Sleeping bag
- Bear canister
- Food (including emergency supply)
- Water purifier
- Stove and fuel
- Pots, pans and utensils
- Pocket knife
- Shorts and a light shirt
- Long-sleeved shirt
- Warm, long pants
- Fleece or down jacket
- Light but warm hat and gloves
- First-aid kit
- Waterproof matches or lighter
- Flashlight (preferably a headlamp)
- Garbage bag
- Toilet paper
- Mosquito repellant

Additional overnight gear

- Sleeping pad
- Small trowel (available for $3 from Wilderness centers)
- Soap/toiletries
- Toothbrush and toothpaste
- Small towel
- Tarp/ground cover
- Journal
- Entertainment: books, playing cards, etc
- Camp shoes (light sandals work best)
- Fishing gear (and license)
- Bathing suit
- Flask

We've listed suggestions for the remaining gear you might want to bring along in the box opposite, but keep in mind that your pack will only get heavier with every step. Food in particular can weigh you down: eschew heavy packaging – especially bottles and cans – in favor of dried foods.

Overnight hikes

The following hikes cover a wide spread of Yosemite's topography and anyone keen enough to complete the lot can consider themselves enough of a Yosemite expert to venture into the really wild country in the very north of the Park. We've listed these hikes according to their trailhead location; the Valley first, then Tioga Road and finishing with Tuolumne Meadows.

H44 Pohono Trail–Panorama Trail Combo

Difficulty Very strenuous
Distance 23 miles one way
Estimated time 2–3 days
Elevation gain 3600ft ascent, 4000ft descent
Season mid-June to Oct
Trailhead location Map p.48, Tunnel View a mile and a half west of Bridalveil Fall.
Comments One entire Valley rim but with a welcome break at Glacier Point.

This hike combines the **Pohono Trail** (Hike 40, here tackled in reverse) with the **Panorama Trail** (Hike 39) to take in a full west-to-east span of Yosemite Valley from the south rim, without resorting to messy shuttle transfers. It is not entirely a wilderness experience – the two trails meet at Glacier Point – but this does have the advantage of assuring hikers access to food, potable water and flush toilets along the way. Be aware, however, that there is **no camping** within four miles of Glacier Point. A good strategy is to catch the Glacier Point Hikers bus as far as the Pohono trailhead at Tunnel View, then camp early before

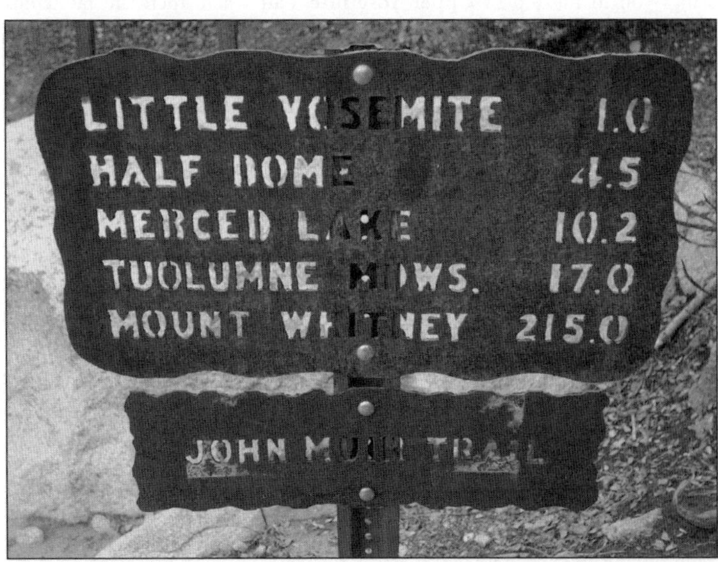

▲ Sign along the John Muir Trail

Glacier Point's exclusion zone (Bridalveil Creek makes a good spot). The second day is long, passing through Glacier Point for supplies before hiking the Panorama Trail, perhaps camping a short distance off the trail at Little Yosemite Valley. Day three can then be spent exploring (maybe hiking up Half Dome) and then descending along the Mist Trail or JMT. By pacing yourself this way you'll always be camping by water, a significant consideration in late summer.

H45 North rim of Yosemite Valley

Difficulty Very strenuous
Distance 30 miles one way
Estimated time 2–3 days
Elevation gain 5700ft ascent, 6700ft descent
Season Late May to Oct
Trailhead location Map p.48, Big Oak Flat Road, 6 miles southeast of Crane Flat.
Comments Lots of unpopulated miles and great views.

The summit of El Capitan, Eagle Peak, the top of Upper Yosemite Fall and North Dome can all be linked together in one lengthy traverse of the Valley's north rim. Apart from the section near the top of Yosemite Fall, you'll see few people, making this a more solitary undertaking than the rest of the overnight hikes listed here. Though possible throughout the summer and fall, timing is everything: too early and you'll have to cope with patches of snow; too late and most streams will have dried up. July and August are the most suitable months.

The best bet is to start at the trailhead on the Big Oak Flat Road two hundred yards uphill from the Foresta turn-off: in season you can catch the Tuolumne Meadows Hikers Bus. The route crosses a couple of minor streams then meets a disused section of Old Big Oak Flat Road (Hike 14) and follows it downhill for a little over half a mile. Logs across the road mark the resumption of the track, which climbs to the summit of **El Capitan**, then undulates along the Valley rim with a short spur trail to the summit of **Eagle Peak**. A short descent brings you to the top of **Upper Yosemite Fall** where there are numerous camping spots located a quarter-mile back from the rim. Even when Yosemite Falls is dry, water can be obtained from deep pools above the fall.

The way ahead climbs out of the valley cut by Yosemite Creek to reach **Yosemite Point** then heads away from the Valley rim to sidle around the head of Indian Canyon. Follow signs for **North Dome** and make a short detour to its summit. You then double back and head south again for the steep descent down Snow Creek which eventually brings you past Mirror Lake and back to the Valley settlements.

H46 John Muir Trail: Yosemite Valley to Tuolumne Meadows

Difficulty Strenuous
Distance 20 miles one way
Estimated time 2 days
Elevation gain 6100ft ascent. 1500ft descent
Season Late June to Oct
Trailhead location Map p.52, shuttle stop 16 near the Nature Center at Happy Isles.
Comments Yosemite's most famous overnight hike.

Several routes from Yosemite Valley lead to Tuolumne Meadows, but one of the best, and certainly the most popular, follows the **John Muir Trail**: reserve a permit early. In two fairly easy days you'll be rewarded with some of the best hiking available, with views to match. The track starts at the Happy Isles trailhead and follows the Merced River to Nevada Fall, mostly keeping away from the river and switchbacking up the canyon wall before traversing along the head of the fall. The major features of this region are discussed in Hikes 1–3 which follow the Mist Trail, parallel to the JMT.

From Nevada Fall, the JMT skirts around Liberty Cap to reach the popular wilderness campground (and composting toilets) at **Little Yosemite Valley**. Soon after, the JMT becomes more peaceful as most hikers head for the summit of Half Dome. The JMT now follows Sunrise Creek climbing fairly steeply to crest a ridge revealing your first startling views of the Cathedral Range. A short descent

The John Muir and Pacific Crest trails

Yosemite is traversed by two of the best-known **long-distance trails** in the western United States: the John Muir and Pacific Crest trails. The 211-mile **John Muir Trail** links the Happy Isles trailhead in Yosemite Valley with the 14,497ft summit of Mount Whitney, the highest peak in the contiguous 48 states. Along the way it passes through Tuolumne Meadows and Lyell Canyon, leaves the Park at Donohue Pass and continues through the John Muir and Ansel Adams wildernesses and Kings Canyon and Sequoia National Park before reaching Whitney's peak. It is all beautiful country with 13,000 and 14,000ft peaks, alpine meadows and pure, rushing streams.

The trail is traditionally tackled from south to north (with a net descent of 4000ft), and the bulk of people still go this way, but it is worth considering going north to south: the terrain is easier around Yosemite so you can break yourself in gently, and gradually get accustomed to the higher altitudes further south. At the end of the trail you still have another 11 miles down to Whitney Portal trailhead (a 6000ft descent) making a total of 222 miles. Most hikers cover eight to twelve miles a day, making it a **three-week trek**. July and August are the most popular months when temperatures are warmest and there is little chance of snow. It is pretty much a wilderness experience, so you'll need to carry everything on your back, though every few days there is an opportunity to buy food or pick up supplies you've sent ahead. For more information check Ⓦwww.pcta.org/about_trail/muir/over.asp and obtain the *Guide to the John Muir Trail* by Thomas Winnett and Kathy Morey (see "Books," p.252).

The **Pacific Crest Trail** is a much more serious undertaking, running 2650 miles from Mexico to Canada through the Mojave Desert and across all the major western ranges following the JMT through southern Yosemite then striking through the north of the Park. Expect everything from scorching deserts of Southern California to damp old-growth rainforests of the Pacific Northwest and the artic-alpine country of the Sierra Nevada.

Every year around 300 people attempt the entire trail in one season – so-called thru-hikers – starting at the Mexican border in early spring and hiking north, always keeping a week or two behind the receding snowline. Around sixty percent successfully turn up at the Canadian border just before winter sets in. Most take five to six months in all, assuming a pace of around 20 miles a day and including a reasonable number of (much needed) rest days. PCT hikers can often be found at the Tuolumne Store in early July, ripping into the food parcels they shipped to the post office.

It often takes longer to plan the trip than to do the hike, and timing is all-important, especially if you don't want to worry about carrying an ice ax or crampons. You'll also want to start off with a good level of physical fitness, and should consider honing skills covered in Ray Jardine's *The Pacific Crest Trail Hiker's Handbook*. One such skill is keeping clean in cold water: you might only get half a dozen hot showers over the entire route.

Typically wilderness permits are issued by the agency (National Park, State Park, National Forest or whatever) that manages the area in which you start your hike and these are valid for the entire hike no matter where you roam. For hikers covering over 500 miles, **permits** can be issued by the Pacific Crest Trail Association (Ⓣ916/349-2109, Ⓦwww.pcta.org), which is a superb source of information.

leads to the **Sunrise Lakes HSC**, beautifully set by a meadow overlooked by Merced Peak and with a striking view of Mount Clark to the south. There's a wilderness campground beside the camp, basic supplies are generally available, and if you've booked in advance you can even eat your meals here.

Edging around the meadow the trail continues into mixed country of forests and meadows to the shallow saddle of **Cathedral Pass** and a virtually unsurpassed view of the stegosaurus back of the **Cathedral Range**: Cathedral Peak, Echo Peaks and the sinuous Matthes Crest. It is all beautifully set off by **Upper Cathedral Lake**, the next significant feature along the way. From here, the trail follows Hike 24 in reverse to the trailhead. Immediately before the trailhead, turn right and follow the JMT parallel to Tioga Road for the last two miles to Tuolumne Meadows.

H47 Merced Lake HSC

Difficulty Very strenuous
Distance 27 miles round trip
Estimated time 2–3 days
Elevation gain 3300ft ascent
Season June–Oct
Trailhead location Map p.52, shuttle stop 16 near the Nature Center at Happy Isles.
Comments Lovely meadows and cascades (with plenty of swimming opportunities), and the chance to summit Half Dome.

Though **Little Yosemite Valley** is one of the Park's gems, few bother to explore its three miles of glacier-sculpted two-thousand-foot walls, lush meadows and feathery waterfalls. It is too far from the Happy Isles trailhead to allow full exploration in one day, so is best tackled by spending a night or two at **Merced Lake**, either camping or at the High Sierra Camp. Tack on an extra night at the *Little Yosemite Valley* campground and you could also summit Half Dome.

From Happy Isles follow Hikes 1–4 as far as the Little Yosemite Valley campground. Here you leave the Half Dome and JMT hikers and follow the Merced River as it winds its way across mostly level ground around the massive lump of **Bunnell Point**. The river slithers over **Bunnell Cascade**, one of many falls, gorges and slides along this active part of the Merced. The meadows of **Echo Valley**, just beyond, herald the liveliest stretch of the river, a mile-long tumbling torrent where springtime eddies have hollowed out great bathing spots. Merced Lake lies a bit further, along with the campground and HSC just a bit further, though neither sits right by the lake. The campground has a treated water supply and toilet, and the HSC has a limited range of supplies and can offer meals to those who've booked in advance.

H48 Ten Lakes

Difficulty Strenuous
Distance 22 miles
Estimated time 2 days
Elevation gain 4500 ft ascent, 3500ft descent
Season June–Oct
Trailhead location Map p.82, 20 miles east of Crane Flat and 20 miles west of Tuolumne Meadows.
Comments A one-way overnighter requiring transport, but well worth the extra effort.

It is hard to say exactly which of the multitude of lakes make up the **Ten Lakes** area, but you'll hardly care when camped out in this beautiful environment. The hike starts on the north side of Tioga Road approximately twenty miles east of the Crane Flat road junction, and initially follows Yosemite Creek, crossing side streams and alternating between forest and open manzanita for a few miles. Climbing all the way you pass the pretty Half Moon Meadow (where camping is possible), and the junction for a two-mile side trip to Grant Lakes. After a total of five miles on the main trail you top out at Ten Lakes Pass, affording fabulous views down into the Grand Canyon of the Tuolumne River and to the innumerable mountains beyond.

Descending you soon catch the first four of the ten lakes strung out in a sequence that earns them the occasional title of the Paternoster Lakes for their similarity to the beads on a rosary. Most people camp over the next few miles on spots near (but not right next to) one of the lakes. Throughout summer you won't be alone, but can usually find a peaceful enough spot.

After joining the South Fork of the Tuolumne River, the trail climbs again, almost reaching 10,000ft on the shoulder of Tuolumne Peak before descending towards May Lake. As you enter the forest before May Lake, look out for tiny Raisin Lake, which makes a good spot for a dip: note that swimming is not allowed in May Lake. From May Lake follow Hike 19 back to the May Lake parking lot.

The hike is slightly inconvenient in that it ends ten road miles from the starting trailhead: either organize a driver, shuttle cars, or time your finish so that you can walk the extra two miles to Tioga Road in time to meet the Valley-bound YARTS or Tuolumne hikers bus (see p.26) back to your vehicle.

H49 Grand Canyon of the Tuolumne River

Difficulty Very strenuous
Distance 28 miles one way
Estimated time 2–3 days
Elevation gain 4000ft ascent, 4800ft descent
Season June–Oct
Trailhead location Map p.86, Lembert Dome parking area at Tuolumne Meadows.
Comments One of the longest river hikes in the Park; remote and rewarding.

The **Grand Canyon of the Tuolumne River** is probably the most-used overnight backpack route north of Tioga Road, but you'll see far fewer fellow hikers here than in the popular areas between Yosemite Valley and Tuolumne Meadows. It is unlike other hikes in the Park, following a single river for over twenty miles as it cuts deep into a granite canyon, alternately erupting into wild cascades, then easing to deep, bottle-green pools. Vegetation changes from stunted lodgepole pines to lowland forests then back to alpine up the relentless four-thousand-foot climb out to White Wolf.

The hike is best divided into three sections with nights spent at Glen Aulin and Pate Valley. With the trail wedged between river and cliff for much of the way, there are few other legal places to camp, though the authorities have a grudging acceptance of the use of "heavily impacted" sites where hikers have obviously camped before.

From Tuolumne Meadows the first five miles follow Hike 30 to the **Glen Aulin HSC** and campground; good sunbathing and swimming possibilities abound a quarter of a mile downstream. Beyond the camp you're on ground covered by Hike 32 as far as **Waterwheel Falls**. Just beyond that is the confluence of the Tuolumne River and Return Creek, an attractive shaded spot with an impacted camping area. You now climb away from the river for a couple of hours as it negotiates **Muir Gorge**.

It is then a steep descent to Register Creek where a pleasant waterfall makes a good place to recover. Ten minutes after Register Creek you cross Rodgers Creek and rejoin the Tuolumne at a collection of attractive impacted camping spots. Here, down below five thousand feet, the canyon traps the heat of summer, allowing black oak to predominate and encouraging **rattlesnakes** to sunbathe: keep your eyes peeled. The trail levels out beside languid pools as you approach **Pate Valley** and a legal camping spot ideal for recuperating before tomorrow's big ascent.

A mile after crossing the Tuolumne you start uphill on a series of switchbacks. Towards the end of summer there's no flowing water along the way, though several streams have stagnant pools that can be pressed into service: fill up whenever possible. About halfway up you cross the biggest stream, **Morrison Creek**, then five minutes beyond arrive at a camping spot with nice views down to Hetch Hetchy and **Kolana Rock**. After a final series of switchbacks the terrain eases and, after a couple of trail junctions, hits **Harden Lake**, a pleasant waterside camping area. From here it is three miles to **White Wolf**, described in reverse in Hike 15.

H50 The High Sierra Camp Loop

Difficulty Moderate
Distance 47 miles one way
Estimated time 6 days
Elevation gain 8000ft total ascent and descent
Season Camps open late June to early Sept.
Trailhead location Map p.86, at Tuolumne Meadows Lodge.
Comments The classic tour of the Yosemite high country.

The most civilized way to spend time in Yosemite's backcountry is to make a **loop of the five High Sierra Camps** (see p.174), all situated at least seven thousand feet up and linked by a wonderful high-country circuit that passes through some of the very finest landscapes the Park has to offer. If you are unlucky with the HSC lottery (see box, p.174) or simply prefer to rough it a bit more, the campgrounds beside each camp make convenient and beautifully sited alternatives. All have toilets and most have potable water. Locations are spaced just six to ten miles apart (eight on average) making it an easy circuit, especially if you're not carrying camping gear.

Most people start in Tuolumne Meadows and make a counterclockwise loop, perhaps spending the first night at *Tuolumne Meadows Lodge* (actually an original HSC, though with vehicle access it is now rather different). The first stop is the **Glen Aulin HSC**, reached along a dramatic stretch of the Tuolumne River by following Hike 31. From there, the route doubles back slightly to join a trail heading southwest, eventually depositing you at the **May Lake HSC**, exquisitely sited by the lakeshore with Mount Hoffmann reflected in its waters. Follow the day hikers down to a parking area, then cross the road to descend through forest to Tioga Road. From here, turn left to get to the Sunrise trailhead at the western end of Tenaya Lake. You now pick up Hike 20 as far as Sunrise Lakes junction; turn left to get to the **Sunrise Lakes HSC**, also with a nice lakeside location.

From Sunrise Lakes, follow the JMT half a mile north, then turn right and swing south for eight miles to Echo Valley where you meet Hike 47 for the delightful final two miles to the **Merced Lake HSC**. For many the next day is the toughest, only eight miles but with a 3000-foot elevation gain to the **Vogelsang HSC**, perched high in alpine country with gorgeous tarns and barren mountains all around. There's a choice of routes: the shorter, steeper and more popular Fletcher Creek trail to the west, and the quieter and more scenic **Lewis Creek** track to the east. From Vogelsang it is a relatively easy amble down through forests and meadows beside Fletcher Creek to meet a section of the JMT for the final mile or so into Tuolumne Meadows.

6

Summer activities

While hiking is by far the Park's most popular summer activity, it is by no means the only one. Anyone seeking more adventure can get off trail **scrambling** up the more accessible peaks, experience technical **rock climbing** with the Yosemite Mountaineering School, or try a little summer snow climbing on the Park's highest peaks.

Most people are content with more sedentary pastimes: **horseback riding**, gentle **rafting** down the Merced River or lolling on its banks occasionally indulging in a little gentle **swimming**. It is also great fun **cycling** around the Valley floor, something we've covered under "Getting around" on p.28, and Wawona even has a **golf course** (see p.98).

Rock climbing and scrambling

Even for the most sluggish couch potato it's hard to visit Yosemite without becoming fascinated by the antics of **rock climbers**, particularly in Yosemite Valley where the sound of climbers calling out to one another is often heard around the base of the cliffs. Though it is always courteous to ask, climbers are generally happy to have an audience. Some of the most accessible areas in the Valley for **watching climbers** in action are: Swan Slab, just north of *Yosemite Lodge*; Church Bowl, between Yosemite Village and *The Ahwahnee*; and El Cap Meadow. In Tuolumne Meadows, walk to the base of Lembert Dome where there are almost always ropes strung up the cliff. In addition, there are sometimes interpretive shows as part of the ranger program; check *Yosemite Today* for details.

You'll also catch people **bouldering**, a kind of low-level climbing without ropes where the thrill is in tackling ridiculously hard moves while barely leaving the ground; and **scrambling**, also rock climbing without ropes, but practiced on less steep sections of the high peaks.

Climbing practicalities

The main rock climbing **season** runs from April to October with most of the action concentrated in the Valley outside the hot summer months of July to September When it gets too hot, climbers often migrate to the cooler Tuolumne Meadows, which sees the majority of the climbing from July to September. In spring and fall, virtually all climbers stay at the bohemian *Camp 4*, near *Yosemite*

Mountain biking

Off-road **mountain biking** is forbidden inside Yosemite National Park, but there's good trail riding just outside the Park near Briceburg (see p.205) and excellent single-track and downhill riding around Mammoth Lakes (see p.220).

Lodge, a trampled, dusty and noisy site often entirely taken over by climbers. It is relatively cheap, with a great sense of camaraderie, and an excellent **bulletin board** for teaming up with climbing partners, selling gear, organizing a ride and the like. Normally you can only stay for seven nights at a stretch, but from mid-Sept to April you're allowed to settle in for a month.

Boulderers are especially well supplied with a bunch of great rocks near the campsite, including the famous Columbia Boulder right at the heart of *Camp 4*. On its overhung eastern side one route, "Midnight Lightning" – given the extremely hard bouldering grade of V7 – defeats most who spend their afternoons trying to conquer it.

Climbing lessons and guided tours

The following lessons, run by the **Yosemite Mountaineering School** (April to mid-Nov; ⓣ209/372-8344, ⓦwww.yosemitemountaineering.com), follow a logical progression and can be taken in sequence to achieve a high level of proficiency. Try to reserve at least a few days in advance, especially in August.

Group climbing lessons

All classes last around **seven hours**, and start at 8.30am either from the Mountain Shop in Curry Village or from outside the Tuolumne Sport Shop in Tuolumne Meadows. All climbing equipment is provided except for climbing shoes, which can be rented ($7 a day).

Go Climb a Rock Here's where you start. Seven hours learning the ropes, so to speak. $117 for three to six people, $156 for two, and $217 for one.

Crack Climbing Much of the climbing in Yosemite follows crack lines: you'll get nowhere without some basic skills in this area. Ideal for gym climbers hitting the rock for the first time. $118 for three to five people, $158 for two, and $217 for one.

Anchoring Learning how to safely set up anchors to facilitate multi-pitch climbing. $118 for three to five people, $158 for two, and $217 for one.

Leading and Multi-pitch climbing Do away with the security of a top-rope and start leading. Now you're really climbing. $140 each for three people, $165 for two, and $235 for one.

Self-rescue and Aid Climbing Start your training for The Nose learning the basics of aid climbing. $118 for three to five people, $158 for two, and $217 for one.

Big Wall Climbing Seminar A two-day seminar covering all you need to know to make an assault on one of Yosemite's mightier cliffs. These take place on nine weekends throughout the summer: check the website for details. $280 each for three people, $330 for two, and $470 for one.

Private classes and guided climbs

Small group or individual guiding on some of the world's finest rock routes allows you to test your limits without overstepping the mark, and is available for all skill levels. These are effectively private lessons and are often booked weeks in advance in midsummer.

3/4-day Up to six hours of climbing covering six to eight pitches. What you tackle depends very much on the ability of the party. $135 each for three people, $158 for two, and $221 for one.

Full-day Eight hours covering around eight pitches, or a shorter route with a long walk-in. $192 each for three people, $210 for two, and $283 for one.

Extreme day A big ten-hour day out. $237 each for two people, and $317 for one.

Overnight climbs Dream of that big wall, but never thought you could do it? For around $500 per person per day you can give it a try: El Capitan goes for $3200 and Half Dome costs $2665. Maximum two climbers per guide.

Attempts to ease long-standing tensions between climbers and park rangers include discussions over free coffee between climbers and the "**climbing ranger**". These typically take place beside Columbia Boulder on Sunday mornings in spring and fall: check noticeboards for times. Another good source of general information about the climbing scene, along with discussion of climbing ethics and details of the latest closures either for rockfall or ecological reasons, can be found at Ⓦwww.nps.gov/yose/wilderness/climbing.htm.

Websites, guidebooks, gear and lessons

There's a wealth of information on climbing in Yosemite, particularly on the **web**, where Terra Galleria (Ⓦwww.terragalleria.com/mountain/info/yosemite/index.html) is a helpful resource for rock climbers with everything from suggestions for beginners to the latest beta on aid routes. It has great photos and useful links as well.

We've listed climbing and bouldering **guidebooks** on p.254, principally the Falcon Guides by Don Reid, and Chris McNamara's Supertopos series. To catch something of the spirit of the scene, read Steve Roper's *Camp 4* and Galen Rowell's *The Vertical World of Yosemite* (for both see p.252). All should be available at the Mountain Shop in Curry Village.

Rock climbing **gear** is available from the Tuolumne Meadows Sport Shop (summer only), and the well-stocked and competitively priced Mountain Shop

The Yosemite Decimal System

It is human nature to want to classify, and hikers and climbers are especially keen to measure their achievements, if only to gauge how to progress. It is for these people that the **Yosemite Decimal System** (YDS) was developed. It essentially divides all vertical endeavors into six categories of increasing difficulty:

Class 1 General hiking along well-established trails both flat and steep. The 50 hikes listed in this guide are all Class 1.

Class 2 Cross-country hiking requiring some route-finding and using hands for balance over rough ground or over fallen trees.

Class 3 Both hands are required to get over rough, steep ground. Some may want a rope in case of a fall.

Class 4 As for Class 3 but on steeper terrain where a fall would likely cause serious injury or death. Most people will want to be roped.

Class 5 Free rock-climbing grades – see below.

Class 6 Aid climbing, where climbing hardware and the rope are used to climb the cliff, not just for protection.

In practice, classes 1 and 2 are seldom used while 3, 4 and 6 get mentioned in some hiking and rock-climbing guides. The only class that is widely used is Class 5. Historically this was divided into ten subclasses – 5.0, 5.1 up to 5.9 – but as rock climbs got harder new grades were invented – 5.10, 5.11, etc – with each class subdivided into four letter categories. The world's hardest climbs are now 5.15a: the hardest climb in Yosemite is 5.13c.

The class of each rock climb (or hike) is defined by its hardest section. A simple hike with a short section of steep scrambling may be Class 3, and a rock climb that is generally 5.8 but has one 5.11a move will be classed as 5.11a. Rock climbs are typically rated (and named) by the first person to climb the route, though the rating may be adjusted as subsequent ascents are made and other climbers pass judgment on how hard it is.

in Curry Village (daily 8am–6pm or later). For a more organized introduction to the climber's craft or to brush up on a few skills, engage the services of the **Yosemite Mountaineering School** (see box, p.148, for details), based at the Curry Village Mountain Shop from spring to fall. During the warmest months (late June to Aug), they also operate from Tuolumne Meadows Sport Shop located in the gas station near the Tuolumne Meadows Store. Private lessons can be arranged in both locales, weather permitting.

Summer snow and alpine climbing

Tuolumne is the venue for the Yosemite Mountaineering School's instruction in **summer snow climbing**, an essential skill for backcountry adventurers covering safe travel through snow country, avalanche avoidance, and the use of ropes and ice axes on steep terrain. There are just nine one-day courses each summer ($200 for one person, $140 each for two, $125 each for three, $105 each for four to six) from mid-June to late July (call or check the website for exact dates).

Scrambling

Anyone who likes to get off trail but lacks the skill or inclination to go rock climbing should consider **scrambling**, essentially low-grade rock climbing on terrain where you feel tolerably comfortable without a rope. All you need is a head for heights, a pair of strong boots and a detailed topographic map of the area, plus the ability to read and understand it. Just be sure you know your abilities, and discuss your proposed route with a ranger in one of the wilderness centers before you start.

With so many exposed ridges and dramatic peaks in Yosemite, it is beyond the scope of this book to cover scrambling in any detail, but an obvious starting point is Tuolumne's **Cathedral Range**; scrambling heaven. Here, in 1869, the 31-year-old John Muir scaled Cathedral Peak and never commented on any difficulties encountered. Even by modern climbing standards, most people would want a rope to scale the final summit block, but scramblers can easily reach the spectacular saddle between the true summit and its attendant Eichorn Pinnacle. Cast your eyes along the horizon from here and numerous other possibilities present themselves: Unicorn Peak from Elizabeth Lake, Echo Peaks, and much more.

Horseback riding

Yosemite has a long heritage of **horse** travel. Ahwahneechee natives went on foot, but when the Mariposa battalion first entered Yosemite Valley they were pursuing the Ahwahneechee on horseback. Until the development of stage roads, and the eventual arrival of automobiles, all long-distance travel was by horse or mule, and the tradition continues today with three sets of stables accommodating everyone from beginners to those prepared to tackle a six-day circuit of the High Sierra Camps.

Yosemite's stables

Unless you're bringing your own horses and gear into Yosemite, **horseback riding** is limited to trips from the three stables. There are two-hour rides (several daily; $53), four-hour rides (8am & 1pm; $69) and full-day rides (Sun and by special arrangement; $96).

For beginner-oriented short rides you can usually just show up, but **reservations** (☎209/372-4386) are recommended for longer excursions. No

Banned in the Park

It often seems that the Park Service takes a dim view of adventure sports; hardly surprising when they have to organize rescues, and then pick up the pieces (sometimes literally). While rock climbing has become a mainstream activity, its very nature seems to encourage an anti-authoritarian streak, and relations between the climbing community and the Park authorities have always been strained.

With this in mind it should come as no surprise that **BASE jumping** was banned in Yosemite virtually as soon as it came on the radar screen. The sport first hit the headlines in 1978 when free-fall photographer, Carl Boenish, and some friends jumped off El Capitan and produced a film of their escapades. The Park Service did experiment with legal jumps for a couple of months in 1980, but the rules were so badly abused that a complete ban has been in place ever since. That doesn't stop people jumping, even though they risk a large fine, jail time and confiscation of their equipment. Still, that's nothing compared to the risk of things going wrong; and they do. Some have hit the rock face, while one jumper in 1998 drowned in the Merced River while trying to escape from rangers after a successful jump.

That same year there was even a day of civil disobedience when BASE jumpers did a deal with the Park Service where they would jump and voluntarily surrender in return for reduced fines. As a BASE jumping promo it backfired badly when one jump veteran, in full view of the media, failed to open her chute and died. Undoubtedly jumps still take place, but it is a secretive pursuit.

Dan Osman wanted to up the ante even further and pioneered **free falling**, using a cat's cradle of climbing ropes, pulleys and anchors to allow huge jumps that would be halted just a few feet above the ground. Often dubbed crazy, or worse, Osman had spent ten years gaining a reputation for fearlessness, always pushing the boundaries. His antics had begun to crop up on extreme videos – *Masters of Stone 4* for example – and even commercials. The Park Service was not amused, though his sport remained legal. On a November evening in 1998, Osman was standing atop the Leaning Tower about to make his biggest jump, a free fall of 1100ft designed to be stopped just 150ft above the deck. He called friends on his mobile from the top then jumped: several seconds later his friends were still waiting for his usual exalted shouts.

experience is necessary, but all riders need to be at least seven years old, over 44 inches high and weigh less than 225 pounds, and should additionally wear long pants and closed-toed shoes. Be sure to arrive at least 45 minutes early to complete paperwork and get matched up with an appropriate horse, or more likely, mule.

The most extensive facilities are at **Yosemite Valley Stables** (late April to Sept), which offers two-hour rides into Tenaya Canyon up to Mirror Lake; four-hour rides along the John Muir Trail with views of Vernal and Nevada falls; and strenuous all-day rides to Quarter Dome on the shoulder of Half Dome.

In the summer months, splendid scenic riding can be done from the **Tuolumne Meadows Stables** (late June to Sept), who offer two-hour rides around Tuolumne Meadows and along Young Lakes trail (see Hike 30) to a perfect vista of the Cathedral Range and Mammoth Peaks; four-hour rides along the Tuolumne River; and all-day outings to Waterwheel Falls.

In the south of the Park, **Wawona Stables** (early May to Sept) offers perhaps the least scenic range of horseback trips including two-hour rides around the Pioneer Yosemite History Center and Wawona Meadows; and various half-day rides.

Horseback rides are also available just **outside the Park** near the southern entrance at Fish Camp with Yosemite Trails Pack Station, (Ⓣ559/683-7611,

Ⓦwww.yosemitetrails.com). Along with one-hour ($35) and two-hour ($60) rides, they run an entertaining five-hour ride ($95) into the Mariposa Grove of giant sequoias.

High Sierra saddle trips

An excellent way to spend several days in the high country is to join one of the **High Sierra saddle trips** (July to early Sept; Ⓣ559/253-5674) four- and six-day journeys with professional guides and packers who look after your mount and tend to the mules which carry the gear. They're based at Tuolumne Meadows Stables and make a loop of the High Sierra Camps (see box, p.174) with all accommodation and meals included in the price: $832 for four days (Wed & Sat departures) and $1315 for six days (Sun departures). Customized guided excursions can also be arranged with groups of three to five paying $185 a day for a guide/packer and $94 a day for pack mules.

Going it alone

The park service makes considerable provision for people bringing horse and pack animals into the Park. You're allowed on most of the Park's trails, and there are **stock camps** at Wawona, Tuolumne Meadows, Bridalveil Creek and Hetch Hetchy (one night maximum), with each site accommodating six people and six head of stock, and costing $20. Two sites at a time can be reserved as much as five months in advance using the campsite reservation system (see box, p.173). Rules and regulations can be found at Ⓦwww.nps.gov/yose/wilderness/stock.htm.

Anyone wanting to rent animals and equipment outside the Park for use in Yosemite should contact either Eastern High Sierra Packers Association, 690 N. Main Street, Bishop, CA 93514 (Ⓣ760/873-8405) or West Side Packers Association, c/o P.O. Box 100, Fish Camp, CA 93623 (Ⓣ559/683-7611 in summer; Ⓣ559/683-5919 in winter).

Rafting and canoeing

While commercial whitewater rafting isn't permitted in Yosemite National Park, there's still plenty of **low-key boating activity**, chiefly on the relatively calm waters of the Merced River in Yosemite Valley. At Curry Village you can **rent** rafts (late May to late July; $20.50 per person per run, $13.50 for under-13s; Ⓣ209/372-8319), which hold up to six adults and come with buoyancy aids, and paddles so that you can guide yourselves around fallen trees and sandbanks. There's no hurry, so make a day of it by taking lunch then getting onto the river at Sentinel Bridge from where you float three miles down to El Capitan and ride the free transport back to Curry Village. Kids must weigh 50 pounds to go in the rafts.

There are no other watercraft rental facilities in the Park but if you bring your own canoe, kayak, or **inflatable plaything** you are free to use the Merced River between Stoneman Bridge and Sentinel Beach (daily 10am–6pm) and the South Fork of the Merced in Wawona from Swinging Bridge down to the Wawona campground (daily 10am–6pm). In the high country the only feasible venue is Tenaya Lake, which lends itself to exploration by kayak or canoe, though it is exposed in windy conditions.

Top-class **whitewater rafting** takes place *outside* the park from April to late June on the Merced River (Class III–IV; see box, p.205) and the Tuolumne River (Class III–V; see box, p.200).

Fishing

Yosemite isn't really a **fishing** destination. None of the rivers and lakes are stocked (though many once were), and over half of Yosemite's lakes have no fish at all. That said, there is some pretty decent trout fishing along the 58 permanent streams, notably at lower elevations such as along the Merced River in Yosemite Valley and along the Tuolumne River above the Hetch Hetchy reservoir. The Merced offers enjoyable fishing all summer and into the winter where the descendents of hatchery-raised brown and rainbow trout are the main attraction.

To fish, anyone sixteen or over needs a California sport fishing license ($18.65 for a two-day permit), which must be visibly attached to your upper body. These are sold at the Tuolumne Meadows store, the Wawona store and the Sport Shop in Yosemite Village, which has the best supply of fishing **gear**. It is open season year-round on lakes and reservoirs, and the stream- and river-fishing season (the last Sat in April–Nov 15) excludes Frog Creek and Lake Eleanor which both open on June 15.

Bag limits vary with location, and you should check with the Park Service rangers, but along the popular Happy Isles to Pohono Bridge stretch of the Merced, you can only fish with artificial lures or flies with barbless hooks. A daily bag of five brown trout is permitted, but rainbow trout are strictly catch-and-release. For more details visit the California Department of Fish and Game site at Ⓦwww.dfg.ca.gov/fishing.

Keen fishers might consider engaging the services of Yosemite Guides (Ⓣ1-866/922-9111, Ⓦwww.yosemiteguides.com), who run personalized catch-and-release **fly fishing trips**. A full day costs $225 for the first person and $50 each for up to two more, and includes tackle and lunch. Half a day goes for $175 plus $50 for each extra person.

▲ Trout fishing on the Tuolumne River

Yosemite's top natural swimming spots

Yosemite Valley and Little Yosemite Valley

Clark Bridge Though swimming is officially banned, proximity to the *North Pines*, *Lower Pines* and *Upper Pines* campgrounds makes this Merced River swimming hole a perennial favorite. Watch for strong currents early in the season.

Housekeeping Camp A pleasant beach and swimming spot frequented mostly by *Housekeeping Camp* guests.

Sentinel Beach A lovely and peaceful spot just off Southside Drive.

Emerald Pool Another officially illegal, but perennially popular, swimming hole above Vernal Falls.

Merced Lake to Little Yosemite Valley There are dozens of gorgeous swimming spots along this lively backcountry stretch of the Merced River.

Northern Yosemite

Tenaya Lake The lake boasts cool waters at 8000ft, but there's a lovely beach at the northeastern end, and a more secluded one at Murphy Creek on its north side.

Glen Aulin Trail The water is too pushy here in spring and early summer, but come this way (following Hike 31) in fall and you'll find numerous beautiful swimming holes.

Southern Yosemite

Wawona Campground The South Fork of the Merced River makes an ideal, gentle and popular place for watery frolics in summer.

Swinging Bridge A gorgeous and relatively little-used pool just over a mile upstream from Wawona.

Outside the Park

Mono Lake By being salty and very alkaline, Mono Lake allows you to float like few other places: see p.215.

Hot springs Hot springs in the Owens Valley are covered on p.225.

Swimming

Your enthusiasm for **swimming** in Yosemite will be dictated largely by your pain threshold: the Park's rivers, streams and lakes are generally icy-cold. Even in the middle of summer the languid waters of the two most popular swimming rivers – the Merced River in Yosemite Valley and the South Fork of the Merced River in Wawona – could hardly be called warm. Still, when the sun is beating down and temperatures are in the nineties, half a day at one of the riverside beaches can become very alluring. The period from mid-July to mid-September is best, when the days are hot and early season snowmelt has abated: perfect for washing away the sweat of tired hikers.

Be aware that **currents** can still be deceptively swift and submerged logs can be a hazard. Always keep away from tempting pools above waterfalls, and remember that kids should have some form of floatation device on them or nearby.

As well as the natural swimming areas listed above, there are public outdoor **swimming pools** (mid-May to mid-Sept; guests free, others $5) at *Yosemite Lodge* and Curry Village. Both the *Wawona Hotel* and *The Ahwahnee* have pools as well, though these are only open to guests.

Winter activities

From sometime in November until around the middle of April much of Yosemite is cloaked in a mantle of snow and looks even more magical than it does the rest of the year. Anywhere over 5500ft has an almost continuous coating during these months, but even in lowland areas like the Valley, pines and cedars are frequently bowed with the weight of snow, waterfalls glisten with icicles, and Half Dome is topped by a thick white cap. The cold days are often sunny though conditions can change rapidly with clouds rolling in only to pull back, revealing tantalizing glimpses of snow-capped peaks.

If your vehicle is equipped with tire chains, you can experience the Valley, Wawona, and a limited number of other areas from the road, but to fully appreciate Yosemite at its seasonal best you'll need to indulge in some **winter activities**. Much of the action at this time takes place at the **Badger Pass Ski Area**, but skaters glide around the outdoor **ice rink** in Curry Village, and **snowshoe** and **cross-country ski** enthusiasts have virtually the whole Park at their disposal. In practice, most gravitate to the snow play areas at Crane Flat and Mariposa Grove where you can ski among the giant sequoias and even camp out under their towering canopy.

Downhill skiing and snowboarding

Yosemite isn't really about **downhill skiing and snowboarding**. The Park's only tows are those at the family-friendly Badger Pass (see p.156), which is seldom crowded, and has runs best suited for beginner and intermediate skiers. The **vertical drop** is a modest 800ft, with nine runs fed by five lifts (one triple-chair, three double chairs and one cable tow). Only around fifteen percent of the terrain is suitable for advanced skiers.

Lift tickets cost $38 a day, with a one-ride ticket going for $5 and a full-season pass $376. Half-day tickets (12.30–4.30pm) are $28, and there are kids' tickets (7–12 years inclusive) costing less than half the adult rate. Seniors (65 and up) get a free lift pass on weekdays but pay almost the full adult fare on weekends and holidays. **Equipment rental** costs $24 (12 & under $15) for downhill skis, boots and poles; $30 (kids $10) for snowboarding gear.

Beginners and those needing to brush up on their technique should enlist the services of the Badger Pass Ski School, which has been providing ski instruction for over seventy years. Lessons typically start at 10am, 11am and 2pm daily. Novices should take the **Guaranteed Learn-to-Ski Package** ($59, kids aged 7–12 $49), with two two-hour group lessons plus ski rental and beginners' lift ticket: there's also a snowboarding equivalent ($69, kids $59). Those looking to improve technique will want the **Next Step Package** with a two-hour lesson, gear rental and a full lift ticket. There are skiing ($72, kids

Badger Pass

The **Badger Pass Ski Area** (generally mid-Dec to March daily 9am–4pm; recorded snow conditions on ⓣ209/372-1000, information desk on ⓣ209/372-8430) lies at 7200ft, a forty-minute drive from the Valley on the road to Glacier Point. It is home to Yosemite's only **downhill ski area** and is the Park's gateway to subalpine cross-country activities, specifically **cross-country skiing** and **snowshoeing**, with 350 miles of skiable trails (90 of them marked) and 25 miles of machine-groomed track fanning out into the backcountry. Expect **temperatures** in the 30–60°F range.

In winter, Glacier Point Road is kept open as far as Badger Pass, which is accessible by a free one-hour **shuttle** starting from Curry Village (8am & 10.30pm), then calling at Yosemite Village (8.10am & 10.40am), *The Ahwahnee* (8.15am & 10.45pm) and *Yosemite Lodge* (8.30am & 11am). Shuttles depart Badger Pass at 2 and 4pm. Once there, you'll find gear rental, a tuning shop and a couple of basic **restaurants** – the *Skiers Grill* and the *Snowflake Room* – that'll keep you supplied with burgers, sandwiches, pizza slices, salads, sodas, beer and wine without breaking the bank.

The best source of advance **information** is the Activities/Badger Pass section of the DNC website (ⓦwww.BadgerPass.com), which includes full details of facilities, rental prices, lessons and trips, along with links to the snow report and any special deals. People traveling with **children** will appreciate the Badger Pups Den (9am–4.30pm; $8 an hour, $50 a day), a kind of crèche for kids aged three to nine that only requires you to provide and eat lunch with your kids. Those aged four to six can also attend one-hour group ski lessons (one lesson $39; two lessons $59).

$46) and boarding variants ($82, kids $52). In addition there are one-hour **private lessons** (daily 9am) charged at $63 for one person, $83 for two, $103 for three and $113 for four.

Cross-country skiing

Perhaps the best way to get a true impression of Yosemite in winter is to head out **cross-country skiing** into the backcountry. Seeing the domes, spires and meadows cloaked in a mantle of snow from some viewpoint miles from anyone else is an experience to treasure. Almost the entire Park is open to skiers, though most activity is concentrated around areas with easy access to winter facilities, particularly **Badger Pass** (see box above) with its gear rental, lessons and guided trips. Touring skis, boots and poles **rental** goes for $22 (kids $12), and you'll pay a couple of dollars more for skate skis, and a couple more again for telemark gear.

Complete **beginners** should take the Learn to Ski Package (daily 10.15am; $31) which includes gear rental and two consecutive two-hour group lessons. Tuition in telemark skiing (Wed, Sat & Sun 10.15am & 2pm; $32, $42 including

Winter wilderness camping

Winter backcountry regulations are essentially the same as for summer. You still need a wilderness permit (advance reservations not needed) and those leaving Yosemite Valley must reach the Valley rim before camping. The Tuolumne Grove of giant sequoias is still off-limits, but in winter (Dec to mid-April) you can **camp in Mariposa Grove** as long as you are uphill from the Clothespin Tree. Although bears do spend long periods sleeping, they don't hibernate and can be after your food at any time.

rentals), and skate skiing (Thurs & Sat 10.15am & 2pm; $30, $40 including rentals) are also available. One-hour private lessons cost $30 for the first person and $16 each for up to three others.

You're free to follow the groomed trails that meander through the forests around Badger Pass, but experienced skiers might want to join a **guided day tour** ($75), designed to improve your off-track skills.

Elsewhere in the Park, most of the cross-country action happens at **Crane Flat** and in the **Mariposa Grove**, each of which has marked trails for all levels of ability ranging from a half-mile loop to sixteen-mile backcountry epics. Maps are available from visitor centers and ranger stations. More advance skiers and snowshoers might want to tackle **Snow Creek Trail** from Yosemite Valley to Tioga Road near Tenaya Lake. You must be competent in backcountry winter travel, winter camping and avalanche assessment, and you'll need to register at the Yosemite Valley Visitor Center. Alternatively, consider joining one of the excellent guided overnight trips run by the Cross-country Ski Center; see the box below for details.

Snowshoeing

Snowshoeing isn't much harder than walking, and if you're in Yosemite in winter you should grasp the opportunity it gives to explore the backcountry. Anywhere that's open to cross-country skiers – virtually the whole Park – is potential snowshoeing territory: just don't walk in the tracks the skiers have

Guided cross-country ski trips

The following **trips** are run by the Cross-country Center & Ski School (☎209/372-8444): book several weeks in advance if possible.

Glacier Point Overnight Ski Trip This is one of the Park's most popular intermediate-grade cross-country trips, and deservedly so with the chance to sleep at Glacier Point and wake up to a winter sunrise over Half Dome. Under skilled guidance you negotiate a 21-mile round trip along Glacier Point Road to Glacier Point, where there's accommodation at a new ski hut, with dormitory accommodation and hearty meals provided. Your personal gear and a sleeping bag (rentals available) are all you need. Midweek $160 for one night, $240 for two; weekends $192 for one night, $288 for two.

Glacier Point Midweek Tour Package This is the obvious solution for those without the confidence to jump straight in with the "Glacier Point Overnight Ski Trip." You get two cross-country ski lessons on the first day, practice on the trail on the second day then an overnight trip to Glacier Point staying at the *Glacier Point Ski Hut* with all meals provided. Five people minimum; $245.

Snow Camping Learn the basics of snow travel (ski or snowshoe) and winter camping skills on this guided overnight trip. You'll need previous ski or snowshoe experience and will have to carry a pack carrying some of the food and communal camping equipment (supplied). Bring or rent skis or showshoes. Three person minimum; $246.

Trans-Sierra Ski Tour An excellent advanced intermediate six-day ski tour through the Sierra Nevada journeying from the east to the Ski School hut in Tuolumne Meadows then exploring the pristine high country. You'll need to be fairly fit to enjoy this. Three person minimum; $800.

Tuolumne Meadows Hut Tour This six-day tour is slightly less demanding than the Trans-Sierra Ski Tour but still includes several days skiing around Tuolumne Meadows. Two tours starting Sunday in late March and/or early April; $800; three person minimum.

Ostrander Ski Hut

Skiers and snowshoers who fancy a night out but don't relish sleeping in a tent or joining one of the guided trips might like staying at the stone-built **Ostrander Ski Hut** (Ⓦwww.ostranderhut.com) located nine miles southeast of Badger Pass. The hut is open from just before Christmas to mid-April and costs $20 per person per night: reserve through the Yosemite Association (Ⓣ209/372-0740 Mon–Fri 9am–4pm Pacific time). Weekends and holidays are in high demand: if you want to stay at these times, get in touch before the beginning of November to be entered into the lottery for spaces.

Whenever you go, take everything you need for camping. The trail to the hut can be treacherous in winter and visitors need to be prepared to snow camp if caught in bad weather along the way.

carefully grooved. Snowshoes can be rented ($19.50 all day, $16.50 half-day) at **Badger Pass** (see box, p.156) where Park Service naturalists lead frequent two-hour **snowshoe walks** (free; snowshoe rental $5) teaching about the dynamics of snow and plant and wildlife adaptations to winter. On the four evenings leading up to full moon (if clear) there are two-hour **Full Moon Snowshoe Walks** (Jan–March; $9.75 including snowshoe rental if needed) involving over two miles of walking up a ridge to a viewpoint: check *Yosemite Today* for times and sign up at the *Yosemite Lodge* Tour Desk (Ⓣ209/372-1240).

In the rest of the Park you are only limited by your imagination and your knowledge of winter wilderness travel and survival, route finding and avalanche safety. The hiking trails (see chapters 4 & 5) are obvious candidates for those sufficiently skilled, but most snowshoers head for the winter trails at Crane Flat and Mariposa Grove, both described on maps available from the visitor centers. For anything ambitious you'll need winter camping equipment, the main exception being the Ostrander Ski Hut (see box above).

▲ Ranger-led snowshoe walk

Snowtubing, sledding and ice skating

Badger Pass has traditionally been a little stuffy in its approach but they have now fashioned a new groomed area for **snowtubing**, where young kids can ride specially designed inner tubes. Two-hour sessions run daily from 11.30am and 2pm and cost $11 per person per session. **Sledding** is not allowed at Badger Pass, but is permitted at the snow play area at the *Crane Flat* campground. Here sledding, tobogganing and inner-tubing are all encouraged. There are no rentals, so bring your own toys.

Though plenty of enthusiasts ski and snowshoe around the Valley, the most popular winter activity is **ice skating** at the open-air rink at Curry Village (typically mid-November to mid-March; ⓣ209/372-8319). Two-and-a-half-hour sessions cost $8 (kids $6; skate rental $3) and run daily from 3.30pm & 7pm with additional sessions from 8.30am and noon on Saturday, Sunday and holidays. Comforts include a warming hut, a fire pit and a snack service.

Listings

Listings

8

Accommodation

On most trips to Yosemite, **accommodation** will be your biggest expense, and procuring it could easily become a huge headache unless you reserve well in advance, especially on summer weekends and holidays. Even in spring and fall, visitors find themselves paying more than they had hoped or accepting accommodation below their standards. The monopoly held by the Park concessionaire keeps prices high for what you get, and even simple canvas tent cabins cost what you would pay for a reasonable motel elsewhere. Service isn't always efficient either, but at their best these places can be comfortable and welcoming. The best advice is to plan as early as possible, or resign yourself to being flexible.

Most people prefer to stay **in the Park** with the scenic splendor and hiking trailheads close at hand. All of the accommodation options within the Park are listed within this chapter, with most concentrated in Yosemite Valley – the choice ranging from comfortable lodges and hotels to cabins and campgrounds.

While there is an obvious benefit to staying right in Yosemite, heavy demand for accommodation within the Park drives many visitors to consider staying **outside the Park** in one of the small towns along the main access roads. A couple of these towns are interesting in their own right (see chapters 12–15), but most should be regarded simply as jumping-off points for the Park. The best accommodation in all these towns is listed in the following pages as well.

We've divided the accommodation into two main sections with hotels, motels, lodges and B&Bs grouped together, and campgrounds and RV parks in

Price Codes

All the accommodation listed in this book has been categorized into one of nine price codes, as set out below. The prices quoted are for the **cheapest available room for two people in the high season**, and do not include taxes. These are generally 8–12 percent, though there is no tax at Park campgrounds. For campgrounds, and hostels that offer individual beds or bunks, we have given the per person price (excluding tax) along with a code for any private rooms.

In the **off season**, particularly the quiet months from December to March, prices drop by up to forty percent in the hinterland towns and along the highways approaching the Park, though inside the Park reductions are only five to ten percent.

- ❶ up to $45
- ❷ $46–60
- ❸ $61–80
- ❹ $81–100
- ❺ $101–140
- ❻ $141–180
- ❼ $181–240
- ❽ $241–300
- ❾ $301 and over

a subsequent section. Visitors looking for low cost "indoor" accommodation should also check under "Campgrounds and RV Parks" as several of the places listed rent out budget cabins.

Within the Park, most of the lowland hotels and lodges (and even some of the campgrounds) stay **open all year**, though snow restricts access to high-country lodges such as those at Tuolumne Meadows and White Wolf.

Hotels, motels, lodges and B&Bs

Virtually all noncamping accommodation **in the Park** is managed by the Park concessionaire, Delaware North Companies in Yosemite (DNC: see below). The most basic and cheapest lodging is at Curry Village, *Housekeeping Camp*, *White Wolf Lodge* and *Tuolumne Meadows Lodge*, where most guests are housed in either canvas-walled tent cabins, or three-sided concrete "cabins." Standard hotel- and motel-style rooms predominate at the *Wawona Hotel* and *Yosemite Lodge*, and for those who want to splurge, there are gorgeous rooms and suites at *The Ahwahnee*.

Near Wawona, *The Redwoods in Yosemite* is the only non-DNC accommodation in the Park, but a dozen or so B&Bs can be found at **Yosemite West**, a small enclave just outside the Park boundary accessible only from inside the Park off Wawona Road. This is also the closest accommodation to Badger Pass Ski Area. There are more vacation homes at the private village of **Foresta**, right on the western Park boundary, eight miles from Yosemite Valley, and again, only accessible from within the Park.

Outside the Park the choice becomes wider, with numerous motels and B&Bs lining all three highways from the west, and many more pack the surrounding towns of Groveland, Coulterville, Mariposa and Oakhurst. In the east, only Lee Vining has much in the way of accommodation with a few motels. The budget conscious should also be aware of **hostel** accommodation at the excellent *Yosemite Bug*, ten miles east of Mariposa and the only such place easily accessible from the Valley. See the "Yosemite and Around" map on p.198 for the locations of accommodation outside the Park.

Yosemite is popular year-round, but most places offer slightly reduced prices during the **winter season** (mid-Nov to mid-March excluding holidays). In the Park, Curry Village and *Yosemite Lodge* both drop their rates, saving you 10–15 percent on standard prices, perhaps a little more midweek. Outside the Park, savings tend to be greater with most places dropping at least one price code, though at weekends prices can remain close to high-season levels.

It is also worth looking out for discount **lodging packages** through the DNC website, which frequently offers off-season long-weekend or midweek deals.

DNC reservations

Almost all accommodation in the Park is operated by the Park concessionaire Delaware North Companies in Yosemite (**DNC**). Reservations can be made up to a year and a day in advance (though a few weeks is adequate at most times) either online (Ⓦwww.yosemitepark.com), or by phoning Ⓣ559/253-6535.

In the Valley

The Ahwahnee Shuttle stop 3; reserve with DNC, front desk ⓣ209/372-1407; open all year. Undoubtedly the finest place to stay in Yosemite, *The Ahwahnee* (described in detail on p.61) lies just a short distance from Yosemite Village, set among the trees and meadows below the Royal Arches. Despite rates which start around $425, you'll have to book months in advance to obtain one of the spacious rooms, each decorated with the hotel's running Native American and Oriental motifs. They come equipped with top-quality furnishings and bedding along with TV, phone, and in many cases a wondrous view. For the same price you might prefer one of the two-dozen guest cottages out amid the pines and cedars and with a rustic tenor, but with all the expected facilities plus, in some, a fireplace. The top floor of the hotel has been converted into four gorgeous suites in English Country style, all with antique furniture, old photos of Valley life, real log fires and fresh flowers. It feels like you're staying in someone's very luxurious home, and so it should for $900–1000 a night. Though grand *The Ahwahnee* avoids stuffiness, exuding a surprisingly low-key lived-in quality that more modern places find difficult (or impossible) to achieve. During the day guests wander through in hiking gear, though to eat in the superb restaurant (p.179) you'll need to dress up. There's also a separate bar (see p.179), and a welter of other facilities including a seasonal tennis court, an outdoor pool (heated year-round), free coffee and pastries in the morning, and free tea and cookies with piano accompaniment at 4pm daily in the Great Lounge. Special weekend deals are listed on the DNC website. ⑨

Curry Village Shuttle stops 13, 13a, 13b, 14, 20 & 21; reserve with DNC; open all year but tent cabins limited in winter. Largest of all the accommodation areas in the Park, Curry Village can accommodate well over a thousand people. It dates back to 1899 when it was opened as the budget Camp Curry (see p.64), and continues its tradition of catering largely to families. Consequently it is seldom peaceful; but it is handy for shops, swimming pool (free to guests; otherwise $3), ice rink, bike and raft rental and more. Unlike *Housekeeping Camp* (see p.166), there are no self-catering facilities, so you'll appreciate the proximity of the

▲ Cabins at Curry Village

Coffee Corner, *Pavilion Buffet*, *Pizza Patio* and *Taqueria*. And being on the shady side of the Valley, this is the coolest accommodation on hot summer days.

Most people stay in one of the 400-plus canvas-walled tent cabins (mid-March to Nov nightly, Dec to mid-March Fri, Sat and holidays only) that sleep two, three or five. All come with wooden floors, an electric light and a propane heater for winter use (extra $4). Beds are made up at the beginning of your stay but you do your own housekeeping thereafter. One step up are the carpeted four-person cabins with table and heater, but no private bathrooms. Other options include: larger and vastly more appealing rustic cabins with bath and a small deck in a quiet area; sixteen standard rooms fashioned from what was originally the 1904 dance hall; and a few specialty cottages all decorated to a higher standard. None of the accommodation options here has a phone and only the specialty cottages have a TV. Children twelve and under stay free in the motel rooms and hard-walled cabins, but are charged $6 each in tent cabins. Third and fourth adults in a tent or room cost $10–14. Cottages ❼, rooms ❻, cabins with bath ❺, cabins without bath ❹, tent cabins ❸

Housekeeping Camp Shuttle stop 12; reserve with DNC; April to mid-Oct only. Loved by many, *Housekeeping Camp* is the only Park lodging that gives you the option of doing your own cooking. It comprises a cluster of around 260 strangely primitive concrete and canvas "cabins" located among the pines by a sandy beach on the south bank of the Merced River with good views of Half Dome and Yosemite Falls. Sort of like camping without a tent, you get three concrete walls, a concrete floor, a white plastic roof and one side which opens through canvas curtains onto a cook-out area with outdoor seating made somewhat private by the surrounding fence. Each cabin has a table, a light and electricity supply, an outdoor grill pit for barbecues, a double bed and two fold-down bunks: bring your own bedding or rent for $2.50 per bed, per night. There's access to toilets, showers (8am–10pm), pay laundry and an on-site grocery store; gas stoves can be rented for cooking, and all food must be stored in the bear-proof boxes dotted around. With the addition of a couple of camp beds, each cabin can sleep six, but rates are for up to four. ❸

Yosemite Lodge Shuttle stop 8; reserve with DNC; open all year. Often filled with tour groups, this sprawling site with more than 250 rooms occupies the Valley's middle ground. Accommodation is motel style; comfortable without being anything special, though its proximity to decent restaurants, a bar, swimming pool (free to guests; otherwise $5), bike rental, grocery shop and evening entertainment makes it perhaps the most convenient all-round accommodation in the Valley. Rooms fall into two categories; all have private bathroom, phone and TV but no a/c. The cheapest are the Standard Rooms, some fairly spacious with two double or king-size beds. The Lodge Rooms are generally larger, mostly have ceiling fans, come with a separate dressing area and all have a small patio or balcony with a couple of chairs for taking in the sun and scenery. Children 12 and under stay free in the same room. Standard ❻, lodge ❼

Northern Yosemite

Tuolumne Meadows Lodge Tuolumne Meadows; reserve with DNC; July to mid-Sept. Though in Tuolumne Meadows – 8775ft up and a perfect base for high-country hikes – this isn't really a lodge at all but a large cluster of seventy wooden-framed tent cabins, each with four beds and a wood-burning stove but no electricity and only candles for light. Bedding is supplied but you do your own housekeeping after arrival. This was one of the original High Sierra Camps (see box, p.174) and though much expanded it maintains the same spirit, with hikers still using it as an overnight stop on the full High Sierra Camp Loop.

The lodge is over a mile from the remainder of Tuolumne Meadows facilities, but there's a restaurant on site (see p.181), showers (free for guests), and newspapers are available from boxes. Rates are for two adults; additional adults cost $10, kids $6. ❹

White Wolf Lodge Reserve with DNC; July to mid-Sept. This is the only Park lodging that's away from the main human honeypots of the Valley, Tuolumne Meadows and Wawona. It is only a mile down a side road off Tioga Road, *White Wolf* still feels quite isolated, surrounded by lodgepole pines, and perfect for easy hikes to Harden Lake (Hike 15), Lukens Lake (Hike 16) and longer forays down into the Grand Canyon of the Tuolumne River (Hike 49). It has a homey feel, though with a campground nearby it can still get busy. The 24 spacious canvas tent cabins sleep four, have a wood-burning stove and candle for light, but have no electricity. Bedding is supplied though there is no daily maid service. The four hard-walled cabins are like regular motel rooms with double beds, chairs on the small porch, propane heating, electricity when the generator is running, bed linens and a daily maid service. Communal showers are free to guests and there's a restaurant on site (see p.182). Tent cabins ❸, cabins ❺

Southern Yosemite

The Redwoods in Yosemite 8038 Chilnualna Falls Rd, Wawona; ⓣ1-888/225-666 or 209/375-6666, ⓦwww.redwoodsinyosemite.com; open all year. The only private accommodation in the Park, the *Redwoods* brings together some 130 fully furnished private homes around Wawona, each let for a minimum two nights (three in summer). Some are rustic log cabins, others plush modern homes, but almost all have a spacious deck with barbecue, TV and firewood for your stove or open fire. Bedding, towels and kitchen utensils are all provided but you'll need to supply all your own food. Rates for a one- or two-bedroom cottage are in the $170–260 range per night; well-appointed full-size homes are in the range $350–420. ❼–❾

Wawona Hotel Reserve with DNC, front desk ⓣ209/375-6556; April–Nov nightly, Jan–March Fri, Sat & holidays only. Second in elegance only to *The Ahwahnee* in the Yosemite hierarchy, the New England-style *Wawona Hotel* (see p.98 for historic detail and other services) dates in part back to 1879, a heritage drawn upon for recent renovations. Its various buildings are all painted white, with wide wraparound verandahs scattered with cane loungers and Adirondack chairs, perfect for spotting the deer that occasionally graze on the lawns. Altogether there are over a hundred rooms, over half with private bath, some with clawfoot tubs. The cheapest rooms – located upstairs in the main building – are smallish and with sloping floors, and come supplied with robes for late-night dashes along the corridor to the shared bathrooms. It is a significant step up to the majority of the rooms, which are scattered in various buildings around the grounds. These more expensive en-suite rooms have been restored gracefully and have been fitted with old-style furniture, Victorian patterned wallpaper and ceiling fans. In keeping with the overall tenor, none of the rooms have phone, TV or a/c. Ask to look at a few rooms as they differ greatly: some are well suited to families, with the adults being able to watch the kids in the pool from their balcony; others link together making them ideal for small groups and some are perfect for a private escape – *Moore's Cabin* and *Clark Cottage* (once lived in by Galen Clark) are particularly romantic.

Meals are served in the *Wawona Dining Room* (see p.181), and you can bookend your meal with aperitifs and after-dinner drinks in the lounge listening to Tom Bopp at the piano (see p.99). It always pays to check web specials and deals. Children 12 and under stay free in the same room. Room with bath ❼, room with shared bath ❺

Yosemite West and Foresta

Yosemite Peregrine 7509 Henness Circle, Yosemite West; ⓣ1-800/396-3639 or 209/372-8517, ⓦwww.yosemiteperegrine.com; open all year. A well-appointed B&B (only open Fri & Sat nights) tastefully decorated in both Southwestern and woodsy themes, complete with an outdoor hot tub. Evening refreshments and home-cooked breakfasts are served on the deck if the weather cooperates. The adjacent *Falcon's Nest* (same contact details) has a pair of attractively appointed budget-oriented rooms. Both properties have a two-night minimum (three on holiday weekends). *Peregrine* ❼, *Falcon's Nest* ❻

Yosemite Scenic Wonders 7421 Yosemite Park Way, Yosemite West; ⓣ1-888/967-3648, ⓦwww.scenicwonders.com; open all year. This vacation rental homes company manages over a dozen quality homes sleeping from two to eight making them especially good value for families or two couples traveling together. All are comfortable though some are more luxurious than others with hot tubs, open fireplaces and sundecks; check the website for full details. Most charge

$250–350 a night for two in summer, though *Studio Condominiums* starts at $140. ❻–❾

Yosemite Vacation Homes Foresta; ⓦwww.4yosemite.com. Almost a dozen independently owned vacation homes in the private enclave of Foresta, some with great views. All are well appointed and come fully equipped: just bring food and drink. Choose from: *El Capitan View* (ⓣ1-888/438-3522; ❽) which sleeps six; *Half Dome View* (ⓣ1-866/367-3543; just ❾) which sleeps eight); or *Clouds Rest* (ⓣ1-866/320-1588; ❽) which sleeps four but is perfect for two. Rates are quoted for two people (extras typically pay $30 a head) and there's often a two- or three-night minimum. ❽–❾

Hwy-120 West: Groveland, Coulterville and around

The following establishments are listed in order of their proximity to Yosemite Valley (see map, p.198).

Yosemite Lakes 31191 Hardin Flat Rd, off Hwy-120 West, 5 miles from the Big Oak Flat Entrance and eighteen miles east of Groveland; ⓣ1-800/533-1001 or 209/962-0121, ⓦwww.stayatyosemite.com. This scattered, family-oriented resort benefits from being so close to the Park. Tent sites are well spaced ($29.50, full RV hookups $37), cabins come with a double bed and a set of bunks, and there are conical-roofed canvas-walled yurts with polished wood floors, a pleasant deck, cooking facilities, shower and toilet, which sleep four in considerable comfort. Their "hostel" section has no dorms. Just comfortable but fairly bare private rooms with shared bath and a communal kitchen and lounge. Rates are around ten percent higher at weekends when a two-night stay is required. Cabins ❸, rooms ❸, yurts ❻

Evergreen Lodge 33160 Evergreen Road, Mather, a mile west of the Big Oak Flat Entrance then 7 miles north of Hwy-120 West; ⓣ209/379-2606 or 1-800/935-6343, ⓦwww.evergreenlodge.com. A peaceful, pine-shrouded resort on the road to Hetch Hetchy with 66 cabins scattered around the main lodge and recreation building. Traditional cabins are modernized and very comfortable, and there are even more spacious deluxe models with shower/tub. There's a general store with espresso bar, good restaurant, bar (the only places you'll find TV), and every night in summer the lodge puts on entertainment in the form of a slide show, movie or live music. Cabins ❻, deluxe ❼

Yosemite Riverside Inn 11399 Cherry Lake Rd, eleven miles from the Big Oak Flat Entrance and fourteen miles east of Groveland; ⓣ1-800/626-7408 or 209/926-7408, ⓦwww.yosemiteriversideinn.com. A woodsy set of motel units and riverside cabins located half a mile off the highway, with good fishing and river swimming nearby. Decent doubles come with TV, a/c and slightly dated decor, though you're probably better opting for the cabins with two doubles, a small kitchen and barbecue pit. An extended continental breakfast is included in summer. Rooms ❺, riverview cabins ❻

Yosemite Westgate Lodge 7633 Hwy-120 West, thirteen miles from Big Oak Flat Entrance and eleven miles east of Groveland; ⓣ1-888/315-2378 or 209/962-5281, ⓦwww.yosemitewestgate.com. The closest standard motel to the Park on Hwy-120 West, the *Lodge* is comfortable and comes with all the expected facilities including satellite TV, phone, pool and hot tub. Some deluxe rooms have limited cooking facilities, though there's decent eating next door at the *Buck Meadow's Restaurant*. Two kids under twelve stay free with two adults, and rates drop dramatically in winter. Midweek ❺, weekend ❻

Groveland Motel & Indian Village 18933 Hwy-120, Groveland; ⓣ1-888/849-3529 or 209/962-7865, ⓦwww.grovelandmotel.net. A wide array of accommodation options dotted about pleasantly wooded grounds. Options include fairly basic air-conditioned cabins with cable TV (❹), a couple of mobile homes with small kitchens (❺), and concrete-floored teepees (❶) clustered around a campfire: it's like camping only with a double bed and somewhere to plug in your hair dryer. They also have *in situ* tents with airbeds (❶) and you can pitch your own tent for $15. ❶–❺

Hotel Charlotte 18736 Hwy-120, Groveland; ⓣ1-800/961-7799 or 209/962-6455, ⓦwww.hotelcharlotte.com. This ten-room hotel dating back to 1921 has been lovingly updated and is full of character. Rooms are mostly small and lack phones, but all have beautiful old-fashioned bathrooms and a/c and some have TV. Rates include a good continental breakfast, and there's free Wi-Fi throughout the hotel. ❹

Groveland Hotel **18767 Hwy-120 West, Groveland; ⓣ1-800/273-3314 & 209/962-4000, ⓦwww.groveland.com.** Though originally founded in an adobe house in 1849, this historic hotel now occupies a wooden two-story structure built in 1914 for VIP guests during the damming of Hetch Hetchy. The hotel is now run as a B&B with luxurious antique-filled rooms, most containing high, quilted beds and deep baths. Best are the three suites, complete with fireplace and spa tub. Wicker chairs on the verandah are perfect for catching the early evening sun before dining in the *Victorian Room* (see p.183), which is also used for the buffet breakfast. Rooms ❻, suites ❽

All Seasons Groveland Inn **18656 Main St, Groveland; ⓣ1-800/595-9993 or 209/962-0232, ⓦwww.allseasonsgrovelandinn.com.** Very comfortable lodging in an 1897 house uncharacteristically decorated in primary colors and bold designs, each room with a "dramatic feature," be it a small waterfall, extravagant hand-painted mural, steam room, or a private deck with a telescope. All have fridge and coffeemaker and most have a fireplace and Jacuzzi. A self-serve continental breakfast is included and guests have access to a small kitchen. ❺

Hotel Jeffery **Corner Hwy-49 & Hwy-132, Coulterville; ⓣ209/878-3471, ⓦwww.hoteljefferygold.com.** Classic gold-era hotel used by original Yosemite sightseers as well as Theodore Roosevelt. Accommodation is mostly in smallish old-fashioned but well-kept rooms ranging from those with a bathroom down the hall, through rooms with private bath to two-room suites. All have access to a communal lounge and sunny deck, and ceiling fans keep the place tolerably cool. Free Wi-Fi. Suites ❻, en-suite rooms ❺, rooms ❹

Yosemite Gold Country Motel **10407 Hwy-49, Coulterville; ⓣ1-800/247-9884 or 209/878 3400.** This excellent-value and welcoming motel, half a mile north of Coulterville, has aged, but has well-kept and nicely appointed motel rooms each with a/c, VCR/TV, fridge and microwave. ❸

Hwy-140: El Portal and Midpines

The following are listed in order of distance from Yosemite Valley (see map, p.198).

Yosemite View Lodge **11136 Hwy-140, El Portal, two miles west of the Arch Rock Entrance; ⓣ1-888/742-4371 or 209/379-2681, ⓦwww.yosemiteresorts.us.** Vast and luxurious – though slightly soulless – complex with rooms, suites, moderately priced restaurant, convenience store and several swimming and spa pools located on the Park boundary beside the tumbling Merced River. The modern rooms all have a/c, phone, cable TV and either one king or two queen beds (and most have a balcony of some sort), but you pay a premium to get river view, fireplace, in-room spa tub and kitchenette. The entire place is often booked well in advance, but it may be worth trying for no-shows; winter prices start under $100. Premium rooms ❽, standard rooms ❻

Cedar Lodge **9966 Hwy-140, El Portal, 8 miles west of Arch Rock Entrance; ⓣ1-800/321-5261 or 209/379-2612, ⓦwww.yosemiteresorts.us.** Older and smaller cousin of the *Yosemite View Lodge* (see above) with indoor and outdoor pools, on-site restaurant, a slightly narrower variety of rooms (none of them riverside), and lower prices to match. With over two hundred rooms there's a fair chance of getting something when everywhere else is full. Suites with kitchenettes ❻, rooms ❺

Yosemite Bug Rustic Mountain Resort **6979 Hwy-140, Midpines, ten miles east of Mariposa, 23 miles west of the Arch Rock Entrance; ⓣ209/966-6666, ⓦwww.YosemiteBug.com; office open 7am–11pm.** With a couple of dozen buildings scattered through twenty acres of woodland, this low-cost to mid-range lodge and campground is the handiest budget lodgings near Yosemite. It includes an HI-USA hostel (adhering to their conservation ethics, but generally running along looser, less institutional lines) and has an international atmosphere, though there are separate rooms away from the bustle if you'd prefer. Self-catering facilities exist for those staying in dorms, but there's also the excellent *Café at the Bug* (see p.183) on site. Mixed and single-sex dorms ($15; nonmembers $18) are clean and comfortable, though those wanting a little privacy might prefer the tent cabins (❷) or shared-bath private rooms (❸). Those seeking extra comfort will prefer the en-suite rooms with decks but no phone or TV (❹), all distinctively decorated – Russian, Zulu,

Country French, Austin Powers, etc. Pitching your own tent costs $17 per site. Other facilities include laundry, free Internet and Wi-Fi, trails to a good summer swimming hole, gear rental (bikes $17 a day; snowshoes $8 a day; tire chains $20 a day), and access to a hot tub, sauna, massage and yoga classes. YARTS buses run into the Park from the stop right outside. Reservations essential June–Sept. ❷–❹

Bear Creek Cabins 6993 Hwy-140, Midpines, ten miles east of Mariposa, 23 miles west of the Arch Rock Entrance; ⓣ1-888/303-6993 or 209/966-5253, ⓦwww.yosemitecabins.com. Well-maintained series of cabins including a basic cabin with full kitchen sleeping up to four (❺), larger standard rooms (❹) all with log finish, kitchenette, tub and shower, and very spacious suites (❺) with a separate living room, gas fireplace and a full kitchen. All have access to a deck and barbecue area. ❹–❺

Muir Lodge 6833 Hwy-140, Midpines, 8.6 miles east of Mariposa, 23.2 miles west of the Arch Rock Entrance; ⓣ209/966-2468, ⓦwww.yosemitemuirlodge.com. Old and fairly basic motel units (with TV and microwave) that haven't been upgraded for years but are at least clean and cheap. ❷

Hwy-140: Mariposa

Best Western Yosemite Way Station 4999 Hwy-140 ⓣ209/966-7545 or 1-800/528-1234, ⓦwww.yosemite-motels.com. Large and comfortable chain motel where the fairly large modern rooms all come with shower/tub, cable TV and continental breakfast, and have access to a heated outdoor pool overlooking a small stream. Rates down to $60 in winter. ❺

Comfort Inn 4994 Bullion St ⓣ209/966-4344 or 1-800/221-2222, ⓦwww.yosemite-motels.com. Modern mid-range motel with Wi-Fi and a/c in all rooms, access to an outdoor pool and hot tub, and a continental breakfast included. Some suites with cooking facilities. ❺

Yosemite Inn 5180 Jones St ⓣ1-866/470-7130 or 209/742-6800, ⓦwww.yosemiteinn.net. Good value, recently renovated motel with some new and large a/c rooms, most with two beds; all rooms have shower/tub combos and cable TV. There's a pool and spa, and a good continental breakfast is served. Rates may drop to as little as $55 a night in winter. ❺

Highland House B&B Inn 3125 Wild Dove Lane ⓣ209/966-3737, ⓦwww.highlandhouseinn.com. It's worth the effort to reach this superb B&B tranquilly tucked away amid ponderosa pines and incense cedars around twelve miles northeast of Mariposa. The three elegantly furnished rooms all have private bathroom with tub and shower, and the suite (❻) has a four-poster bed, fireplace and VCR. Breakfasts are delicious, there's a full kitchen for guests' use and the common area even has a pool table. Located off Jerseydale road, but call for detailed directions. Reserve well ahead in summer. ❺

River Rock Inn 4993 Seventh St ⓣ209/966-5793, ⓦwww.riverrockncafe.com. Peaceful, welcoming and good value seven-room budget motel just off Mariposa's main drag with attractively decorated smallish rooms (and a couple of larger suites) all equipped with a/c, fridge and coffee pot. Continental breakfast (included) is served in the adjacent *River Rock Deli*. Suites ❹, rooms ❸

Hwy-140: Merced

HI-Merced Home Hostel Call for pick-up or directions once in Merced ⓣ209/725-0407, ⓔmerced-hostel@juno.com. The best place to stay in Merced if you are relying on public transportation, this reservations-only establishment is a hospitable private home with just two single-sex four-bunk dorms ($15; nonmembers $18). Check-in hours and access hours are limited (7–9am & 5–10pm), but this is a small inconvenience for the benefits of a free ride to and from the train and bus stations, an enthusiastic welcome, as much Yosemite information as you can handle and a free dessert every evening. It is a great place to hook up with Yosemite-bound travelers, maybe teaming up to rent a car for a couple of days exploration. The hostel also rents sleeping bags ($5 a night) and two-person tents ($5).

Holiday Inn Express 730 Motel Drive ⓣ1-800/465-4329 or 209/383-0333. High-standard motel with all the expected facilities including HBO, pool, sauna and free Wi-Fi. ❺

The Hooper House - Bear Creek Inn 575 W N Bear Creek Drive ⓣ209/723-3991, ⓦwww.hooperhouse.com. B&B in a lovely Colonial-style house furnished with polished floors, plain painted walls and an understated smattering of antique furnishings. It is all tastefully done and breakfast is served in a grand dining room. ❺

Slumber Motel 1315 W 16th St ⓣ209/722-5783, ⓔbhaktavb@yahoo.com. The pick of a string of basic, budget motels half a mile west of the Transpo Center (left as you step out of the door), with a small pool, cable TV and free Wi-Fi. ❷

Hwy-41: Fish Camp and Oakhurst

The following are listed in order of distance from the Park's South Entrance (see map, p.198).

Owl's Nest Lodging 1235 Hwy-41, Fish Camp ⓣ559/683-3484, ⓦwww.owlsnestlodging.com; closed mid-Oct to April. Nicely decorated, friendly, and right by a stream, this lodge has large guest rooms for two (❺) and self-contained chalets (❻) that sleep up to seven making them an excellent deal for small groups or large families. Closed mid-Oct to April. ❺

Big Creek Inn 1221 Hwy-41, Fish Camp ⓣ559/641-2828, ⓦwww.bigcreekinn.com. High standards are maintained at this new B&B which features three airy and spacious bedrooms, each with shower/tub combo bathrooms, TV/VCR/DVD and French doors opening onto a large deck. A couple of rooms have fireplaces and extensive breakfasts are served (in your room if desired). ❼

Tenaya Lodge 1122 Hwy-41, Fish Camp, 2.5 miles from the South Entrance ⓣ1-888/514-2167 or 559/253-2005, ⓦwww.tenayalodge.com. A modern and attractive four-star complex that makes a fairly successful attempt to replicate the grand tradition of Western Lodges that's best exemplified by *The Ahwahnee*. It caters to conferences and Yosemite tourists with over 200 modern comfortable rooms, three on-site restaurants open to all-comers, indoor and outdoor pools, sauna, hot tubs and gym, and all sorts of outdoor activities like mountain biking, horse riding, guided hiking and even a kids' entertainment program. In summer (when you should always reserve in advance) rates start around $280, though midweek in winter rates can drop to $120. ❽

Narrow Gauge Inn 48571 Hwy-41, Fish Camp, 4.5 miles from the South Entrance; ⓣ1-888/644-9050 & 559/683-7720, ⓦwww.narrowgaugeinn.com. Attractive 26-room lodge with a wide selection of accommodation, many rooms with a balcony and views over the forest. All rooms come with phone, TV and include continental breakfast. There's also a pool and spa, and a fine on-site restaurant (see p.184). Two-night weekend minimum in summer. ❺

Sierra Sky Ranch 50552 Road 632, Oakhurst, 12 miles from the South Entrance ⓣ559/683-8040, ⓦwww.sierraskyranch.com. This woodsy lodge was started in 1875 on what was the largest cattle ranch in the state. It still has a spacious feel with a verandah-girt main lodge, large cozy lounge with heavy wood furniture, and sunny library plus a pool, creek swimming and fishing on-site. Ageing rooms come without a phone but do have cable TV and Wi-Fi. *Sara's Room* boasts a clawfoot tub. ❺

Hounds Tooth Inn 42071 Hwy-41, almost three miles north of Oakhurst ⓣ1-888/642-6610 or 559/642-6600, ⓦwww.houndstoothinn.com. Modern, luxurious B&B with a dozen individually decorated rooms most with either a fireplace or a spa bath (or both) and all air-conditioned. The friendly hosts provide complimentary wine each evening, delicious buffet breakfasts and there's an extensive video library. Rooms ❺, deluxe ❻

Days Inn 40662 Hwy-41, Oakhurst ⓣ1-800/329-7644 or 559/642-2525, ⓦwww.daysinn.com. The cheapest of Oakhurst's franchise motels, but still done to a high standard with comfortable rooms, HBO, free Wi-Fi, a pool and continental breakfast. Rates as low as ❷ in winter. ❺

America's Best Value Inn 48800 Royal Oaks Drive, Oakhurst ⓣ1-800/658-2888 or 559/658 5500, ⓦwww.americasbestvalueinn.com. Slightly soulless chain hotel but recently refurbished and with large airy rooms, cable TV and access to an outdoor pool and spa. Continental breakfast is included and some rooms have a microwave and fridge. ❸ winter rates. ❺

The Homestead 41110 Road 600, Ahwahnee, 4 miles northwest of Oakhurst along Hwy-49 then 2.5 miles south ⓣ1-800/483-0495 or 559/683-0495, ⓦwww.homesteadcottages.com. Just a handful of very attractive and beautifully outfitted adobe cottages – including a/c, TV and gas barbecue – set amid oak-filled foothills, each with full self-catering facilities, a comfortable lounge area and a deck that's perfect for those relaxing sundowners.

Breakfast ingredients are supplied, and there's a two-night minimum stay at weekends. Small "Star Gazing" loft ❻, 1-bedroom cottages ❼, 2-bedroom cottages ❾

Meadow Creek Ranch Corner Hwy-49 & Triangle Rd ⓣ1-800/853-2037 or 209/966-3843, ⓦwww.meadowcreekranchinn.com. Comfortable B&B inn roughly equidistant from the Park's southern and Arch Rock entrances based around a stagecoach stop dating back to 1858. The two cottages on the grounds are decorated with old-fashioned furnishings, and each has its own entrance but the excellent breakfast is served in the main house. ❺

Hwy-120 East and Lee Vining

The following are listed in order headed east from Tioga Pass (see map, p.198).

Tioga Pass Resort Two miles east of Tioga Pass ⓣ209/372-4471, ⓦwww.tiogapassresort.com; late May to mid-Oct. Streamside mini-resort at 9600ft originally built in 1914 and comprising woodsy, self-contained, shingle-roofed cabins with full bathrooms, and motel units without cooking facilities. There's an excellent little diner on site and even a small grocery and an espresso cart in summer. The place stays open in winter (when the road is closed) at which time you'll need to ski or snowmobile in from the snowline in Lee Vining Canyon. Cabins ❼, units ❺

El Mono Motel US-395, Lee Vining ⓣ760/647-6310, ⓦwww.elmonomotel.com. Basic motel that's the place to go if looking for the cheapest roof over your head around Lee Vining. ❸

Murphey's Motel 51493 US-395, Lee Vining ⓣ1-800/334-6316 or 760/647-6316, ⓦwww.murpheysyosemite.com. Very clean and well-presented motel in the center of town, with cable TV and a/c. Some units have a kitchen at no extra cost, and there are bathrooms with both shower and tub. ❹

Campgrounds and RV parks

As with any national park, **camping** is the best way to really feel part of your surroundings, though this is perhaps less true in Yosemite Valley where the campgrounds are large and crowded, especially from May to September. Around 700,000 people camp in the Valley annually, so rules are strictly imposed and camping outside recognized sites is strictly forbidden. Beyond the Valley, things improve dramatically with a number of delightful road-accessible campgrounds.

Park campgrounds vary in altitude from 4000ft in Yosemite Valley to 8600ft at Tuolumne Meadows. Take note of the altitude listed under each campground: a balmy summer evening in the Valley could easily be decidedly chilly in Tuolumne. Wherever they are, Park campgrounds are all set amid pines and are eternally dusty affairs. They typically offer plumbed toilets and potable water, cost $20, and provide space for up to two vehicles and six people (including children). Several offer more limited facilities but charge less. In addition there is the *Camp 4* walk-in site in the Valley, and a couple of tent-only sites outside. Unless otherwise noted the price quoted is for the site, not per person.

RV campers can use all the main campgrounds but there are currently no hookups in Yosemite. Dump stations are in Yosemite Valley (Upper Pines Campground), Wawona and Tuolumne Meadows (summer only).

Outside the Park there's more variety with a number of commercial campgrounds along the access roads. Most have some tent sites, but generally cater to RVs, offer all manner of facilities and diversions and charge accordingly.

The entire Park is surrounded by National Forests, all offering simple campgrounds that often act as an overspill for the national park. We've mentioned those most convenient for forays into the Park.

Reservations

Bookings are required year-round for campgrounds in Yosemite Valley that remain busy for most of the year, even winter weekends. If you are headed for one of the first-come-first-served campgrounds you'll usually get a place if you arrive before noon, though your chances are better midweek. At bookable campgrounds, **reserve** beforehand through Ⓦwww.recreation.gov which accepts phone and Internet bookings (daily: March–Oct 7am–9pm Pacific time, Nov–Feb 7am–7pm). Within the US and Canada call Ⓣ1-877/444-6777, from outside the US or Canada use Ⓣ518/885-3639, and TDD 1-877/833-6777 or book through the website at Ⓦwww.recreation.gov.

Reservations open in one-month chunks, **five months in advance**, so to book for the month July 15–August 14 you should make contact starting February 15. Popular days between May and September often book out within minutes of becoming available. You'll be required to supply personal contact details, the park and campground you wish to stay at, dates, number of people and pets, indication of tent or RV (including length of vehicle), and any discounts you are eligible for such as Senior Pass or Access Pass (see p.32). After booking, any changes or **cancellations** incur a cost of $10 per reservation.

Those **without reservations** will need to show up very early in the morning and hope for cancellations at one of the reservations offices which all deal with reservations for their own area: either the Curry Village Reservations Office (May to mid-Oct daily 8am–5pm, mid-Oct to April daily 8.30am–4.30pm) or its equivalent in Tuolumne Meadows (July–early Sept daily 8am–5pm), Wawona (May–Sept daily 8am–5pm), and by the Big Oak Flat entrance station (May–Sept daily 8am–5pm).

The same reservation system can be used for groups up to thirty who can book special **group campsites** at Tuolumne Meadows, Hodgdon Meadow, Bridalveil Creek and Wawona.

Campground practicalities

Camping in Yosemite is restricted to one month in any calendar year, but between May and mid-September fourteen days is the **maximum stay**, of which only seven can be spent in the Valley and seven more at Wawona. **Check-out times** are 10am in Yosemite Valley and noon outside the Valley.

All campgrounds in Yosemite have **tent sites**, often well away from the **RV sites**. *Camp 4*, *Tamarack* and *Yosemite Creek* are tent-only campgrounds. **RVs** over 40ft are not permitted in Valley campgrounds and 35ft is the maximum in campgrounds outside the Valley. Currently there are **no hookups** of any sort in Yosemite, and sparing **generator use** is only permitted between 7am and 7pm: **quiet hours** are from 10pm to 6am. Each site accommodates up to six people and two vehicles. For more on camping rules consult Ⓦwww.nps.gov/yose/planyourvisit/campregs.htm.

Free **dump stations** exist in Yosemite Valley by the entrance to the *Upper Pines* campground (open all year); Wawona (open all year) and Tuolumne Meadows (June to early Sept). **Pets** are not encouraged in Yosemite campgrounds but are allowed in most (see Basics, p.36).

For details of **showers** and **laundry** facilities see "Travel essentials" on p.35.

Though no limitations apply in winter, summertime air quality restrictions in the Valley only allow **campground fires** between 5 and 10pm from May to September. For ecological reasons, neither firewood nor kindling (including pine cones and needles) can be gathered in the Valley, so you'll need to either bring

High Sierra Camps

Hikers who fancy carrying a light load and ending the day with a hot shower, a comfortable bed, and a hearty meal might consider staying at one (or all) of the five **High Sierra Camps**, spectacularly sited complexes of tent cabins about a day's walk apart (6–10 miles) in the Tuolumne backcountry. Located at Glen Aulin (Map, p.82; 7800ft), May Lake (Map, p.82; 9270ft), Sunrise (Map, p.82; 9400ft), Merced Lake (Map, p.92; 7150ft), and Vogelsang (Map, p.82; 10,300ft), each camp sleeps thirty to sixty people in four- to six-bed dormitory-style tents. They come with steel-framed beds, mattresses, pillows and blankets, so all you need to bring is sheets or a sleep sack, towel and personal items. Don't forget that hip flask for a relaxing sundowner: none of the HSCs sell alcohol. **Merced Lake** is the largest and often has openings when others are full: there's fishing and swimming nearby.

Unfortunately, the season is short (late June until after the second weekend in Sept) and the demand is high, so aspirants have to enter a **lottery** to stay in the HSCs. Applications are made between November 1 and January 15 using a form downloadable from the Ⓦwww.yosemitepark.com website under "Lodging." The site also included details of obtaining the requisite form by phone or mail.

Applicants are notified by the end of February, and cancellations become available on April 1; check the website for availability, phone Ⓣ559/253-5674 or call at the front desk at *Tuolumne Meadows Lodge* which also keeps a list of vacancies for the current week.

Successful applicants pay $136 a night (excluding tax; kids 7–12 $85, children under seven not allowed) for bed, three-course dinner, an energy giving breakfast served family style, and hot **showers** (except at Glen Aulin and Vogelsang where showers are not available). Tents are usually single-sex, though members of a party can be accommodated in the same tent. **Dinner** and **breakfast** may also be available to nonguest hikers who reserve in advance ($36 for both meals; Ⓣ559/253-5674). A sack lunch is also available ($10.50): order at the camp.

The camps are mostly frequented by older, moderately well-heeled hikers who often combine the camps into a circuit known as the High Sierra Camp Loop (see p.146): either book the nights in whatever order you choose, or join a guided hike (see p.135), or a guided mule-back saddle trip (see p.152).

wood with you from outside the Valley or buy supplies (around $9 a box) from the stores in Yosemite Village and Curry Village. Fires can be started with newspaper, which produces less smoke than pine needles. Campfires are permitted at all times in other parts of the Park, but only dead and down wood may be collected, and not in the giant sequoia groves nor above 9600ft. Outside the Valley you can buy firewood at the Wawona and Tuolumne Meadows stores.

In the valley

Camp 4 Walk-In Shuttle stop 7; 4000ft; open all year; space for 210 people; $5 per person. First-come-first-served site west of (and away from) the other Valley sites, and very popular with rock climbers. It is a fairly bohemian (some would say squalid) place with sites just a few yards from the dusty parking lot and shared by six people. The campground is non-reservable and often full by 9am, especially in spring and fall when climbers are here in numbers. A ranger staffs a small kiosk at the site to register campers at around 8.30am each morning, but such is the demand you may have to join the line at 7am and still may not get a place. There's piped water and flush toilets, but there are no showers and the already inadequate washing facilities are rendered more so by climbers not looking after them. A few years back, climbers succeeded in getting the Park Service to recognize their historic name and ditch the previous title of *Sunnyside*. As in the rest of the Valley camping here is limited to 7 days in the summer season

(May to mid-Sept), a regulation that is increasingly heavily enforced. No pets.

Lower Pines Shuttle stop 19; 4000ft; late March–Oct; 60 tent and RV sites; $20. One of three almost identical Valley campgrounds (along with *North Pines* and *Upper Pines*), surrounded by evergreens and with the Merced River running along one side, and Stoneman Meadow on the other. This is the only Valley campground specifically designed with wheelchair accessible sites (with electric wheelchair charging outlets), and also has an RV and tent site with tap water, flush toilets, picnic tables and fire pits. The Curry Village showers are close at hand, and there's an amphitheater for camp ranger programs.

North Pines Shuttle stop 18; 4000ft; April–Sept; 81 tent and RV sites; $20. Similar to *Lower Pines* (see above) but slightly more isolated from Curry Village, closer to the stables and a touch quieter.

Upper Pines Shuttle stops 15 & 19; 4000ft; open all year; 238 tent and RV sites; $20. Easily the biggest of the Valley campgrounds with pine-shrouded sites, toilets, water and fire rings; especially popular with RVers. It has the Valley's only RV dump station, which can be used by guests at the other campgrounds.

Yosemite Valley backpacker campground Shuttle stop 18; 4000ft; open all year; 20 sites; $5 per person with wilderness permit. Small, peaceful campground only available to hikers setting off on, or returning from backcountry trips. There's a one-night maximum stay, and campers must have a valid wilderness permit for the next or previous night. The main access is through the *North Pines* campground.

Northern Yosemite

Crane Flat 6200ft; July–early Oct; 166 tent and RV sites; $20. Northwest of the Valley, at the beginning of the Tioga Road, this large but appealing reservation-only campground is particularly handy for the Tuolumne and Merced groves of giant sequoias. There's piped water, flush toilets, fireplaces and picnic tables.

Hetch Hetchy backpacker campground 3800ft; open all year; $5 per person with wilderness permit. Small campground only available to hikers setting off on, or returning from backcountry trips. There's a one-night maximum stay, and campers must have a valid wilderness permit for the next or previous night.

Hodgdon Meadow 4900ft; open all year; 105 tent and RV sites; $14–20. Relatively quiet creekside campground with flush toilets right on the Park's western boundary beside Hwy-120 West. Reservations are required from mid-April to mid-Oct when it costs $20, but for the rest of the year when piped water is turned off it becomes a $14 first-come-first-served campground.

Porcupine Flat 8100ft; July to mid-Oct; 52 tent and RV sites; $10. Beautifully sited primitive campground along the Tioga Road, nearly forty miles from the Valley but close to Tuolumne Meadows and some important trailheads. Though small it is often one of the last to fill at busy times, partly because facilities are limited to pit toilets, and stream water that should be treated. No pets.

Tamarack Flat 6300ft; late June–Sept; 52 tent sites; $10. Small first-come-first-served site two miles down a rough road off the Tioga Road, 23 miles from the Valley and with only limited RV access. As with *Porcupine Flat*, there are pit toilets and stream water that should be treated. No pets.

Tuolumne Meadows 8600ft; July–late Sept; 304 tent and RV sites; $20. Yosemite's largest campground by far, but still an attractive affair beside a subalpine meadow right by the Tuolumne River where there's reasonable trout fishing. Popular with both car campers and backpackers, half the sites are available by advance reservation, half available by same-day reservation at the office near the entrance. Flush toilets, piped water and a dump station are all on site, and showers are available at *Tuolumne Meadows Lodge* for $4 (see p.166). Sites along Loop A are closest to the river but are generally smaller than on other loops.

Tuolumne Meadows backpacker campground 8600ft; open all year; $5 per person with wilderness permit. One section of the main *Tuolumne Meadows* campground is restricted to hikers setting off on, or returning from backcountry trips. There's a one-night maximum stay, and campers must have a valid wilderness permit for the next or previous night.

White Wolf 8000ft; July to mid-Sept; 74 tent and RV sites; $14. Forest-shrouded first-come-first-served tent and RV campground a mile north of the Tioga Road midway between the Valley and Tuolumne Meadows. It is a particularly pleasant site with good hiking all around (see Hike 15 & Hike 16), but can be plagued by mosquitoes in July. Proximity to *White Wolf Lodge* (see p.166) where you can buy meals and limited groceries adds to its attraction. Maximum RV length 27 feet.

Yosemite Creek 7700ft; July–early Sept; 40 tent sites; $10. First-come-first-served tent-only site that's five miles down a rough road and consequently enough off the beaten track to discourage all except those keen on a bit of solitude. It is often one of the last places to fill up but can still be packed on summer weekends. Pit toilets, and stream water that must be treated are available.

Southern Yosemite

Bridalveil Creek Glacier Point Road; 7200ft; July–early Sept; 110 tent and RV sites; $14. A high-country, first-come-first-served site just off Glacier Point Road that makes a cooler midsummer alternative to the Valley sites. Set beside Bridalveil Creek, there are meadows all around that are gradually being invaded by lodgepole pines, and access to wilderness trails is excellent.

Wawona 4000ft; open all year; 93 tent and RV sites; $14–20. The only site in the southern sector of the Park, approximately a mile north of the *Wawona Hotel*, this campground is located right by the South Fork of the Merced River on a site occupied by the US cavalry for sixteen summers from 1890. Less secluded and shaded than many Park campgrounds, it is nonetheless handy for the Merced Grove of giant sequoias and the Pioneer Yosemite History Center. Reservations are required from May to Sept when it costs $20, but for the rest of the year when piped water is turned off it becomes a $14 first-come-first-served campground. The campground reservation office is beside the stables.

Hwy-120 West: Stanislaus National Forest, Groveland and Coulterville

The following are listed in order of distance from Yosemite's Big Oak Flat entrance.

Dimond O Stanislaus National Forest; Evergreen Rd, 25 miles east of Groveland and one mile west of the Big Oak Flat Entrance. 4400ft; late April to early Oct; 38 sites; $19. The nearest forest campground to the Valley, located six miles north of Hwy-120 West and with tent and small RV sites, pit toilets, piped water and fishing on the Middle Fork of the Tuolumne River. Some sites first-come-first-served, others reservable (Ⓣ1-877/444-6777, ⓦRecreation.gov).

Lost Claim Stanislaus National Forest; Hwy-120 West, twelve miles east of Groveland and fourteen miles west of the Big Oak Flat Entrance; 3100ft; May–early Sept; 10 sites; $14. Small first-come-first-served tent and RV site with pit toilets and hand-pumped water.

The Pines Stanislaus National Forest; Hwy-120 West, nine miles east of Groveland and seventeen miles west of the Big Oak Flat Entrance; 3200ft; open all year; 11 sites; $12. Standard first-come-first-served forest service campground near the Groveland Ranger Station with RV and tent sites amid the pines, toilets and piped water. For kids there's the short Little Golden Trail running through the so-called Children's Forest.

Yosemite Pines RV Resort Half mile off Hwy-120, one mile east of Groveland and twenty-five miles west of the Big Oak Flat Entrance; 3000ft; Ⓣ1-800/368-5368 or 209/962-5042, ⓦwww.yosemitepinesrv.com; open all year; 160 sites; $20–40. Major RV park with heaps of activities including pony rides, gold panning and bike rentals. Tent sites ($20), and full hookups ($35–40) are available, and there's also an array of cabins and units; bedding included. Deluxe cabin ❻, standard cabin ❸

Hwy-140: El Portal, Midpines and Mariposa

The following are listed in order of distance from Yosemite's Arch Rock Entrance (see map, p.198).

Indian Flat RV Park 9988 Hwy-140, 8 miles west of the Arch Rock Entrance; 1400ft; Ⓣ209/379-2339, ⓦwww.indianflatrvpark.com; open all year, 50 sites; $20–35. The nearest hookups to the Valley are at this simple RV park with a separate and reasonably shady tent area, fire rings, picnic tables and a clean shower block ($3 for non-guests). Rates start at $20 for two tenters, going up to $30 for power and water, and $35 for waste hookup.

McCabe Flat Turn off Hwy-140 near the Briceburg Information Center, 20 miles west of the Arch Rock Entrance; 1200ft; open all year, 14 sites; $10. The handiest of three first-come-first-served $10-a-night BLM campgrounds situated at around 1000ft along the Merced River each with pit toilets and river water that must be treated. They're all accessed by a fairly rough road along a former trackbed of the Yosemite Valley Railroad (1906–45): *McCabe Flat* is 2.3 miles along, *Willow Placer* 3.6 miles and *Railroad Flat* 4.5 miles.

Yosemite-Mariposa KOA 6323 Hwy-140, Midpines, six miles east of Mariposa, 25.7 miles west of the Arch Rock Entrance; 2600ft; ⓣ1-800/562-9391 or 209/966-2201, ⓦwww.yosemitekoa.com; open March to mid-Nov; 46 sites. Full facility RV-oriented site with a separate woodland tent area, laundry, outdoor swimming pool, on-site catch-and-release lake fishing and convenience store. Basic tent sites are $33, full hookup costs $42, there are log cabins (❸), some with decks overlooking the fishing pond, and some relatively luxurious lodge rooms (❻) sleeping up to six.

Hwy-41: Oakhurst and Fish Camp

The following are listed in order of distance from Yosemite's South Entrance (see map, p.198).

Summerdale Sierra National Forest, 1.5 miles south of the South Entrance and half a mile north of Fish Camp; 5000ft; ⓣ1-877/444-6777, ⓦRecreation.gov; June–Oct; 29 sites; $19. Typically wooded site that takes the overflow when Wawona is full, and consequently packed most summer weekends.

Nelder Grove Sierra National Forest, off Sky Ranch Rd, 9 miles east of Hwy-41, follow Road 632 which turns off Hwy-41 4 miles north of Oakhurst; 5500ft; May–Oct; 7 sites; free. Primitive campground with stream water and vault toilet inconveniently sited along winding roads some distance from the Park, but it is free and is close to a grove of sequoias threaded by a nature trail.

High Sierra RV Park 40389 Hwy-41, Oakhurst; 2000ft; ⓣ1-877/314-7662 or 559/683-7662, ⓦwww.highsierrarv.com; open all year, 126 sites; $18–28. Compact RV park in the heart of Oakhurst with clean facilities, tents sites ($19, weekends $22) and electricity and water RV hookups ($28, weekends $31).

Hwy-120 East and Lee Vining

The following are listed in order of distance from Yosemite's South Entrance (see map, p.198).

Tioga Lake Inyo National Forest, one mile east of Tioga Pass Entrance; 9700ft; June to mid-Oct; 13 sites; $17. Located beside Tioga Lake with a real alpine feel, this is the best of the highwayside Inyo National Forest campgrounds. It is a first-come-first-served, RV-dominated site that's always popular and is usually the first to fill when *Tuolumne Meadows* is full. There are flush toilets, pump water, fire rings and picnic tables.

Junction Inyo National Forest, 2.2 miles east of Tioga Pass Entrance; 9600ft; June to mid-Oct; 13 sites; $12. First-come-first-served tent and RV site, ranged around a meadow and popular with fishers. Less appealing than *Tioga Lake* but cheaper and with the pleasant Nunatak Nature Trail just nearby. Pit toilets and treatable stream water available.

Sawmill Walk-in Mile 1.5 Saddlebag Lake Rd; 9800ft; June to mid-Oct; 12 sites; $12. Primitive walk-in campground around four hundred yards from its parking lot, superbly sited amid jagged peaks that feel a world away from the glaciated domes around Tuolumne. Arrive early for the most convenient sites with the best views. No reservations.

Saddlebag Lake Mile 2 Saddlebag Lake Rd; 10,000ft; June to mid-Oct; 20 sites; $17. The highest road-accessible campground in California; a beautiful place to stay and with good hiking nearby. First-come-first-served.

Ellery Lake Inyo National Forest 2.5 miles east of Tioga Pass Entrance; 9500ft; June to mid-Oct; 21 sites; $17. Small first-come-first-served campground among pines and rocks with a high mountain tenor, but contrary to the name it is not right next to a lake. Piped water.

Lee Vining Creek Poole Power Plant Rd, roughly 3.5 miles east of Lee Vining and 9 miles west of the Tioga Pass Entrance; 7800ft; late April to late Oct; $14–17. A collection of near-identical streamside campgrounds, all surrounded by trees and each with a campground host in summer. Choose from *Boulder*, *Aspen*, *Big Bend*, *Moraine*, *Cattleguard* and *Lower Lee Vining*.

Mono Vista RV Park US-395 in Lee Vining; ⓣ760/647-6401; 6400ft; $17–30. Pleasant RV park and campground close to Mono Lake and an easy walk from a couple of decent restaurants. There are RV hookups ($24–30), space for tents ($17), and showers which are available to nonguests ($2.25 for 5min; daily 9am–6pm).

Eating and drinking

With the notable exception of the *Ahwahnee Dining Room* and the *Mountain Room Restaurant*, **eating** in Yosemite is more a function than a pleasure. Dishes at the better places can be tasty and decent value (relatively speaking), but food, whether in restaurants or in the grocery stores, is around twenty percent more expensive inside the Park than out.

By judicious selection, even those on a tight budget can get by. The cheapest option is to make your own meals buying groceries outside the Park – Mariposa (see p.207) has the closest large supermarket – or in some of Yosemite's stores. The largest and most varied is at Yosemite Village, and there are narrower selections at Curry Village, Wawona, Crane Flat and Tuolumne Meadows (summer only). All these places are fine for putting together a picnic lunch, but you can also order **box lunches** from some of the Park hotels by calling the front desk the night before.

There are enough restaurants and snack bars in Yosemite Valley to satisfy most needs, and many of the more upscale restaurants have alcohol licenses. Most of the Valley's real **drinking** action, though, takes place in the *Mountain Room Lounge* at Yosemite Lodge, with outdoor possibilities at the *Pizza Deck and Curry Village Bar* in Curry Village, and more refined imbibing at the *Ahwahnee Bar*.

As Yosemite's restaurant and bar choices are limited, you may be tempted to stray **beyond the Park**. In the gateway towns of Groveland, Mariposa, Oakhurst and Lee Vining you'll find plenty of good eating establishments charging reasonable prices, as well as a smattering of bars.

We've listed all eating options within the Park and a selection of the best places in the surrounding area. **Normal summer opening hours** are given; expect shorter hours in shoulder seasons and occasional winter closures. Even in summer few places serve much later than 9pm.

Supermarkets

If you're planning to self-cater during your Park visit, or even just need picnic supplies and snacks, you can save money (and ensure more choice) by doing your grocery shopping outside the Park. The best bets nearby are the Pioneer Market in Mariposa (see p.207) and one of the large supermarkets in Oakhurst. For details of stores inside the Park, see Chapter 11, beginning on p.191.

▲ Dining at The Ahwahnee

Inside the Park

Yosemite Village and The Ahwahnee

Ahwahnee Bar *The Ahwahnee*; shuttle stop 3; daily 11am–11pm. Food served to 9pm. Intimate piano bar where you sit at the bar, at tables out on the terrace, or in the cozy recess at one end and try one of their draft beers and microbrews, or indulge in something more sophisticated. Attentive bar staff will rustle up one of their classic martinis ($15), a classy Manhattan ($9), or perhaps something from their selection of single malts (mostly $12–26), Cognacs, Armagnacs and ports. Light meals such as Caesar salads ($9), antipasto plates for two ($21) and wild boar chili con carne ($9) are served, plus there's espresso coffees and live music most Fri and Sat nights, usually something subdued.

Ahwahnee Dining Room *The Ahwahnee*; shuttle stop 3; reservations essential for dinner (☎209/372-1489); breakfast 7–10.30am, lunch 11.30am–3pm, dinner 5.30–9pm,

Sun brunch 7am–3pm. Quite simply one of the most beautiful restaurants in the US, designed in baronial style with 34-foot high ceilings of exposed sugar pine beams, rustic iron chandeliers, and floor-to-ceiling leaded windows that look out into the forest. Tables graced with starched white tablecloths and tall candles provide the setting for what is by far the best food in Yosemite – though you'd expect something pretty special when main courses range from $25–43 and appetizers are $15–18. Dinner might consist of an Atlantic salmon terrine with dill and crème fraîche, or an endive and watercress salad followed by hot seared Ahi tuna with shoyu butter and wasabi, all washed down with something striking from the extensive and not-too-pricey California-heavy wine list. They charge $30 corkage if you've got that special bottle you want to bring along.

Earlier in the day, expect simpler dishes such as a breakfast wrap ($16) or Eggs Benedict ($17) for breakfast, then a Portobello mushroom and sun-dried tomato roll ($12) or a smoked duck Caesar salad ($15) for lunch. The Sun brunch ($32) is particularly stupendous.

Casual dress is permitted during the day, and even at dinner the old jacket-and-tie requirements have been loosened. It is enough for men to wear long pants, a collared shirt and closed shoes; women should be similarly smartly attired.

The hotel and Dining Room also host a number of annual events that are usually booked out way in advance. See the Annual Events box, pp.186–187 for details of the Chefs' Holidays (Jan & Feb), Vintners' Holidays (Nov & Dec), and the Bracebridge Dinner (Dec).

Degnan's Café Yosemite Village; shuttle stop 4; June to mid-Sept daily 7am–5pm. Slightly pricey espresso coffees and specialty teas plus a selection of danishes, cinnamon rolls (all under $3), scoop and soft-serve ice cream served inside or out. There are newspaper boxes outside and Internet kiosks within.

Degnan's Deli Yosemite Village; shuttle stop 4; daily 7am–6pm. Some of the best take out in the Valley with bowls of soup ($2.75–3.75) and chili ($4–5), and massive sandwiches, burritos and salads for around $7 – try the Yosemite Sam, with pastrami, onion, Swiss cheese, lettuce, tomato and mustard, which is big enough for two small appetites. There's also a good selection of snacks and drinks along with a more limited supply of groceries.

Degnan's Loft Yosemite Village; shuttle stop 4; mid-April to June, Sept & Oct Mon–Fri 5–9pm, Sat & Sun noon–9pm, July & Aug Mon–Fri 5–9pm, Sat & Sun noon–9pm. Though lacking the atmosphere of the *Pizza Deck* in Curry Village, this is the place for gourmet pizzas ($14–18 for medium; $17–22 for a large) such as chicken pesto or "The Mountain" laden with pepperoni, sausage, ham, tomato, olives and more. You can also build your own, and select from soups, salads, a variety of draft beers and bottled wines.

Village Grill Yosemite Village; shuttle stop 2; April–Oct daily 11am–5pm. Fast food Yosemite-style, with the likes of double cheeseburgers ($5.50), fish sandwiches ($5), and burger-fries-and-drink combos ($6–8) to eat out on the deck.

Yosemite Lodge

Mountain Room Lounge *Yosemite Lodge*; shuttle stop 8; Mon–Fri 4.30–11pm, Sat & Sun noon–11pm. The Valley's only straightforward drinking bar that's good anytime for a few beers, but especially convivial in cooler or inclement weather when everyone huddles around the huge circular central fireplace heated by a big brazier. Seats outside in warmer weather are perfect for escaping the continual sports TV inside. There's full bar service along with light snacks – chicken pesto wrap ($6.50), spinach artichoke dip ($7) – which are available until around 9pm.

Mountain Room Restaurant *Yosemite Lodge*; shuttle stop 8; reservations at *Yosemite Lodge* front desk ⓣ209/372-1281; daily 5.30–9.30pm. Second only to the *Ahwahnee Dining Room* in Yosemite's culinary hierarchy, the *Mountain Room* offers semi-formal dining in a more modern setting with huge picture windows that afford an outstanding view of Yosemite Falls from nearly every seat: dine early outside midsummer or you'll miss the view. A short menu is offered which includes soup ($3.25–5.25), then perhaps an appetizer of mushroom strudel ($9), then sesame Ahi tuna fillet with wasabi mash ($25), followed by a flourless chocolate almond torte ($7). There's also a kids' menu and a decent wine and cocktail list.

Yosemite Lodge Food Court ***Yosemite Lodge* at the Falls; shuttle stop 8; breakfast 6.30am–11am; lunch & dinner 11.30am–9pm; coffee and snacks served all day.** Bright and cheerful self-serve café/restaurant that sees the bulk of the dining action around *Yosemite Lodge*. It serves a full range of cold and cooked breakfasts ($3–7), muffins, Danishes and espresso, plus lunches and dinners that range from a grilled chicken sandwich, pizza or gyro platter (all $7) to pasta and meatballs ($9) or chicken, vegetables and rice ($9). There is some outdoor seating where assorted small forest creatures will try to steal your meal.

Curry Village

Coffee Corner Curry Village; shuttle stops 14 & 20; April–Nov and winter weekends 6am–10pm. Simple coffee bar serving light breakfasts, bagels, Danishes, pastries, muffins, moderately palatable espresso coffees and ice cream starting from $1.70.

Pavilion Buffet Curry Village; shuttle stops 14 & 20; April–Oct daily; breakfast 7–10am, dinner 5.30–8pm. Attractive wood-paneled cafeteria decorated with old photos and aquatints of Camp Curry and serving all-you-can-eat breakfast and dinner. Breakfast ($10) is particularly good value with plenty of fresh fruit, juices, eggs, bacon, hash browns, breakfast burritos, waffles, pancakes, French toast, yogurt, muffins and coffee. Dinner ($12) suffers a little from over-cooked vegetables and sloppy preparation but you can still fill up on salads, build-your-own tacos, chicken fried steak, corn, chow mien, simple pasta dishes, cake, fruit cobbler and sodas. Buy a beer or wine at the adjacent bar and carry it through.

Pizza Deck and Curry Village Bar shuttle stops 14 & 20; mid-April to Nov. Pizza and drinks daily noon–10pm. Very much the place to repair on a balmy evening after a hard day of hiking. Fight for an outdoor table while you wait for a pretty decent build-your-own pizza (from $18 for twelve slices), and maybe a pint of quality draft beer ($5) or a daiquiri, margarita or two ($7.50).

Taqueria Curry Village shuttle stops 14 & 20; April–Sept daily 11am–5pm. Hole-in-the-wall take-out joint with deck seating and simple menu of basic Tex-Mex concoctions. Choose from a taco ($3.25), beef and bean burrito ($4-5), or taco salad ($8.25) and a selection of sodas.

The rest of the Park

Tuolumne Meadows Grill Tuolumne Meadows; mid-June to late Sept Sun–Thurs 8am–5pm, Fri & Sat 8am–6pm. Basically a canvas-roofed shed harboring a take out fast-food counter with outside seating; reasonably good value, and always popular with hungry hikers. Eggs, bacon, hash browns and biscuits ($7) are served until 11.30am, then it is cheeseburgers ($5), grilled chicken sandwiches ($6), and chili dogs ($5) until closing. Filter coffee and soft-freeze ice cream are on offer all day, and the Tuolumne Store, next door, sells a decent range of groceries plus firewood, ice and beer.

Tuolumne Meadows Lodge Dining Room Tuolumne Meadows; mid-June to mid-Sept. Breakfast 7–9am (no reservation necessary); dinner 5.50pm and 8pm (reserve on ☎209/372-8413). Family-style tent dining room that mainly caters to lodge guests but also serves nonguests with hearty breakfasts such as bacon and eggs or pancakes and bacon (both $7) and an equally filling choice of dinners. The range extends from a cheeseburger and baked potato ($14) to the likes of pistachio-crusted trout ($19) and cilantro shrimp kebabs ($23). Beer and wine are served, and they'll also prepare box lunches ($6) if requested before 8pm the night before.

Wawona Dining Room Wawona; April–Nov nightly, Jan–March Fri, Sat and holidays only. Dinner reservations for parties of eight or more ☎209/375-1425; breakfast 7.30–10am, lunch 11.30am–1.30pm, dinner 5.30–9pm, cocktails 5–9.30pm. White linen tablecloths, candles, chunky silverware and uniformed waitresses in a grand century-old room lend the *Dining Room* a semi-formal atmosphere, though neither the food nor service is particularly special. Still, the decor and views across the lawns are appealing and you can dine reasonably well during the day on the likes of soup ($3), chicken alfredo, ratatouille, or a club sandwich ($9). In the evening they request smart attire and collared shirts while you tuck into dishes such as pan-fried trout ($21) or chicken picatta ($21) followed by raspberry nut cake ($5). In summer you can eat on the broad verandah.

Look out too for the wonderful Sun brunch buffet (Easter–Thanksgiving 7.30am–1.30pm), which costs $14 if you arrive before 10.30am, $19 afterwards when extra meat dishes are added. The hotel also has a Lawn Barbecue on summer Saturdays (late May to early Sept 5–8pm; for reservations ☎209/375-6572) where you buy whatever meats you want and eat from gingham tablecloths.

White Wolf Lodge White Wolf; mid-June to mid-Sept; breakfast 7.30–9.30am, dinner 6–8.30pm. Dinner reservations required on ☎209/372-8416. Just off Hwy-120 East on the way to Tuolumne Meadows, this simple lodge serves large portions of good-value American food in rustic surroundings: at wooden tables on a broad verandah or, on those cool Sierra evenings, inside beside a roaring fire. Standard breakfasts are available ($10) and the fixed menu dinner ($23) changes nightly and always comes with soup, salad, vegetables, rice or pasta and a roll. Expect the likes of grilled chicken lasagna or steak with sautéed mushrooms, though there's always a vegetarian dish, a short children's menu ($8), and the place is licensed for beer and wine sales. Guests can order box lunches ($6) and the adjacent store has ready-made sandwiches.

Outside the Park

Hwy-120 West: Groveland, Coulterville and around

Café Charlotte 18959 Hwy-120 West, Groveland ☎209/962-6455; Thurs–Sun 5.30–9pm. Excellent little restaurant where the casual atmosphere belies a serious approach to the quality of the food. There's everything from pasta (including vegan and kids' dishes) to chicken Jerusalem (with artichokes and mushrooms) and succulent steaks (all $13–23) plus lip-smacking desserts. Licensed and BYO with $8 corkage.

Cocina Michoacana 18370 Hwy-120 West, Groveland; daily 10am–9pm. Authentic and low-priced Mexican food, specializing in dishes from immediately west of Mexico City. Eight bucks will get you a great breakfast of perhaps scrambled eggs with strips of steak or one of the daily lunch specials, and later in the day they serve a full range of Mexican favorites including great fajitas ($21–25 for two) and melt-in-your-mouth breaded shrimps ($12).

Iron Door 18761 Main St, Groveland ☎209/962-6244; daily 11am–9pm or later; bar nightly to 1am or later. Push through the swing doors into the dim world of what is reliably claimed as one of the oldest saloons in California, dating back to 1852. It was originally a general mercantile and later served as a post office but has been a dedicated bar since 1937 and comes festooned with paraphernalia on the walls, baseball caps and dollar bills pinned to the ceiling, and a pool table in the corner. Most weekends, as you sit at the bar or in booths enjoying one of the microbrews, there's some kind of live music.

The saloon may be the star, but this is also a good place to eat with the *Iron Door Grill* serving the likes of chicken Portabello ravioli ($18), ribeye steak ($22), or salmon teriyaki ($20) all nicely prepared and presented.

Magnolia Saloon *Hotel Jeffery* Corner Hwy-49 & Hwy-132, Coulterville; ☎209/878-3471; daily 11am–midnight or later. The hotel's *Magnolia Saloon* is a classic old-West watering hole, here since 1851 and laden with character. Horse tack and mining paraphernalia hang from the ceiling, old aquatints and prints cover the walls, and there might even be someone bashing away at the honky-tonk piano in the corner. The food is pretty good – burgers, steak sandwiches, ribs and the like – but for fancy dining, repair to *Cherylann's Dining Parlor* (Wed–Sun 5–9pm) where you might have salmon cakes with honey mustard sauce ($10) followed by pan-seared salmon ($16) served on white linen tablecloths. Get your espresso fix at the coffee counter, also on the premises.

Mountain Sage Café 18653 Hwy-120 West; summer Sun–Thurs 7am–6pm, Sat & Sun 7am–7pm. One corner of the Mountain Sage store, devoted to great espresso, bagels and fine breakfast burritos. Free Wi-Fi hotspot.

Stan's "Que" Outdoor Grill 18745 Back St, Groveland ☎209/962-0806; May–Oct Sat 11am–4pm, Sun 11am–6pm. Convivial outdoor barbecue with meats pit-grilled over almond wood. Sink your teeth into a tri tip dinner ($17), half a chicken ($14) or an equally juicy burger or sandwich ($7). Fill up on salads and corn-on-the-cob, and wash it all down with bottled beer or sodas.

Two Guys Pizza Pies 18955 Ferretti Rd, Groveland ☎209/962-4897; daily summer 11am–10pm winter 11am–9pm. Basic sit-in or take out pizzeria with tasty gourmet and traditional pizzas ($15 for one feeding 2–3), plus microbrews.

Victorian Room *Groveland Hotel*, 18767 Hwy-120 West ☎209/962-4000; summer daily 5.30–9pm, winter generally Thurs–Sun. The best restaurant in town (and for miles around), decorated in keeping with the rest of the *Groveland Hotel*, and featuring a seasonally changing menu plus nightly chef's specials. Dishes might include crab cakes with cilantro and caper sauce, and honey-glazed baby back pork ribs. Expect to pay $40–45 for three courses plus something from their extensive wine list. Reservations suggested in summer.

Hwy-140: El Portal and Midpines

Café at the Bug *Yosemite Bug Rustic Mountain Resort*, Midpines; breakfast 7–10am, lunch 7am–3pm, dinner 6–9pm; bar until around 10.30pm. Superb-value licensed café with the emphasis on quality food at a good price. Wholesome breakfasts ($4.50–6.50), packed lunches ($6) and dinners ($7–13) are served to all-comers, so if you are staying anywhere around Mariposa and don't mind the slightly frenetic hostel atmosphere, it is definitely worth the drive. Expect the likes of slow-roasted Cajun pork or baked trout fillet with butter pecan sauce, each with salad roll, rice and vegetables. Good microbrews on tap and a deck to sit out and knock it back. Also free Wi-Fi and Internet access.

Yosemite View Restaurant 11136 Hwy-140, El Portal, two miles west of the Arch Rock Entrance ☎209/379-2183; breakfast buffet 7–11am, dining room 5.30–11pm, pizza parlor 5–10pm. Decent and moderately pricey restaurant that's part of *Yosemite View Lodge* and is designed with the needs of its several hundred guests in mind. There's a breakfast buffet, then a range of sandwiches, soups, salads, plus pizza (in traditional and specialty combinations), steaks for around $20–27, and ribs and chicken dishes for a little less.

Hwy-140: Mariposa

Charles Street Dinner House 5043 Hwy-140 ☎209/966-2366; nightly plus Sun brunch. Mariposa's premier fine dining establishment in a former doctor's rooms, now converted to a dim interior with booths. Discerning diners might kick off with a Portobello ravioli parmesan ($15) and follow with a scallop and abalone blend served with toasted almonds and lemon butter ($20), though the wise will leave space for the mocha ice cream pie ($6). There's a full wine list, and all dishes are cooked to order, so set the evening aside.

49er Club 5026 Hwy-140 ☎209/742-4000; noon–midnight or later. A dark bar with table football, pool and a line of bar stools.

Happy Burger 5120 Hwy-140 at 12th St ☎209/966-2719; daily 5.30am–8pm. A huge array of good, cheap diner food – breakfast burrito ($4.50), tuna melt ($5.50), teriyaki chicken salad ($6) – to take out or eat in at Formica booths. There's a fine jukebox and the entire place is decorated with tragic Seventies album covers.

High Country Café Corner Hwy-140 & Hwy-49; Mon–Sat 9am–3pm. Health food café with sandwiches for vegetarians and omnivores ($6–7) along with salads, burritos, fruit smoothies and filter coffee. There's also a health food store next door (Mon–Fri 9am–6pm, Sat 9am–5pm) offering good bread, organic fruit and goodies in bulk bins that are great for making up trail mix.

Mariposa Pizza Factory 5005 Hwy-140 ☎209/966-3112; daily 11am–10pm. Basic eat-in and take-out pizza joint with traditional toppings as well as gourmet combos in five different sizes. Filling and fairly cheap with something around $15 usually sufficient for two.

Savoury's 5027 Hwy-140 ☎209/966-7677; Wed–Sun 5–9pm. The pick of Mariposa's mid-range restaurants, offering a relaxed atmosphere with a touch of class: modern decor, black linen tablecloths and a secluded patio out back for those warm summer evenings. Choose from the likes of chipotle chicken ($16), roasted garlic cream scallops ($23), and spinach and pine nut pasta ($16), perhaps followed by chocolate bread pudding ($5). Wine is available by the glass.

Hwy-140: Merced

La Nita's 1327 18th St at T ☎209/723-2291; Mon–Sat 9am–9.30pm, Sun 8am–9.30pm. Authentic Mexican dining about ten blocks from the bus station offering all the expected south of the border staples along with *menudo* (tripe and hominy soup) and *albondigas* (both $7). Lunch specials change daily and there are hearty combination plates for under $10.

Paul's Place 2991 G St at Alexander ⓣ209/723-1339; daily 6am–midnight. Very popular diner offering a broad range of ethnic and American dishes at very reasonable prices; try the Portuguese *linguica* sausage omelette.

Wired 450 W 18th St at Canal ⓣ209/386-0206; Mon–Fri 6.30am–2pm. Downtown Internet café handy for the Transpo Center, with good coffee, muffins, bagels and fast Internet access.

Hwy-41: Oakhurst and Fish Camp

Jackalopes Bar & Grill ***Tenaya Lodge*** (see p.171), **1122 Hwy-41, Fish Camp ⓣ559/683-6555; daily 7am–11pm.** Probably the pick of the restaurants at *Tenaya Lodge*, where you can sit outside (around the brazier if there's a chill in the air) and order from a menu laden with soups, salads, sandwiches, burgers, pizza and pasta dishes at only slightly inflated prices. Next door, the *Sierra Restaurant* is more formal and a good bit pricier.

Mountain House Junction of Hwy-41 & Bass Lake Rd, five miles north of Oakhurst ⓣ559/683-5191; daily 6am–9pm. The best of the local diner-style restaurants with tasty and well-prepared burgers, sandwiches and pasta along with breakfast blintzes ($8), New York steak ($24) and charbroiled trout ($17). Always reliable and with friendly and efficient service.

The Narrow Gauge Inn 48571 Hwy-41, Fish Camp ⓣ559/683-6446; mid-April to mid-Oct only, Wed–Sun 5.30–9pm. Fine dining in an Old World setting with candlelight and a warming fire make this one of the picks on the south side of the Park. Start by dipping sourdough into a rich fondue and continue with charbroiled swordfish or filet mignon. Expect to pay $40 each, more with wine.

Three Sisters Café 40291 Junction Drive, off Hwy-49 behind Raley's supermarket, Oakhurst ⓣ559/642-2253, ⓦwww.threesisterscafe.com; daily 9am–9pm, closed Mon & Tues in winter. Classy but casual restaurant run by a husband and wife team who run a tight ship. Try the wild mushroom eggs Florentine for breakfast ($9) or perhaps a prawn and asparagus Caesar for lunch ($10). Check out the $12 Earlybird dinner specials (Weds & Thurs 4–5.30pm) or come later for the likes of pork medallions in a blue cheese sauce ($23) or braised lamb shanks ($22).

Yosemite Coffee & Roasting Company 40879 Hwy-41, a mile north of Oakhurst ⓣ559/683-8815; Sun–Thurs 6.30am–7pm, Fri & Sat 6.30am–11pm. This local java joint with mismatched chairs, old tables and newspapers to read makes a relaxed setting for digging into breakfast burritos, toothsome muffins, sandwiches, cakes and good espresso at modest prices. Also operates as a bar often with live music at weekends.

Hwy-120 East and Lee Vining

Mono Inn Restaurant 55620 US-395, almost five miles north of Lee Vining ⓣ760/647-6581, ⓦwww.monoinn.com; mid-May to Oct daily except Tues 5–9pm. Classy but relaxed restaurant owned and run by Ansel Adams' granddaughter, featuring lovingly prepared meals served on the patio or inside, both with a superb lake view. Dinner might start with roasted artichoke and goat's cheese tart with leeks ($11) followed by salmon with wild boar tenderloin ($31). There's a good (mostly Californian) wine list, though few are sold by the glass.

Nicely's US-395 in Lee Vining ⓣ760/647-6477; daily 6am–9pm, closed Tues & Wed in winter. Great Fifties vinyl palace serving up reliable diner food to tourists and dedicated locals. All your favorites are there including a three-egg omelet ($8), Jumbo burger and fries ($8), breaded steak ($12) and the obligatory slice of one of their many fruit pies ($3.50).

Tioga Pass Resort Two miles east of Tioga Pass ⓣ209/372-4471; late May to mid-Oct 7am–9pm. Cozy wood-paneled diner with the usual range of egg and pancake breakfasts ($6–9), burgers and sandwiches ($7–10) and a superb line in fruit pies and cobblers made on the premises ($5).

Whoa Nellie Deli Inside the Tioga Gas Mart at Corner of Hwy-120 East & US-395 ⓣ760/647 1088; daily 8am–9pm, closed Nov–March. The best quick food for miles around is served in this less than inspiring location, though in summer you can sit at tables outside. There's always a lively atmosphere and they dish up great tortilla soup, jambalaya ($10), fish tacos ($10), burgers and steaks, along with espresso coffees, microbrews and margaritas. There's also pizza by the slice and on evenings in July & Aug there is usually live music outside. Closed Nov–March.

10

Organized events and entertainment

With boundless opportunities for sightseeing, hiking and other outdoor pursuits, most of Yosemite's visitors have little trouble keeping busy, but your experience can be greatly enhanced by taking advantage of some of the Park's organized activities and entertainment, the majority of which are in the form of **ranger programs** and include walks, talks and campfires. Put on by the Park Service (often in conjunction with DNC or the Yosemite Association), most are informative, fun and free. The bulk of what's available takes place in Yosemite Valley, but the rest of the Park isn't ignored with events in Wawona, Tuolumne Meadows, at Glacier Point, and even at a couple of the popular campgrounds.

Activities vary with the seasons, with most happening from June until the end of September. There are also **films**, **slide presentations**, and **musical acts**, which generally take place at night.

Yosemite can be a great place for **kids**, what with all the adventuring, camping and swimming to be done – just don't expect them to thank you for dragging them on long treks. Most of the standard ranger programs are suitable for **kids** – star gazing, learning about bears – but there are also programs designed especially for young families such as campfire sing-alongs, storytelling and even kids' art classes. Children might also enjoy the hands-on and basket-weaving sections of the Yosemite Museum (see p.58) and can become either a Junior Ranger or Little Cub (see box below). **In winter**,

Junior Ranger Program

One of the best ways to prepare kids for exploring Yosemite is to enroll them in the summertime **Junior Ranger Program**, designed to bring the sheer scale of Yosemite down to something tangible to the young mind. To become a Yosemite Junior Ranger (and earn the Junior Ranger patch) you'll need to attend a guided program with a ranger, pick up a bag of litter, and complete an educational booklet ($3.50). Younger kids (aged 3–6) can earn the **Little Cubs** button by completing their own self-guided booklet ($3).

Both booklets are available from visitor centers around the Park and from the **Nature Center at Happy Isles** (see p.66), which is specifically set up to introduce children and their parents to what's out there alongside the trails.

the Badger Pass Ski Area is a great place for families, with an extensive kids program (see box, p.156).

The best source of current information for all these programs is the *Yosemite Today* newspaper, though you might also go direct to the *Yosemite Lodge* and Curry Village tour desks, and keep your eye open for bulletin boards as well. The Park concessionaire's website (Ⓦwww.yosemitepark.com) also has full details of events.

Daytime programs

From early in the morning until the sun goes down there's an unending array of organized activities to keep Valley visitors entertained. Beyond the confines of its cliffs, the choice diminishes, but careful timing should still allow you to join something interesting: Glacier Point has particularly enticing sunset talks. The core of the daytime ranger programs are the general **ranger walks** though variations include specific **photography walks**, a **Historic Ahwahnee Tour** and some free art classes out in the meadows.

Kids are equally well catered for in the Valley, though in the rest of the Park you'll be best served in Wawona where the popular horse-drawn stage rides are run (see p.99).

Annual events and activities

Yosemite's concessionaire doesn't need to do much Park promotion during the summer months, but in the off season they pull out all the stops to try to fill the hotels. The well-heeled are lured to high-end dinners and wine tastings with many staying in great comfort at *The Ahwahnee*, where the bulk of events are held. In addition, there are end-of-winter celebrations at the Badger Pass Ski Area, and a couple of music festivals just outside the Park.

January

Chefs' Holidays Early Jan to early Feb; reservations Ⓣ559/253-5635, Ⓦwww.yosemitepark.com. Put off that post-Christmas diet and visit gastronomic heaven for a couple of days. Some of America's top chefs lead cooking demonstrations, conduct behind-the-scenes kitchen tours and finish off with a fabulous five-course gala dinner ($155 by itself) in the *Ahwahnee Dining Room*. Two-person packages range from $570 including two nights at *Yosemite Lodge* and the gala dinner, up to $1076 with three nights at *The Ahwahnee*.

February

Nordic Holiday Race Ⓣ209/371-8444. California's oldest cross-country ski race takes place at Badger Pass on the last Saturday of February or the first in March. The morning Nordic race is followed by a Telemark race in the afternoon followed by a big party.

March

Spring Fest Ⓣ209/371-8444. A traditional winter carnival at Badger Pass on one of the last Sundays of the ski season (usually late March or early April). Dual slalom racing, costume contests, cross-country skiing, obstacle course races and more.

May

Strawberry Music Festival Ⓣ209/984-8630, Ⓦwww.strawberrymusic.com. Camp Mather, just outside the Park near Hetch Hetchy, plays host to this three-day, start-of-summer festival of bluegrass, swing, rock, blues and gospel. Pretty much everyone camps on site making for a celebratory atmosphere. It takes place over Memorial Day weekend (the last in May) and is important enough to lure relatively big names: Michael Franti and Lucinda Williams in 2007. Call to book as far in advance

Mostly for adults

Art Classes Mid-April to Oct Mon–Sat 10am–2pm; free. Yosemite can be so overwhelming that the sheer grandeur obliterates the small beauties. One way to re-focus on particular elements is to spend time painting – waterfalls and dogwood blooms in spring; the lazy serenity of the Merced River in summer; and the colors of the oaks and maples in fall. The Yosemite Art & Education Center (Yosemite Village; shuttle stop 2; ⓣ209/372-1442) runs informal outdoor art classes for adults in a range of media – watercolor, acrylic, pen and ink, etc – with each class led by a visiting artist: for the current schedule go to ⓦwww.yosemite.org/visitor/AAC.html. Bring your own art supplies, or buy at the Yosemite Art and Education Center. Genuinely interested children aged ten and over are welcome at the adult classes.

Historic Ahwahnee Tour All year, check with *The Ahwahnee* concierge for times; free. A chance to spend an hour wandering around Yosemite's grandest building learning something of its history and admiring its fine furnishings.

Mariposa Grove Nature Walk June Sat & Sun 2pm, July & Aug 3–4 weekly 2pm; free. An hour-long stroll through the big trees with a ranger.

Parsons Memorial Lodge Summer Series Mid-July to late Aug Sat & Sun 2pm; free. This series of one-hour seminars in a historic lodge in Tuolumne Meadows encompasses a broad sweep, from storytelling walks to slide presentations on the cycles of stream flow along the Tuolumne River. Allow time for the 30min walk from the Lembert Dome parking lot or the Tuolumne Meadows Visitor Center.

Photography Walks All year; prices vary. The Ansel Adams Gallery offers a wide-ranging

as you can and expect to pay $165 for three days including camping. There's a repeat performance in fall.

August

Tuolumne Meadows Poetry Festival Usually third weekend; free. Local poets and musicians get together at Parsons Memorial Lodge in Tuolumne Meadows for entertaining morning (Sat & Sun 10–11.30am), afternoon (Sat & Sun 2–3.30pm) and evening (Sat 7.30–10pm) sessions. Allow 30min to walk from Lembert Dome parking lot of Tuolumne Meadows visitor center.

September

Strawberry Music Festival ⓣ209/984-8630, ⓦwww.strawberrymusic.com. The end-of-summer equivalent of May festival (see above) takes place over Labor Day weekend (the first in Sept).

November

Vintners' Holidays Early Nov to early Dec; reservations ⓣ559/253-5635, ⓦwww.yosemitepark.com. As fall turns into winter *The Ahwahnee* puts on these two- and three-day wine appreciation seminars with panel discussions and tastings led by industry experts. Several top wineries are represented and there's a last-night, five-course, candlelit dinner where you can dine with the winemakers in the *Ahwahnee Dining Room*. Two-person packages at *Yosemite Lodge* (two nights $550, three nights $659) and *The Ahwahnee* (two nights $886, three nights $1132) include tastings and the dinner.

December

Bracebridge Dinners Dec 15–26; reservations ⓣ559/253-5635, ⓦwww.yosemitepark.com. Christmas at *The Ahwahnee* centers on these four-hour, seven-course feasts held in the Dining Room, which is decked out to look like a seventeenth-century English manor as described in Washington Irving's novel *Squire Bracebridge*. There's much song and revelry with staff dressed in period costume and guests in tuxedos and ball gowns. Two-night accommodation packages for two, including the dinner and a gift, go for around $1100 at *Yosemite Lodge*, over $1600 at *The Ahwahnee*.

slate of photography walks and courses. See "Photography" (p.36) for full details.

Ranger Walks All year; check *Yosemite Today* for times; free. Spend an hour and a half with a ranger, perhaps learning about Yosemite's first people, wandering to Mirror Lake or exploring the Valley's geology. Every walk is different and depends largely on where you are. Look out too for the twilight strolls making the best of the golden hour, usually passing some great photo ops. Most walks take place in the Valley but there are less frequent walks in Tuolumne Meadows and at Glacier Point.

Yosemite Association field seminars All year; prices vary. The nonprofit Yosemite Association (see p.40) runs a series of small-group outdoor education "field seminars" from June through to Oct. Mostly two to four days long, they cover specific topics – Hetch Hetchy Wildflowers, Miwok basketry, Capturing Light and Color in the Landscape, etc – predominantly in the fields of natural history, birding, day hiking, backpacking, photography, drawing, painting and writing. Prices are typically $200–300, and some seminars have reserved campgrounds and/ or hotel rooms at an additional cost. The website has a full seminar listing.

Mostly for kids

Arts & Crafts see *Yosemite Today* for times; free. The Yosemite Art & Education Center (Yosemite Village; shuttle stop 2; ⓣ209/372-1442) runs dedicated outdoor classes aimed at introducing budding artists aged nine and up to sketching, watercolor and charcoal drawing.

Explore Yosemite Family Program July & Aug 3–4 weekly; up to two adults go free, first child $12.50, additional kids $10. These three-hour morning sessions encourage families to interact with and learn about Yosemite through hands-on activities, games with an educational message and stories. You'll be walking 2–3 miles so bring a carrier for the wee ones. Check *Yosemite Today* for current schedules. Tickets can be bought at the Curry Village tour kiosk or the *Yosemite Lodge* tour desk; meet at the Curry Village Amphitheater.

Story Time All year; see *Yosemite Today* for times; free. Lasting little more than half an hour, these storytelling sessions are aimed at those twelve and under. They take place either on the Ansel Adams Gallery porch or the *Ahwahnee* lawn.

Wee Wild Ones All year 2–3 weekly, check *Yosemite Today* for times; free. Though aimed specifically at those six and under, parents are encouraged to participate in these 45-minute sessions using games and stories to learn about Yosemite wildlife and geology. Held at the outdoor amphitheaters in *Yosemite Lodge* and Curry Village when warm enough, otherwise by the huge fireplace in Great Lounge at *The Ahwahnee*.

Evening programs

Few come to Yosemite expecting more from their **evening entertainment** than a few stories and a beer or two around the campfire, but there's actually plenty more to do when night falls. Much of the action in the Valley is concentrated around the amphitheaters at Curry Village and *Yosemite Lodge*, where a full **evening program** of talks, slide shows and films take place. At Yosemite Village the Valley Visitor Center Theater is put to good use for a series of **live performances**, mostly for a small fee.

Outside the Valley, the eternal mainstay is the Old Fashioned Campfire, an hour-long talk around a raging campfire that takes place most nights in summer (and weekends in spring and fall); and the *Wawona Hotel* lounge plays host to pianist Tom Bopp and his "Vintage Songs of Yosemite."

Live performances

All the following shows take place in the Valley Visitor Center theater: reserve through any tour desk in the Park (ⓣ209/372-1240) or buy a ticket at the auditorium half an hour in advance. Check *Yosemite Today* for current schedules.

Return to Balance: A Climber's Journey Check *Yosemite Today* for details; adults $8, kids 5–12 $4. Stunning shots of Yosemite and brilliant rock-climbing photography are the highlights of this video, presented by rock-climbing superstar Ron Kauk who views rock climbing as a way of life and a means to discover the beauty and mystery of nature. Suitable for those 8 and older.

Stories of a Pioneer Woman Mid-May to Sept 2–3 weekly 8pm; adults $8, kids 5–12 $4. Connie Stetson assumes the role of the

▲ Sunset ranger talk at Glacier Point

spirited and entertaining Yosemite pioneer, Sarah Hawkins, a synthesis of several real pioneer women woven together from the diary entries and anecdotes of women who came to the wilds of California during the Gold Rush. Many a good yarn is spun as she relates her times with her first three husbands and contemplates taking on a fourth. The show lasts around ninety minutes and is recommended for those seven years and older.

Wild Stories with John Muir Mid-May to Sept 2–3 weekly 8pm; adults $8, kids 5–12 $4. A collection of fun one-man shows featuring the well-honed talents of actor Lee Stetson, who has been impersonating John Muir since 1982. Muir's entertaining and inspiring adventures are explored through four different performances. In summer, "Conversations with a Tramp" explores Muir's conservationist philosophy and his lifelong battle to defend his beloved Yosemite; "Stickeen & Other Mortals" follows his encounters with wild animals in the Sierra and Alaska, and "The Spirit of John Muir" relates Muir's wild adventures. In winter, Stetson concentrates on tales of Muir in the snow and ice. These shows last around ninety minutes and are recommended for those eight years and older.

Other evening activities

Evening Programs All year, mostly 8pm; free. During the warmer months the amphitheaters at *Yosemite Lodge*, Curry Village and the *Lower Pines* campground are usually packed for these hour-long talks and slide shows which might cover topics as varied as early twentieth-century Yosemite through the eyes of a Buffalo soldier, the secret life of bats, or the Firefall (see box, p.67). In winter they take place at *Yosemite Lodge* and *The Ahwahnee*.

LeConte Memorial Lodge Late May to Sept Fri–Sun; free. Valley-based evening programs that are a little more academic than those elsewhere in the Park and might include a slide show or talk by some luminary: check *Yosemite Today* for details.

Old Fashioned Campfire & Sing-along June–Sept 3–5 weekly, typically 7.30pm; adults and kids $5, families $20. This family-oriented event involves spending an hour and a half around the campfire toasting marshmallows as the ranger tells entertaining tales and leads campfire songs. In Yosemite Valley you can expect a short walk through the woods near Curry Village; access is difficult for strollers and wheelchairs. Purchase tickets at the *Yosemite Lodge* and Curry Village tour desks. Outside the Valley there are regular summer campfire sessions at the campgrounds at Wawona, Tuolumne Meadows, White Wolf and Crane Flat.

Starry Skies Over Yosemite June–Sept 8pm or 9pm; adults and kids $5, families $20. Yosemite's policy of using minimal lighting makes for brilliant starry skies even in relatively populated Yosemite Valley. Wander out into the meadow, lie down and listen to the tales, which mostly depend on the interests of the ranger involved – celestial navigation, native folklore, constellations, distant galaxies, etc. Starry Skies typically takes place three times a week in Yosemite and once a week in Wawona: check *Yosemite Today* for details.

Vintage Songs of Yosemite *Wawona Hotel*; free. Tom Bopp plays the piano in the lounge at this hotel, occasionally accompanied by a Yosemite-oriented slide show. For more details see p.99.

11

Shopping

When you find yourself looking for that perfect Yosemite souvenir, you'll find numerous places to avail yourself of a "Go Climb a Rock!" T-shirt or Half Dome paperweight. Yosemite National Park is certainly no **shopping** paradise but is far better supplied than most national parks, and you can satisfy most practical needs. Groceries, film, books, clothing, hiking and camping needs are all adequately supplied.

The vast majority of shops are in Yosemite Valley with only the bare minimum found elsewhere: Crane Flat has a grocery store and gas station; Tuolumne Meadows has the same along with a climbing/camping shop; and Wawona boasts a couple of grocery stores. **Prices** for groceries and incidentals are around twenty percent higher than you might expect outside the Park, and souvenirs range from cheap trinkets to elegant and expensive native crafts. Throughout this chapter we've quoted normal summer **opening hours**: expect shorter hours in May, June, September and October, and occasional winter closures.

Outside the Park, gateway towns offer a much wider selection of supplies. The best bets are Mariposa (on Hwy-140 to the west) and Oakhurst (on Hwy-41 to the south). Both have large supermarkets and a range of specialist stores (though none dedicated to the needs of hikers, campers and climbers).

All-purpose shops: Groceries, film and firewood

Any road-accessible spot in the Park that humans congregate will have a **general store**, typically selling basic groceries, film, firewood, beer, wine, ice cream and usually some Yosemite-branded clothing and trinkets. Yosemite Village has the only **supermarket** in the Park and is the best bet for fresh fruit and vegetables.

Yosemite Valley

Ahwahnee Sweet Shop *The Ahwahnee*; daily 7am–10pm. A little nook selling newspapers, stamps, film, sodas, local wine and drinks.

Curry Village Store shuttle stops 14 & 20; daily 8am–10pm. Though strong on gifts, beer, ice and firewood, its grocery selection leans heavily on ready-to-eat snack food rather than the raw materials for genuine cooking.

Housekeeping Camp Store shuttle stop 12; April to late Oct daily 9am–5pm, later in peak season. A convenience store stocked with *Housekeeping* campers' needs in mind: basic groceries, beer, ice and firewood.

Yosemite Lodge Store shuttle stop 8; daily 8am–10pm. A decent range of books, gifts, snacks and drinks but fairly meager supplies of real groceries.

Yosemite Village Store shuttle stops 2 & 10; daily 8am–10pm. Easily the biggest shop in the Valley, with a huge gift store, a book corner, and what amounts to a small supermarket stocking the best selection of groceries, beer and wine and even fresh fruit and vegetables (something virtually unheard of elsewhere in the Valley). Nearby, there's a smaller selection of snacks at *Degnan's Deli* (see "Eating," p.180).

Outside the Valley

Crane Flat Store daily 8am–8pm. Gas station (24hr with credit card) and general store stocked with film, postcards, Yosemite books, assorted snacks and a grocery selection wide enough for modest needs, including ice, beer and wine and firewood.

Glacier Point Gift Shop June–Sept 9am–6pm. A few snacks and ice creams but mostly a gift store specializing in film, clothes and gifts relating to geology and astronomy. Bizarrely it is usually closed when large numbers of people hit Glacier Point at sunset.

Tuolumne Meadows Store mid-June to late Sept 8am–8pm. Much used by campers and hikers restocking for the next leg of their trek, this seasonal tent store stocks a decent selection of supplies (even a limited range of fresh fruit and vegetables) plus postcards, Yosemite books, simple camping equipment, Coleman fuel, camping gas canisters, bear-resistant food canisters, ice, beer and wine and firewood.

Wawona Store June–Aug 8am–8pm, Sept–May 8am–7pm. A modest supply of groceries, beer, wine, ice, firewood and camping supplies but mostly snacks, clothing, gifts, film and books.

White Wolf Store mid-June to mid-Sept 8am–8pm. A basic hole-in-the-wall store with a skimpy supply of essentials.

Books, prints and newspapers

All the stores mentioned above sell postcards, magazines and Yosemite-related guides and videos, but a couple of places offer a more specialist selection of **books**. First stop should be the Yosemite Bookstore (see below), which has a wide range of maps and Yosemite related non-fiction covering flora and fauna, Native legends and a good deal of social history.

Newspapers – the *New York Times*, *LA Times*, *San Francisco Chronicle*, *USA Today*, *Fresno Bee* and others – are available from boxes outside *Degnan's* in Yosemite Village, Yosemite Village Store, in front of the Curry Village Store, near the front desk at *Yosemite Lodge*, and from the Ahwahnee Sweet Shop, inside *The Ahwahnee*.

Yosemite Bookstore Yosemite Village; shuttle stops 4, 5 & 9; daily 9am–5pm. Vies with the Ansel Adams Gallery as the Park's best bookstore with everything from kids' books to climbing guides and lovely coffee table picture glossies.

Ansel Adams Gallery Yosemite Village; shuttle stops 4, 5 & 9; daily 9am–6pm; ⓦwww.anseladams.com. The excellent selection of Ansel Adams books, calendars, postcards and posters is supplemented by other quality photography books, and top-quality photographic prints. They also stock a range of novels and non-fiction that's a cut above what's available elsewhere in the Park, most of them outdoor and ecology-based books on the Sierra and the wider American West.

Yosemite Art & Education Center Yosemite Village; shuttle stops 2 & 10; mid-April to Oct daily 9.30am–5pm. Sells a good range of art and painting supplies along with a modest stock of fine art books.

Mountain Shop Curry Village; shuttle stops 14 & 20; summer daily 8am–8pm. The Park's best stock of hiking and climbing guidebooks.

Outdoor equipment

While cost-conscious hikers and campers should bring their **gear** with them, almost all the **backpacking supplies** you're likely to need can be bought within the Park at higher but not unreasonable prices.

Yosemite Valley

Curry Village Mountain Shop shuttle stops 14 & 20; daily 8am–8pm. The best-stocked shop for serious outdoor gear, always full of tents, sleeping bags, thermal and waterproof clothing, camp cooking gear and fuel, dried meals, and bear-resistant food canisters, plus a full range of aid and free-climbing equipment at competitive prices.

Village Sport Shop shuttle stops 2 & 10; daily 8am–6pm. A modest range of fishing gear plus a fair selection of non-specialist outdoor gear such as freeze-dried meals, day packs, hiking shoes, lanterns, Coleman fuel, camping gas canisters and books.

Outside the Valley

Badger Pass Sport Shop mid-Dec to late March daily 9am–5pm. Winter-only shop selling ski clothing, sunglasses, waxes and other incidentals.

Tuolumne Sport Shop early June to late Sept daily 9am–5pm or 6pm. This smaller cousin of the Curry Village Mountain Shop primarily caters to the needs of Tuolumne hikers and climbers. It is located at the gas station close to the *Tuolumne Meadows Grill* and stocks quality brands of tents, packs, climbing gear and outdoor clothing.

Wawona Golf Shop May–Sept daily 9am–5pm. Stocks a limited supply of golfing essentials and tennis requisites for use on the nearby courts and the golf course across the road.

Specialist Gifts

The **gift** sections of the grocery stores in Yosemite Village, Curry Village and at *Yosemite Lodge* (see "All-purpose shops" above) mostly stock uninspired souvenirs such as stuffed bears and Yosemite baseball caps. Some of it borders on collectable kitsch – a Half Dome snow dome springs to mind – but for something a little more imaginative try the following, all in Yosemite Valley.

Ahwahnee Gift Shop *The Ahwahnee*; daily 8am–10pm. Quality and prices are a notch or two higher than the Yosemite norm in this flagship store, which comes artfully arrayed with authentic Native American jewelry along with handicrafts, rugs, leather goods, works by local artists, prints, books, CDs and a good deal more. If you like the signature ziggurat patterning the *Ahwahnee*'s restaurant plates, drop in here and buy your own set.

Habitat Yosemite Yosemite Village; shuttle stop 4; May–Sept daily 9am–5pm. A small shop stocking Yosemite-branded clothing and Native artworks along with postcards, posters, kids' books and stuffed bears.

The Nature Shop *Yosemite Lodge*; shuttle stop 8; daily 10am–6pm or 8pm. A nature-oriented range of postcards, DVDs and books along with Yosemite-branded clothing and Native artworks.

Yosemite Museum Shop Yosemite Village; shuttle stops 5 & 9; daily 9am–noon & 1–5pm. A good bet for Native handicrafts with small but appealing displays of beadwork, chokers and necklaces, silver and bead jewelry, soaproot baskets, Miwok charm-stones and Native books. Some is high quality and pricey, but much is quite affordable, and all is made in the US and bought directly from Native Americans with its provenance fully documented.

Out of the Park

Out of the Park

Northwest of Yosemite: Hwy-120 West and around

The most direct route linking Yosemite and the Bay Area follows Hwy-120 West, which cuts through a couple of interesting towns on the southern fringes of the California Gold Country, and opens up some stupendous whitewater rafting on the Tuolumne River.

On the immediate outskirts of the Park, almost every building along Hwy-120 West seems to have geared itself to Park visitors. There are several decent places to stay along here, but the nearest towns that make realistic bases for exploring the Park are the tiny but characterful **Groveland**, and the slightly less convenient but equally atmospheric **Coulterville**. Beyond these two towns, the decrepit **Chinese Camp** and lively **Oakdale** warrant brief stops.

Along Hwy-120 West

Leaving the Yosemite boundary at Big Oak Flat, there's immediate temptation with Evergreen Road heading off north to **Hetch Hetchy** (see p.73). Sticking with Hwy-120 West it's a 24-mile run to Groveland, a pretty enough drive but with little reason to stop for long unless you fancy the convenience of one of the highwayside lodgings. Apart from an overpriced gas station, a couple of general stores and one restaurant there isn't much in the way of facilities.

Pause for views down to the Tuolumne River from the **Rim of the World Viewpoint**, twelve miles west of Big Oak Flat, then continue four miles to the **Groveland Ranger Station** (Mon–Fri 8am–4.30pm Sat & Sun 8am–3.30pm, winter closed Sat; ⓣ209/962-7825), home to all sorts of information on the surrounding Stanislaus National Forest, including a handy "Hiking Trails" leaflet with weeks' worth of suggested trails. On the other side of Hwy-120 West, the La Casa Loma River Store is the meeting place for most companies running

Hotel, campsite and restaurant **listings** for the towns covered within this chapter begin on pages 168, 176 and 182 respectively.

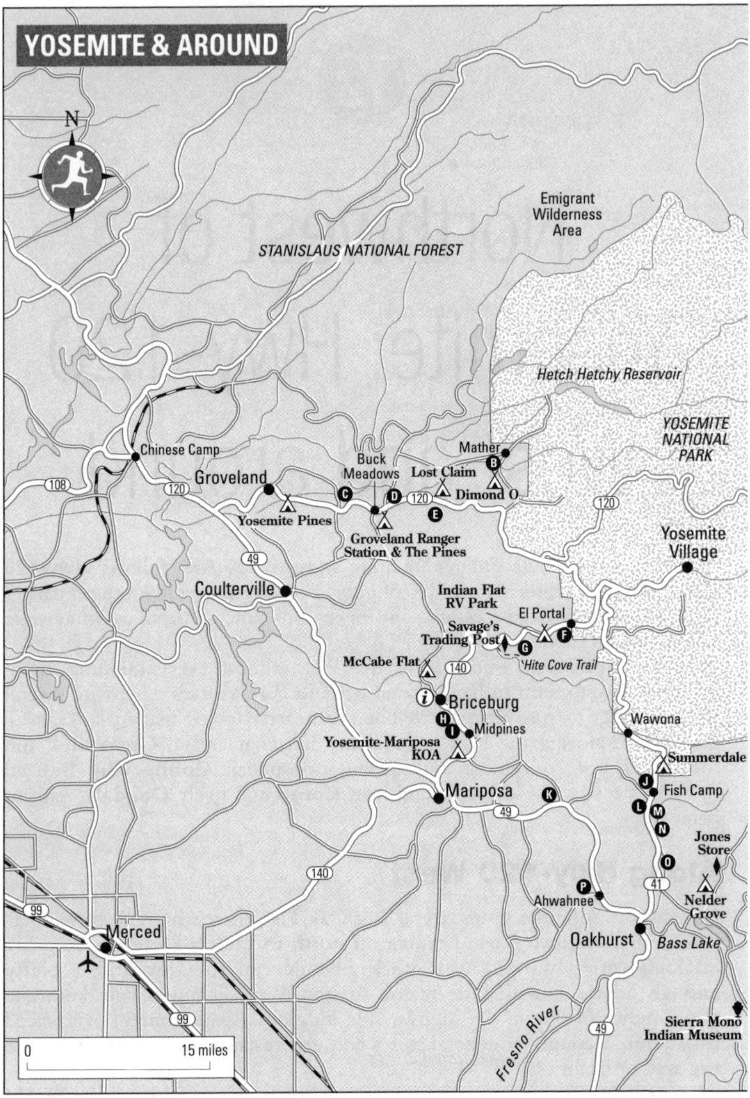

whitewater rafting trips on the Tuolumne River (see box, p.200). From here it is a further eight miles into Groveland.

Groveland

Probably the single most appealing town in the vicinity of Yosemite is diminutive **GROVELAND**, almost fifty miles west of the Valley. With its old-time tenor, some good places to stay and eat, and a cracking old bar

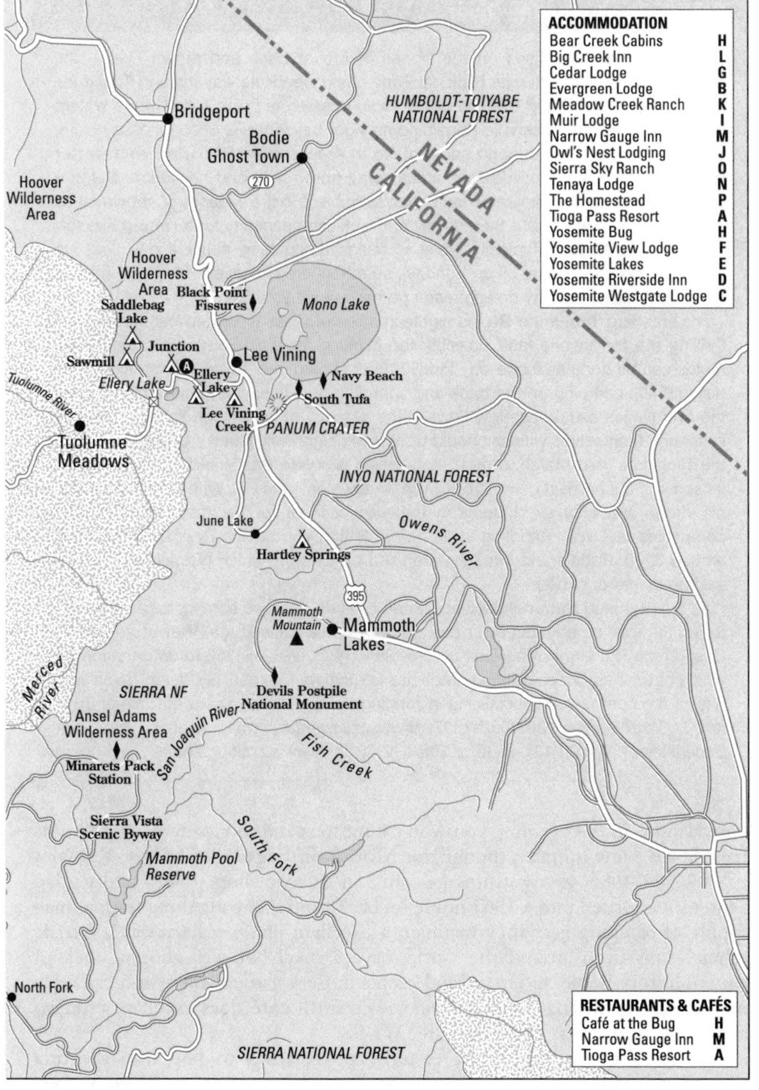

called the *Iron Door Saloon* (see p.182), you can hardly go wrong. Groveland came into being in 1849 when gold was discovered nearby on the delightfully named "Garrote Creek," and the town has bumbled along ever since. Even today the town has only 1500 residents scattered across the Sierra foothills at a mild 2800ft.

Groveland runs for half a mile on either side of Hwy-120 West, its short central section retaining the verandahs and wooden sidewalks of its early days. A couple of old hotels and the saloon add to the character but, appealing as

Rafting the Tuolumne River

The **Tuolumne River** rises on the slopes of Mount Dana and Mount Lyell – the highest mountain in Yosemite National Park – then wends its way through Tuolumne Meadows and the Grand Canyon of the Tuolumne before being stilled in the waters of the Hetch Hetchy reservoir. Regaining its vigor below the O'Shaughnessey Dam, the river then tumbles through some of North America's most exalted **whitewater rafting** runs, mostly in wilderness areas away from roads and habitation. Being a dam-release river, the Tuolumne isn't quite as subject to the vagaries of snowmelt as some of its nearby kin, but there is still only sufficient capacity for a **rafting season** from April to August. Typically water is released for three hours a day (less on Saturday and often not at all on Sunday), so rafters are effectively riding a bubble of water as it makes its way downstream: go midweek if you can.

The standard **Tuolumne Run** is eighteen miles of Class IV whitewater, making it a thrilling trip for anyone (and possibly too exciting for timid or novice rafters). The rapids can be done as a one-day trip ($220) or spread over two ($430) or even three days ($540), camping on the bank and spending time fishing and mucking about in the river (which usually has low flows in the evening and morning). Those interested in scaring themselves witless should opt for the eight-mile **Cherry Creek** section of the Tuolumne (mid-March to mid-Sept), which is solid Class V and widely regarded as some of the hardest commercially run whitewater in the US. With long fast rapids, big drops and only short pools in between, it's not for the faint-hearted: most companies test your paddling skills before letting you on the river. Day-trips cost around $290. Paddle and oar rafts are used on all trips, which typically end with a salmon dinner or similar.

As a designated **National Wild and Scenic River**, only two companies are allowed to run the river on any particular day, so **contact** La Casa Loma River Store, 24000 Casa Loma Rd, eight miles east of Groveland (ⓣ209/962-5435), for information on which of the half-dozen rafting companies is running. Alternatively, get in touch with one of the companies specializing in running the Tuolumne: Sierra Mac River Trips (ⓣ1-800/457-2580 or 209/532-1327, ⓦwww.sierramac.com) or Zephyr Whitewater Expeditions (ⓣ1-800/431-3636 or 209/532-6249, ⓦwww.zrafting.com).

Groveland is in the evening, you won't want to spend too many daylight hours here. Spare a few minutes, though, for **Mountain Sage**, 18653 Hwy-120 West (ⓣ209/962-4686, ⓦwww.mtnsage.com), an eclectic shop, gallery and garden center shoehorned into a 1867 house set back from the road. Along with a small supply of camping gear they maintain a excellent photo gallery, sell fair-trade ethnic crafts from around the world, have a small but well-chosen stock of natural history books and maps, and keep a nursery garden where you can relax in a hammock among the grape vines. The small **café** does excellent espresso and breakfast burritos and there's free Wi-Fi.

Consider also heading to the eastern end of town to pop into the tiny **Groveland Museum**, 18990 Hwy-120 West (daily except Tues 1–4pm; free; ⓣ209/962-0300, ⓦwww.grovelandmuseum.org), which has changing exhibits of local history, often with contributions from the area's artists. The adjacent **library** (Mon–Thurs 2–6pm, Fri & Sat 10am–2pm, ⓣ209/962-6144) has free **Internet access**. For more **information** contact the Highway 120 Chamber of Commerce, 18583 Highway 120 (ⓣ1-800/449-9120 or 209/962-0429, ⓔinfo@groveland.org), which keeps fairly sporadic opening hours. They'll supply you with a leaflet containing the "Groveland Historic Building Tour" map highlighting existing mid-nineteenth-century structures, and the simple neoclassical **Groveland Jail**, which you can still peer into.

If you're driving into the Park, **gas** up with fairly cheap fuel a couple of miles west along Hwy-120.

Coulterville

The tiny, ancient gold town of **Coulterville** was once an important waystation on the main route between the Bay Area and Yosemite. John Muir brought Theodore Roosevelt this way in 1903 when they were heading up to the Park for a little camping, but as other routes into Yosemite were developed and later paved, the old stage road through Coulterville declined. The town hasn't fared much better and is a shadow of its former self, though that's the very reason you should make the brief detour here. The entirety of the town's diminutive heart, with its sagging wooden buildings and covered boardwalks, has been listed as a State Historical Site.

Some travelers stayed at The Coulterville Hotel, now transformed into the small **Northern Mariposa County History Center** (Wed–Sun 10am–4pm; donations welcome; ⓣ209/878-3015), which tells the history of the founding of Coulterville and the early Gold Rush years of the 1850s. Others – Theodore Roosevelt among them – stayed across the road at *Hotel Jeffery* (see p.169). Built in 1851 it remains the centerpiece of the town, and after a few minutes following the self-guided tour around the old town you should definitely repair to the long wooden bar of the hotel's swing-door *Magnolia Saloon* (see p.182). Other than that there's just three or four low-key antique-cum-knick-knack stores, a post office, and a couple of restaurants.

You can obtain tourist information at the small **Coulterville Visitor Center**, 5007 Main St (mid-May to mid-Sept Wed–Mon 8am–5pm, mid-Sept to mid-May Thurs–Sun 9am–4.30pm; ⓣ209/878-3074).

Chinese Camp

Driving westbound from Groveland it is just fourteen miles to another former Gold Rush town, **Chinese Camp**, that's easily missed off the main road. It was here that the center of the worst of the Tong Wars between rival factions of Chinese miners took place in 1856, after the Chinese had been excluded from other mining camps in the area by white miners. Racism was rampant in the southern Gold Rush camps, something which accounts for its most enduring legend, the story of the so-called Robin Hood of the Mother Lode, **Joaquin Murieta**. Murieta was an archetype representing the dispossessed Mexican miners driven to banditry by violent racist abuse at the hands of newly arrived white Americans and likely never existed. Now there's little evidence of the violent past amid the run-down shacks and trailers other than a historic marker on the main road. Explore a little further and you'll find the still-standing remains of the 1854 stone-and-brick post office, St Xavier's church (built in 1855 and restored in 1949) and several other buildings ripe for restoration.

Oakdale

Another thirty miles west along Hwy-120 sits the bustling small town of **Oakdale**. For years tourists flocked here for the tours of the Hershey's chocolate factory on the outskirts of town, but since their suspension after September 11 all you now get is the **Hershey's visitor center**, downtown at 120 S Sierra Ave (Mon–Sat 9am–5pm, and Thurs to 7pm; ⓣ209/848-8126). It is little more than a chocolate-lover's gift shop, but there's some compensation if you're here over the third weekend in May when the town holds its family-oriented **Chocolate Festival**. Beside the Hershey's visitor center is the **Oakdale Cowboy Museum** (Mon–Sat 10am–2pm; $1), exploring the town's ranching roots in a room full of tooled-leather saddles and rodeo photos.

If you need to stay, head for one of the numerous convenient **motels** along Hwy-120, and consider joining the **Sierra Railroad Dinner Train**, 220 S Sierra Ave (Ⓣ1-800/866-1690, Ⓦwww.sierrarailroad.com), which runs a regular summer schedule of three-hour, three-course dining trips ($54) along a sixteen-mile stretch of track through the surrounding agricultural country, mostly in restored 1930s carriages. For something simpler, go for a good Mexican **meal** at *El Jardín*, 137a S Sierra Ave, right by the Hershey visitor centre.

Beyond here, it's about a hundred miles to San Francisco, a drive of a little over two hours.

13

Southwest of Yosemite: Hwy-140 and around

There is an obvious benefit to staying right in the Park, close to everything you want to see, and with numerous trailheads on your doorstep. Heavy demand for accommodation within the Park, though, drives many to consider staying outside. The most convenient selection for doing so is along Hwy-140, the fastest road into Yosemite and the one least likely to be closed by snowfall. At **El Portal** (on the Park boundary), a couple of large hotels supply several hundred rooms, while a few miles further out, Midpines has the *Yosemite Bug*, an excellent lodge with the only backpacker **hostel** facilities in the region. Beyond that, the former gold town of **Mariposa** makes an attractive and convenient base, though the transport nexus of **Merced** is considerably less well situated.

The road from Mariposa into Yosemite was only completed in 1926 by convict labor. It was the last of the current access roads to be built, but the first to be kept open year-round. Most people blast quickly through, or stop only to secure accommodation at one of the motels, campgrounds or lodges that line the highway. Come in March and you'll find the **redbud** trees in vibrant bloom, a herald for the snowmelt season from April to June when the river becomes a foaming torrent – this is the best time to come **whitewater rafting** on the Merced. By July the river is typically fairly placid and can be little more than a trickle by late summer.

Along Hwy-140

Leaving Yosemite Valley, Hwy-140 descends gradually to a parking lot where it is worth a brief stop to admire **The Cascades**, which fall five hundred feet in a fairly untidy flight, best seen in spring. The descent then steepens for seven miles dropping from the 4000ft Valley floor to less than 2000ft at the Park boundary

Hotel, campsite and restaurant **listings** for the area covered within this chapter begin on pages 169, 176 and 183 respectively.

at El Portal. Along the way you pass through the **Arch Rock** entrance station where Yosemite-bound vehicles pass between overhanging rocks that just touch at the top to form a rough arch. The Merced River cascades beside the road here, forming a raging torrent during the spring snowmelt.

El Portal and around

The region's largest concentration of rooms with quick access to Yosemite Valley is at **El Portal**, just 14 miles from Yosemite Village. There is barely a town to speak of, just the El Portal Market grocery store beside the highway, a pricey gas station, and the massive *Yosemite View Lodge* complex (see p.169). Tucked away behind the trees is the former eastern terminus of the **Yosemite Valley Railroad**. From here early twentieth-century tourists were decanted into charabancs for the relatively brief but bone-shaking ride into Yosemite Valley. The railhead is now marked by a short section of track supporting a black locomotive originally used on the Hetch Hetchy Railroad during the building of the O'Shaughnessey Dam, and later employed for hauling lumber near here. Close by is a signal box which houses the offices of the Yosemite Association (no public access), a post office and a fair bit of housing for Park workers who are increasingly being relocated outside the Valley.

Continuing west, Hwy-140 heads into the **Merced River Canyon** hugging the south side of the Merced, and after eight miles reaching the confluence of the main branch of the Merced and the South fork which drains the hills around Wawona. In the early days this was an important meeting point for Miwok, and once the Gold Rush hit it was deemed a propitious spot for **Savage's Trading Post** where gold miners flocked to swap their gold dust for clothing, supplies and hooch. It was established in 1849 by James Savage who two years later became one of the first to enter Yosemite Valley as part of the Mariposa Battalion, though he was far less a hero than the sign here would have you believe. The trading tradition continued into the twenty-first century, but the gift store has now closed and doesn't look to be reopening in the near future. In spring it is still worth stopping, if only to hike the **Hite Cove Trail** (see box below).

Casting your eyes over to the north bank of the Merced you can see the level trackbed used by the **Yosemite Valley Railroad** to carry passengers between Merced and El Portal from 1907 until its abandonment in 1945. Recently the trackbed has had to be put into service as a major **rockfall** in 2006 blocked the

Hite Cove trail

If in the Merced River Canyon between February and April, find time for the moderate hike up to **Hite Cove** (7 miles round trip; 3–5hr; 300ft ascent), highly regarded throughout the Sierra for its wildflowers. Some sixty varieties have been recorded, and if you time it right the orange California poppies are sensational. Poison oak (see p.30) is almost equally common in the river canyon and there may be rattlesnakes, so keep your eyes peeled.

This popular hike follows the South Fork of the Merced River, initially across private land and eventually to the former site of Hite's Mine, a small town that produced over $3 million in gold. The story goes that when prospector John Hite was caught in a snowstorm he was nursed back to health by Maresa, the daughter of a Miwok chief, who later showed him the rich quartz vein. John later married her sister, Lucy, used Chinese labor to extract the gold and became very rich.

The trail is often closed in summer and fall due to the elevated fire risk.

Rafting the Merced

Yosemite Valley offers rafting on the Merced River, but it is a far cry from the white-water frolics on offer just outside the Park. The frenetic cascade between the Valley and the Park boundary abates to a raftable level at El Portal, the beginning of the most commonly run section. Rafted during the spring snowmelt **season** (late April to early July), the **Cranberry Gulch to Briceburg** section of the Merced is graded Class III–IV, quite manageable for first-timers but still fun for those who have rafted before. It is usually at its rollicking, drenching best in May and early June, and the river runs right beside the road so, for better or worse, you never feel too isolated. Day-trips here cost $120–140 midweek, $130–160 at weekends.

When the water levels drop (say mid-June to July) companies operate on the 25-mile, two-day **Cranberry Gulch to Bagby** run, which extends the standard trip with several miles of exciting whitewater. You'll camp beside the river and can expect to pay $310 for a Saturday start, $285 for any other day.

For details, contact rafting companies such as the non-profit ARTA River Trips (Ⓣ1-800/323-2782, Ⓦwww.arta.org), Whitewater Voyages (Ⓣ1-800/400-7238 or 510/222-5994, Ⓦwww.whitewatervoyages.com) or Zephyr Whitewater Expeditions (Ⓣ1-800/431-3636 or 209/532-6249, Ⓦwww.zrafting.com).

main highway. Temporary bridges now divert you across the river for a few hundred yards to circumvent the slip: expect delays of up to 15min.

Briceburg and around

Nine miles on at **Briceburg**, a suspension bridge over the Merced River announces a **visitor center** (May–Aug Fri 1–6pm, Sat & Sun 9am–6pm; Mariposa BLM Ⓣ209/966-9414) that contains some moderately interesting natural history displays along with material on the area's Gold Rush history and notes on local **mountain biking**. The 1920s suspension bridge behind the center provides vehicular access to the river's right bank where the old trackbed has been turned into a rough road heading downstream past three $10-a-night **campgrounds** – *McCabe Flat*, *Willow Placer* and *Railroad Flat* (see p.176) – all prettily sited beside the river. Continuing west on Hwy-140 the road soon passes through the scattered community of Midpines, then on to Mariposa, ten miles beyond.

Mountain biking around Briceburg

National Park restrictions severely limit **mountain biking** within Yosemite, forcing keen riders to explore elsewhere. One of the best areas is just across the Merced River from the Briceburg Visitor Center where there's a range of rides for different abilities. Guests of the nearby *Yosemite Bug* can rent bikes for use here, but unfortunately there is **no other bike rental** nearby.

Park on the south side of the river and unhitch your bike before crossing the suspension bridge and letting loose.

The **easiest trail** simply follows the dirt road downstream from the bridge, an almost completely flat five-mile ride past the aforementioned campgrounds to a metal bridge where there's a locked gate. In summer, once the high spring flows have abated and the river has warmed up (July–Sept), you'll find plenty of inviting swimming holes. For something tougher, go for the **Briceburg Bike Loop** (15 mile loop; 2–3hr; 500ft ascent), using a map available from the visitor center; the loop follows a fire road around the hills above the Merced River Canyon. There are great views and it is all quite manageable, though in summer it is best done in the early morning or around dusk to avoid the midday heat. The loop is accessed by the Burma Grade (Bull Creek Road), classed for 4x4s though high clearance two-wheelers can make it in good conditions. Of course, you can cycle up to the loop as well (5 miles; 1500ft ascent), though it is a real slog only partially compensated by the excellent downhill to get back to your rig.

Mariposa

The nearest town of any size on Yosemite's western flanks is **MARIPOSA**, 45 miles from the Valley and a former gold town that has turned its hand to mining the rich vein of tourists passing through. Modern developments have mostly swamped the old town center, but Hwy-140 still rattles through a short stretch of covered walkways and two-story gold-era buildings, the best being the 1859 adobe former **Schlageter Hotel** on the corner of Fifth Street. Though the retail core increasingly consists of wayside restaurants and knick-knack/antique shops, Mariposa remains an attractive enough place.

The most historic structure is the **Mariposa County Courthouse**, corner of Jones and 10th streets (45min tours late May to early Sept Fri 5.30–8.30pm, Sat 10am–8.30pm, Sun 10am–4pm, reservations essential ⓣ209/966-7081; free), the oldest law enforcement building west of the Mississippi still in continuous use. Built without nails, the lumber was rough-cut from a nearby stand of white pine, and you can still see the saw marks on the hand-planed spectator benches.

The town's heritage is further celebrated at the **Mariposa Museum & History Center**, corner of Jesse and 12th streets (March–Oct daily 10am–4.30pm, Nov, Dec & Feb daily 10am–4pm, Jan closed; $3), which wedges in a mildly diverting mock-up of a gold-era street (drug store, saloon, dress shop, etc) and has a corner devoted to the local Miwok people with some fine examples

▲ Mariposa County Courthouse

of basketwork. Scattered around the outside is large-scale mining paraphernalia, including a stamp mill that is occasionally fired up for group tours. It all means a lot more if you can engage one of the docents to show you around; they might even show you the 1901 stagecoach that is still used a couple of times a year.

In truth, you're better off at the **California State Mining and Mineral Museum**, two miles south on Hwy-49 (May–Sept daily 10am–6pm, Oct–April daily except Tues 10am–4pm; $3; Ⓦwww.parks.ca.gov), which revels in the glory days of the mid-nineteenth century with realistic reconstructions of a mine, assay office and stamp mill, plus the **Fricot Nugget**, the largest surviving specimen of crystallized gold from the Gold Rush era in California, a thirteen-pound chunk valued at over $1 million. An impressive geology section brings together samples from all over the state, including a beautiful piece of malachite looking like three melting candles, and a case of fluorescent rocks glowing green, yellow and blue. The use of minerals in daily life is also explored along with suitably unearthly looking meteorites.

Practicalities

The helpful **Mariposa County Visitor Centee**, 5158 Hwy-140 (mid-May to mid-Sept Mon–Sat 7am–8pm Sun 8am–5pm, mid-Sept to mid-May Mon–Sat 8am–5pm Sun closed; Ⓣ209/966-7081, Ⓦwww.mariposa.org), concentrates on those Yosemite-bound but also has the handy "Historic Walking Tour" map of the key heritage buildings. Perhaps more important to those heading on to Yosemite is the extensive Pioneer Market **supermarket** (daily 8am–9pm) at the eastern end of town, complete with in-store bakery. The **library**, 4978 10th St (Mon & Sat 9.30am–2pm, Tues & Thurs 9.30am–6pm, Wed & Fri 9.30am–5pm), has free **Internet access**.

Merced

Some eighty miles southwest of Yosemite Valley, **MERCED** is too far from the Park to be considered a good base for exploring, but is very handy for its **transport connections**, and has a few minor sights.

The best thing about this sleepy town is its courthouse, a gem of a building in the main square that's maintained as the **County Courthouse Museum**, corner of N Street and W 20th Street (Wed–Sun 1–4pm; free; Ⓦwww.mercedmuseum.org). This striking Italian Renaissance-style structure, with columns, elaborately sculptured window frames, and a cupola topped by a statue of the Goddess of Justice (minus her customary blindfold), was raised in 1875 when it completely dominated the few dozen shacks that comprised the town. Impressively restored in period style, the courtroom retained a legal function until 1951, while the equally sumptuous offices were vacated in the 1970s, leaving the place to serve as storage space for local memorabilia – most exotic among which is an 1870s Taoist shrine, found by chance in a makeshift temple above a Chinese restaurant. You might also pass a pleasant half-hour in the mostly contemporary galleries in the **Merced Multicultural Arts Museum**, 645 W Main St (Mon–Fri 9am–5pm, Sat 10am–2pm; free; Ⓦwww.artsmerced.org).

Six miles northwest of Merced, close to the dormitory community of **Atwater** – and signposted off Hwy-99 – lies the **Castle Air Museum** (daily: May–Sept 9am–5pm; Oct–May 10am–4pm; $10; Ⓦwww.castleairmuseum.org). Forty-odd military aircraft from WWII to Vietnam – mostly bulky bombers with a few fighters thrown in, including the world's fastest plane, the SR-71 – are scattered outdoors, while inside there's a static B52 simulator, assorted military paraphernalia and a collection of some 120 model planes crafted by one enthusiast from redwood. Route #8 of Merced's transit system, "The Bus" (Mon–Sat only; ⓣ1-800/345-3111, ⓦwww.mercedthebus.com), runs out here about every ninety minutes for $2 each way.

Practicalities

None of these sights are much of a reason to visit Merced, though the convenient **bus links to Yosemite** are. Greyhounds from Bakersfield, Sacramento and San Francisco stop downtown at the **Transpo Center** on W 16th St at N Street, where you'll find **Merced California Welcome Center**, 710 W 16th St (Mon–Sat 8.30am–5pm Sun 9.30am–3.30pm ⓣ1-800/446-5353, ⓦwww.yosemite-gateway.org), which covers the region but has some local info. The **Amtrak station** is somewhat isolated at 24th and K streets, about ten blocks away on the opposite side of the town center: follow K Street off W 16th Street.

YARTS buses (see p.23) pick up at the Transpo Center and train station on their way to Yosemite, and there are several **car rental** agencies in town (see p.20). Most people pass straight through Merced, but in case you need to stop over, we've detailed some lodging and eating options in the appropriate chapters of the guide (see p.170 & p.183 respectively).

South of Yosemite: Hwy-41 and around

After exploring southern Yosemite's Wawona and the big trees in Mariposa Grove, it's worth spending a little time in the country just south of the Park. Should you have trouble securing accommodation in the Park, you may also find yourself staying out this way either in the roadside cluster known as **Fish Camp**, a couple of miles south of the Park entrance or the growing town of **Oakhurst**, not a pretty place, but with all the necessary facilities.

Leaving Yosemite's South Entrance you soon pass the Forest Service's convenient *Summerdale* campground, and tiny Fish Camp followed by the entrance to the grand *Tenaya Lodge*. Onwards it's downhill all the way to Oakhurst, a fast winding road leading initially through pines then coming out into the oak-studded grasslands of the Sierra foothills. To the east, roads fan out to **Bass Lake** and the secluded **Sierra Vista Scenic Byway**.

Fish Camp

The tiny huddle of houses and lodging making up **Fish Camp** lies just two miles from the Park's South Entrance and fourteen miles north of Oakhurst, making it a convenient base for exploring Wawona and around. Most visitors spend their days in the Park, but Fish Camp has something to keep the kids quiet in the form of **Yosemite Mountain Sugar Pine Railroad**, 56001 Hwy-41 (mid-March to Oct 9.30am–3pm or 4pm; ⓣ559/683-7273, ⓦwww.ymsprr.com). Two miles of narrow-gauge track wend their way into the forest along a line used by the Madera Sugar Pine Lumber Company who, from 1899 to 1931, hauled out almost one and a half billion board feet of timber. For a real sense of what it must have been like, ride "The Logger" (April–Oct Mon–Fri 1–3 daily, Sat & Sun 2–4 daily; adults $17, kids 3–12 $8.50), a train of open cars hauled by a vintage oil-burning Shay steam locomotive; extra services are hauled by "Jenny" cars (adults $13, kids $6.50) powered by ancient Model A Ford engines. *The Logger* is also fired up for the family-oriented Moonlight Specials (May & Sept to mid-Oct Sat, June–Aug Wed & Sat; adults $45, kids $22.50; reservations essential), which

Hotel, campsite and restaurant **listings** for the area covered within this chapter begin on pages 171, 177 and 184 respectively.

includes a steak barbecue dinner, live music by the Sugar Pine Singers then a night ride on the train.

Fish Camp also has **horseback riding** at Yosemite Trails Pack Station (see p.152), with rides into Mariposa Grove, and there's a range of activities at *Tenaya Lodge* (see p.171), though these are mostly aimed at guests of the hotel.

Oakhurst

In the last few years, **OAKHURST**, sixteen miles south of the Park's South Entrance and fifty miles south of the Valley proper, has become a booming huddle of malls and sky-high signs for chain hotels and fast-food joints. It makes little of its pleasant setting in the Sierra foothills, but the abundance of lodging and restaurants does make it a handy base both for Yosemite and for Bass Lake (see opposite). There is no useful public transportation to or from Oakhurst, but with your own wheels you can easily explore the southern section of the Park, and day-trips into the Valley are by no means out of the question.

The town and around

Most of the malls in Oakhurst cluster around the junction of Hwy-41 and Hwy-49. From the intersection, Hwy-41 heads north towards the Park passing most of the hotels and restaurants and, after two miles, the **Yosemite Sierra Visitors Bureau**, 41969 Hwy-41 (Mon–Sat 8.30am–5pm, Sun 9am–1pm; ⓣ559/683-4636, ⓦwww.yosemite.travel), which has armloads of information on Yosemite. Look out for the misleadingly titled *Yosemite Sierra Visitors Guide*, which concentrates on the area immediately south of Yosemite National Park – useful if you're planning to explore Bass Lake and the Sierra Vista Scenic Byway.

Between the highway junction and the visitors bureau, Road 426 leads east to Road 427 (aka School Road) and the **Fresno Flats Historical Park** (daily dawn–dusk; free), half a mile out, where a cluster of relocated vernacular buildings scattered among the oaks recalls the original 1850s settlement of Fresno Flats where Oakhurst now stands. A self-guided tour leads around the exteriors, but it all makes more sense when you visit the **museum** (March–Dec Mon–Fri 10am–3pm, Sat & Sun noon–4pm, Jan & Feb closed; free; ⓦwww.fresnoflatsmuseum.org), fashioned from two 1870s homes. Guided tours take place at weekends (Sat & Sun noon–4pm).

Apart from the wide selection of places to stay (see p.170) and eat (see p.184), Oakhurst has the region's most functional array of shops and services including the **Oakhurst Branch Library**, 49044 Civic Circle (Mon–Thurs 10am–6pm, Fri & Sat 10am–2pm; ⓣ559/683-4838), which has **free Internet access**. Keen cyclists should visit Yosemite Bicycle & Sport (ⓣ559/641-2453, ⓦwww.yosemitebicycle.com), behind the *McDonald's* at 40120 Hwy-41, who **rent bikes** (from $30 a day) and give great advice on all manner of local rides.

For **entertainment**, first-run movies play at the Met Cinemas (ⓣ559/683-1234), corner of Hwy-49 and Hwy-41, and family-oriented, nineteenth-century **melodramas** are staged at the volunteer-run Golden Chain Theatre on Hwy-41 two miles north of Oakhurst (ⓣ559/683-7112, ⓦwww.goldenchaintheatre.org; $12): come to cheer the hero and boo the villain.

Bass Lake and the Sierra Vista Scenic Byway

It is easy to be seduced by Yosemite and focus entirely on the Park, but the beauty doesn't stop on its boundaries. In fact, the surrounding national forest can often be just as beautiful, less crowded and free from the more stringent regulations applied in national parks. A case in point is the **Sierra Vista Scenic Byway**, which loops east and north of Oakhurst into the wilds of the Ansel Adams Wilderness on the southern flanks of Yosemite.

Bass Lake

Just seven miles west of Oakhurst lies the biggest tourist attraction in the area, **BASS LAKE**, a pine-fringed man-made lake at 3400 feet. A stomping ground of the Hell's Angels in the 1960s – the leather and licentiousness memorably described in Hunter S. Thompson's *Hell's Angels* – Bass Lake is nowadays a family resort, crowded with boaters and anglers in summer, though the best fishing is in winter and spring. It makes a good spot to rest up for a day or two, probably staying in one of the lakeside campgrounds.

Road 222 runs right around the lake. At the main settlement, **Pines Village**, you can buy groceries, eat well and spend the night at the swanky *Pines Resort* (Ⓣ559/642-3121 or 1-800/350-7463, Ⓦwww.basslake.com; chalets, suites ⑧) in luxurious two-story chalets with kitchens or even more palatial lakeside suites. By the southwestern tip of the lake, *Miller's Landing Resort*, 37976 Rd 222 (Ⓣ559/642-3633 or 1-866/657-4386, Ⓦwww.millerslanding.com; cabins ②, deluxe cabins ⑦), offers rustic cabins without bathrooms, and a range of fancy chalets fully equipped with kitchen, barbecue and satellite TV: many are booked by the week throughout summer, but nightly stays are possible. *Miller's Landing* is also the best place to rent aquatic equipment – including **fishing boats** ($60 for 6hrs) and **jet skis** ($100 an hour) – and they have public showers and laundry.

The western side of Bass Lake is slung with $21-a-night family **campgrounds**, most oriented towards long stays beside your camper. In summer, book well in advance (Ⓣ1-877/444-6777, ⓌRecreation.gov), though no-shows are sometimes available at the Bass Lake Recreation Area office, 39900 Rd 222, on the lake's southwest side (late May to early Sept daily 8am–8pm; Ⓣ559/642-3212). For tent campers, the best site is *Lupine* ($21), just north of *Miller's Landing*.

Sierra Vista Scenic Byway

If Bass Lake is too commercial and overcrowded for you, the antidote starts immediately to the north. The **SIERRA VISTA SCENIC BYWAY** makes a ninety-mile circuit east of Hwy-41, topping out at the Clover Meadow Ranger Station (7000ft), which is the trailhead for much of the magnificent **Ansel Adams Wilderness**. Apart from trailheads and campgrounds, there's not a great deal to the road, though the views are fantastic and people are scarce. A straight circuit (snow-free July–Oct at best) takes five hours, and is especially slow going on the rough dirt roads of the north side. Stock up on supplies before you start: there are a couple of stores and gas stations dotted along its length but they're not cheap and the range is limited. Accommodation on the circuit is largely limited to campgrounds, all (except two free sites) costing $16.

The best source of information on the circuit is the **Bass Lake Ranger District** office (Mon–Fri 8am–4.30pm; Ⓣ559/877-2218) in the hamlet of North Fork at the southern end of Bass Lake, where you can pick up a **map** – important, as there are numerous confusing forestry roads and few signposts. Before setting off, consider a **meal** at *La Cabaña*, 32762 Road 222 in North Fork (Ⓣ559/877-3311), a nondescript shack serving excellent and authentic Mexican dishes and burgers, most for under $7.

The south side

Before setting out from North Fork, check out the **Sierra Mono Indian Museum** (Tues–Sat 9am–4pm; $5), with some good examples of local Native American basketry and beadwork, as well as a lot of stuffed animals in glass cases. Once on your way, the first point of interest is the **Jesse Ross Cabin**, 15 miles along, a 1860s hewn-log original that has been restored and brought to the site. It is left open so you can poke around inside. Ten miles on, **Mile High Vista** reveals endless views of muscle-bound mountain ranges and bursting granite domes stretching back to Mammoth Mountain (see p.220). A little further on, an eight-mile side road cuts south to the dammed **Mammoth Pool**, where anglers boat on the lake and smoke their catch at one of the four **campgrounds**. The quietest of them are *Sweetwater* ($16; 3800ft) and *Placer* ($16; 4100ft), away from the pool but by streams.

Back on the Scenic Byway, you'll pass the rather disappointing **Arch Rock**, where the earth under a slab of granite has been undermined to leave a kind of bridge, and continue climbing to a small ranger outpost (late June to Sept occasionally staffed; ⓣ559/877-2218), and the Minarets Pack Station (mid-June to Sept; ⓣ559/868-3405, ⓦwww.highsierrapackers.org/min.htm). Apart from a general store and reasonable meals, the station offers simple lodging ($13 per person) and **horseback trips** from $55 a day. It's a great base for wilderness trips, many of which start by the **Clover Meadow Wilderness Station**, a couple of miles up a spur road (late June to mid-Sept daily 9am–5pm; permits available). Nearby are two free and wonderfully sited campgrounds, *Clover Meadow* and *Granite Creek*, both at 7000ft, the former with potable water.

The north side

The Minarets Pack Station marks the start of the descent from the backcountry and the end of the asphalt; for the next few miles you're on rough dirt, generally passable in ordinary passenger vehicles when clear of snow. The hulking form of **Globe Rock** heralds the return to asphalt, which runs down to **Beasore Meadow**, where the summer-only **Jones Store** (open mid-June to mid-Oct) has supplied groceries, gas and basic meals (8am–8pm) for the best part of a century, and offers showers to hikers. A short distance further on you reach Cold Springs Meadow, the junction with Sky Ranch Road (follow it left to continue the loop) and a spur to the wonderful *Fresno Dome* campground ($16; no water; 6400ft), a great base for a moderately strenuous walk to the top of the exfoliated granite namesake.

The Scenic Byway then passes several $16 campgrounds, most without running water, en route to the **Nelder Grove Historical Area** (unrestricted entry), a couple of miles north along a dirt road. Over a hundred giant sequoias are scattered through the forest here, though the overall impression is of devastation evidenced by the number of enormous stumps among the second-growth sugar pine, white fir and cedar. The mile-long "Shadow of the Giants" interpretive walk explains the logging activities that took place here in the 1880s and early 1890s and, with its low visitor count, offers a more serene communion with these majestic trees than in Yosemite. A second interpretive trail leads from the nearby, wooded *Nelder Grove* campground (free; 3500ft; stream water) to **Bull Buck Tree**, which with its base circumference of 99ft was once a serious contender for the world's largest tree. Though slimmer in the base Sequoia National Park's General Sherman Tree, is taller and broader at the top, so taking the prize. From here it's seven twisting miles back to Hwy-41, reached at a point around four miles north of Oakhurst.

15

East of Yosemite: Mono Lake, Bodie and Mammoth Lakes

Snow typically blocks Hwy-120 East from early November until late May, cutting off the bulk of Yosemite National Park from the eastern Sierra. For the rest of the year, however, the Tioga Road (as it is known) shouldn't be missed.

From the Park boundary at Tioga Pass Hwy-120 East plunges fourteen miles down the Lee Vining Grade (see p.87) past numerous good campgrounds to the small town of Lee Vining. The scenery changes rapidly from Yosemite's granite domes and alpine lakes to a land that feels a million miles away. Here in the rain shadow of the mountains you're on the fringes of the Great Basin, semi-arid uplands that stretch away across Nevada to Utah. Snowmelt streams coursing down the Eastern Sierra each spring have created the alkaline **Mono Lake**, an almost otherworldly disc shining amid miles of scrubby sage brush. Around its shore, tufa towers make a photogenic, if unnatural, sight. On the lake's western flank, tiny **Lee Vining** is the district's service town and the only place on the eastern side of the Sierra that's close enough to be used as a base for visiting the Park. You wouldn't want to drive daily into Yosemite Valley, sixty miles distant, but Tuolumne Meadows is within easy striking distance.

The barren hill country thirty miles to the north of Lee Vining appears to be an inhospitable place to live, and the twenty thousand people who once called **Bodie** home wouldn't contest that. As soon as the gold ran out, so did the people, leaving behind what many consider the most atmospheric **ghost town** in the West. It is a great spot for anyone needing a break from hiking, or looking for more boom-time history than Yosemite can supply.

There's a very different feel to **Mammoth Lakes**, located forty miles' drive south of the Park's Tioga Pass Entrance Station. Although it's too far away to be a suitable jumping-off point for the Park, the resort town could very well end up stealing a few nights from your Yosemite itinerary, especially if its superior mountain-biking and fishing opportunities strike a chord. Come winter, Mammoth transforms into one of the state's finest alpine skiing and snowboarding destinations, though highway closures turn the three-hour summer drive from Yosemite Valley into a six-hour odyssey.

Mono Lake and Lee Vining

The blue expanse of **MONO LAKE** sits in the middle of a volcanic desert tableland, its sixty square miles reflecting the statuesque, snowcapped mass of the eastern Sierra Nevada. At over a million years old, it's an ancient lake with two large volcanic islands – the light-colored **Paoha** and the black **Negit** – surrounded by salty, alkaline water. It resembles nothing more than a science-fiction landscape, with great towers and spires formed by mineral deposits ringing the shores; hot springs surround the lake, and all around the basin are signs of lava flows and volcanic activity, especially in the cones of the Mono Craters, just to the south.

The lake's most distinctive feature, the strange, sandcastle-like **tufa** formations, were increasingly exposed from the early 1940s to the mid-1990s as the City of Los Angeles drained away the waters that flow into the lake (see box, p.216). The towers of tufa were formed underwater, where calcium-bearing freshwater springs well up through the carbonate-rich lake water; the calcium and carbonate combine as limestone, slowly growing into the weird formations you can see today.

Lee Vining, overlooking Mono Lake, is the only settlement anywhere nearby, offering the usual range of visitor services but not a great deal more. Hotel, camping and restaurant **listings** for the area begin on p.172, p.177 and p.184 respectively.

Arrival and information

The most useful public transport calling at Lee Vining is the summer-only YARTS **bus** service (see p.23) between Mammoth Lakes and Yosemite Valley. The shuttles stop in the center of town, visit the Mono Basin Scenic Area Visitor Center (see opposite) and call at the Tioga Gas Mart at the start of Hwy-120 East. There's also the year-round CREST service (Ⓣ760/872-1901 or 1-800/922-1930), which follows US-395 along the Owens Valley linking Ridgecrest in the south and Reno, Nevada, in the north. Both towns have onward connections. Buses generally have bike racks or space onboard.

Before striking out for a close look at the lake and its tufa, call in at both of the excellent visitor centers. In the heart of Lee Vining, the town's **Mono Lake Committee Information Center** (daily: July & Aug 9am–10pm; rest of year 9am–5pm; Ⓣ760/647-6595, Ⓦwww.leevining.com and Ⓦwww.monolake.org) is partly the showcase for the committee's battle for Mono Lake, featuring an excellent twenty-minute video presentation, but also has helpful staff and an excellent bookstore concentrating on the environment and the Eastern Sierra. There's even a tasteful gift shop and **Internet access**.

A mile north along US-395, the **Mono Basin Scenic Area Visitor Center**, a mile north of Lee Vining beside US-395 (daily May–Oct 9am–4.30pm; Nov–April generally closed; Ⓣ760/873-2408, Ⓦwww.r5.fs.fed.us/inyo) has exhibits and a good short film detail the lake's geology, and rangers give talks on various aspects of its ecology.

Accommodation and **eating** establishments around Lee Vining are covered on p.172 and p.184 respectively.

Exploring Mono Lake

Everyone's first stop is **South Tufa**, five miles east of US-395 via Hwy-120 ($3; valid one week), the single best place to look at the tufa spires. Boardwalks and trails lead around and among these twenty-foot-high limestone cathedrals and along the lakeshore where photo ops turn up around every corner. About a mile to the east lies **Navy Beach** (free), where there are a few more (though less spectacular) spires, and the opportunity to float in water at least twice as buoyant as (and a thousand times more alkaline than) sea water. Even towards the end of summer the water is chilly, and some find that the salt stings.

To add an educational component to your explorations, join one of the **guided walks** (July to early Sept daily 10am, 1pm & 6pm) run by the Mono

A thirsty city and the battle for Mono Lake

Mono Lake is one of the oldest on the continent and has survived several ice ages and all the volcanic activity that the area can throw at it, but the lake's biggest threat has been the City of Los Angeles, which owns the riparian rights to Mono Lake's catchment.

From 1892 to 1904, the fledgling city of Los Angeles experienced a twelve-year drought and started looking to the Owens River as a reliable source of water that could be easily channeled to the city. Under the auspices of the Los Angeles Department of Water and Power, the city bought up almost the entire Owens Valley, then diverted the river and its tributaries into a 223-mile gravity-fed aqueduct to take this water to LA. Farms and orchards in the once-productive Owens Valley were rendered useless without water, and Owens Lake near Lone Pine was left to dry up entirely.

The aqueduct was completed in 1913 but the growing city demanded ever more water. Consequently, in 1941, LA diverted four of the five streams that fed Mono Lake through an eleven-mile tunnel into its Owens Valley Aqueduct. This was an engineering marvel, dug through the volcanically active Mono Craters, but it has been overshadowed by the legal battle surrounding the depletion of the lake itself, long one of the biggest **environmental controversies** raging in California.

Over the next fifty years, the **water level** in Mono Lake dropped over forty feet, a disaster not only because of the lake's unique beauty, but also because Mono Lake is the primary nesting ground for **California gulls** and a critical resting point for hundreds of thousands of migratory eared **grebes** and **phalaropes**. The lake was down to roughly half its natural size, and as the levels dropped, the islands in the middle of the lake where the gulls lay their eggs became peninsulas, and the colonies fell prey to coyotes and other mainland predators. Also, as less fresh water reached the lake, the landlocked water became increasingly saline, threatening the unique local ecosystem. About all that will thrive in the harsh conditions are brine shrimp and alkali flies, both essential food sources for the birdlife. Humans are not immune to the harmful effects – winds blowing across the salt pans left behind by the receding lake create alkaline clouds containing selenium and arsenic, both contributors to lung disease.

Seemingly oblivious to the plight of the lake, the City of Los Angeles built a second aqueduct in 1970 and the water level dropped even faster, sometimes falling eighteen inches in a single year. Prompted by scientific reports of an impending ecological disaster, a small group of activists set up the **Mono Lake Committee** (Ⓦwww.monolake.org) in 1978, fighting for the preservation of this unique ecosystem partly through the courts and partly through publicity campaigns – "Save Mono Lake" bumper stickers were once de rigueur for concerned citizens. Though the California Supreme Court declared in 1983 that Mono Lake must be saved, it wasn't until 1994 that emergency action was taken. A target water height of 6377ft above sea level (later raised to 6392ft) was grudgingly agreed to make Negit Island once again safe for nesting birds. Streams dry for decades are now flowing again, and warm springs formerly located by lakeside interpretive trails are now submerged. The target level – 18 feet higher than its recorded minimum, but still 25 feet below its pre-diversion level – won't be reached at least until 2014 when the agreement is up for re-negotiation, something that concentrates the ongoing efforts of the Mono Lake Committee.

Basin Scenic Area Visitor Center around the tufa formations, or sign up for the Mono Lake Committee's regular hour-long **canoe trips** (mid-June to early Sept Sat & Sun 8am, 9.30am & 11am; $24; reservations recommended ⓣ760/647-6595), on which you'll paddle around the tufa towers and learn all about their formation along with details of migrating birdlife and the brine shrimp they feed off.

Otherwise, you can go by kayak with Mammoth Lakes-based Caldera Kayaks (ⓣ760/934-1691, ⓦwww.calderakayak.com), who run half-day natural history tours on Mono Lake ($95, $70 each for groups of 3 or more) and rent sit-on-top kayaks for $40 a day (doubles $60). Both trips require reservations as far in advance as you can manage.

Adjacent to the south shore of the lake stands **Panum Crater**, a 700-year-old volcano riddled with deep fissures and fifty-foot towers of lava, visited on **Plug Trail** and **Rim Trail**, two short and fairly easy trails. This is the most recent of the **Mono Craters**, a series of volcanic cones that stretch twelve miles south from here towards Crowley Lake. This constitutes the youngest mountain range in North America, entirely formed over the last forty thousand years.

On the north shore of the lake, three miles along US-395, a side road leads to **Mono County Park**, where a guided boardwalk trail leads down to the lakefront and the best examples of mushroom-shaped tufa towers. A further five miles along this (mostly washboard gravel) side road is the trailhead for the **Black Point Fissures**, the result of a massive underwater eruption of molten lava some thirteen thousand years ago. As the lava cooled and contracted, cracks and fissures formed on the top, some only a few feet wide but as much as fifty feet deep. You can explore their depths, but pick up a directions sheet from the Visitor Center and be prepared for hot, dry and sandy conditions.

Bodie Ghost Town

In the 1880s, the gold-mining town of **BODIE**, eighteen miles north of Lee Vining then thirteen miles (three of them dirt) east of US-395, boasted three breweries, some sixty saloons and dance halls, and a population of nearly ten thousand. It also had a well-earned reputation as the raunchiest and most lawless mining camp in the West. Contemporary accounts describe a town that ended each day with a shootout on Main Street, while the firehouse bell, rung once for every year of a murdered man's life, seemed never to stop sounding. The town boomed for just four years, starting in 1877, when a rather unproductive existing mine collapsed and exposed an enormously rich vein. Within four years this was the second-largest town in the state after San Francisco, even supporting its own Chinatown. By 1885, gold and silver currently valued at around $1.2 billion had been extracted, but a drop in the gold price made mining largely unprofitable. The town dwindled and then was virtually destroyed by two disastrous fires, the last in 1932. The school finally closed in 1942, but a few hardly souls stuck it out until the early 1960s when the site was taken over by the State of California.

What remains has been turned into the **Bodie State Historic Park** (daily: June–early Sept 8am–7pm; early Sept–May 9am–4pm; $3; ⓣ760/647-6445, ⓦwww.parks.ca.gov), where lack of theme-park tampering gives the place an authentically eerie atmosphere absent from other US ghost towns. Bodie is almost 8400ft above sea level and, although the park is open throughout the year, snow often prevents vehicular access between December and April; call for road conditions. If you can get in during that time, bundle up: Bodie is often cited on the national weather report as having the lowest temperature in

▲ Bodie Ghost Town

the US. Whenever you go, remember to bring all you need: there are no services at the site.

A good self-guided tour booklet ($1) leads you around many of the 150-odd wooden buildings – about six percent of the original town – surviving in a state of arrested decay around the intact town center. Some buildings have been re-roofed and others supported in some way, but it is by and large a faithful preservation: even the dirty dishes are much as they were in the 1940s, little damaged by sixty years of weathering. The **Miners' Union Building** on Main Street was the center of the town's social life; founded in 1877, the union was the first in California, organized by workers at the Standard and Midnight mines. The building now houses a small **museum** (June–Aug daily 9am–6pm; May & Sept daily 9am–5pm; free), which paints a graphic picture of mining life. Various **tours** depart from here in the summer, particularly on weekends, though schedules are flexible and you should call ahead if you have specific interests.

The history talk is free, but there's also a fifty-minute tour of the **Standard Consolidated Stamp Mill** (generally June–Aug daily 11am & 2pm; $5) otherwise off-limits, and one along a ridge ($5) which offers some of the best views of Bodie. Other highlights of the town include the **Methodist church** with its intact pipe organ, the **general store** with its beautiful pressed-steel ceiling, the **saloon** and the **cemetery** on the hill where lie the remains of Bill Bodey, after whom the town was (sort of) named.

Mammoth Lakes and around

You'll need to head 25 miles south from Mono Lake along US-395 to reach the first town of any significance, **MAMMOTH LAKES**, and the associated skiing, snowboarding and mountain biking hotspot of **Mammoth Mountain**. Jointly they make up the Eastern Sierra's biggest resort, and one that is only challenged in California by those around Lake Tahoe. During the winter months, masses of weekend skiers speed through the Owens Valley on their way to some of the state's premier pistes, but snow and ice block direct access from Yosemite over Tioga Pass. Because of this, for Yosemite visitors Mammoth is best considered for its fishing and wonderfully accessible mountain-biking terrain – along with fine hiking and horseback riding the opportunities in the unlikely case you tire of the Park's options.

Despite its popularity with LA weekenders, Mammoth has always been a fairly low-key resort, but in recent years the involvement of a major corporate resort owner has propelled Mammoth into the ranks of the winter sports mega-resorts like those at Vail in the Rockies, and Whistler/Blackcomb in Canada. One company now owns the ski operation, large chunks of Mammoth real estate, and the new **Village at Mammoth** development, complete with pricey hotels, swanky stores, and linked to the mountain by the Village Gondola. Lots of new lodging has been built along with Mammoth's second golf course, and there are advanced plans for a much-expanded airport with scheduled flights.

Residents are torn between enthusiasm for the new opportunities presented and nostalgia for the way things used to be, but for the moment Mammoth remains unbeatable for outdoor activities and is scenically as dramatic as just about anywhere in the Sierra. You may find the testosterone overload oppressive and the town overpriced, but it is easy to escape to the hills during the day and return each evening to good food, lively bars and even a couple of movie theaters.

Arrival, information and accommodation

Hwy-203 runs three miles west from US-395 into the town of Mammoth Lakes, from where it continues six miles to the Main Lodge for Mammoth Mountain, then ascends the San Joaquin Ridge and drops down to the Devils Postpile National Monument. From June to September the **YARTS bus service** to Tuolumne Meadows and Yosemite Valley (see p.23) departs from *Mammoth Mountain Inn*, opposite the skifield Main Lodge, at 7am and returns that evening around 9pm. There's also the year-round **CREST buses** (☎760/872-1901 or 1-800/922-1930) which stop three times a week in the *McDonald's* parking lot on Hwy-203.

If you happen to be here during the ski season, the five-route **Mammoth Shuttle** goes everywhere you'll want to. During the rest of the year, those without their own transport will have to **rent a bike** (see "Listings," p.225). There's also the **Devils Postpile shuttle** between main ski lodge and Devils Postpile National Monument, some fifteen miles west of town.

The best source of practical information for the area is the combined US Forest Service and Mammoth Lakes **visitor center** (daily 8am–5pm; ☎760/924-5500, Ⓦwww.visitmammoth.com) on the main highway half a mile east of the town center.

Accommodation

About every second building in Mammoth is a condo, but there are numerous other **accommodation** opportunities (including a hostel and some welcoming B&Bs), so beds are at a premium only during ski-season weekends. Winter prices are highest, summer rates (quoted here, and still fairly high) come next, and in the months in between some relative bargains can be found. If you fancy staying in a **condo** try contacting Mammoth Mountain Reservations (☎1-800/223-3032, Ⓦwww.mammothreservations.com).

There is also mile upon mile of backcountry (see "Hiking" box, p.221) in which to pitch a tent, and plenty of family sites with campers almost overwhelmed by choice. There are some twenty **campgrounds** within a ten-mile radius of town; the two main concentrations being around Twin Lakes and along the Devils Postpile–Reds Meadow road. Almost all come with water, cost $15–16, and are rented on a first-come-first-served basis. The *Mammoth Lakes Welcome Center Visitor Guide* (available free from the visitor center) has full details along with rules for free dispersed camping on national forest lands around about.

Hotels and B&Bs

Cinnamon Bear Inn **113 Center St ⓣ760/934-2873 or 1-800/845-2873, ⓦwww.cinnamonbearinn.com.** Reasonably priced, 22-room B&B inn close to downtown with comfortable rooms, all with TV and phone (and some with VCR), use of hot tub, wine-and-nibbles happy hour on arrival, and a full breakfast. Check the web for low-cost specials. Midweek ❺, weekends ❻

Davison Street Guest House **19 Davison St ⓣ760/924-2188, ⓦwww.mammoth-guest.com.** Mammoth's only backpacker hostel is in a wooden A-frame chalet with mountain views from its deck. There's a spacious lounge, good communal cooking facilities, bunks in fairly compact dorms (summer $28, winter weekdays $40, winter weekends $50), three-bed rooms (summer ❷, winter weekdays ❸, winter weekends ❹), and one en-suite room for an extra $25–35.

The M Inn Mammoth **75 Joaquin Rd ⓣ760/934-2710, ⓦwww.mammothcountryinn.com.** Welcoming boutique inn located in a quiet neighborhood, with ten modern and tastefully themed rooms, all with private baths and some with Jacuzzis. There's wine and hors d'oeuvres on arrival, and full and delicious breakfasts. Midweek ❺, weekend ❻

Motel 6 **3372 Main St ⓣ760/934-6660 or 1-800/466-8356, ⓦwww.motel6.com.** Basic modern motel close to the town center with all you really need at an affordable price. ❸

Sierra Nevada Rodeway Inn **164 Old Mammoth Rd ⓣ760/934-2515 or 1-800/824-5132, ⓦwww.mammothsnri.com.** At the cheaper end of Mammoth motels but still with large comfy rooms, pool, spa and sauna, and on-site restaurant. ❺

Tamarack Lodge & Resort **Lake Mary Rd ⓣ760/934-2442 or 1-800/626-6684, ⓦwww.tamaracklodge.com.** Away from the town and with a woodsy setting right by Twin Lake on the edge of a cross-country ski area, this luxurious lodge in rustic style offers lodge rooms (shared bath ❹; private bath ❻), rustic cabins (❻) with fully equipped kitchens, refurbished cabins (❼) and some gorgeous deluxe cabins costing around $320. (❾)

Camping and RVs

Convict Lake **Open late April to Oct; 7600ft.** Wooded, lakeside National Forest campground just west of US-395 around four miles south of the Mammoth turn-off, with the longest opening season in the area. Showers are available at the nearby *Convict Lake Resort* (ⓣ760/934-3800, ⓦwww.convictlake.com; $2 for two minutes). $18

Devils Postpile **Open July–Sept; 7500ft.** National Park Service campground half a mile from the rocks themselves along the Devils Postpile–Reds Meadow road, and a good base for hikes to Rainbow Falls or along the John Muir Trail. $16

Hartley Springs **Open early May–Oct; 8400ft.** Just one of several primitive waterless campgrounds in the area, this one located 1.5 miles west of US-395 along Glass Flow Road around eleven miles north of the Mammoth turn-off. Free

Mammoth Mountain RV Park **Hwy-203 ⓣ760/934-3822 or 1-800/582-4603, ⓦwww.mammothrv.com.** Year-round fully featured RV park right in town opposite the visitor center, with indoor spas, kids' play areas, tent sites ($28) and a range of partial and full hookup sites ($45–51).

New Shady Rest **Open mid-May to Oct; 7800ft.** Large and busy campground close to town with flush toilets and a dump station. Several sites can be reserved on ⓣ1-877/444-6777 or ⓦwww.recreation.gov. $18

Reds Meadow **Open mid-June to Oct; 7600ft.** National Forest campground along the Devils Postpile–Reds Meadow road and within easy hiking distance of Devils Postpile, Rainbow Falls and a nice nature trail around Sotcher Lake. It also comes with a natural hot-spring bathhouse open to all (donations appreciated). $16

Twin Lakes **Open mid-May to Oct; 8700ft.** The longest-opening of five near-identical sites in this area of glacially scooped lake beds, a mile southwest of Mammoth Lakes township. Lakeside setting among the pines and plenty of hiking trails nearby. $19

Mammoth: biking, hiking and other activities

Mammoth is all about getting into the outdoors. Aside from eating, drinking and mooching around the sports shops and factory clothing outlets, you'll find little reason to spend much time in town, though anyone interested in Mammoth's gold-mining and timber-milling origins may fancy a visit to the small **Mammoth Museum**, 5489 Sherwin Creek Rd (June–Sept daily 10am–6pm; free), located in a 1920s log cabin. Winter sports fans will find more of interest in the **Mammoth Ski Museum**, 100 College Parkway (Tues–Sun noon–5pm; $3; ⓣ760/934-6592, ⓦwww.mammothskimuseum.org), a small but well-presented collection of skiing-related paraphernalia most of it amassed over sixty years by one Mason Beekley. There's the expected racks of old skis, a chair from the original Mammoth chairlift and a 450-year-old book by a Swedish monk which illustrates skiing, but the museum's strength is in the graphic arts. The walls come lined with vintage ski posters, photos (some by Ansel Adams) and even woodcuts: many are reproduced and available at the gift shop.

There's more fun to be had four miles west of the center up on the slopes of the dormant volcano that is **Mammoth Mountain**, where the **Panorama Gondola** (all year except Oct to mid-Nov daily 9am–4.30pm; $20 round trip) will whisk you to the top of Mammoth Mountain in eight minutes, for fine mountain views seen through telescopes from a new interpretive center at the top.

If you'd rather work up a sweat there are a number of ways to do just that: mountain biking (see below), hiking (see opposite), plus stacks of people willing to get you mobile: **mountain biking**, and **rock climbing** are both covered in "Listings" on p.226.

Mountain biking

Once the ski runs have freed themselves of the winter snows, the slopes transform into the 3500-acre **Mammoth Mountain Bike Park** (late June to Sept daily 9am–4.30pm; ⓣ760/934-0706, ⓦwww.mammothmountain.com) with over eighty miles of groomed singletrack trails. Chairlifts quickly give you and your bike an altitude boost, allowing you to hurtle down the twisting sandy trails, brushing pines and negotiating small jumps and tree roots. The emphasis here is definitely on going downhill, and when you're transported to the rarefied 11,000ft air at the top of the chairlift you very quickly appreciate the logic of this. The bike park produces a color map of the mountain showing the lifts and trails in three grades of difficulty, and indicates X-Zones where they've created enhanced freeriding terrain for the more aggressive riders. Beginners often take the **Downtown** run into Mammoth (from where a bike shuttle bus returns you to the bike park), while those with a little more skill or ambition might opt for the **Beach Cruiser**, which carves its way down the western side of the mountain from near the summit. Experts and those with a death wish can tackle the **Kamikaze**, scene of the ultimate downhill race that has traditionally formed the centerpiece of the annual World Cup racing weekend (usually around late Sept), at which competitors hit speeds of sixty miles per hour.

The basic **park use fee** ($10) gives you access to the trails, and you can rent bikes for $39 a day. In addition there's a complex selection of deals such as the Park Pass (one day $37, two days $66), which gives all-day access to the Panorama Gondola to the summit and the bike shuttle from town. Gondola and bike rental combos include a two-hour package ($40) giving bike rental and gondola access, and a full-day unlimited deal ($76).

If you don't fancy forking out for use of the bike park, or just prefer something a little gentler, there is plenty more **trail riding** around the resort, made comfortable by midsummer temperatures reliably in the seventies. Several bike stores around town will point you in the right direction and rent bikes (see p.225) that can also be taken to the bike park. Likely candidates include: the relatively gentle Shady Rest Park, close to central Mammoth; the Lakes Basin area near *Tamarack Resort*; and Inyo and Mono craters. The visitor center offers free trail maps and a brochure on route descriptions and trail ethics.

Hiking

Interwoven among the bike trails on Mammoth Mountain are a couple of **hiking paths** which top out at the summit. The views are stupendous but, in common with many volcanoes, the hiking isn't the best and you're better off riding the gondola to the summit (see p.221) and saving your legs for hikes elsewhere.

Listed in the box below are some of the best of the **short hikes** around Mammoth. No permits are required for these, though you'll need to obtain a free **wilderness permit** if you want to spend the night in the Ansel Adams or John Muir wilderness areas to the south and west. On all trailheads into the wilderness there is an overnight quota season from May to October when the number of overnight hikers setting off from each trailhead is limited. Call the Wilderness Reservations Office in Bishop (Ⓣ760/873-2483, Ⓕ873-2484, Ⓦwww.r5.fs.fed.us/inyo) up to six months and at least two days in advance; there is a $5 reservation fee.

Hikes around Mammoth Lakes

Crystal Lake (3.5 miles round trip; 2hr; 650ft ascent). From the Lake George trailhead the path skirts high above Lake George revealing increasingly dramatic views as you climb towards Crystal Lake, hunkered below Crystal Crag. Fit hikers can tack on the Mammoth Crest Trail (a further 2.5 miles round trip; 2–3hr; 1000ft ascent).

Panorama Dome Trail (1 mile round trip; 30min; 100ft ascent). Great views over the town and the Owens Valley reward this short sylvan trail from Twin Lakes on Lake Mary Road.

Sky Meadows Trail (4 miles; 1.5–2hr; 1200ft ascent). Starting at the southern end of Lake Mary, this delightful hike along the wildflower-flanked Coldwater Creek passes Emerald Lake on its way to Sky Meadow at the foot of the striking Blue Crag.

Rainbow Falls Trail (5 miles; 2hr; 300ft ascent). Moderate hike that combines the two key features of the Devils Postpile National Monument. Start from the *Devils Postpile* campground and stroll to the monument itself, then continue to the top of Rainbow Falls.

Fishing

There is no actual Mammoth Lake, but the town of Mammoth Lakes makes a great base for reeling in brook, rainbow and brown trout in the dozens of lakes all about. During the main summer season many anglers head for Mary Lake, the largest hereabouts, where you can rent boats and spend the day hooking fish in beautiful surroundings. You won't be alone, but with a little imagination it is easy enough to find a peaceful spot. Pick up information from one of the many fishing shops in town, such as Kittredge Sports, 3218 Main St (ⓣ1-760/943-7566, ⓦwww.kittredgesports.com), which rents gear and has a board outside giving the latest on the region's fishing spots along with fly and spinner advice.

The artificial **Crowley Lake** (see p.216) is also a popular spot and is just twelve miles south along US-395. For **river fishing**, the San Joaquin, over the hill near the Devils Postpile, is a winner for those in search of trout.

Horseback trips

For those wanting to explore the High Sierra without carrying all food and camping gear, help is at hand in the form of pack stations offering **horseback trips** ranging from a single night to seven-, ten-, or even twenty-day trips over the Sierra Crest and into Yosemite or Kings Canyon national parks. Cheapest are custom **spot trips**, where you and your gear are taken to a suitable campsite then picked up at some prearranged time. Rates depend on numbers and distance traveled, but taking a group of four to a destination 4–6 hours

Winter and spring in Mammoth

With one of the longest Californian seasons (from early Nov often until well into June), three thousand vertical feet of skiing, and more than its fair share of dreamy deep powder, **Mammoth Mountain** (daily 8.30am–4pm; ⓣ1-800/626-6684, lift and snow conditions ⓣ1-888/766-9778, ⓦwww.mammothmountain.com) ranks as one of California's premier ski mountains. Unfortunately for Yosemite visitors, its season coincides almost exactly with the time when Tioga Pass is closed so the quickest way to drive between Yosemite Valley and Mammoth is via Hwy-88 just south of Lake Tahoe. In the process you pass close to several other downhill resorts making the whole enterprise a bit pointless.

Still, should you be in the area during the snowy season you'll find a well-balanced resort with roughly equal areas of beginner, intermediate and expert terrain, plus some of the very best terrain parks and halfpipes in North America. Add to that a cat's-cradle of intersecting gondolas and chairlifts – seemingly being added to each year and now numbering over thirty – bundles of snow-making equipment, and a whole resort of bars and restaurants designed with après-ski in mind, and you can hardly go wrong. As if this weren't enough, your lift ticket is also valid at June Lake (see map, p.198), a few miles north.

Pick up **lift tickets** ($79) from the Main Lodge on Minaret Road, where you can also rent **equipment** ($32 for basic skis, boots, and poles or snowboard and boots), and book **lessons** ($70 per half-day).

Off the mountain there are stacks of **cross-country skiing** trails; *Tamarack Lodge Resort* (see "Accommodation," p.219) offers ski packages, including instruction, tours and rentals, and charges $25 a day for access to the trails.

If you prefer a motorized approach to the white stuff, you can rent gear and clothing from DJ's Snowmobile Adventures (ⓣ760/935-4480, ⓦwww.snowmobilemammoth.com) who have one-hour (single $65, double $85), two-hour ($116/156) and half-day ($232/312) rentals.

away, you might expect to pay $500–800 each round trip. Multi-night **trail rides** with a guide usually work to a schedule advertised in advance and are likely to cost close to $200 a day. For these you'll generally be teaming up with others. Most outfitters also rent stock for carrying gear and will even use horses to drop off gear for you at a specified location. If interested, contact either Mammoth Lakes Pack Outfit (ⓣ760/934-2434 or 1-888/475-8748, ⓦwww.mammothpack.com) or Reds Meadow (ⓣ760/934-2345 or 1-800/292-7758, ⓦwww.redsmeadow.com), the later located right by Devils Postpile.

Along Minaret Road: Devils Postpile National Monument

From the ski area, the narrow and winding **Minaret Road/Reds Meadow Road** (typically open mid-June to Oct) climbs briefly to a nine-thousand-foot pass in the San Joaquin Ridge, then plummets into the headwaters of the Middle Fork of the San Joaquin River, ending some eight miles beyond at the Reds Meadow pack station. This is the only road access into the evocatively named **DEVILS POSTPILE NATIONAL MONUMENT** (free but see "shuttle bus" below; ⓦwww.nps.gov/depo), which centers on a collection of slender, blue-gray basalt columns ranged like hundreds of pencils stood on end. Some are as tall as sixty feet, others are twisted and warped; while vulnerable sections are shorter where the brittle rock has cracked and the upper sections have fallen forward to form a talus slope of shattered rubble. It was formed as lava from a vent near Mammoth Mountain cooled and fractured into multi-sided forms, a phenomenon best appreciated by skirting round to the top of the columns. The Postpile itself is a half-mile stroll from the *Devils Postpile* campground where there is a small **visitor center** (mid-June to mid-Sept daily

▲ Devils Postpile National Monument

9am–4pm), from where rangers guide daily walks at 11am and lead free evening campfire programs (twice weekly at 8pm).

The second highlight of the National Monument is **Rainbow Falls**, where the Middle Fork of the San Joaquin River plunges 101ft into a deep pool, the spray refracting to earn its name, especially at midday. It is two miles away through Reds Meadow, reached on a pleasant hike (see box, p.221).

Throughout the summer, Minaret Road/Reds Meadow Road is closed to private vehicles during the day and you must access Devils Postpile by **shuttle bus** (daily 7.15am–8.30pm, last bus leaves the Postpile 7.45pm; day-pass $7 per person, three-day pass $14, Federal Lands Senior and Annual passes not accepted), which leaves every thirty minutes from the Mammoth Mountain Main Lodge Gondola Building. Campers are allowed vehicular access at all times, and in the early morning (before 7am) and evening (after 7.30pm) others can drive along Minaret Road/Reds Meadow Road; drive over before 7am and you can come back whenever you wish. In theory, drivers and their passengers still have to pay but there is unlikely to be anyone to take your money.

During the day, the furthest you can drive without taking the shuttle bus is **Minaret Vista**, a parking lot high on the San Joaquin Ridge with wonderful views of the **Minaret Peaks**, a spiky volcanic ridge just south of pointed Mount Ritter – one of the Sierra's most enticing high peaks.

Eating and drinking

Mammoth offers by far the widest selection of **restaurants**, **cafés** and **bars** (some with **live music**) on this side of the Sierra. If you're just after replenishing your cooler, pick up **groceries** at Von's, in the Minaret Village mall, and healthy goodies at Sierra Sundance Earth Foods in the Mammoth Mall.

Angel's Main St at Sierra Blvd ☎760/934-7427. The menu has a Southwestern kick at this broadly appealing and family-friendly restaurant. The Angel's salad ($4) and jalapeño corn fritters ($6) are very good and there is a decent selection of burgers ($8–9) and $10 mains such as spinach and mushroom lasagna, and chicken pot pie, all washed down with Mammoth Brewing Company microbrews.

Base Camp Café 3325 Main St ☎760/934-3900. Great low-cost café usually bustling with the outdoors and active set here for the hearty breakfasts ($4–7), tasty soups and sandwiches, bargain daily specials, organic espresso coffees and microbrews. Also open for dinner (Thurs–Sun to around 8pm).

Giovanni's Minaret Village Mall, Old Mammoth Rd ☎760/934-7563. The favorite local stop for low-cost dining; three out of ten for decor and ambience but very good pasta and pizza (a 12-inch from $13), and great lunchtime deals.

Good Life Café The Mammoth Mall ☎760/934-1734. Doesn't cater to vegetarians and vegans as well as they'd like you to believe, but probably the best around with freshly made veggie burritos ($9), good salads ($7–9), and vegetable wraps as well as plenty of burgers and egg dishes ($8–9), all served inside or on the sunny deck. Daily 6.30am–3pm.

Grumpy's 361 Old Mammoth Rd ☎760/934-8587, ⓦwww.grumpysmammoth.com. Sports bar with 35 TVs, pool table and a good grill serving the likes of the half-pound Grumpy Melt with ortega chilies and grilled onions ($11), and a fine halibut and chips ($12).

Lakefront Restaurant *Tamarack Lodge* ☎760/934-2442. Superb lake views accompany dishes from a menu with French-Californian leanings, which might include wild mushroom strudel ($12), walnut-crusted chicken breast ($24), and a sumptuous selection of desserts and ports.

Looney Bean Coffee House The Mammoth Mall ☎760/934-1345. The most vibrant of Mammoth's coffee bars with good coffee, muffins and the like, served up to dedicated regulars either inside (where there's a stack of magazines) or out front. Stays open late in the ski season and the free Wi-Fi is very popular.

Nevados **Main St and Minaret Rd ⓣ760/934-4466.** Another favorite with the foodies with an eclectic menu from crisp nori-wrapped shrimp with wasabi to hazelnut crust rack of lamb and a $38 prix fixe deal for an appetizer, main and dessert.
Schat's Bakery & Café **3305 Main St ⓣ760/934-6055.** Easily the best range of baked goods in town, either to take out or eat in with a coffee. The crisp danishes, baklava, and handmade chocolates are all toothsome.
Thai'd Up **587 Old Mammoth Rd ⓣ760/934-7355.** Terrible name but tasty food is served in this diminutive Thai restaurant. Try summer rolls (served cold; $5) followed by Panang curry ($10). Lunch Wed–Sun, dinner daily except Tues.
The Stove **644 Old Mammoth Rd ⓣ760/934-2821.** Long-standing Mammoth favorite for its traditional country cooking, serving egg, waffle and pancake breakfasts (around $8), sandwiches and full meals later on – all in massive portions.
Whiskey Creek **Main St and Minaret Rd ⓣ760/934-2555.** Traditional American dining in one of the town's better restaurants, which particularly excels with its seafood, Sierra Ranch salad ($6.50) and meatloaf ($19). Upstairs is one of the livelier bars in town, serving its own Mammoth Brewing Company beers (daily happy hour: June–Oct 5–6.30pm, rest of year 4–5.30pm) and often putting on bands, on winter weekends.

Listings

Banks Several around town (all with ATMs) including the Bank of America, corner of Main St and Old Mammoth Rd.
Bookstores Booky Joint in the Minaret Village Mall (ⓣ760/934-2176) has the best all-round selection.
Cinemas First-run Hollywood fare at the Minaret Cinema in the Minaret Village Mall (ⓣ760/934-3131).
Festivals During the annual Jazz Jubilee, held over four days around the second weekend in July (details on ⓣ760/934-2478, ⓦwww.mammothjazz.org), bars, restaurants and impromptu venues around town pack out with predominantly trad-jazz types. Blues fans should come later for the Festival of Beers and Bluesapalooza (ⓣ760/934-0606, ⓦwww.mammothevents.com), held over the first weekend in Aug.
Internet access The library (see p.226) has free surfing for an hour at a time, and unlimited Wi-Fi. There's also access and Wi-Fi at the *Stellar Brew* coffeehouse, 3280 Main St ⓣ760/924-3559.
Laundry Aloha Sudz, corner of Main St and Old Mammoth Rd. Also coin-op machines at *Mammoth Mountain Inn* (7am–9pm).

Mammoth area hot springs

One of the pleasures of any extended visit to the Owens Valley is soaking your bones in one of the numerous **hot springs**. None is well signposted, and most are primarily used by locals who are welcoming enough if you are respectful. Most springs are tucked away miles down some rutted dirt road and often comprise little more than a ring of rocks or a hollowed-out tub into which people have diverted the waters to create pools of differing temperatures.

The most convenient springs are those at the **Hot Creek Geological Site**, on Hot Creek Hatchery Road which spurs off Hwy-395 three miles south of the exit for Mammoth Lakes. Once very popular, these are currently off-limits for bathing after a geyser erupted in the waters in 2006.

Aficionados in search of an alternative will want to get hold of either *Hot Springs of the Eastern Sierra* by George Williams III or *Touring California and Nevada Hot Springs* by Matt Bischoff (Falcon). Both have full descriptions and detailed directions of places such as Keough's Hot Springs, Travertine Hot Springs and Buckeye Hot Springs, all within an hour's drive of Mammoth. Most are **clothing-optional**, but you'll stand out as a tourist if you don't strip off.

Library The public library is located at 960 Forest Trail (Mon–Fri 10am–7pm, Sat 9am–5.30pm) and has Internet access.
Mountain biking Footloose Sports, corner of Main St and Old Mammoth Rd (ⓣ760/934-2400, ⓦwww.footloosesports.com), rents front and full suspension bikes ($6–9/hr, $32–39/day), plus the latest demo models ($18/78) and organizes weekly group rides; Mammoth Sporting Goods, Sierra Center Mall (ⓣ760/934-3239, ⓦwww.mammothsportinggoods.com), offers slightly better rates for a similar range of machines and also run-summer-only group rides (July–Oct Wed 5.30pm & Sat 9am) and a Fri evening night ride starting at 9pm.
Photographic supplies Speed of Light Photo & Video, Minaret Village Mall ⓣ760/934-8415.
Post office 3330 Main St (Mon–Fri 8.30am–5pm). The zip code is 93546.
Rock and alpine climbing Mammoth Mountain run family-oriented sessions on a 32-foot artificial climbing rock (late June to Sept daily 10am–5pm; single climb $10, or $20 an hour, shoes $5) in front of the *Mammoth Mountain Inn*. To get out on the real stuff, contact Southern Yosemite Mountain Guides (ⓣ1-800/231-4575, ⓦwww.symg.com) who offer a rock and alpine guiding service at $365 a day for up to six people. The Bishop-based guide services also run trips in the Mammoth area.
Showers In Mammoth township try *Mammoth Mountain RV Park* (daily 9am–5pm; $5).

In the Devils Postpile area, head for the natural hot-spring bathhouse at the *Reds Meadow* campground (donations appreciated).

Contexts

Contexts

History

Yosemite's written history dates back only 150 years, when Gold Rush pioneers chased the native Ahwahneechee from their home in what is now Yosemite Valley in 1851. Since then its scenic splendor has drawn ever more people: John Muir for its wild beauty, Ansel Adams for its picture-perfect rocks and trees, and millions more to hike, climb the magnificent granite monoliths, or stroll through the meadows. Of course, the story starts well before that: we've covered the early **geology** and mountain forming under "Geology, flora and fauna" from p.236.

The Ahwahneechee

Native Americans have been visiting Yosemite for over seven thousand years, with the **Ahwahneechee** tribe (see box, p.60) living in and around the Park for the last three thousand years, maybe longer. Up until approximately 2500 years ago, the tribe relied on spear-hunting deer, catching trout and foraging for seeds, but as they grew more sophisticated they shifted to efficient bow and arrows, and added acorns to their diet. Grinding holes for pounding acorns have been found throughout Yosemite Valley, though their locations are not widely advertised. Clam shells found in archeological digs indicate contact with coastal tribes, and the Ahwahneechee also developed trade with the Paiute people on the eastern side of the Sierra, trading pinyon nuts and obsidian. Typically they would move with the seasons, spending the cooler months in the fertile valleys, following the deer up to higher (and cooler) elevations in summer.

Historical evidence shows that a couple of generations before the arrival of white folk, a devastating plague swept through the Ahwahneechee, possibly a European disease that had spread inland from the Spanish on the coast. The few survivors teamed up with neighboring tribes leaving Yosemite Valley vacant. Though raised among the Mono Lake Paiutes, **Chief Tenaya** had heard tell of a "deep, grassy valley" and after visiting Yosemite decided to lead the remnants of his people – perhaps only two to three hundred of them – back.

Early exploration

In the early half of the nineteenth century, what we now know as central California was still loosely under **Spanish** control, ruled from Mexico. Despite over a hundred years of exploration along the Californian coast, non-natives had yet to penetrate more than a few miles inland, and certainly not far enough to set eyes on Yosemite. Spanish Army lieutenant **Gabriel Moraga**, who was the first white man to explore the Californian interior, didn't see the Merced River meandering through Yosemite Valley, but when he stumbled on its lower reaches on Sept 29, 1806 (5 days after the feast of Our Lady of Mercy) he dubbed it "El Río de Nuestra Señora de la Merced."

Over the next few decades, European Americans started straying into Alta California, as it was known, from the east. The first to penetrate the Sierra was a Wyoming fur trapper, **Jedediah Smith**, who crossed the mountains in 1827, and whose tales of good trapping in the California sun inspired others. Among these adventurers was one Joseph Walker, leading what is now known as the **Walker Party** over the mountains from Nevada in late 1833. Deep snows claimed the lives of many horses and the party members were in a sorry state when they became the first whites to enter the Yosemite region. They recorded seeing giant sequoias (probably the Tuolumne or Merced groves) and may have been the first to sight Yosemite Valley from one of the surrounding ridges, though their accounts are too vague to be sure.

The 49ers and the Mariposa Battalion

The **discovery of gold** in central California in 1848 changed everything. Suddenly argonauts from all over the United States and beyond were flooding into the region and the delicate balance that had existed between the Spanish and the Indians was destroyed. While the gateway towns of Groveland and Mariposa were important gold settlements, the 49ers left Yosemite alone as there was little to indicate the source of gold lay in that direction. But traders and pastoralists followed the gold diggers, and whites were soon encroaching on native territory, threatening their supply of game, stealing land and using superior firepower to remove anyone who stood in their way. To protect Ahwahneechee interests, raiding parties were dispatched to nearby encampments, and by 1851 the whites in the surrounding towns were losing patience. An initial punitive foray in January 1851 was led by **James Savage**, a trading post owner at the settlement of Big Oak Flat on the Tuolumne River. It met with little success and a month later the fledgling state of California sanctioned the formation of a vigilante group, subsequently dubbed the **Mariposa Battalion**. With Savage installed as "Major" and chief scout, they followed the South Fork of the Merced River to present-day Wawona where some Ahwahneechee were captured and others surrendered. The battalion pursued the rest to their villages and became the first non-native Americans to set foot in Yosemite Valley.

The group's surgeon, **Dr Lafayette Bunnell**, became the first of many to lyrically describe the Valley, later writing that "none but those who have visited this most wonderful valley can even imagine the feelings with which I looked upon the view that was there presented. The grandeur of the scene was but softened by the haze that hung over the valley – light as gossamer – and by the clouds which partially dimmed the higher cliffs and mountains. This obscurity of vision but increased the awe with which I beheld it, and as I looked, a peculiar exalted sensation seemed to fill my whole being, and I found my eyes in tears with emotion." The party camped in Bridalveil Meadow and Bunnell proposed that the valley be known as "Yosemite," incorrectly honoring what he thought to be the Ahwahneechee name for the area (see box opposite).

A second expedition by the Mariposa Battalion, under Captain **John Boling**, tracked down the rest of the Ahwahneechee, capturing their chief, **Tenaya**, on the shores of what is now Tenaya Lake. Defeated, most of the remaining population was relocated to the baking San Joaquin Valley near Fresno, where many succumbed to European diseases before the rest were allowed back. Chief Tenaya was effectively forced into signing a treaty with the whites, but even the US Senate subsequently determined that it was invalid. The Indians still

Naming Yosemite

The Ahwahneechee people had always known Yosemite Valley as **Ahwahnee**, meaning "land of the gaping mouth" – an apt description of Yosemite Valley when seen from its western end. When the Mariposa Battalion arrived in 1851, they camped in the Valley and agreed to call it Yosemite, wrongly believing it to be the native name for the area. There seems to be some dispute about how this misunderstanding came about. Some claim it is a corruption of *uzumati*, which means "grizzly bear" and probably refers to the dominant subtribe within the Ahwahneechee. Others contend the battalion misheard the Ahwahneechee word *yohemite* or *yohometuk*, which translates to "some of them are killers," and may have been a reference to the battalion itself.

officially owned the land, but white violence and murder soon drove the remaining Ahwahneechee away, clearing the path for white settlement.

White settlement and early tourism

White foresters and farmers established themselves in Yosemite Valley by using the high-country grasslands, particularly Tuolumne Meadows, for summer grazing. Lured by tales of great waterfalls, the first 48 **tourists** arrived in the summer of 1855. Among them were San Francisco writer (and later Yosemite hotel owner) **James Mason Hutchings** and artist **Thomas Ayers**, whose publicizing works were just the first of many. The famed editor of the *New York Tribune*, Horace Greeley, added his effusive praise and upper-class Americans began to realize that what they had at home was as good as their traditional stomping grounds in the European Alps. Despite the lack of anything more than a horse trail, numbers of visitors increased steadily, though in the first decade the number of hotel registrations was still only 653.

Another one of those 1855 tourists was mining company employee **Galen Clark**, who the following year quit his job for health reasons and homesteaded 160 acres at what is now Wawona.

Clark had heard rumors of enormous trees in those parts, and in May 1857 "discovered" Mariposa Grove and cut a trail to them as an added attraction for the fledgling tourist industry. Clark subsequently guided pioneer landscape photographers Charles Weed and Carlton Watkins and the painter **Albert Bierstadt**, all critical in getting out the message of Yosemite's wonders.

As the giant sequoias became an essential tourist sight, the first stagecoach road was routed this way and visitors spent the night in Wawona before continuing towards Yosemite Valley. In the latter half of the 1850s several hotels sprang up in Yosemite Valley and a few homesteaders started to take up residence, at least during the warmer months of the year. One was **James Lamon**, who built a cabin at the eastern end of the Valley, tended a garden and planted an orchard that still produces fruit near Curry Village. Meanwhile, many of the remaining Ahwahneechee had filtered back to the Valley, the men adopting European dress and working as guides, wranglers and woodcutters. The women retained more traditional ways, adapting their basket making to the demands of souvenir hunters. Towards the end of the 1860s, visitor numbers rose to over a thousand a year, and as the focus of tourism shifted progressively towards the Valley new and more direct roads were pioneered, most of them being cut in the early 1870s.

Protection and administration

As academic interest in California grew, the California State Geological Survey (always known as the **Whitney Survey**) was sent, under Josiah D. Whitney, to explore the Sierra Nevada. In the early 1860s they named Mount Whitney along with numerous mountains and features in Yosemite, and developed theories on how glaciers helped shape much of the landscape. They were adamant, though, that Yosemite Valley could only have been caused by a great cataclysm or devastating earthquake. Into this framework strode **John Muir** (see box, p.84), who arrived in 1868 and spent much of the next ten years living in or frequently visiting Yosemite, soaking up everything it had to offer and expanding on his theory of the Valley's glacial formation. Muir also became a vociferous advocate for the protection and preservation of the land he had come to love.

Around the same time, hoteliers were converting meadows into hay fields and cutting down trees. This didn't sit well with public-spirited men of influence, and in 1864 senator John Conness convinced congress to establish the **Yosemite Land Grant**, with Yosemite Valley and Mariposa Grove transferred from federal to state ownership under the guardianship of Galen Clark. As the first area expressly set aside to protect wilderness, it became the template for the first national park, Yellowstone, which was established eight years later. Illegal homesteaders were forced to leave or sign a lease, but most refused. Hutchings even took his claim to the US Supreme Court and lost, though the California legislature saw fit to award him the princely sum of $60,000 as compensation for the land he never had any right to in the first place.

Though the Yosemite Land Grant afforded some protection, Muir wasn't happy with the logging and sheep grazing taking place. In 1889, he met Robert Underwood Johnson, editor of the influential *Century* magazine. They camped together in Tuolumne Meadows just after some sheep had eaten their way through, and Johnson convinced Muir to write a couple of articles stating his case. These, and Underwood's machinations in Washington, helped bring about the creation of **Yosemite National Park**, which in 1890 became the nation's third (after Yellowstone in Wyoming, and Sequoia, not too far south of Yosemite in California).

Here comes the cavalry

Yosemite came under the jurisdiction of the Department of the Interior, who sent in the **cavalry** to help drive out illegal homesteaders, poachers and hopeful prospectors. They stayed in Yosemite until 1914, their role gradually changing from enforcement to management. In 1903, troops of African American "**Buffalo soldiers**" became some of the first "rangers" to be assigned to protect the Park. After a short unregulated period, the cavalry were replaced in 1916 by rangers from the newly formed **National Park Service**.

The Park's protection was also high on the agenda for the **Sierra Club**, the environmental campaigning organization jointly formed by Muir in

1892. He became its first president, and continued in that role for 22 years until his death. Muir's reputation by now was huge, so it was no surprise when President **Theodore Roosevelt** asked Muir to accompany him on his tour of Yosemite. Muir took the opportunity to bend Teddy's ear about the parlous state of Yosemite Valley, which at this stage was still part of the Yosemite Land Grant and managed by the State of California. His arguments obviously had some effect, and in 1905 the Valley and Mariposa Grove were finally incorporated into the national park.

But all was not rosy at the Sierra Club headquarters. The same bill also reduced the size of Yosemite National Park by chipping away at sections to the southwest and on the eastern boundary, which were deemed strategic by mining and forestry interests. Buoyed by their success in reducing the size of Yosemite, commercial interests now set their sights on building a dam inside the Park boundary at **Hetch Hetchy** (see box, p.75). After twelve years of battles, Congress finally authorized the construction of the O'Shaughnessy Dam in 1913. Though a defeat for Muir and the Sierra Club it galvanized opposition to such projects elsewhere, helping mark a turning point in government attitudes to protection inside national parks.

Promoting the Park

Yosemite had initially been visited by the relatively well-off, but with its designation as a national park, and the existence of several coach roads, numbers increased rapidly to include tourists from a broad spectrum of social classes. In 1899, David and Jennie Curry established **Camp Curry**, the forerunner of today's Curry Village (see p.64), to cater to these new arrivals in modest fashion, and their business grew quickly. With the arrival of the railroad at El Portal in 1907 and the Park's legalization of automobile traffic in 1913, Yosemite became truly accessible to the public. By 1916, the Curry Company had been awarded the concession to run services in Yosemite for the annual influx of 35,000 visitors.

During his twelve-year tenure as director of the National Park Service from 1917 to 1929, **Stephen T. Mather** sought to further increase visitor numbers with an aggressive policy of **park development** that led to now unthinkable proposals. He championed the building of the Wawona golf course, the ice rink at Curry Village, made an unsuccessful bid to host the 1932 Winter Olympics at Badger Pass, and even proposed building a road beside Vernal and Nevada falls to Tuolumne Meadows. The Curry Company quickly fell in line, promoting the idea of building a dam on the stream above Yosemite Falls so the flow could be regulated and the tourist season extended. Luckily few of these proposals came to pass, though **bear feeding** was introduced for the edification of tourists. Garbage was spread out for bears each evening in front of visitors arrayed on specially built platforms. Bears, of course, took a liking to easy meals provided by humans, and 81 people were treated for bear-related injuries in 1929 alone. The bears were the ones blamed, and many were relocated or even killed before the feeding practice was halted in 1940. At much the same time, the few Indians still left in the Valley were encouraged to perform **native dances**, often involving teepees and feather headdresses that had nothing to do with the life of their forebears.

By 1930, half a million people were visiting Yosemite each year, and the Park Service was forced to impose controls. Camping in and driving through meadows was banned, and there were greater efforts to manage development. Nonetheless, numbers continued to grow steadily – though the group that initially laid claim to the lands was on its way out. By the late 1960s, the last of the Ahwahneechee residents were effectively forced out of the Valley and their village razed (see box, p.60). Meanwhile, the Park's image was growing exponentially thanks in part to the efforts of **Ansel Adams** (see box, p.64), who had begun photographing the Park to matchless effect as far back as the late 1920s. He also campaigned to maintain Yosemite's ecological values, mainly through his role as a director of the Sierra Club, which he held throughout the mid-century.

It was in the late 1960s, near the end of Adams' tenure, that climbers began arriving in droves to scale the great rocks of Yosemite; the era lives on as the Golden Age of Yosemite climbing. The counterculture ethic espoused by many climbers flowed through the next decade when **hippies** started arriving in Yosemite Valley, camping in the meadows, hanging out and generally getting up the noses of uptight rangers. Matters came to a head leading up to Independence Day in 1970 with the **Stoneman Meadow Riots**, when mounted rangers fought a pitched battle with the hippies to clear them out of the meadows. A few dozen were jailed for a short time but both sides compromised and peace returned to the Valley.

Modern Yosemite

In recent decades the Park's foremost issue has become balancing environmental concerns with the demands of increased visitor numbers. Recognizing that Yosemite was unable to cope with the strain of almost three million tourists a year, the Park Service released the **General Management Plan** in 1980, a document that engendered much talk but little action. At this point there were well over a thousand buildings in the Valley so the Plan called for reducing visitor accommodation by seventeen percent and more than halving employee housing. In addition the Wawona tennis courts and golf course were to go, and the Curry Village ice rink was to be pulled up, all by 1990. Almost none of this happened.

Various other plans and impact statements kept the ball rolling for the next few years, but still nothing much happened until several rockfalls close to Valley lodging were followed by some devastating floods in January 1997. These caused the Valley to close for ten weeks and speeded up production of the **Final Yosemite Valley Plan**, which looked set to dictate the Park's development over the next couple of decades. Again the emphasis was on coping with increased visitor numbers, though as the plan came out it was only just becoming apparent that **Park visitation** numbers were actually going down. After peaking in 1996 at 4.2 million, numbers dropped steadily, with 2006 recoding only around 3.2 million. The summer weekend crowds haven't exactly disappeared, but the administration is now less worried about congestion than spreading the reduced revenue across all the projects that are underway or planned.

Several factors are cited as reasons for the decline including: the downturn in the economy; reduced travel after September 11, 2001; historic bad press over crowding in Yosemite Valley; incorrect rumors about not being allowed to drive into Yosemite Valley; and images of devastation after the 1997 flooding. Visitation to most western national parks has been on the slide over the same period but one Yosemite-specific factor was the brutal slayings of four women – three tourists and a worker – in 1999 by Carl Stayner, an employee at one of the motels in El Portal, just outside the Park. These so-called **Yosemite Murders** hit headlines across the nation and undoubtedly dented Yosemite's appeal.

For most of the last decade, the Park Service has struggled to implement the Final Yosemite Valley Plan, which has come under sustained legal challenges from local minority interest groups. Piecemeal progress has been achieved, principally with the introduction of new hybrid shuttle buses, meadow and riparian restoration along the Merced River, and improvements at the base of Lower Yosemite Fall.

Plans for a new Ahwahneechee interpretive center on the site of the last Indian village in the Valley are dependent on clearing legal obstacles.

Geology, flora and fauna

Yosemite sits astride the Sierra Nevada, a 400-mile-long range that rises steadily from the San Joaquin Valley in the west then drops away steeply almost 10,000 feet into the Owens Valley. The Park's landscapes stretch from semi-arid foothills in the west to the alpine summits of the Sierra Nevada in the east, with much of the intervening country covered by mature evergreen forests that John Muir felt were the "grandest and most beautiful in the world." Along with the meadows, streams and lakes, the forests provide habitats for eighty-odd species of mammals, hundreds of varieties of plants and wildflowers, a hundred and fifty bird species, and dozens of types of reptiles and amphibians.

Geology

Yosemite National Park is defined by its distinctive granite architecture of domes, spires and waterfall-strung cliffs, much of which was shaped by deep rivers of ice over the last million years. But the formation of the rock itself dates back 500 million years to a time when what is now central California was under a primordial sea. Over the eons, marine sediments were deposited on the sea floor to form **sedimentary rocks**.

Around 200 million years ago, plate tectonics came into play as the Pacific plate started to slide under the North American plate. As the Pacific plate was subducted, the rock melted, welled up, then cooled some six miles underground into dome-shaped blocks of granite known as **batholiths**. Granite is part of the **plutonic igneous** family of rocks characterized by large crystals formed as the molten rock cooled extremely slowly. There are seven different types of granite in Yosemite Valley alone, all with slightly different colors and chemistry, the hardest and most weather-resistant forming the steepest cliffs. Half Dome is actually made from one of the youngest types of rock, just 87 million years old.

By 50 million years ago, the sea had receded, leaving a gentle landscape of rolling hills with the Merced River winding through hardwood forests on a bed of sedimentary rock with no granite in sight. Over the next forty million years or so, rivers and streams gradually eroded away the overlying sedimentary and metamorphic rock, while the Merced River cut a V-shaped valley three thousand feet deep. The removal of this overburden of rock allowed the granite to expand forming cracks parallel to the surface, a process still evident today at road cuttings in the high country where distinctive onion-layers are evident. As the rock peeled away, the classic granite domes were formed.

Yosemite' glacial wonderland

As the last glacier receded, it left a terminal moraine just west of El Capitan. Behind this moraine the waters of the Merced River created the prehistoric Lake Yosemite, a shallow, five-mile-long lake that over the millennia filled with sediment carried down by the river. Eventually it formed the flat Valley floor we see today, with the Merced River gently winding its way through.

Yosemite' glacial wonderland

A few permanent ice fields tucked away high on remote mountains is all that remains of the huge **glaciers** that once carved Yosemite's granite into the wonderful forms we see today. Some 250,000 years ago, the entire Park was covered by a thick sheet of ice which chiseled out **U-shaped valleys** such as Yosemite Valley, a classic example which contrasts with the unglaciated V-shape of the Merced River Canyon further downstream.

As the ancient glaciers melted, rock carried along with the ice was deposited to form a **terminal moraine**, which typically held back a lake. Over the millennia these lakes filled with sediment to form the characteristic **flat floor** of glaciated valleys. Tributary glaciers fed into the large glaciers but carved shallower channels which, when the ice melted, left **hanging valleys** and fabulous waterfalls such as Upper Yosemite Fall, Bridalveil Fall and Ribbon Fall.

Even in the depths of the Ice Ages when glaciation was at its maximum extent, the very highest peaks stood above the ice sheet as unglaciated **nunataks**, forming spiky mountaintops such as Tuolumne's Cathedral and Unicorn peaks. As the ice ground its way across the land, rocks embedded in its base scraped across the bedrock leaving telltale parallel scarring known as **striations**. In places the effect is so pronounced that large patches of rock were rubbed smooth to form **glacial polish** that gleams in the sunlight. Pothole Dome in Tuolumne is a prime example.

As the world warmed and the glaciers melted, rocks carried along with the ice were randomly deposited as **erratics**, and large hunks of ice left behind by retreating glaciers melted to form **kettle lakes** in the deep impression they created. Dana Meadows, east of Tuolumne, contains numerous classic examples.

None of this was even suspected until the middle of the nineteenth century, but when **John Muir** arrived in Yosemite in 1868 he began to apply the emerging theories of glaciation to his new home. He came against stubborn resistance from learned geologists who had long believed Yosemite Valley was created in a gargantuan earthquake, but by relentlessly publishing treatises on the matter he eventually won over academia.

The redwood forests and much of the vegetation familiar today was already established when the Ice Ages began around a million years back. The first wave of glaciation lasted until 250,000 years ago and covered the entire Yosemite area with glaciers forging down the V-shaped river valleys, scouring away the weaker rock to form the classic glacial **U-shaped valley**. Most of the overlying sedimentary rock was ground away, leaving the awe-inspiring granite features we now know as Half Dome and El Capitan. Thirty thousand yeas ago, the most recent Ice Age brought the Yosemite Glacier into Yosemite Valley to add the finishing touches.

Ecosystems and flora

Because of the huge range of elevations – 2000 to over 13,000 feet – Yosemite contains a vast diversity of flora that can be loosely divided into forest **ecosystems** or zones. As elevation increases moisture levels broadly increase while average temperatures drop, creating zones where different tree species tend to dominate. Smaller flora also change along with the fauna it supports, but it is the large trees by which the zones are characterized. Generally porous soils and uneven precipitation makes Yosemite more suited to relatively drought-resistant evergreens, but deciduous trees can be found wherever there is an abundant water supply, generally close to lakes and streams and in moist meadows. The area where meadow meets the oaks and conifers forest is known as an **ecotone**, and it is here that you'll find the greatest wildlife diversity.

The foothills

Yosemite is approached from the west through the Sierra **foothills**, which range between 500 and 4000 feet in altitude. This encompasses the countryside around all the western gateway towns, the western fringes of the Park (which start at around 2000 feet), and extends up into Yosemite Valley (covered in more detail on p.45). This is a region characterized by wet, cool winters that give way to a moist spring when most of the new growth takes place. Summers are relatively hot and dry, so most species are adapted to cope with fairly frequent **fires** (see p.246).

Outside the Park you'll travel through open **grasslands** mostly comprising exotic grasses like wild oat and foxtail fescue. Green in spring they brown off through summer, and when fires strike the perennial grasses can re-sprout from the root crowns. Here you might expect to see wildflowers such as the bright orange **California poppies**, distinctive patches of **baby blue-eyes**, and **lupines**, a species found all over Yosemite.

In riparian woodlands like those along the Merced River Canyon and into Yosemite Valley, deciduous species predominate. The shrubby **Western redbud** provides a riot of magenta blooms from February to April, and you'll also come across black cottonwood, California sycamore, big-leaf maple and Pacific dogwood (see below).

Shallow well-drained soils provide a perfect terrain for **chaparral**, Spanish for "scrub oak." Low thickets of **canyon oak** are usually interspersed with species of smooth red-barked **manzanita**, a plant with small, thick leaves that resist moisture loss. The scrubby **ceanothus** shares these characteristics along with the ability to sprout from the root crown after fire. Such fires, fuelled by oils in the plants themselves, burn very hot and tend to kill larger trees ensuring the continued dominance of these species. Manzanita and ceanothus also exist at much higher elevations

Between 2000 and 4000 feet, you'll find **savannah** woodlands dominated by the deep-rooted **blue oak**, which thrives in dry climates.

Yosemite Valley and Wawona

The bulk of Yosemite's indoor accommodation and campsites are around the 4000-foot mark, mostly in **Yosemite Valley** and at **Wawona**. This interzone region marks the upper reaches of the foothills where chaparral merges with the mixed coniferous forests that predominate higher up. Among these **transition forests**, the dominant features are **meadows** such as those found on the Yosemite Valley floor.

Black oak woodlands and evergreens

As the Valley's post-glacial lake dried out, the Valley floor was colonized by forests of **black oak**, a large deciduous tree with big, yellow-green leaves and a dark trunk. It is an important source of acorns for squirrels and mule deer, but the tree's bounty was likewise appreciated by the Ahwahneechee, who encouraged its growth by using fire to keep conifers at bay.

Since then, **fire suppression** (see below) has caused the balance to shift towards **evergreen** species, whose saplings shaded the young oaks and quickly

▲ Wawona

outgrew them. One of the most drought-resistant evergreens is the tall **ponderosa pine**, easily identified by its irregular scaly plates of reddish-yellow bark and long needles in clusters of three. Well adapted to fire, it has thick bark and high first branches that make it hard for fires to "ladder" up to the crown where more damage can be done. Ponderosas range up to around 8000 feet but start as low as Yosemite Valley and Wawona where they were once the dominant evergreen. That mantle has now passed to the more shade-tolerant **incense cedar**, which with its feathery cinnamon red bark can sometimes be confused with a young sequoia. The name comes from its soft, lacy foliage that is fragrant when crushed. Wetter locales, such as side canyons off Yosemite Valley and against north-facing cliffs, are ideal for **Douglas fir**, with its soft, inch-long needles and numerous, distinctive three-pronged bracts which protrude from the brown, egg-shaped cones.

Scattered among these other trees you'll find **sugar pines**, the largest of the Sierra pines and with the biggest cones, some a massive eighteen inches long. With their long, straight trunks, sugar pines are a target species for loggers who have removed most trees outside protected areas such as Yosemite. During the decades of fire suppression, these majestic conifers have gained an understory of shade-loving **white fir**, which has thin, gray bark and branches that sweep to the ground making it susceptible to fire.

Riparian areas and meadows

Along riverbanks, beside lakes and in shady, moist side canyons the **Pacific dogwood** thrives. Catch it in late April and May and few are unmoved by the display of large, creamy white blossoms. These trees seldom grow taller than thirty feet, but their elegant shape makes a beautiful contrast to the backdrop of pines. The dogwood often has the company of the **big-leaf maples**, which populate the talus slopes at the foot of the Valley cliffs. It is distinguished by palm-shaped leaves up to a foot across, which turn golden yellow in fall. Look too for the smaller **mountain maple**, with much smaller but equally pretty leaves.

The meadows of Yosemite Valley and Wawona are prime **wildflower** habitats. You may not get the visual impact of some of the higher meadows, but here you'll find the longest wildflower season (roughly April to August) and a more diverse selection than anywhere else. Wildflower buffs return year after year to experience the meadows at slightly different seasons, but if here from May to July look out for the **shooting stars**, which take the Latin name *Dodecatheon*, meaning "Twelve Gods." The idea is that the pattern of yellow, pink and purple is so delicate it must have taken a dozen Greek gods to complete the job. Visit El Cap Meadow from May to July for the display of the lilac and white **wild iris**, which also goes by the name Western Blue Flag. Other favorites include the purple **elegant brodiaea** and the even deeper purple **winecup clarkia**, but there are really too many gorgeous examples to mention.

Middle elevations

Elevations between 6000 and 8000 feet support the so-called **mid-elevation forests**, which benefit from higher levels of snow and rainfall. Temperatures are cooler, though, and these two factors combine to favor a different set of dominant trees, easily seen from Tioga Road. **White pines** find their greatest expression in the middle elevations, where they can form stands that are up to eighty percent pure. These tend to be intermixed with **Jeffrey pines**, easily confused with ponderosa pines though distinguished by their larger cones (5–8 inches) with prickles that turn inwards at the ends of the scales. The two species don't overlap much, and Jeffrey pines have darker and more furrowed bark with bunches of three needles over eight inches long. At higher elevations they often appear stunted and twisted. A fairly narrow band between 6500 feet and 8000 feet – where there is reliable moisture year-round – is now the sole preserve of the **giant sequoias** (see box, p.102). There are only three groves of these magnificent trees in the Park, which are usually found mixed with white fir and Jeffrey pine.

Many of the wildflowers mentioned above exist at these higher elevations, but also look out for the brilliant magenta **mountain pride penstemon**, which grows in roadside clusters on low bushes, and the scarlet **Indian paintbrush**.

The high country

Between 8000 and 10,000 feet you're in Yosemite's **high country**, commonly experienced around Tuolumne Meadows and Tioga Pass. This **subalpine** zone receives the heaviest snowfall, meaning dominant species are moisture loving. **Red fir**, also evident in the middle elevations, become ever more prevalent above 8000 feet. They often grow in pure stands, their cinnamon-colored trunks rising to a dense canopy that shades the ground allowing snow to remain well into summer. Like all firs, their cones grow upright on the branches, in this case rising six to eight inches.

Shallower, drier soils (often in glacially scoured basins) support near-pure stands of **lodgepole pines**, the pines within the Sierra with two needles per cluster. Paradoxically these trees also favor boggy ground and can range right up to the tree line. The lodgepole takes its name from close cousins that were used for teepee poles by Plains Indians, though the Sierran lodgepole is usually too stout. Fire is often required to open the cones, but once achieved, lodgepoles are quick to root in burned or disturbed areas. Little grows in the lodgepole

Wild Yosemite

With an area the size of Rhode Island, 95 percent of it designated "wilderness," and hunting not permitted, wild animals have a good life in Yosemite. Bears, mule deer, marmots and numerous small forest creatures are common sights, though you can consider yourself lucky if you spy a mountain lion or California bighorn sheep. These animals are free to roam the Park from the hot and dry foothills through the mid-elevation forests to the icy Sierra peaks. Wherever you go you'll see an abundance of wildflowers: wonderful en masse but especially fascinating when you get down on your knees for closer inspection.

Wildflowers

California poppies ▲

Sequoias ▼

Yosemite boasts a huge array of wildflowers. In the foothills at 2000ft they start blooming with the arrival of spring in early March, but up around 9000ft, in the beautiful Tuolumne Meadows, the short growing season forces them into a burst of color from July to early September. In the high alpine regions around 13,000ft, the last of the wildflowers won't seed until October, just before the first snows.

Purple **lupin** have adapted wonderfully to just about every ecological niche. Other species are much more picky. The bright orange **California poppy** – the official state flower – is found in open areas and along roadsides up to 4000ft, while the vibrant lilac wild iris favors marshy meadows from 4000 to 8000ft. Other favorites include **shooting stars**, whose heads have yellow and black tips with purple petals that appear like the trailing tail of a meteorite, and **Indian paintbrush**, whose low-growing clusters of red flowers look like they were dipped into a paint pot.

Sequoias

The **giant sequoia** (a cousin of the coastal redwood) is the earth's most massive living thing. Up to 300ft high and 30ft in diameter, some of these arboreal monsters weigh in at a whopping 1000 tons, courtesy of a broad trunk that barely tapers from base to crown. Some live for 3000 years, partly due to the thick, cinnamon-colored bark that protects the sapwood from the periodic forest fires, and gives the tree its redwood tag. Once common throughout the western Sierra Nevada, sequoias are now only found in around 75 isolated groups of between 5000ft and 8500ft. They occupy three main groves in Yosemite (Mariposa, Tuolumne and Merced) but early residents also planted several in Yosemite Valley – some by the chapel and others in the cemetery – though none is yet above six feet in diameter.

Marmots

In the Yosemite's high country above 10,000ft, the evergreens are getting thinner and more stunted, and wildlife seems scarce ... except for the **yellow-bellied marmot**. These shy and shaggy ten-pound rodents waddle about the talus slopes searching for grass, flowers, bugs and even bird eggs, their favorite food.

At the slightest danger, they whistle to their mates, which has earned them the nickname of "whistle pig." Quickly they dive for cover into one of several burrows fashioned among the loose rocks. Coyotes and golden eagles are what they're really worried about, but a swift movement on your part and they'll be gone – though you'll soon see their inquisitive noses poking out to test if the coast's clear. After all, they've got a lot of fattening up to do before they hibernate through the worst of the winter snows.

▲ Marmot

▼ Mule deer

Mule deer

Around dawn and dusk **mule deer** browse the meadows around Yosemite Village, seemingly oblivious to all the tourist traffic. They seem pretty tame and will often let you get quite close, but they are wild animals. Deer cause more injuries than bears in the Park.

Easily identified by their mule-like ears, white rump and black-tipped tail,

Yosemite National Park ▲

Black bear ▼

they weigh in at 100 to 200 pounds and a full-grown buck is tall enough to look you in the eye when standing on all fours.

Mule deer are typically content to browse on berries and herbaceous plants; when disturbed they bound away landing on all four feet at each leap. Fences are no obstacle.

Bears

Despite its prominence on the state flag, the grizzly bear has been extinct in California since 1895 when the last specimen was shot at Crescent Lake, east of Wawona. In Yosemite you'll only come across the smaller **black bear**, whose fur might range from anything between blond or cinnamon to black or brown. Females weigh around 250 pounds, with males averaging as much as a hundred pounds heavier, though the largest recorded was a mighty 700 pounds.

With around four hundred resident bears, they are relatively common all over the Park, but can be hard to spot at times. They generally rest in the shade or go about their business quietly during the day, so you're more likely to spot them around dawn or dusk when they are feeding. Backcountry sightings are relatively rare but, perhaps counter-intuitively, you'll often see them where people congregate, particularly around campgrounds or prowling around the parking lots after dark in search of human food. The Park Service goes to great lengths to discourage this behavior: see box, p.11. In winter, bears den for short periods to conserve energy, but don't truly hibernate and hikers should never assume there are no bears around.

forest except the shrubby **Labrador tea**, which bears white flowers from June to August, and **red mountain heather** with its pink, bell-shaped flowers.

Lodgepole forests are frequently intermixed with **mountain hemlock**, which prefers cool, shaded habitats where winter snowdrifts pile deep. Identifiable by their drooping tip, they can be best spotted between Tenaya Lake and Tuolumne Meadows. Other relatively common species at these elevations include the five-needled **western white pine**, which is similar to the sugar pine but with cones half as long, and the squat and stunted **whitebark pine**, common around the 10,000-foot mark. Perhaps even more gnarled, the **western juniper** also occupies some of the highest ground, clinging to whatever crevices it can get its roots into. According to John Muir it seemed to live on just "sunshine and snow," but some manage to hang on for over a thousand years, becoming beautifully weathered in the process. Among all these evergreens it might seem strange to find groves of deciduous trees, but in the upper regions close to the tree line

▲ Yosemite Cemetery

you'll see groves of **aspen**, with its smooth, white bark and heart-shaped leaves that seem to flutter earning it its usual moniker of "quaking aspen."

Along with some of its most beautiful forests, Yosemite's high country boasts the most abundant lakes, typically either in bedrock hollows scoured by ancient glaciers or kettle lakes. The surrounding **meadows** are usually too wet for substantial trees to grow, but they make wonderful areas for **wildflowers**. Many favorites from lower elevations crop up (albeit in slightly different forms), but are supplemented by the **camas lily**, with its gold anthers, the bell-shaped **leopard lily**, and many more.

Above 10,500 feet is the **Alpine zone**, which contains few trees but does have plants adapted to a very short growing season. They mostly grow low to the ground in cushions or mats such as **moss campion**.

Fauna

Yosemite's rich diversity of **wildlife** is largely the result of its wide-ranging ecosystems, which support a variety of animals. Most visitors to the Park don't make any special effort to look for wildlife, but almost everyone sees plenty. Spend a few hours in Yosemite Valley, around Wawona or in Mariposa Grove, for example, and you'll more than likely spot mule deer grazing.

Large mammals

On any visit to Yosemite you'll almost certainly see a few campground critters, but other mammals are often hard to see. The most common sightings are **mule deer**, which are found throughout the Park, though they migrate throughout the year, favoring the lower valleys in cooler seasons and the high country in summer. That said, even in July you'll see their distinctive mule-like ears and black-tipped tail around Yosemite Valley and Wawona as they graze the meadows virtually oblivious to human activity. For the best viewing head towards shaded areas in the morning and evening.

Also common throughout the Park are **black bears** (see color section, and Smarter Than the Average Bear box on p.11). At 250–350 pounds they're the largest mammals in the Park, and are most commonly seen foraging around campgrounds at dusk.

Wolves have been wiped out locally, but **mountain lions** survive, always keeping a very low profile, usually alone in the high country. Five feet long (plus a three-foot, black-tipped tail) and weighing up to two hundred pounds, they are very rarely seen, though you may come across their four-toed clawless footprints or scratch marks on trees. Mountain lions mainly hunt for deer and smaller animals, but when they get the chance they're happy to chow on **bighorn sheep**. Before white settlers came to the Yosemite region, these High Sierra grazers were relatively common, but loss of habitat, disease and hunting eradicated them from the Park by 1914. Attitudes changed, and in 1986 twenty-seven bighorns were reintroduced to Lee Vining Canyon, east of Tioga Pass. Initial success and a top-up introduction of more sheep saw numbers peak around eighty in the early 1990s, but a couple of harsh winters and continued mountain lion and coyote predation has seen the population settle back to just a handful of breeding pairs. Your best chance of seeing one is in Lee Vining Canyon, where the light brown fur is a suitable camouflage, though the male's massive curved horns give the game away.

Other largish mammals include: stumpy-tailed **bobcats**, which hunt small game in scrub and chaparral; the voracious small-bear-like **wolverine**, which hunts and scavenges mostly in alpine and subalpine regions; the silver-gray **coyote**, which eats just about anything it can find as it ranges from the foothills to the tree line; and a couple of species of **fox** (the gray and the rare red) only found in oak woodlands, chaparral and lowland forests.

Smaller critters

Smaller mammals are almost too numerous to mention, and wherever you go in the Park you'll be visited by scavenging creatures of some description. **Chipmunks** show up everywhere in the Valley, especially around campgrounds, where you might also see tree squirrels such as the white-chested **Douglas squirrel** and the **Western Gray squirrel**, with its impressive bushy tail. During the spring mating season, look out for the Western Grays chasing each other and fighting.

There's an abundance of **mice**, **shrews**, burrow-digging **moles**, **bats**, **wood rats**, **weasels**, **martens** and **voles** but only a few are of much interest to the non-specialist. **Raccoons** inhabit riparian areas at lower elevations, **badgers** range through the open forests over a wide elevation range, and **skunks** ferret around the foothills.

Up in the high country you may spot the **Belding's ground squirrel**, which is usually known as the "picket pin" for its habit of sitting bolt upright and whistling sharply when disturbed. They inhabit the red fir forests and high country meadows and hibernate through winter. Another high-country resident is the guinea-pig-sized **pika**, which lives among rocks gathering hay so that it can survive through the winter snow without hibernating. You'll probably hear its distinctive "enk" whistle before you see it. The highest-living of the mammals is the ten-pound **yellow-bellied marmot**, a large rodent at home in extensive rock piles where it can often be seen sunning itself, though not when any coyotes or golden eagles are around.

▲ Chipmunk

Birds

A quarter of all North American **bird species** have been recorded in the park, though only around 150 species are regular visitors. Of all campground foragers, the boldest and most raucous is the **Stellar's jay**, a western cousin of the blue jay, with its bright blue sides and black topknot. Its distinctive caw-like screech and year-round presence means it seldom goes unnoticed. **Woodpeckers** can be heard among the trees, especially the pilated, acorn, downey and white-headed varieties, and soaring high on the cliffs you might even spot acrobatic **peregrine falcons** which have recently returned to Yosemite in small numbers. They can sometimes be seen near El Capitan and around Glacier Point, where around a dozen birds are regularly tending a handful of nests built on narrow rock ledges high above the Valley floor. With keen eyesight it can dive at almost 200mph capturing its prey in midair. Removed from the federally endangered list in 1999, the peregrines are just one of four species of falcon in the Park (along with the prairie falcon, kestrel and merlin), and can be identified by its hood of dark feathers and light underside.

Other raptors found in the Park are **golden eagles**, occasionally seen in the Valley but more commonly at higher elevations. Look for a very large dark brown bird that holds its broad wings flat when soaring, though juveniles have white area on the wings and tail. One bird you probably won't see is the endangered **great gray owl**, though you've a better chance of seeing it in Yosemite than just about anywhere else, most likely on forest margins near meadows.

Fish, amphibians and reptiles

Historically Yosemite had virtually no **fish** in the rivers and streams above 4000 feet, but early promoters saw the opportunity to attract anglers to the Park. Hatcheries were built in Wawona (1895) and Happy Isles (1927), and streams and lakes were stocked with introduced trout – brown, brook, cutthroat and golden – which supplemented the native **rainbow trout**. All species grow to ten pounds under favorable conditions. Over the same period, migratory salmon and steelhead have been prevented from spawning in Yosemite streams as their passage has been halted by dams downstream. High-country lakes are no longer stocked for sport, but self-sustaining populations keep the occasional fishermen interested.

The presence of introduced trout has had a detrimental impact on **amphibians** as small frogs form a major part of the trout diet. Still, Yosemite has more than a dozen species of frogs, toads and salamanders. Found in or near water, the two most interesting are the **Mount Lyell salamander** and the **limestone salamander**, both largely endemic to Yosemite, the latter very rare and only discovered in 1952. The half-dozen species of **lizard** between them inhabit virtually the whole Park, with the Northern Alligator lizard favoring forested areas up to the Alpine zone.

Snakes are also well represented with over a dozen species. The only poisonous representative is the **Western rattlesnake**, most common below 5000 feet though the occasional rattler has been seen at double that elevation. Well camouflaged in forest, they often sun themselves on rocks. Though they may look dangerous, there's nothing to fear from other snakes. A case in point is the attractive California **mountain kingsnake** with its black, white and red banding. It is occasionally seen crossing the road. Another pretty example is the **ringneck snake**, which has an orange-yellow ring around its neck and a red, yellow and orange belly.

Ecology

Changes are afoot in Yosemite. It has long been recognized that Yosemite is poorly set up to safely cope with almost three and a half million visitors a year while maintaining its ecological and scenic integrity. While plans to redress this go back to 1980, matters really came to a head in the mid-1990s after a couple of major **rockfalls** threatened buildings and devastating **floodwaters** swept through the Valley wiping out large sections of some campgrounds and sluicing away lodging. You can still see markers around the Valley showing the astonishing level the floodwaters reached.

The need to site buildings away from the cliffs and out of the Merced River's floodplain presented the National Park Service with a golden opportunity to make big steps towards restoring the balance.

The Yosemite Valley Plan

After extensive consultation with local businesses and wilderness advocacy organizations the **Final Yosemite Valley Plan** was finished in November 2000, just as the Clinton administration was packing its bags. Since then, political changes in Washington DC combined with a series of local lawsuits from interests opposing some of the changes have virtually halted progress. Still, improvements have been made around the base of Lower Yosemite Fall, the shuttle bus system has been extended, and over the next ten to fifteen years some Valley roads will be removed to allow meadow restoration, and lodging and campgrounds will be sited away from flood-prone areas. The plan also calls for supplying some campgrounds with electrical hookups to reduce generator noise; installing more walk-in and walk-to campsites; altering and removing bridges to rehabilitate natural river flow patterns; and constructing an Indian Cultural Center on the site of the last occupied Indian village in Yosemite.

For more info, consult the Park's frequently updated planning website Ⓦwww.nps.gov/yose/planning.

Restoring the balance

Over the last four thousand years, human activity has had a significant impact on Yosemite's environment. The most obvious ongoing impact is in Yosemite Valley, changed in numerous ways by both Miwok and white settlement. The most significant changes made by **Miwok** was with fire (see below) which changed the balance between black oaks to conifers. **European Americans** then arrived and started messing around with the Merced River. During the wetter months of the year, early Valley visitors and residents had to contend with wet feet and slippery boardwalks as they made their way between hotels. The Park's guardian, Galen Clark, solved the problem in 1878 by **dynamiting the moraine**, thereby lowering the water table. The trouble was, this dried out the Valley too much, and ever since, trees have been invading the meadows. In other places early settlers placed boulders and barriers in the river, deepening and widening it and changing the flows for various purposes: fishing, boating, even to create a source of ice which was stored in a nearby icehouse. River users and hikers wandering along the banks had a detrimental effect on the riparian environment accelerating **erosion** and limiting shelter for riverlife. In recent years, the Park Service has been striving to return the Merced River to something like its natural condition: barriers have been removed, rafters are encouraged to stick to designated access and egress points, and fallen trees which were previously removed are now left in place.

The adjacent **meadows** act like a sponge, soaking up water during the snowmelt period then gradually releasing it over the dry months of summer and fall. Tourism has brought the Valley millions of people who wander across the meadows, compacting the soil and increasing run-off. Until the 1930s, horses and cows were allowed to graze the meadows further exacerbating the situation.

Heavy-footed hikers also crush plants, damage nests and kill small animals. Less obviously, the survivors find it difficult to rebuild in the compressed soil. Visitors are now encouraged to stick to boardwalks and the meadow margins, while restoration projects have removed old drainage ditches, dug up former roadbeds, and sensitive areas have been protected by fences so that native plants have a chance to regain their toehold.

Elsewhere, **non-native plants** have been removed, black oak saplings have been protected from grazing deer, buildings have been moved out of flood zones and swimmers have been directed to less vulnerable beaches.

As yet there are no moves to return grizzly bears to Yosemite, but the long absent **peregrine falcons** have returned, though still in very small numbers. Access to rock climbs in falcon nesting areas is restricted in spring. Up in the high country, the once-numerous **California bighorn sheep** were largely killed off by hunting, disease and competition for food from grazing sheep. Now, the few remaining groups on the far eastern fringes of the park are protected and there are attempts to boost the population.

Fire: friend or foe?

Summer visitors to Yosemite often wonder why there are several fires burning with no one trying to put them out. While often thought of solely in terms of the harm they do, fires don't destroy a forest, but are an important part of the forest ecosystem that keeps the ratio of species in balance and recycles nutrients to the soil.

Historically, **lightning strikes** have started fires which would burn at relatively cool temperatures and sweep slowly through the forest singeing the base of the trees and the lower branches. With the forest canopy still largely intact, the forest could then regenerate quite quickly. Some species even evolved to benefit from this process, and certainly the giant sequoias can't regenerate without periodic fires (see box, p.102). Over a period of twenty to fifty years a patchwork of fires would tidy up the whole forest.

Into this dynamic but relatively stable scene stepped the **Miwok** people, about four thousand years ago. They relied on oak trees for their acorn supply and made abundant use of meadow plants for food, medicinal and ceremonial purposes. Fire became an important tool for clearing conifers and creating open oak woodlands and meadows where milkweed, dogbane, sedge root and bunch grass would grow. When **European Americans** started living in Yosemite Valley in the 1860s, black oaks predominated, but settlers put an end to Miwok burns.

Fire suppression has since drastically reduced the number of black oaks, and over the next hundred years the meadows were colonized particularly by white fir which is normally kept at bay by fire. Thick-barked trees which benefit from fires – Douglas fir, incense cedar, red fir and Jeffrey pine – were progressively crowded out. The once open groves where Muir liked to walk "along sunny colonnades and through openings that have a smooth park-like surface" have become much harder to find. For an idea of what the Valley once looked like you'll need to search out the oak woodland close to Pohono Bridge, though the Park Service is giving the black oaks a chance to re-establish themselves by fencing off natural oak nurseries to stop people trampling the soil, and protecting the young shoots with plastic tubes to keep out the grazing deer. Look for examples around Yosemite Village.

Decades of fervent fire suppression left dangerous levels of **debris accumulation** on the forest floor, and any fire would quickly become a raging **crown fire** killing everything in its path. Forests now took many years to regenerate. It wasn't until the late 1960s, after over a century of fire suppression, that ecologists recognized fire's pivotal role in forest regeneration and started revising their approach. The current fire policy has two facets. **Lightning-strike fires** are left to burn themselves out, so it is not uncommon to find backcountry fires burning throughout summer and fall. This puts some areas (and trails) off-limits for months, and Valley visitors can wake to find the Valley full of **smoke** which gradually lifts and blows away as the day wears on. If such fires threaten human life or property they are extinguished as quickly as possible, so you're unlikely to find wildfires close to Yosemite Valley, Tuolumne Meadows or Wawona. In such populated areas where no fires have occurred for long periods, the Park Service removes the forest floor debris by **prescribed burns**, which are intentionally set when light winds are blowing in the right direction and moisture levels are high enough to limit the risk of a raging blaze. They are closely monitored as they slowly clear out the woody debris.

Rock Climbing in Yosemite

Yosemite Valley and Tuolumne Meadows are renowned for their excellent granite walls and domes, and fine weather – a combination that has made Yosemite National Park the Mecca for **rock climbers** from all over the world.

For many, the pinnacle of climbing achievement is the three-thousand-foot face of **El Capitan**. The routes are highly convoluted, but what is probably the world's most famous climb, **The Nose**, lies straight ahead, tracing a line up the prow of the El Capitan past the relative luxury of El Cap Towers. This twenty-foot-by-six-foot patio, over 1500 feet above the Valley floor, is used as a bivouac spot by climbers who typically spend three to five nights on the route. Dozens of other routes follow barely imaginable routes up the cliffs to the left and right. To the right lies the **North American Wall**, where a route of the same name passes directly through a large mark on the rock looking like a map of North America. Left of The Nose is the **Salathé Wall**, named after one of the Valley's pioneer climbers.

For practical details of rock climbing – including courses and guided climbs – see Chapter 6, "Summer activities."

The early years

John Muir was Yosemite's first climber; some would say he was also Yosemite's first climbing bum as he effectively dropped out of society in the early 1870s to be among the mountains. While he never bothered with ropes, his explorations took him to places many people can barely reach today, even with a full rack of climbing gear. Perhaps his finest ascent was **Cathedral Peak**, south of Tuolumne Meadows, which when he left it was a natural and pristine as before.

At much the same time, Scottish trail builder and blacksmith **George Anderson** became the first person to stand on the top of **Half Dome** after he had drilled holes, five to six feet apart, all the way up its northeast shoulder. This was Yosemite's first aid climb, and the divergent climbing ethics of these two Scotsmen set a pattern for the future.

Yosemite has long captured the imagination of climbers but technical rock climbing didn't kick off here until the early 1930s. In 1933, four Bay Area climbers reached what is now known as the Lunch Ledge, 1000 feet up Washington Column – the tower opposite Half Dome. That same year, Yosemite climbing pioneers Dick Leonard, Jules Eichorn and Bestor Robinson made two abortive attempts on **Higher Cathedral Spire** having used Ansel Adams' photographs of the spire to plan a likely route up. A third, successful, attempt in April 1934 is considered Yosemite's first landmark climb.

In these primitive times, heavy steel pitons were used for driving into cracks and weighty karabiners attached the pitons to ropes that were so weak the protection they provided was mostly psychological. Still, climbers continued to knock off new climbs, including the fifteen-pitch **Royal Arches** route, which weaves its way up the ledges and slabs behind *The Ahwahnee*. On this ascent, Morgan Harris became the Valley's first recorded practitioner of the pendulum traverse.

Bathooks and bugaboos

Many of the most celebrated routes in Yosemite are what's known as "Big Wall" routes, tackled by **aid climbing**, where bits of metal are hammered into cracks and hauled on to achieve upward movement. The demands of ever harder climbs have pushed the development of an extensive armory that's totally baffling to the uninitiated: bathooks, birdbeaks, bongs, bugaboos, circleheads, fifi hooks, a funkness device, lost arrows and RURPs are all employed either to grapple a ledge or wedge into cracks of different sizes. The scale of Yosemite's walls is such that few cracks can be followed from bottom to top and to get from one crack to another, climbers employ death-defying **pendulums**, and repeatedly sweep across the face gaining momentum until they can lunge out at a tiny flake or fingertip hold. All this "nailing" and swinging takes time and most Big Wallers are forced to spend nights slung in a kind of lightweight camp bed known as a **portaledge**. Food, gallons of water, sleeping bags, warm clothing and wet-weather gear must all be lugged up in haul sacks, along with a well-loaded iPod – after all, it can get a bit tedious hammering away up there for hours on end. As Yosemite veteran John Long writes: "Climbing a wall can be a monumental pain in the ass. No one could pay you enough to do it. A thousand dollars would be too little by far. But you wouldn't sell the least of the memories for ten times that sum."

During World War II, many climbers enlisted in the army helping form its 10th mountain division, enabling them to keep climbing. After being demobbed, climbers employed newly developed, tough nylon ropes and lightweight safety equipment to push standards to new levels, and pipe dreams became realistic propositions. An early conquest, in 1947, was **Lost Arrow Spire**, rising to the right of Yosemite Falls and easy to spot in the early morning and late afternoon light when the spire casts a shadow on a nearby wall. This was the first route intentionally approached as a multi-day ascent, much of the groundwork being laid by Swiss-born blacksmith **John Salathé**. He was at the cutting edge of climbing, putting up technically demanding aid routes through the late 1940s and early 1950s, and even fashioning his own tougher carbon-steel pitons from the axles of a Model A Ford. These were put to good use in 1950 when Salathé and another Valley leading light, **Allen Steck**, made the first ascent of the face of Sentinel Rock. This was Salathé's last major route and was done in typically pure style, only drilling a protection bolt into the rock when it was absolutely necessary.

Scaling the big cliffs

For the next twenty years, two talented climbers with widely divergent styles assumed Salathé's mantle. Classical purist **Royal Robbins** followed Salathé's ethical approach, whereas hard-living **Warren Harding** was prepared to drill a bolt just about anywhere if it would help him get up something new. Little love was lost between them, though they did team up for the first, unsuccessful attempt on the Northwest Face of **Half Dome**. Months later, in 1957, when Robbins led a different team up the route, Harding got wind of their ascent and was on the summit to congratulate them. It was a magnificent effort and ranked as the hardest climb in North America at the time. Yosemite became an international forcing ground for aid climbing, and Americans were suddenly matching, and even surpassing, the achievements of previously dominant Europeans.

Now even the mighty El Cap seemed possible and Harding, having been robbed of the prize of Half Dome, had the strongest incentive. **The Nose** was the most obvious line but refused to submit for seventeen months, even after Harding used four massive pitons fashioned from stove legs scavenged from the Berkeley city dump and drove them into what are still known as the Stoveleg Cracks. Harding and two colleagues finally topped out in 1958 after a single thirteen-day push, the culmination of 47 days' work on the route.

These siege tactics didn't sit well with Robbins who, in 1960, pulled together a team that climbed The Nose in a self-contained seven-day effort. This team included up-and-coming youngsters, **Chuck Pratt** and **Tom Frost**, who joined Robbins the following year to put up a route on the **Salathé Wall** to the left of The Nose. It wasn't until 1965 that a two-man team completed an El Capitan route, the **Muir Wall**, which was then climbed a year later by Robbins, solo.

The Golden Age

With these critical ascents completed, climbers' aspirations broadened and the 1960s became the **Golden Age** of climbing in the Yosemite Valley, when it drew a motley collection of dropouts and misfits, many ranking among the world's finest climbers. For some, climbing had now become a lifestyle, and Park residency rules were ignored as people learnt to get by on next to nothing if it meant they could stay in *Camp 4* for months and climb. With this level of commitment, climbing standards shot up. Almost all the major walls and hundreds of minor routes were completed at this time, but the old guard

Naming rights

Generally the first people to climb a route get **naming rights**. Traditionally names were straightforward descriptions such as Northwest Face and East Buttress, but very soon a little more imagination was required. Good climbing guidebooks often explain the sources of names like *Left Rabbit Ear Route* and *Ephemeral Clogdance*, but many more get lost in time. One story from 1967 tells of Royal Robbins eschewing the traditional use of pitons and adopting the new European practice of climbing using non-intrusive metal wedges known as "nuts" for protection. He put up a brilliant five-pitch route and called it *Nutcracker Sweet* (now known simply as *The Nutcracker*). Robbins' long-time rival, Warren Harding, found the whole Tchaikovsky reference preposterous and immediately set about climbing a new route nearby, which he then named *Cocksucker Concerto*. It now goes by the abbreviated moniker of *CS Concerto*.

was still at work. In 1967 **Liz Robbins** became the first woman to climb Half Dome when she climbed it with her future husband, Royal. Women climbers were still a rarity in the Valley at this time, but by 1973 El Capitan had been topped by the first all-women team.

The final chapter in the Robbins/Harding saga took place in 1970 when Warren Harding and Dean Caldwell climbed a new El Capitan route called the **Dawn Wall**. It became controversial after they'd been on the wall about three weeks and worried friends called for a rescue. The climbers were fine and refused the rescue, finally topping out a week later to a full media welcome. Their faces were plastered all over the national newspapers. Harding had placed over three hundred bolts on the climb, something Robbins felt was totally unjustified and would set a bad precedent as new climbs could basically be constructed from a long series of bolts. To make his point he started climbing the route cutting out most of the bolts as he went. He soon had to acknowledge that the quality and difficulty of the climbing on the route justified the bolting, and he climbed the rest without cutting any more bolts.

The Stone Masters and their disciples

By the mid-1970s, all the obvious lines and the major cliffs had been climbed, and some of the originality had seeped out of the climbing. The new breed were searching for something new and as the Golden Age came to an end, the so-called **Stone Masters** began demolishing old standards. According to one of the original Stone Masters, **John Long**, the requirements were "one, you had to climb Valhalla which is 5.11, one of the hardest routes in the country; two, you had to be a young, arrogant punk; and three, you had to have the capacity to smoke enormous amounts, prodigious amounts, of really, really, bad marijuana; and we all had those talents, and so that was the glue that held the whole thing together." Somehow, Long, head Stone Master **Jim Bridwell**, and Billy Westbay kept their heads together long enough to complete the first **one-day ascent of The Nose** on midsummer's day 1975. Meanwhile languid afternoons and "rest" days back in *Camp 4* were spent trying to climb the boulder problem known as "Midnight Lightning" on the Columbia Boulder in the middle of the campground. Finally, in 1978, **Ron Kauk** sent the final move and set the standard for the thousands who have tried to follow his example.

As the 1980s dawned, the creation of new, sticky rubber climbing shoes helped make climbing even more athletic. Purists became disenchanted with the artificiality of aid ascents and began to concentrate on **free climbing**, only using their body to climb the rock, but still using ropes and climbing hardware to provide protection in case of a fall. Jim Bridwell, John Long, Ron Kauk and others had "freed" about half of Salathé Wall back in 1975, but it wasn't until 1988 (27 years after Robbins' first ascent) that Todd Skinner and Paul Piana completed the first free ascent of the whole route.

The culmination of years of cutting-edge climbing, and months of route-specific training was **Lynn Hill**'s ground-breaking free ascent of The Nose in 1993, praised and admired by all, if ruefully by some in Yosemite's traditionally macho climbing community. Hill repeated the climb in a day the following year, something not matched until **Tommy Caldwell's** 2005 ascent in under 12hr.

Speed climbing, enchainment and free soloing

There is always scope for new routes, and variations are being put up all the time, but much of the cutting-edge action in Yosemite in recent years has been in **speed climbing** (usually a combination of free and aid climbing). It is not something to be undertaken lightly. To shave time off a climb, practitioners both climb together with a length of rope between them, the leader placing gear for protection that is later taken out by the second. Eventually the leader will run out of appropriate gear and they'll regroup before continuing. When **simul-climbing** in this way there may only be one or two pieces of protection between the climbers and a mistake could result in a fall of a hundred feet or more, with the obvious risk of serious injury or death.

Speed climbing goes hand in hand with **enchainment**, linking together two or more big climbs in a day. In 1986, Yosemite hardmen **Peter Croft** and **John Bachar** set a landmark by climbing both El Capitan and Half Dome in a day. Then in 1993 Croft hooked up with **Hans Florine** for an ascent of The Nose in an impressive 4hr 22 min. Since then, the time has been progressively knocked down to an incredible 2hr 48min 50sec, done in 2002 by Yuji Hirayama and Hans Florine.

Throughout the 1990s younger climbers were increasingly attracted to **bouldering**, effectively free solo climbing with no ropes or equipment. Typically boulder problems don't get more than a few feet off the ground, but there is a venerable tradition of **free soloing** far longer routes. Peter Croft, John Bachar and **Dean Potter** are all renowned for their bold solo climbs where one false move would mean certain death. The sport's fans rave about the Zen calmness that descends as a way of overcoming the fear, while its detractors regard this sub-branch of rock climbing as something of a dead end.

Climbing Back

In 1989, **Mark Wellman** made history by becoming the first paraplegic to climb El Capitan. Paralyzed from the waist down after a mountaineering accident, Wellman was determined to climb again. With the help of climbing partner Mike Corbett, who has climbed El Cap over fifty times, Wellman was able to ascend The Nose by doing over seven thousand pull ups over seven days. He followed this feat by an ascent of Half Dome in 1991 and a second El Cap assault in 1999. Now a motivational speaker, his exploits are detailed in *Climbing Back* (Mark Wellman and John Flinn; Globe Pequot Press), which tells of his return to climbing, and the inspirational video "No Barriers," which also features the skiing and kayaking adventures of other disabled athletes.

Books

Most of the following **books** are widely available in stores in Yosemite National Park and the surrounding towns, but may be harder to find further afield and are virtually unseen outside North America. All are available through the major Internet booksellers, but first try the Yosemite Store section of the Yosemite Association's website (®www.yosemitestore.com), which has all worthwhile Yosemite-related books. Particularly recommended books are marked with the symbol.

Travel and Impressions

John Muir *The Yosemite* (North Books). There are various paperback versions of this Muir classic, but it is worth splurging on this large-format version ($25), which includes a hundred excellent color photos by Galen Rowell. It contains the full text, a wonderful introduction to the Park, its history, flora, fauna and plenty of full-blooded tales of Muir's adventures.

John Muir *The Wild Muir: 22 of John Muir's Greatest Adventures* (Yosemite Association). Some readers find Muir's more wordy moments a little heavy going, but this volume boils it all down to 22 thrilling and often death-defying adventure stories: riding an avalanche from the Valley rim, scaling Mount Ritter, experiencing a windstorm from atop a tree, and playing chicken with the wind-swayed Upper Yosemite Fall.

John Muir *The Eight Wilderness Discovery Books* (Diadem). The Muir completist's Bible, containing over a thousand pages including the full text of *The Story of my Boyhood and Youth, A Thousand Mile Walk to the Gulf, My First Summer in the Sierra, The Mountains of California, Our National Parks, The Yosemite, Travels in Alaska* and *Steep Trails.*

Steve Roper *Camp 4: Recollections of a Yosemite Rock-climber* (Mountaineers Books). The Yosemite veteran tells an entertaining and engaging tale about Yosemite's Golden Age of rock climbing during the 1960s and 1970s. Catches the spirit of the times wonderfully.

Galen Rowell *Vertical World of Yosemite* (Wilderness Press). Well-written and nicely photographed book covering the epic drama of many of the classic Yosemite rock climbs, often described by those who made the first ascents. First published in 1979 it is getting a little long in the tooth, but still a worthwhile read.

Yosemite Once Removed – Portraits of the Backcountry (Yosemite Association). Claude Fiddler's photos, and accompanying essays by renowned Yosemite mountaineers and hikers make this picture book come alive. The emphasis is on the vast majority of the Park that is outside Yosemite Valley and you can hardly flick through without wanting to go just about everywhere.

History, people and society

Ansel Adams *An Autobiography* (Bulfinch). Written in his final years, this is a fascinating insight into the man and his work (both photographic and environmental); liberally illustrated with Adams' own photographs.

Hank Johnson and Martha Lee *Guide to the Yosemite Cemetery* ($3.50). Slim tome on who is interred in the Yosemite Cemetery near the museum.

Margaret Sanborn *Yosemite* (Yosemite Association). Probably the best all-round book on Yosemite history, eschewing the sequential timeline in favor of focusing on specific events and the lives of the key players in the Park's development.

Shirley Sargent *Yosemite's Innkeepers* (Ponderosa Press). Sargent, a prolific historian, profiles the life in Yosemite's many early inns; an interesting if somewhat specialist read.

Jonathan Spalding *Ansel Adams and the American Landscape: A Biography* (University of California Press). An important biography of Adams, fully documented and researched, but lacking any of the great man's photos.

Dwight Willard *A Guide to the Sequoia Groves of California* (Yosemite Association). Yosemite's three sequoia groves, and 61 others along a narrow band of the Sierra Nevada are covered. Includes color photos, full details of each grove and the historical framework of their exploitation and preservation.

Native life and legends

S.A. Barrett and E.W. Gifford *Indian Life of the Yosemite Region: Miwok Material Culture* (Yosemite Association). An academic but readable depiction of Miwok life after European contact, researched in the early 1900s and published in 1933. Learn about herbal medicines, basket-making, food production and much more.

Frank La Pena, Craig D. Bates and Steven P. Medley *Legends of the Yosemite Miwok* (Yosemite Association). Contains what are thought to be the most authentic versions of Miwok legends about the Park geology and environment. Nicely illustrated too.

Robert D. San Souci *Two Bear Cubs – A Miwok Legend from California's Yosemite Valley* (Yosemite Association). Probably the best Yosemite-related kids' book, telling the tale of the creation of El Capitan (see box, p.47) with lovely illustrations.

Landscapes: geology, flora and fauna

Gary Brown *The Great Bear Almanac* (The Lyons Press). Exhaustive tome, full of photos and facts, providing everything you always wanted to know about all types of bears, not just the black variety found in Yosemite.

Richard Ditton and Donald McHenry *Yosemite Road Guide* (Yosemite Association). Just about every wayside point of interest (and many of little interest) along all of Yosemite's roads. It reads a bit dated but only costs $3.

David Gaines and Keith Hansen *Birds of Yosemite and the East Slope* (Artemesia Press). The best guide to the birds of Yosemite and the Mono Lake region, fully illustrated with location and occurrence maps, drawings and photos, plus full coverage of species found in the area.

N. King Huber *Geologic Story of Yosemite National Park* (Yosemite Association). The most current and authoritative description of how Yosemite was formed, with a minimum of pointy-headedness.

Lynn Wilson, Jim Wilson and Jeff Nicholas *Wildflowers of Yosemite* (Sierra Press). Handy and easy-to-use guide to identifying Yosemite's wildflowers, with lots of color photos, comprehensible text and maps to illustrate the range of many species.

Outdoor activity guides

Alan Castle *The John Muir Trail: Through the Californian Sierra Nevada* (Cicerone Press). Comprehensive guide to the JMT including additional access routes, ascent profiles, numerous maps and full trip-planning details.

Michael Frye *Photographer's Guide to Yosemite* (Yosemite Association). Color guide to photographing the Park, with numerous technical tips, suggestions for different seasons and times of day, and recommended locations.

Ray Jardine *The Pacific Crest Trail Hiker's Handbook* (Adventurelore Press). Though focused on completing the Pacific Crest Trial, Jardine's ultra lightweight backpacking techniques can be applied for any overnight hiking. You can probably ignore some of his more offbeat ideas but overall it is a great book.

John Moynier *Backcountry Skiing California's High Sierra* (Falcon Guides). A collection of day and overnight backcountry skiing and snowboarding routes, including multi-day classics and most of the important descents.

Don Reid *Yosemite: Free Climbs* (Falcon Guides). The definitive guide with general route descriptions for a huge number of free climbs in the Valley and nearby. *Tuolumne Meadows* and best-of *Yosemite's Select* round out the series.

Jeffrey P. Scheffer *Yosemite National Park: A Natural History Guide to Yosemite and its Trails* (Wilderness Press). True to its subtitle, with flora, fauna and geology notes to a hundred hikes through the Park, plus a supplementary topographic map.

Supertopo (®www.supertopo.com) A series of guides giving highly detailed route descriptions for selected climbs. They're mostly available in both print and downloadable eBook form (PDF), and titles include *Yosemite Valley Free Climbs, Tuolumne Free Climbs, Yosemite Big Walls, Yosemite Valley Bouldering* and *The Road to The Nose.*

Michael C. White *Snowshoe Trails of Yosemite* (Wilderness Press). Meticulous details of over forty of the Park's most scenic trails for a range of abilities.

Glossary

Ahwahnee Native Miwok name for Yosemite Valley and now the name of its best hotel.

Ahwahneechee The local subtribe of the native Miwok people.

Ahwiyah Miwok name for Mirror Lake, meaning "quiet water."

Aid climbing Placing climbing hardware in cracks and on ledges then using them to gain upward movement.

BASE jumping Parachute jumps from Buildings, Antennae, Structures and Earth.

Big Wall Large cliffs scaled by rock climbers; El Capitan and the face of Half Dome are obvious examples.

Bivvy Short for bivouac, this usually refers to a tent-free night under the stars, or many hanging on one of the Big Wall climbs.

Cairn Small pile of rocks used to mark trails and trail junctions, also known as a "duck."

Cholok Miwok name for Yosemite Falls.

Cirque Amphitheater of rock walls at the head of an ancient glacier.

Dikes Feldspar and quartz intrusions that leave 4–8-inch-wide straight lines scarring smooth sheets of gray granite.

DNC Delaware North Company, the Park concessionaire which runs lodging, restaurants, tours, etc.

Duck See "Cairn."

Erratic A boulder carried by an ancient glacier then dumped far from its original home as the glacier melted.

Exfoliation Geologic process where, over millennia, bands of rock peel off like layers of an onion.

Free climbing Using your body to climb the rock, but still utilizing ropes and hardware to provide protection in case of a fall.

Glacial polish Shiny, almost reflective rock worn smooth by glaciers. Good examples are found on Lembert Dome (see p.125) and Pothole Dome (see p.122).

Hanging valley Side valley high on the rock walls of the larger valley where a side glacier once met the main branch. Most of Yosemite's highest waterfalls – Bridalveil, Upper Yosemite, etc – cascade from such hanging valleys.

HSC High Sierra Camp (see p.174).

JMT The 211-mile John Muir Trail from Yosemite Valley to Mount Whitney (see box, p.143).

Kettle Lakes Lakes formed in depressions created by large lumps of ice left behind when ancient glaciers receded.

Kosuko Miwok name for Cathedral Rock.

Moonbow Nighttime rainbow created by moonlight shining on the spray from waterfalls.

Moraine Mass of glacially transported rubble.

Nailing Aid climbing (see above).

Nunatak Jagged mountain top which was never subject to glacial smoothing, always standing above ancient ice sheets.

Pohono Miwok name for Bridalveil Fall, meaning "puffing wind."

Portaledge A light kind of camp bed used by climbers which can be slung from the rock wall for overnighting on climbs.

Redwood Large trees of the sequoia family. "Redwood" is usually reserved for the tall but relatively slender coastal redwoods.

Roche moutonnée A smooth lump of rock (literally a "sheep rock") formed by glaciers grinding over their surface leaving a gentle slope on the upstream side, and a steeper face downstream. Lembert Dome is a large example and there are several smaller ones in the meadows towards Tioga Pass.

Sequoia Large trees of the sequoia family. "Sequoia" typically refers to the immense trees found in the Sierra Nevada.

Soloing Rock climbing with no ropes or gear for protection.

Striations Parallel scratch marks in smooth bedrock ground by rocks embedded in the base of ancient glaciers.

Talus Piles of rocky rubble at the base of cliffs, the product of millennia of rockfall.

Terminal moraine A barrier of rock rubble left behind at the furthest extent of an ancient glacier.

Tis-sa-yak Miwok name for Half Dome (see box, p.47).

Tu-tok-a-nu-la Miwok name for El Capitan (see box, p.47).

U-shaped valley Flat-floored, vertically walled valley carved out by a glacier. In dramatic contrast to the river-formed V-shaped valley.

Wakalla Miwok name for the Merced River.

People

Ansel Adams (1902–84) The finest photographer Yosemite has ever had. See box, p.64.

George Anderson (see p.248) Scottish blacksmith who made the first ascent up the shoulder of Half Dome in 1875.

Galen Clark (1814–1910). Yosemite's first guardian and early resident of Wawona.

James Lamon (1817–75) Early Yosemite Valley settler known for his apple orchard in what is now Curry Village.

Joseph LeConte (1823–1901). Important geologist who spent time in Yosemite with John Muir. The Le Conte Memorial is named after him.

John Muir (1838–1914) Scottish naturalist and adventurer. See box, p.84.

Frederick Law Olmsted (1822–1903). The first chairman of the Yosemite Park Commission and joint architect of New York City's Central Park. Olmsted Point is named after him.

Gilbert Stanley Underwood (1890–1960) Architect of The Ahwahnee.

Joseph Walker (1798–1876). Leader of the Walker Party, the first group of whites to travel through the Yosemite region.

Small print and
Index

A Rough Guide to Rough Guides

Published in 1982, the first Rough Guide – to Greece – was a student scheme that became a publishing phenomenon. Mark Ellingham, a recent graduate in English from Bristol University, had been traveling in Greece the previous summer and couldn't find the right guidebook. With a small group of friends he wrote his own guide, combining a highly contemporary, journalistic style with a thoroughly practical approach to travelers' needs.

The immediate success of the book spawned a series that rapidly covered dozens of destinations. And, in addition to impecunious backpackers, Rough Guides soon acquired a much broader and older readership that relished the guides' wit and inquisitiveness as much as their enthusiastic, critical approach and value-for-money ethos.

These days, Rough Guides include recommendations from shoestring to luxury and cover more than 200 destinations around the globe, including almost every country in the Americas and Europe, more than half of Africa and most of Asia and Australasia. Our ever-growing team of authors and photographers is spread all over the world, particularly in Europe, the USA and Australia.

In the early 1990s, Rough Guides branched out of travel, with the publication of Rough Guides to World Music, Classical Music and the Internet. All three have become benchmark titles in their fields, spearheading the publication of a wide range of books under the Rough Guide name.

Including the travel series, Rough Guides now number more than 350 titles, covering: phrasebooks, waterproof maps, music guides from Opera to Heavy Metal, reference works as diverse as Conspiracy Theories and Shakespeare, and popular culture books from iPods to Poker. Rough Guides also produce a series of more than 120 World Music CDs in partnership with World Music Network.

Visit www.roughguides.com to see our latest publications.

Rough Guide travel images are available for commercial licensing at www.roughguidespictures.com

Rough Guide credits

Text editor: Anna Owens
Layout: Jessica Subramanian
Cartography: Jai Prakash Mishra
Picture editor: Chrissy McIntyre
Production: Rebecca Short
Proofreader: Karen Parker
Cover design: Chloë Roberts
Photographer: Paul Whitfield
Editorial: **London** Ruth Blackmore, Alison Murchie, Karoline Densley, Andy Turner, Keith Drew, Edward Aves, Alice Park, Lucy White, Jo Kirby, James Smart, Natasha Foges, Róisín Cameron, Emma Traynor, Emma Gibbs, Kathryn Lane, Christina Valhouli, Monica Woods, James Rice, Mani Ramaswamy, Joe Staines, Peter Buckley, Matthew Milton, Tracy Hopkins, Ruth Tidball; **New York** Andrew Rosenberg, Steven Horak, AnneLise Sorensen, April Isaacs, Ella Steim, Sean Mahoney, Courtney Miller, Paula Neudorf; **Delhi** Madhavi Singh, Karen D'Souza
Design & Pictures: **London** Scott Stickland, Dan May, Diana Jarvis, Mark Thomas, Nicole Newman, Sarah Cummins, Emily Taylor; **Delhi** Umesh Aggarwal, Ajay Verma, Ankur Guha, Pradeep Thapliyal, Sachin Tanwar, Anita Singh, Nikhil Agarwal
Production: Vicky Baldwin
Cartography: **London** Maxine Repath, Ed Wright, Katie Lloyd-Jones; **Delhi** Rajesh Chhibber, Ashutosh Bharti, Rajesh Mishra, Animesh Pathak, Jasbir Sandhu, Karobi Gogoi, Amod Singh, Alakananda Bhattacharya, Swati Handoo
Online: Narender Kumar, Rakesh Kumar, Amit Verma, Rahul Kumar, Ganesh Sharma, Debojit Borah, Saurabh Sati
Marketing & Publicity: **London** Liz Statham, Niki Hanmer, Louise Maher, Jess Carter, Vanessa Godden, Vivienne Watton, Anna Paynton, Rachel Sprackett, Libby Jelie; **New York** Geoff Colquitt, Katy Ball, Nancy Lambert; **Delhi** Ragini Govind
Manager India: Punita Singh
Reference Director: Andrew Lockett
Operations Manager: Helen Phillips
PA to Publishing Director: Nicola Henderson
Publishing Director: Martin Dunford
Commercial Manager: Gino Magnotta
Managing Director: John Duhigg

ROUGH GUIDES

SMALL PRINT

Publishing information

This third edition published June 2008 by
Rough Guides Ltd,
80 Strand, London WC2R 0RL
345 Hudson St, 4th Floor,
New York, NY 10014, USA
14 Local Shopping Centre, Panchsheel Park,
New Delhi 110017, India
Distributed by the Penguin Group
Penguin Books Ltd,
80 Strand, London WC2R 0RL
Penguin Group (USA)
375 Hudson Street, NY 10014, USA
Penguin Group (Australia)
250 Camberwell Road, Camberwell,
Victoria 3124, Australia
Penguin Books Canada Ltd,
10 Alcorn Avenue, Toronto, Ontario,
Canada M4V 1E4
Penguin Group (NZ)
67 Apollo Drive, Mairangi Bay, Auckland 1310,
New Zealand

Cover concept by Peter Dyer.

Typeset in Bembo and Helvetica to an original design by Henry Iles.

Printed and bound in China

272pp includes index

A catalogue record for this book is available from the British Library

ISBN: 978-1-85828-393-7

1 3 5 7 9 8 6 4 2

Help us update

We've gone to a lot of effort to ensure that the third edition of **The Rough Guide to Yosemite National Park** is accurate and up to date. However, things change – places get "discovered", opening hours are notoriously fickle, restaurants and rooms raise prices or lower standards. If you feel we've got it wrong or left something out, we'd like to know, and if you can remember the address, the price, the hours, the phone number, so much the better.

Please send your comments with the subject line "**Rough Guide Yosemite National Park Update**" to ⓔ mail@roughguides.com. We'll credit all contributions and send a copy of the next edition (or any other Rough Guide if you prefer) for the very best emails.

Have your questions answered and tell others about your trip at ⓦ community.roughguides.com

Acknowledgements

Paul Whitfield: Thanks go out to all those who contributed to this book in any way; sharing hikes and bar room tales, voicing opinions, and helping out with logistics. Assistance from Kenny Karst at DNC and Scott Gediman at the Park Service was especially appreciated, as was the help of all those rangers and visitor centre staff who contributed: you know who you are. Special thanks go out to Wendy and Phil for icy swims, precipitous rock climbs, photo modeling, long days on the trail and welcome meals at the Ahwahnee as reward. Also to Chris Kapka for a home from home in San Fran, a sympathetic ear and more beers than were entirely necessary. A big debt of gratitude too to those at the Rough Guide office in New York, particularly Anna Owens who helped make this edition what it is. Thanks also to Jessica Subramanian, Chrissy McIntyre, Katie Lloyd-Jones, and Jai Mishra. And lastly to Marion for support back home when the writing days got long and indexing became mind-numbingly boring. Thanks.

The editor thanks Paul, whose work was so well done and a joy to edit; and in the RG offices: Steven Horak, Andrew Rosenberg, Chrissy McIntyre, Jessica Subramanian, Jai Mishra, Katie Lloyd-Jones, and all other staffers in London, Delhi, and New York.

Readers' letters

Thanks to all the readers who have taken the time to write in with comments and suggestions (and apologies if we've inadvertently omitted or misspelt anyone's name):

Pam Clements, John DeGrazio, Julie Sykes, and Joe Toska.

Photo credits

All photos © Rough Guides except the following:

Things not to miss

01 Sunset at Glacier Point © Chris Pancewicz /Alamy

06 Winter in Yosemite © Golden Gate Images /Alamy

10 Horseback riding © Diane Cook & Len Jenshel/Corbis

12 Hiking Half Dome © Terry Husebye/Getty Images

Black and whites

p.66 Oak Tree, Snowstorm © Ansel Adams /Corbis

p.86 John Muir © Rights and Reproductions /Library of Congress

p.100 Mariposa Grove, 1905 © Rights and Reproductions/Library of Congress

p.113 Hiking Half Dome, 1904 © Rights and Reproductions/Library of Congress

p.136 Camping in 1902 © Rights and Reproductions/Library of Congress

p.223 Devils Postpile © Dennis Frates/Alamy

p.239 Wawona Covered Bridge © Rights and Reproductions/Library of Congress

p.240 Chipmunk © Rolling Verlinde/DK Images

Color insert: Wild Yosemite

Black Bear © Frank Leung/iStock

Poppies © W. Cody/Corbis

Index

Map entries are in color.

D

E

Day hikes

INDEX

J

K

L

M

INDEX

N

O

Overnight hikes

P

R

S

T

I

INDEX

U

V

W

Y

Map symbols

maps are listed in the full index using colored text

State boundary
Yosemite National Park boundary
Interstate highway
US highway
State highway
Limited-access road
Other road
Recommended hiking trail
Other trail
River
Tram route & stop
Park entrance
Ranger station
Peak
Viewpoint
Waterfall
Spring
Ski area
Ski hut/High Sierra camp

Point of interest
Information office
Internet access
Regional airport
International airport
Accommodation
Road-accessible campground
Backcountry campground
Post office
Toilets
Shuttle bus stop
Building
Chapel
Parking
Gas station
Golf course
Sequoia grove
Mine